DICTIONARY OF
SHAKESPEARE

DICTIONARY OF
SHAKESPEARE

by
Louise McConnell

FITZROY DEARBORN PUBLISHERS
CHICAGO • LONDON

Using the Dictionary

The dictionary entries use various type styles to indicate different cross-references.

> Word or phrase in *Italic* is the name of play.

> A word or entry (used in a description) that is defined elsewhere in the book is written in SMALL CAPITALS.

> A cross-refence to another entry is indicated by '*See xxx*'

Acknowledgements

As an enthusiast venturing into the arena of Shakespearean study, I owe an immeasurable debt of gratitude to the wealth of scholarship that has gone before. I have drawn on the work of Shakespearean critics from Dr Johnson to Professor Stanley Wells. I shall always be grateful to my father and his infectious passion for Shakespeare. Like A C Bradley, he believed that 'Shakespeare wrote primarily for the theatre and not for students'. He took me to my first Shakespeare plays when the Old Vic theatre was in its heyday in the 1950s, and today's stars such as Judi Dench and Alec McCowan were beginning their careers. They were unforgettable performances. I should like to thank Lucy Cocker who inspired this project; Profesor Kirpal Singh who gave me so much encouragement; friends, too numerous to mention, but in particular Rita Adam who kept my spirits up when they flagged; and family, my Mother, Ella Joyce, and my children, Charlotte, William and Graham, without whom I would neither have begun nor finished the book. I have been greatly helped by Christopher Bangs who generously gave me leave from my work with him, Violet Small who kept me organised at home, and my cat Lily, a constant companion at the word processor. My thanks are due to John Mclaughlin and to Peter Collin for getting the book into print. Most of all, I must thank my husband Louis James, for his practical kindnesses and colossal patience. I could not have done it without him.

Dedication

For Charlotte and William

Aa

Aaron

A character in *Titus Andronicus* and one of Shakespeare's most evil and unrepentant villains. He is a Moor, who says of himself that his soul is as black as his face. Aaron is Queen Tamora's servant and lover, who is delighted when she marries the Emperor Saturnius because he forsees the possibility of advancement for himself. Aaron takes pleasure in cruelty, and his elaborate scheming is central to the spiral of killing in the play. He engineers Lavinia's rape, and plots to kill her husband Bassianus, framing Titus' sons for the murder. Aaron tricks Titus into cutting off his hand as the price he must pay for his sons' lives, and as a macabre and cruel joke returns the sons' heads and the severed hand to Titus on a dish. Aaron is incapable of pity except to his infant son whose life he spares. Ironically, the baby's cries alert Titus' sons to Aaron's whereabouts, and he is captured. In order to save the child, Aaron makes a full confession; he is condemned to be buried alive up to his neck and left to starve.

Abergavenny, Lord

A historical figure (c. 1461-1535) and a minor character in *King Henry VIII*, Lord Abergavenny is arrested with the Duke of Buckingham, falsely accused of treason by Wolsey, whom Abergavenny has been criticising. He is resigned to the future, trusting in God and the King.

Abbot of Westminster, The

A minor character in *King Richard II*, The Abbot of Westminster is one of the conspirators against Bolingbroke. After Bolingbroke has seized the crown and deposed Richard, the Abbot plots with the Bishop of Carlisle and the Duke of Aumerle to kill him. Aumerle's part in the conspiracy is discovered and while his treachery is pardoned by Bolingbroke, now crowned King Henry, the Abbot is condemned to death, but dies of a guilty conscience before he is executed.

Abhorson

A minor comic character in *Measure for Measure*, Abhorson is an executioner who takes his profession very seriously. When the prisoner Barnadine is due to be executed, Abhorson is perplexed when his victim refuses to cooperate, on the grounds that as he has been drinking all night he has not had time to prepare himself for death.

Abram

A minor character in *Romeo and Juliet*, Abram is a servingman in the Montague household who fights with the Capulet servants in the opening scene of the play. The brawl establishes the long-running feud that exists between the two households.

accent
Another word for STRESS.

Achilles
A hero from Greek legend and a character in *Troilus and Cressida*, Achilles is the greatest of the Greek warriors but fame has made him arrogant and he refuses to fight. Sullen and uncooperative, he lazes in his tent where his only companions are his friend Patroclus, who makes fun of the Greek commanders, and the spiteful Thersites. The Greeks are worried that Achilles' disobedience will spread through the army; Ajax, another great warrior is already showing signs of similar behaviour. Achilles' real reason for refusing to fight is his secret and treacherous love for Polyxena, the daughter of his enemy, the Trojan King. When Achilles sees that his reputation is at stake, he challenges the Trojan hero Hector to fight. When Hector kills Patroclus, the fight becomes a personal one, and Achilles dishonourably murders Hector while he is unarmed, and then drags Hector's body behind his horse.

act
A division of a play, which is further subdivided into scenes. Shakespeare's plays were written to be performed straight through, without any break; it was later editors of his plays, such as Nicholas ROWE, rather than Shakespeare himself, who were responsible for the five act division of his texts, following the convention of Classical Roman DRAMA.

action
The course of events that is developed in a narrative and enacted on stage. When incidents that have occurred OFF-STAGE, before or during the course of the play, are related to the characters by, for example, a messenger, this is called REPORTED ACTION.

action, unity of
See UNITIES.

actors and acting
In the 16th century, when for the first time acting in England became a professional rather than an amateur occupation, actors were more usually called PLAYERS. The profession was legitimized in 1574 by Royal Warrant when the actor Richard BURBAGE was given a licence to perform 'Comedies, Tragedies, Interludes and Stage plays' with the company of players, LEICESTER'S MEN, and from 1581 it was regularized by the authority of the MASTER OF THE REVELS. English actors, some of whom travelled as far afield as the Continent to perform (a troupe of actors is recorded as performing at ELSINORE in Denmark), were regarded as the best in the world.

Under an act of 1598, actors performing in public risked imprisonment for vagrancy [homelessness] unless they could prove that they belonged to a company of actors formed under the patronage of a nobleman, as part of his retinue of entertainers. Their status validated, actors might wear a special livery or a badge provided by their patron, but they were not paid a regular wage. They had to live on what they could earn from audience takings as they toured the country, performing in great houses, INN-YARDS or on makeshift staging on village greens. In the Induction [introduction] to *The Taming of the Shrew*, a touring company of players arrives at the Lord's country house. They are warmly welcomed by the Lord who recalls an earlier visit and gives them hospitality before they perform *The Taming of the Shrew*.

Life on the road for most provincial travelling players was harsh and they made a meagre living but members of established companies based in London fared better. While minor actors, HIRELINGS, were poorly paid (in 1579 their wages were six shillings a week), leading players, who shared in the company's profits, might earn as much as £90 a year. Successful actors like Richard BURBAGE and Edward ALLEYN certainly prospered financially, becoming celebrities who specialized as comedians or tragedians, and for whom parts were specifically written.

It was not until the mid-17th century in England that women were legally permitted to perform in public (see WOMEN ACTORS). In Shakespeare's time, despite the censure of the Puritans (see PURITAN) who regarded the practice as highly immoral, boys whose voices had not yet broken took the female roles. No Elizabethan audience would have found it strange to watch a boy player in the part of Cleopatra, although there is a story told that a performance of *Othello* was once delayed because the boy actor playing Desdemona needed to shave. Boy actors were recruited from choir schools and grammar schools and were apprenticed to established actors who provided for them and taught them their art. The younger boys would have taken the parts of children in the plays, for example the little princes in the tower in *King Richard III* or parts such as the fairies in *The Merry Wives of Windsor*. Although the names of adult actors appeared in contemporary cast lists, boy actors were never named.

Productions of plays were mounted with a minimum of rehearsal time and each actor in a company would appear in every production, often playing more than one part. Because of the REPERTORY system that operated with its fast turnover of plays, an actor would have been required to learn and remember a daunting number of roles; actors needed to be skilled improvisers in order to mask any lapses of memory. They were also required to be competent in singing, dancing and fencing.

We can only speculate about acting styles, but specific attitudes and gestures belonged to certain STOCK CHARACTERS and 16th-century acting would probably seem stylized to modern audiences used to a more naturalistic technique. It is believed that the verse lines were spoken with the accents on the words strongly stressed in order to preserve the METRE. Hamlet discusses the conventions of acting, advising the players who visit Elsinore to 'suit the action to the word and the word to the action'. *See also* BOY COMPANIES; COMPANIES OF ACTORS; PLAY PRODUCTION; PLAYHOUSES.

actresses
See WOMEN ACTORS.

act tunes
Musical interludes between the acts of plays.

Adam
A character in *As You Like It*, Adam is a servant in the household of the scheming Oliver, and served Oliver's father before him. Honest and good-hearted, he is now an old man, and says he has been with the family for so long that he has lost most of his teeth in their service. When Oliver turns Orlando out of his house, Adam pledges his loyalty to Orlando, promising that despite his age he will be of use, and generously

offering to share his life's savings. In fact, Adam does feel his age, and is overcome with tiredness and hunger on their travels. Orlando is seeking food for him in the Forest of ARDEN, when he meets Duke Senior, whose entourage he eventually joins, after which Adam disappears from the play. Adam says that the reason for his healthy old age is that he lived a moderate life in his youth.

Admiral's Men, The or The Lord Admiral's Men
One of the most successful COMPANIES OF ACTORS in the Elizabethan theatre from 1576, and rivals to Shakespeare's company the LORD CHAMBERLAIN'S MEN. Originally called Lord Howard's Company after their patron, they were renamed the Admiral's Men in 1585 when he was appointed Lord High Admiral. They toured the provinces led by the actor Edward ALLEYN until they eventually established themselves in London in 1585, playing at the Theatre, the Rose Theatre and later at the Fortune Theatre under the financial control of the theatrical entrepreneur Philip HENSLOWE. During the reign of James I (1603-25) they became known as PRINCE HENRY'S MEN when the King's son became their patron.

Adrian
A minor character in *Coriolanus; see* VOLSCIANS.

Adrian and Francisco
Two minor characters in *The Tempest*, Adrian and Francisco are Lords attending Alonso, King of Naples, who are shipwrecked with him on Prospero's magic island. Francisco tries to comfort Alonso, who believes his son Ferdinand has drowned, by saying that he saw Ferdinand swimming strongly towards the shore. Adrian is instructed by Gonzalo to prevent Alonso, who is heartbroken at the loss of his son and under Prospero's spell, from doing himself any harm.

Adriana
A character in *The Comedy of Errors*, Adriana is married to Ephesus Antipholus. When her husband is late returning home one day, Adriana becomes anxious, and despite her sister Luciana's attempts to pacify her, Adriana becomes increasingly angry, ignoring Luciana's advice that patience and submission are what is required of a wife. Unknown to Adriana, her husband's identical twin brother, Syracuse Antipholus, is in town and a series of encounters with the man Adriana believes to be her husband, but who in fact is her brother-in-law, leave Adriana extremely confused. As the behaviour of her husband grows apparently more and more bizarre, she begins to think he has gone mad, and hires an eccentric magician to exorcise the spirits that possess him. Adriana is jealous, angry, forgiving, and bemused in turns for most of the play, but she is ultimately a loving wife who is restored to her husband in the end.

Aediles
Several minor characters in *Coriolanus*, The Aediles act as messengers and assistants to the Roman tribunes [civil officers]. They round up the crowds to demonstrate against Coriolanus and are told by the tribunes, Brutus and Sicinius, to instruct the crowd to shout and heckle Coriolanus when he addresses them.

Aegeon
A minor character in *The Comedy of Errors*; *see* EGEON.

Aemilia (Emilia)
A minor character in *The Comedy of Errors*, Aemilia is the mother of the two Antipholuses. She was separated from her husband Egeon, and one of her sons, when the family was shipwrecked, and has become an Abbess in a priory at Ephesus. Aemilia is a stern figure who tells Adriana in no uncertain terms that her unwifely and jealous behaviour towards her husband is the cause of his madness. It is Aemilia, who is able finally to explain all the confusions, after which she invites everyone into the priory to celebrate the happy reunions.

Aemilius (Emilius)
A minor character in *Titus Andronicus*, Aemilius is the messenger who tells Saturnius that the Goths, led by Lucius, are preparing to attack; Saturnius sends him back to Lucius with a request for a meeting to discuss peace. After Saturnius' death, Aemilius hails Lucius as the new Emperor. See also LEPIDUS.

Aeneas
A hero from Greek legend and a minor character in *Troilus and Cressida*, Aeneas is one of the Trojan commanders who is sent to tell Troilus about the plan to exchange Cressida for the Greek prisoner Antenor. Aeneas is a model of courtesy and honour who seems to regard war as a kind of sport.

Agamemnon
A legendary figure and a character in *Troilus and Cressida*, Agamemnon is the Greek commander-in-chief but a weak leader who lacks authority. He is slow and pompous and his commands are largely ignored, most particularly by Achilles who takes no notice of Agamemnon's orders to fight Hector.

Agincourt
A village in northern France, and the site of a battle in 1415 between the French and English armies which is enacted in *King Henry V*. The English army was outnumbered by the French but won a notable victory at Agincourt largely due to the skill of the English bowmen. The anniversary of the battle was still celebrated in Shakespeare's time.

Agrippa
A minor character in *Antony and Cleopatra*, Agrippa is a commander in Caesar's army. Although Agrippa is well aware of the hold Cleopatra has over Antony, he suggests that in order to seal the fragile peace made between Antony and Caesar, Antony should marry Caesar's sister, Octavia. When the peace has broken down, Agrippa is ordered by Caesar to capture Antony alive at Alexandria. Learning of Antony's death later, Agrippa praises him, observing that, as with all men, Antony had faults.

Agrippa, Menenius
A character in *Coriolanus*; *see* MENENIUS AGRIPPA.

Aguecheek, Sir Andrew
A comic character in *Twelfth Night*, Sir Andrew Aguecheek is Sir Toby Belch's gullible friend. Sir Andrew is something of a laughing-stock; as tall as any man in Illyria, he is described as having lank hair that hangs 'like flax on a distaff'. Sir Andrew however,

who says wistfully that he was 'ador'd once', sees himself as something of a ladies' man and sets out to court the Countess Olivia. She spurns him in favour of Cesario (who is Viola disguised as a boy), and Sir Andrew is persuaded by Sir Toby to challenge his rival to a duel. Sir Andrew is terrified by the prospect of the fight, which fortunately is interrupted before any damage can be inflicted on either side. Sir Andrew conspires with Sir Toby in the plot to humiliate Malvolio, but he is himself Sir Toby's pawn. Vain and self-deluding, Sir Andrew has moments of insight. He acknowledges that 'many do call me fool' and wonders if eating too much meat has damaged his mind.

Ajax
A hero from Greek legend and a character in *Troilus and Cressida*, Ajax is a famous Greek warrior who is courageous but brainless, and described by Thersites as 'beef-witted'. While Achilles is sulking in his tent and refusing to fight, the Greek leaders promote Ajax as his replacement. Ajax is absurdly excited and struts around like a peacock. He eagerly takes up the challenge to face the Trojan hero Hector in single combat, and fights bravely, but when Hector reminds him that they are related (Hector is his uncle) Ajax agrees that they should call a truce. Ajax has his own moment of glory when he kills the Trojan general, Aeneas.

Alarbus
A minor character in *Titus Andronicus*, Alarbus is the eldest son of Queen Tamora of the Goths, who is captured with his mother and brothers by Titus and brought to Rome. His death is demanded as a religious sacrifice to the spirits of Titus' sons who were killed in battle. Alarbus is hacked to pieces and his body burned, and his bloody death is the first in a horrific cycle of murder and revenge.

Albany, Duke of
A character in *King Lear*, Albany is the evil Goneril's husband. He is dominated by his wife, who calls him gutless, a 'milk-liver'd man'. Albany shares none of Goneril's ruthless ambition and takes no part in her villainy; when he learns how she has treated her father Lear, he is appalled; he is still more horrified by the cruel blinding of Gloucester, which he vows to avenge. Although he condemns her, Albany remains by Goneril's side when she allies herself with Edmund to fight Cordelia's army, until he learns that Edmund is her lover and that she is planning to kill him. Albany discovers the extent of Goneril's wickedness too late to influence the tragic outcome.

Alcibiades
A historical figure (c. 450-404 BC) and a character in *Timon of Athens*, Alcibiades is a military commander, young and impulsive, but a man of principle and Timon's one real friend. He pleads with the cold-hearted Senators to show mercy to a soldier who killed someone while he was drunk, but his appeal is refused. He responds angrily and is sent into exile like Timon; but where Timon descends into madness, Alcibiades takes the initiative and decides to be revenged on Athens. Alcibiades visits Timon in his cave in the woods, but his offers of help are spurned by Timon. Timon in turn offers him gold, and Alcibiades accepts it, so that than he can pay his men. He marches on Athens but the Senators persuade him to enter the city peacefully. Alcibiades promises to show mercy to his enemies, and vows to make Athens a place where everyone will live in peace and work for the general good of the state.

Alexander
A minor character in *Troilus and Cressida*, Alexander is Cressida's servant. He tells her how the Trojan hero Hector was beaten and humiliated in battle by the Greek warrior Ajax.

Alexander Iden
See IDEN.

Alexas
A minor character in *Antony and Cleopatra*, Alexas is one of Cleopatra's attendants, a humorous character who jokes with his mistress and her maids. When Antony leaves for Rome, he sends Alexas to Cleopatra with a pearl as a parting gift. After the Battle of Actium, Alexas is reported as having defected to Caesar in Rome , where it is said that he is hanged for an earlier act of treachery.

Alice
A minor character in *King Henry V*, Alice is Princess Katherine's lady-in-waiting. When Katherine is to be married to King Henry, Alice gives her English lessons, and she acts as interpreter when Henry first meets his future bride.

Aliena
In *As You Like It*, Aliena is the name that Celia adopts when she lives in disguise with Rosalind in the Forest of ARDEN.

All is True
The title that was probably first given to the play *King Henry VIII*; Sir Henry Wotton, who visited the GLOBE THEATRE in June 1623, wrote a letter describing a play entitled *All is True*, which represented 'some principal pieces of the reign of Henry VIII, which was set forth with many extraordinary circumstances of pomp and majesty, even to the matting of the stage ...'.

allegory
A narrative in which the events or characters, or even the setting, for example a storm, as well as telling a story at a literal level, also represent some abstract meaning (in the case of a storm, chaos and turmoil) or moral qualities. Shakespeare's long poem *The Phoenix and the Turtle* is an example of an allegory. In recounting the funeral of two birds, it also represents a celebration of idealized and spiritual love. See also METAPHOR; SYMBOLISM.

Alleyn, Edward; also known as Ned Allen, (1566–1626)
One of the most successful actors of his time, Alleyn was particularly well known as a tragedian. He formed the ADMIRAL'S MEN company of actors at the Rose theatre before becoming owner-manager of the Fortune Theatre, and subsequently a wealthy man. Alleyn founded Dulwich College (a school in South London), and left the diary and papers inherited from his father-in-law, the theatrical entrepreneur Philip HENSLOWE to the foundation. It has been suggested that Shakespeare may have satirized Alleyn's style of acting in the character of Pistol in *King Henry IV, Part Two*.

All's Well that Ends Well

One of Shakespeare's PROBLEM PLAYS, a comedy written around 1603-05; it was presumably performed during Shakespeare's lifetime but its first recorded performance was not until 1741. It was first published in the First FOLIO edition of the plays in 1623, and there is a theory that it was originally entitled *Love's Labour's Wonne*. The main source for the play was one of the stories in the *Decameron* by the Italian Giovanni Boccaccio (1313-75), which was translated into English in 1566 by William Painter. The play, set in France and Italy, is a moral story about love and sex; it explores themes of snobbery, loyalty and disloyalty, and healing and forgiveness.

SYNOPSIS : Helena's father, a famous doctor, has died and she now lives with the Countess of Rossillion. When the Countess's son, Bertram, leaves for the court in Paris, Helena confesses that she loves Bertram, and follows him. The King of France is incurably ill, but Helena cures him, with an old remedy of her father's, and the King rewards her by allowing her to chose Bertram as her husband. Bertram is appalled at the idea of marrying someone whose social status is so far beneath his own. He protests vigorously, and immediately leaves for the war in Italy and sends Helena back home. He seals his cruel rejection of her with a vow never to consummate the marriage until she fulfils two seemingly impossible tasks. She must take a ring from his finger and, while remaining a virgin, bear him a child. Helena is undeterred, and follows him to Italy where she discovers that he is trying to seduce Diana, a young virgin; Helena asks Diana for her help. Diana pretends to Bertram that she is willing to sleep with him, and asks him to exchange his ring for hers. When Bertram comes to Diana that night, he is unaware that it is in fact Helena with whom he is sleeping and that he is fathering her child. Now that both Bertram's conditions have been fulfilled, Helena circulates a rumour that she has died. Bertram is about to be married to someone else when Diana appears from Florence, appealing to the King for justice because she says Bertram has failed to fulfil his promise to marry her; she produces Bertram's ring as proof. Helena makes a dramatic entrance and explains everything. She and Bertram are reconciled, and as Helena has remarked during the play, all's well that ends well.

alliteration

The repetition of consonants, usually at the beginning of words and in a sequence. The effect can enhance mood or meaning; hard sounds such as a repeated 't' or 'k' might suggest anger or unease; soft sounds, 'f', 'l' and 's' can evoke tenderness, for example: 'Thus far for love my love suit, sweet fulfill' (Sonnet 136). *Compare* ASSONANCE.

allusion

A reference in a work of literature, made either directly or indirectly, to someone or something in a different work or another context. In *King Lear*, Gloucester makes a topical allusion when he speaks of 'these late eclipses in the sun and moon' which it is assumed refers to the eclipses which took place in England in 1605.

Alonso

A character in *The Tempest*, Alonso is the King of Naples and an old enemy of Prospero's. He supported Prospero's treacherous brother Antonio when he seized the dukedom of Milan, and twelve years later, Prospero uses his magic to bring Alonso to his island. Shipwrecked in the storm, Alonso is separated from his son Ferdinand whom he believes has drowned. Ariel, in the guise of a Harpy [a creature with a woman's face and eagle's wings and claws] tells Alonso that his heart-breaking loss is a punishment for his crime. Prospero uses his magic to control Alonso, imprisoning him and his companions in a kind of trance until he feels they have suffered enough. Alonso begs forgiveness for his treachery and he is pardoned by Prospero who reunites him with Ferdinand.

Ira Aldridge as Othello   *Courtesy of the Trustees of the V&A*

Aldridge, Ira (c.1807–1867)

A black American actor, born in New York, Aldridge made his name in England playing the parts of Shakespeare's two central black characters, Aaron and Othello, but he was equally acclaimed in the roles of Lear, Hamlet and Macbeth. His father was a minister and hoped that his son would follow him into the church, but Aldridge had his heart set on the theatre from an early age. At the age of 17, he met the English actor Henry Wallace (1790-1870) who persuaded him to come to England where there was less racial prejudice. Aldridge toured the British provinces and Europe, but his first great success came in 1833 when he replaced Edmund KEAN in the part of Othello at the Covent Garden Theatre in London. He was an eminent figure in the British theatre until his death, never returning to America, and his popularity with audiences increased the awareness of the potential of black Americans at a time when the American Civil War (1861-65) had made black slavery a controversial issue. *See also* BLACK CHARACTERS.

Alençon
A minor character in KING HENRY VI, PART ONE, a French nobleman and commander of King Charles' army fighting the English, Alençon is portrayed as an incompetent soldier who is unprepared when Talbot's English forces attack at Orleans.

Ambassador
A minor character in *Antony and Cleopatra*, whom Shakespeare's source for the play, PLUTARCH, identified as Euphronius; Antony sends the Ambassador to tell Caesar of his terms of surrender after the battle of Actium. When Caesar agrees to spare Cleopatra's life, but not Antony's, Antony sends the Ambassador back to Caesar with a challenge to hand-to-hand combat. The Ambassador is actually the schoolmaster employed to teach Antony's children, and one of Caesar's friends observes that it is a sign of Antony's complete defeat that he is reduced to using such a humble person as his representative.

Ambassadors
Minor characters in *King Henry V*, two French ambassadors visit King Henry's court with a contemptuous message from the Dauphin, and present Henry with the Dauphin's present of tennis balls.

Amiens
A minor character in *As You Like It*, Amiens is a member of Duke Senior's entourage living in the Forest of ARDEN. Amiens is a singer, and most of his songs reflect the Duke's contentment with his simple life in exile, which he prefers to the artificiality of court life. The best-known of Amiens' songs is 'Blow, blow, thou winter wind'.

anachronism
The presence of, or reference to, something in a work which belongs to a different (usually later) period in time. This may include an object or a costume, a style of language, or an event which has not yet occurred. Shakespeare was not always concerned with historical accuracy and one of several anachronisms in his plays is the mention of striking clocks in *Cymbeline* and in *Julius Caesar*; clocks had not been invented either in Ancient Britain or in Caesar's Rome.

anagnorisis
The moment of recognition, or a revelation of the truth by the characters in a play that leads to a resolution. An example in comedy is the moment when Viola reveals her identity at the end of *Twelfth Night*.

anapaest
A metrical FOOT, consisting of two short syllables followed by a long one.

Andromache
A legendary figure and a minor character in *Troilus and Cressida*, Andromache is the Trojan hero Hector's wife. Andromache has an ominous dream about death and, fearing for Hector's safety, she pleads with him not to fight with Achilles.

Angelo[1]
A minor character in *The Comedy of Errors*, Angelo is the goldsmith who makes a gold chain for Ephesus Antipholus to give his wife Adriana. His repeated unsuccessful

attempts to get paid for the chain add to the general confusions in the play, and his state of permanent bewilderment adds to the comedy.

Angelo[2]
A character in *Measure for Measure*, Angelo, a man whom the Duke trusts to be upright and incorruptible, is chosen to rule Vienna in the Duke's absence. The Duke's rule may have been too permissive, but Angelo's is too oppressive. He resurrects an old law against adultery and sentences Claudio to death for making his fiancée pregnant. Angelo is deaf to Isabella's pleading for her brother's life, until he finds himself attracted to her for displaying the very same qualities of inflexibility and restraint that he embodies. Overtaken by a lust that he despises in himself as much as in others, he agrees to spare Claudio's life in exchange for Isabella's sexual favours. Angelo is fooled by the substitution of his ex-fiancée Mariana in his bed, tricked into sparing Claudio, and trapped into confessing his guilt. Ordered by the Duke to marry Mariana, Angelo is redeemed by her love. He is spared from execution and makes a full repentance.

Angus
A minor character in *Macbeth*, Angus is a Scottish nobleman who joins forces with Malcolm against Macbeth.

Anne Boleyn (Bullen)
A historical figure (c. 1505-36) and a character in *King Henry VIII*, Anne is a Maid of Honour to Queen Katharine. She attends a banquet held by Cardinal Wolsey where she instantly charms the King. Anne has a high regard for Katharine and expresses sympathy with her plight; she says, with sincerity, that she herself would not be Queen 'for all the world'. However, Henry plans otherwise. He enobles her with the title of Marchioness of Pembroke, and although the honour makes her uneasy, she is reported soon after as having married the King in secret. Wolsey angrily opposes the marriage, because Anne comes from a Lutheran (Protestant) family, and he fears this will influence the King in his dealings with the Pope. At her coronation, Queen Anne is described by onlookers as having an angelic beauty and saint-like modesty that impressed everyone who saw her, including the crowds of ordinary people who cheered her to the rooftops. Anne's triumph is complete when she provides the King with a daughter.

Shakespeare's portrayal of Allen Boleyn or Bullen, is a piece of political propaganda. As the mother of Queen Elizabeth I, she is portrayed as a paragon of virtue. In fact her history was a chequered one and she probably had a series of love affairs before she married Henry. Certainly, her treatment of Katharine was often positively insulting, and scandalized many at court. Anne failed to produce the male heir to the throne that Henry so desperately needed, and after three years of marriage she was executed, accused of treason and adultery.

Anne, Lady
A historical figure (1456-85) and a character in *King Richard III*, Anne is the widow of the Prince of Wales whom Richard has supposedly killed earlier. Anne is chief mourner at the funeral of her father-in-law, the late King Henry VI, whom she believes was also one of Richard's victims. Richard interrupts the funeral procession and silkily woos Anne over Henry's corpse. Anne's initial hatred of Richard is undermined by his

hypnotic charm and she agrees to marry him, although her feelings for him continue to swing between loathing and fascination. Anne predicts that Richard will kill her, and indeed, when Richard sees that marrying Queen Elizabeth's daughter will make his position as King more secure, he spreads a rumour that Anne is fatally ill. Anne disappears from the scene and is heard of no more. Her ghost appears to haunt Richard on the eve of the Battle of Bosworth.

Anne Page
A character in *The Merry Wives of Windsor;* see PAGE, ANNE.

antagonist
A central character in a play who is in conflict with the hero (the protagonist), the antagonist is usually the villain. An example is Iago in *Othello*.

Antenor
A minor character in *Troilus and Cressida*, Antenor is one of the Trojan commanders. He was captured by the Greeks and is later exchanged for Cressida.

Antigonus
A character in *The Winter's Tale*, Antigonus is a Lord of Sicilia and Paulina's husband. When King Leontes wrongly accuses his wife Hermione of adultery, Antigonus dares to stand up to the King, and protests that Hermione is innocent. Leontes refuses to accept the legitimacy of his infant daughter Perdita, and orders Antigonus to take the baby to some wild coast and abandon her there. Antigonus, humane but ultimately weak, reluctantly obeys the King's command and takes the baby to Bohemia. He condemns himself for collaborating in the King's wickedness, but he is also a victim of Leontes' madness. Antigonus dies, eaten by a wild bear.

anti-hero
A central character in a play who does not embody the conventional virtues of a HERO. An example is Falstaff in *King Henry IV, Part One,* who demonstrates cowardice rather than the courage expected of a hero.

Antiochus
A minor character in *Pericles*, Antiochus is the wicked King of Antioch. When Pericles, in search of a wife, visits Antiochus' kingdom, he is required to first answer a riddle. The answer reveals that Antiochus has an incestuous relationship with his daughter. Antiochus sends an assassin after Pericles to try to ensure his silence. Justice is seen to be done when Antiochus is later reported dying a terrible death with his daughter, killed by the vengeful gods.

Antipholus of Ephesus
A character in *The Comedy of Errors*, Antipholus is the identical twin brother of Syracuse Antipholus *(see below)*, and the son of Egeon and Emilia. Shipwrecked in infancy, the twins were parted, and one Antipholus and his mother were washed up on the shores of Ephesus. Antipholus is now a respected citizen, who is happily married to Adriana and served by his slave, Dromio (who also has a long-lost identical twin). When, unknown to Ephesus Antipholus, his twin brother (also served by a Dromio twin) arrives in town, the identical brothers are repeatedly mistaken for each other in a

comedy of errors. Ephesus Antipholus finds himself called an imposter and barred from his own house. As his bewilderment increases, so does his anger, particularly against his wife. At the pinnacle of his frustration he is declared a lunatic by a Dr Pinch, but he escapes and gets his revenge setting fire to Pinch's beard. The mysteries are eventually solved by the appearance of the Antipholuses' long-lost mother and the twins are reunited.

Antipholus of Syracuse
A character in *The Comedy of Errors*, Syracuse Antipholus is the identical twin brother of Ephesus Antipholus (*see above*). In the shipwreck that separated the infant twins, this Antipholus and his father were washed up in Syracuse. Antipholus is now seeking his lost twin and arrives in Ephesus where, of course, he is repeatedly mistaken for his brother. Syracuse Antipholus, more happy-go-lucky by nature than his brother, is bemused rather than angry at all the confusion, although he begins to think that the town must be bewitched. He is confronted by a 'wife' who thinks he is mad and an angry crowd, who are backing a merchant who says he owes money, and he is forced to seek refuge in a nearby priory. There, the abbess turns out to be his long-lost mother Emilia, who explains away all the confusions.

anti-semitism
Anti-semitism existed in Shakespeare's England, but unlike the anti-semitism behind the Holocaust in the 20th century, 16th-century prejudice was based on religious beliefs, rather than race. English Christians believed that the JEWS had murdered Jesus Christ, but also that if a Jew converted to Christianity he or she would be forgiven. The Jewish character SHYLOCK is ordered to convert to Christianity at the end of The Merchant of Venice. *See also* JEWS, MERCHANT OF VENICE and SHYLOCK.

antithesis
A contrast or opposition of ideas; sometimes the exact opposite of something. An example is Romeo's expression of sorrow at parting from Juliet at dawn: 'More light and light: more dark and dark our woes'. See also OXYMORON.

Antonio[1]
A character in *The Merchant of Venice*, Antonio is the merchant of the title. He is a conventional, melancholic figure who represents an ideal of unselfishness. When his friend Bassanio needs money, Antonio is glad to help. He raises a loan from Shylock, and signs an agreement promising to forfeit a pound of his flesh if Bassanio ever fails to repay the loan. Antonio does not foresee such an event ever arising. However, his fleet of merchant ships are one by one lost at sea, Shylock demands repayment of the loan, and Antonio is arrested. He tries to reach a compromise with Shylock in court, but when he fails Antonio is resigned to Shylock taking his pound of flesh and even his life. When Portia turns the tables on Shylock, and he is stripped of his wealth, Antonio promises that his share of Shylock's money to Shylock's daughter Jessica, and insists that Shylock becomes Christian. At the end of the play Antonio remains single among the pairs of happy lovers.

Antonio[2]
A character in *The Tempest*, Antonio is Prospero's treacherous brother. Supported by Alonso, King of Naples, Antonio seized the Dukedom of Milan from Prospero, and

arranged for him to be cast adrift at sea with his daughter Miranda. Twelve years later, Prospero uses his magic to bring Antonio to his island. Shipwrecked in the storm of Prospero's making, the villainous Antonio encourages Alonso's brother Sebastian to kill Alonso while he sleeps, and snatch the crown of Naples. However, Prospero casts a spell on Antonio and the other survivors of the shipwreck before the murderous plan can be carried out. In the final reconciliation, Antonio returns the Dukedom of Milan to his brother and is forgiven by Prospero, but he is without conscience, and never expresses any remorse.

Antonio[3]

A character in *Twelfth Night*, Antonio is a sea captain, and friend to Sebastian whom he has rescued from shipwreck. Antonio accompanies Sebastian in Illyria, although is own life is in danger because of an old enmity with the ruler, Duke Orsino. Antonio encounters Viola, Sebastian's identical twin sister who is disguised as the page 'Cesario'. Viola/Cesario is about to fight a duel with Sir Andrew Aguecheek and Antonio, mistaking Viola for Sebastian, and anxious to help his friend, stops the fight. Antonio is arrested by Orsino's men, and needing money, he asks Viola for the return of a purse, that he had earlier lent to Sebastian. Viola can make no sense of his request and when she refuses to help him, Antonio feels he has been betrayed by his friend.

Antonio[4]

A minor character in *The Two Gentlemen of Verona*, Antonio is the hero, Proteus' father who sends his son to Milan.

Antonio[5]

A minor character in *Much Ado About Nothing*, Antonio is Leonato's brother and Hero's kindly old uncle. He dances at the masked ball and flirts with Hero's lady's maid Ursula, who recognizes him by his habit of wagging his head and because he has an old man's hands. Antonio joins in the trick of persuading Claudio that Hero has died of grief and angrily threatens to challenge him to a duel. At the end of the play, Antonio happily gives his veiled niece, Hero, in marriage to Claudio.

Antony, Mark

A historical figure (c. 82-30 BC) and a character in *Julius Caesar* and *Antony and Cleopatra*, he is sometimes referred to as Antonio.

In *Julius Caesar*, Antony is a loyal supporter of Caesar. According to Caesar, Antony is a pleasure-seeker, but actually he is ambitious and takes his political duties seriously. When Caesar is assassinated, Antony pours out his grief over Caesar's body and begs to be allowed to address the crowd. His emotional funeral oration is one of extraordinary eloquence and RHETORIC. He captures the imagination of the people, who a moment before had been pledging loyalty to Brutus, and incites them to kill Caesar's assassins. Although he may not have intended to advance himself personally, Antony's fortunes are now in the ascendant. He joins forces with Octavius Caesar and Lepidus to govern the Roman Empire. Octavius and Antony defeat Cassius and Brutus at Philippi, and Antony praises Brutus, describing him as a noble and honest man.

The tragic hero of *Antony and Cleopatra*, Antony is a military hero with many past glories to his name. He is one of the TRIUMVIRS ruling the Roman Empire but, spellbound by Cleopatra's sensual beauty, he has luxuriated and lingered in Egypt and neglected his political duties in Rome. His absence is resented by Caesar, who accuses him of complicity in a rebellion stirred up by Antony's wife Fulvia. Antony and Caesar become reconciled, and Antony makes a diplomatic marriage with Octavia, Caesar's sister, but the magnetic pull of Egypt and Cleopatra prove too strong for Antony to resist and he returns to Alexandria. Once a man of action, Antony is weakened by his passion for Cleopatra and loses the clear-sightedness he needs to fight the ensuing battles with Caesar. Defeated by his enemy, Antony is angry with Cleopatra for deserting him in battle, and disgusted with himself. When he is wrongly informed of Cleopatra's death, he is heartbroken, and commits suicide.

Antony and Cleopatra
One of Shakespeare's ROMAN PLAYS, *Antony and Cleopatra* is a late TRAGEDY written around 1606-08. There is no recorded performance of the play in Shakespeare's lifetime but it almost certainly was performed. It was first published in the First FOLIO edition of 1623, the eleventh play in the tragedy section.

The primary source of the play was a 16th-century English translation of *Lives of the Greeks and Romans* by PLUTARCH. It explores themes of the tension between duty and pleasure, the ordered and military world of Rome versus the passion and luxury of Egypt, and is full of some of Shakespeare's greatest dramatic verse. The fast moving action compresses eleven years of history into a matter of hours and moves from Italy to Egypt and beyond.

SYNOPSIS : Following the assassination of JULIUS CAESAR, the vast Roman Empire is ruled by three 'Triumvirs', Antony, Octavius Caesar and Lepidus. Antony is in Egypt, in love with the famously beautiful Queen Cleopatra, and his absence from Rome is resented particularly because his wife Fulvia has stirred up rebellion against Caesar. When Fulvia dies, Antony is recalled; he leaves the passionate Cleopatra with great reluctance and returns to a tense meeting with Caesar and Lepidus. In order to keep the triumvirate together, Antony agrees to a diplomatic marriage with Caesar's sister, Octavia. During Antony's absence in Egypt, the rebel Pompey has become increasingly powerful; popular with the people, he has made areas in the south of Italy his own. The Triumvirs negotiate a peace with Pompey but before long Caesar breaks the treaty, defeats Pompey and rids himself of Lepidus. Antony can no longer resist the pull of Egypt and Cleopatra, who has been pining for him. She had been furious to hear of Antony's marriage to Octavia and Antony makes amends by granting her part of the Roman Empire. Caesar's power is growing and Antony prepares for war. He makes a bad mistake in choosing to fight Caesar at sea rather than on land, and is defeated at Actium, largely because Cleopatra's fleet of ships sail away from the battle at a crucial moment. After another defeat at Alexandria, Antony begins to lose his grip on affairs, particularly after his friend and advisor, Enobarbus, defects to Caesar. He is angry with Cleopatra, who flees to a monument for safety. Cleopatra sends a message to Antony, announcing her suicide, and although she sends another message later to say that she is alive, it comes too late. Antony has stabbed himself and is already dying. He is taken to Cleopatra and dies in her arms. Cleopatra avoids the humiliation of being paraded as Caesar's prisoner by killing herself with a poisonous asp.

antonym
A word or phrase which means the opposite of another word. For example 'high' is an antonym of 'low'. *Compare* SYNONYM.

Apemantus
A character in *Timon of Athens*, Apemantus is described as a 'churlish philosopher'. He is a cynic, and his role is like a FOOL and CHORUS rolled into one. He attends Timon's banquet, refusing to eat, and announcing that he has just come to observe. Setting himself apart from the other guests, he philosophizes on the insincerity of the company, and human beings in general. He sees clearly what Timon fails to understand, that Timon is surrounded by hypocrites and flatterers. Apemantus visits Timon during his self-imposed exile in the woods and offers his friendship as well as food. He criticizes Timon for being a man of extremes. They exchange insults, and Timon turns on Apemantus and stones him. As he leaves, Apemantus threatens to spread the news of Timon's discovery of gold, news that will ensure that Timon has a stream of greedy visitors.

Apothecary
A minor character in *Romeo and Juliet*, the Apothecary in Mantua is the equivalent of a modern day pharmacist. He sells Romeo the poison with which he plans to commit suicide. The Apothecary is reluctant to provide the poison, as selling poison is punishable by death, but he is driven by desperate poverty to do so.

Apparitions
Minor characters in *Cymbeline*; Apparitions appear to Posthumus in a dream. *See* GHOSTS.

apron stage or thrust stage
A stage, often higher at the back than in the front, that projects into the body of a theatre, with the audience seated on three sides. This type of stage allows an intimacy between the spectators and the actors, who can approach the audience quite closely in a confiding way. Stages in Elizabethan PLAYHOUSES, which projected into the pit, were built to this design.

Arcas
A minor, non-speaking character in *The Two Noble Kinsmen*, Arcas is one of the five COUNTRYMEN who perform the Morris dance for Duke Theseus.

Archbishop of York, Richard Scroop
A character in *King Henry IV, Parts One and Two*; *see* SCROOP.

Archibald, Earl of Douglas
A character in *King Henry IV, Part One*; *see* DOUGLAS.

Archidamus
A minor character in *The Winter's Tale*, Archidamus is a member of King Polixenes' retinue when the King is visiting his old friend Leontes in Sicilia.

Arcite

One of the two Theban heroes of *The Two Noble Kinsmen*, Arcite is Palamon's cousin and inseparable friend. Until they set eyes on Emilia and become rivals for her love, the kinsmen are of one mind about everything. Arcite is freed from jail where the two friends are held as prisoners of war, but banished from Athens by Theseus. He envies his friend who, though still in prison, can watch Emilia from his prison window. Arcite enterprisingly disguises himself, and enters the May Day games in Athens. He has the good fortune to be noticed by Emilia, who admires his nobility and beauty. In the duel fought for Emilia's hand, Arcite defeats Palamon, but, riding in triumph through the streets, he is thrown from his skittish horse. With his dying breath, he gives Emilia to Palamon. Arcite and Palamon, courtly knights, are barely indistinguishable characters, but before the duel, Arcite offers prayers to the god of war, Mars, while Palamon appeals to Venus, goddess of love.

Arden, Forest of

The Forest of Arden is the imagined setting for *As You Like It*. Arden is a kind of Arcadia, a idealized PASTORAL world, where shepherds and shepherdesses fall in love, and where Duke Senior and his companions live in rustic simplicity. However, some of the characters in Shakespeare's invented rural paradise, such as Silvius and Audrey, are comic imitations of figures from the pastoral tradition.

Shakespeare may have got the name from the ancient Arden Forest in Warwickshire, from which his mother's family claimed to derive their name. A large part of the forest still covered the area around Stratford-on-Avon in Shakespeare's own time. Alternatively, it may be the English version of the 'Ardennes', a forested district on the borders of present-day France, Germany, and Belgium.

Arden, Mary (d. 1608)

Shakespeare's mother, Mary Arden was a gentlewoman from a Roman Catholic family living in Wilmcote, a village not far from Stratford-on-Avon, who married John Shakespeare in about 1577. She was the youngest of the eight daughters of Robert Arden, a prosperous yeoman farmer who leased land to Shakespeare's grandfather. Mary inherited a share of land and property from her father, but it was sold in about 1579 when the Shakespeare family were experiencing financial difficulties. Mary is buried in Stratford churchyard. The Arden House at Wilmcote, which remains largely unchanged from the 16th century, can be visited by the public.

Ariel

A character in *The Tempest*, Ariel is a spirit of the air on Prospero's enchanted island. Twelve years before the time of the play, Ariel was punished by a witch, Sycorax, for refusing to obey her. He was imprisoned in a tree trunk until Prospero arrived and released him. Grateful for his freedom, Ariel is duty bound to serve Prospero as his magical assistant, although he yearns to be entirely free. He is commanded by Prospero to raise the storm that drives the boat containing Prospero's enemies onto the island's shores. Invisible to all but Prospero, and sometimes in the guise of sea nymph, Ariel enchants Alonso and his companions with his spellbinding music and draws the drunken villains, Stephano and Trinculo, with invisible strings through the mud. When he has lured everyone to Prospero's cell, Ariel looks forward to the freedom that Prospero has

promised him and sings about the future; his final task is to ensure that the fleet of ships
with everyone aboard has a safe homeward journey.

Aristotle (384–322 BC)
A Greek philosopher whose discourse, *Poetics,* many regard as the first work of
LITERARY CRITICISM. In it Aristotle influentially discussed the nature of poetry and
TRAGEDY, although what he actually said has sometimes been misunderstood. He
argued that a tragedy should have one action only; in other words that there should be
no SUB-PLOT or deviation from the main narrative. A brief remark was taken to indicate
that the action of a play should take place on the stage within the same time it would
take in real life. He did not claim, as is often thought, that the setting of a play should be
confined to a single place. Aristotle described the effect of tragedy as cathartic [purging
emotions of pity and fear]. *See* CATHARSIS; UNITIES.

Armado, Don Adriano de
A comic character in *Love's Labour's Lost*; Armado is a Spanish nobleman. He is
ridiculous and vain, a man of fashion and a gambler, who has taken an oath with the
other noblemen at court to lead a life of celibacy and scholarship for three years.
Armado, a comic version of the Elizabethan STOCK CHARACTER of melancholic lover,
adores Jaquenetta and asks Costard to deliver a love letter to her. Unfortunately, the
letter, which is full of the overblown and extravagant rhetoric that is Armado's
hallmark, is misdelivered by Costard. The King asks Armado to arrange the court
entertainment. In the MASQUE of the Nine Worthies, Armado solemnly takes the part of
the hero Hector, but his performance is rudely interrupted by Costard's announcement
that Jaquenetta is pregnant by Armado. Armado's first response is to challenge Costard
to a fight, but when he has cooled down he promises to reform and to make an honest
woman of Jaquenetta.

Armin, Robert (c. 1568–c. 1615)
A principal actor and comedian who began his working life as an apprentice to a
goldsmith. He may have been trained by the comic actor Richard TARLTON before he
joined the LORD CHAMBERLAIN'S MEN around 1599, replacing the clown Will KEMP.
Shakespeare probably wrote the parts of Feste in *Twelfth Night* and Touchstone in *As
You Like It* for Armin, who is thought to have been a more sophisticated comic actor
than Kemp. He wrote a book of rhyming jokes, and a play *The History of Two Maids of
Moreclack*, c. 1597- 1599.

Arragon, (Aragon) the Prince of
A minor character in *The Merchant of Venice*, the proud Prince of Arragon is one of
Portia's unsuccessful suitors. When he is asked to choose one of the three caskets in
order to win Portia's hand, he decides on the silver casket, believing that only a lesser
man would make the more obvious choice of choosing gold.

Artemidorus
A minor character in *Julius Caesar*, Artemidorus has written a letter to Caesar telling
him about the conspiracy against his life. Artemidorus attempts to give the letter to
Caesar as he passes on his way to the Capitol but Caesar ignores him.

Artesius
A minor character in *The Two Noble Kinsmen*, Artesius is the army officer who is ordered by Theseus to prepare for war with the Thebans.

Arthur
A historical figure (1187-1203) and a character in *King John*, Arthur is Duke of Brittany and King John's nephew. Arthur, a young boy, is the son of Richard I Lionheart, and so is rightful heir to the English throne; but the crown has been taken by John. The French King Philip supports Arthur's mother, Constance, in her determination to see Arthur as King of England and goes to war with the English. King John places the innocent Arthur in Hubert's care with instructions to kill the boy but Hubert is touched by Arthur's pleas for mercy and lets him live. Hubert pretends to John that the boy is dead but in the meantime Arthur, still fearing for his life, dies trying to escape from the castle where he has been held.

Arviragus
A character in *Cymbeline*, Arviragus is the younger of Cymbeline's two sons who were snatched as young children by Belarius in revenge for an old injustice. For twenty years Belarius has brought up the two princes in exile in Wales and has given Arviragus the name 'Cadwal'. Despite their simple lifestyle, Arviragus and his brother Guiderius, have grown into princely young men. They show great kindness to the young boy 'Fidele' (actually their long-lost sister Imogen) who lands in their midst, and Arviragus is overcome with grief when they find 'Fidele' apparently dead. The two young men are determined to fight for their country and join the British forces when the Romans invade. They fight with such bravery that they turn the tide of the battle in favour of the Britons. In the fairy tale resolution to the play, the princes' true identities are revealed and they are reunited with their real father.

As You Like It
One of Shakespeare's pastoral comedies (*see* COMEDY; PASTORAL), *As You Like It* was probably written around 1598-1600; the history of the play's first performance is unrecorded. It was first published in the First Folio of 1623. The source for the play was a prose romance entitled *Rosalynde* by Thomas Lodge (c. 1557-1625) which was printed in 1590.

As You Like It, set mostly in the Forest of ARDEN, contrasts the formality and insincerity of court life with the simple goodness of country life. Shakespeare parodies some of the elements of traditional PASTORAL comedies in his creation of the comic shepherds and shepherdesses. There are a number of songs in the play, including the famous 'Blow, blow thou winter wind', and there is a large proportion of prose.

SYNOPSIS : Duke Frederick has seized the lands belonging to his elder brother, Duke Senior, and banished him to the Forest of Arden with a handful of companions, including the melancholy Jaques. There, they live a life of rural simplicity among romancing shepherds and shepherdesses. Orlando, orphan son of a nearby landowner, has also been cheated out of an inheritance by his brother, Oliver. About to try his luck in a wrestling match against the local champion, Orlando meets Rosalind, Duke Senior's daughter, who remained behind when her father was banished. Orlando and Rosalind fall instantly in love, but Orlando is forced to flee to the Forest of Arden when his brother plots to kill him. He meets up with Duke Senior and his party, and is invited to join them. When Rosalind, too, is banished from Duke Frederick's court, she flees to Arden disguised as a young man, 'Ganymede'. Her friend Celia, Duke Frederick's daughter, goes with her, disguised as 'Aliena'. In the Forest, Orlando cannot get Rosalind out of his mind. He carves her name on trees and decorates the forest with love poems. Rosalind discovers the poems, and when, in the guise of Ganymede, she meets Orlando, she teases him for being lovesick. In order to be cured of his complaint, she persuades Orlando to woo her as if she were really Rosalind, not Ganymede, while she spurns his love. Rosalind plays out an elaborate game, pretending to scorn romance, but in fact falling deeper and deeper in love herself. Oliver arrives in Arden to capture his brother Orlando, dead or alive. However, Orlando saves his brother from an angry lioness, and his unselfish heroism so impresses Oliver, that he is transformed into a loving brother. He falls in love with Celia, and surrenders his wealth to Orlando before marrying her. At their wedding, Rosalind, makes a surprise appearance as herself, and she and Orlando marry.

aside
A remark made by a character to the audience, rather than to another character on stage, and which it is assumed that the other characters cannot hear.

Asnath
The name of the spirit in *King Henry VI, Part Two* who is conjured up to make predictions at the Duchess of Gloucester's seance.

assonance
The repetition of vowel sounds within a sequence of words (but not the rhyming sounds repeated at the end of lines of verse). An example, in contemporary pronunciation, is: Nor Mars his sword nor war's quick fire shall burn' (Sonnet 55). The effect of assonance can be to evoke a particular mood; a burst of short vowel sounds may connote tension, while repeated long vowel sounds can suggest a more relaxed mood. *Compare* ALLITERATION.

Athenian, An Old
A minor character in *Timon of Athens*, the Old Athenian man complains to Timon that his daughter is being courted by one of Timon's servants, Lucilius. Because Lucilius is of a lower social class, the Old Athenian wants Timon to put a stop to Lucilius' visits to the his house, but instead Timon gives his servant enough money to make him an acceptable son-in-law to the old man.

Aubrey, John (1626–97)
The author of a collection of often inaccurate, but always entertaining, anecdotal biographies entitled *Brief Lives* (unpublished until 1898), which includes an apocryphal account of the life of William Shakespeare. Aubrey gleaned much of his information from William BEESTON, an actor whose father had been a member of the LORD CHAMBERLAIN'S MEN. Shakespeare is described as a 'handsome, well-shap't man: very good company, and of a very readie smooth witt'. Aubrey says Shakespeare's father was a butcher, and describes how William as a young apprentice to his father, would kill a calf 'in high style, and make a speech'. He says that 'he had little Latine and lesse Grek ... for he had been in his younger yeares a school-master in the countrey'. Aubrey

also records that in his travels between Stratford-on-Avon and London, Shakespeare
used to make regular visits to an inn where an affair with the inn keeper's wife resulted
in the birth, in 1606, of an illegitimate son, one William DAVENANT, who himself went
on to become a theatre manager.

audiences
Along with bull- and bear-baiting, plays were part of the popular culture of the
Elizabethans, and were enjoyed by audiences from all strata of society, except for the
very poorest. While the prices of seats in private theatres would have been too
expensive for all but the nobility or wealthy theatregoers, audiences in public
PLAYHOUSES would have included people from all walks of life, from nobles to petty
criminals. The audience in a public playhouse was accommodated in three tiers of
roofed seating around the sides of the theatre, and in an open, unroofed area in front of
the stage, known as the yard or PIT. Here the GROUNDLINGS, or poorer members of the
audience, stood, exposed to the elements, on mud and straw or rushes that were often
very wet. They would have paid about one penny, while seats in the galleries would
have cost twice that amount. The more expensive seats were the 'gentlemen's roomes'
and the 'twoe pennie roomes' in the galleries (see GALLERY), which were something
like boxes in a modern theatre. The best seats of all were stools on the side of the stage
itself which could be hired for about sixpence, although it was considered indecent for
women to be seated on the stage. Ale and other refreshments were on sale during
performances and while the spectators were probably attentive and appreciative, there
would have been a great deal of often rowdy audience participation. If they were
displeased with a play the audience would pelt the stage with fruit and nuts, stones or
even benches.

Audrey
A comic character, in *As You Like It*, Audrey is a goatherd in the Forest of ARDEN with
ambitions to be a 'woman of the world'. Audrey is a child of nature, uneducated and
easily confused by words such as 'poetical'. She is aware that she is no beauty either,
but says that if not pretty, she is, at least, honest. Touchstone, who loves and marries
her, describes Audrey as: 'An ill-favoured thing ... but mine own' and says he is glad to
marry her, because no one else will.

Aufidius, Tullus
A character in *Coriolanus*, Aufidius is a general commanding the Volscian army, who
shares Coriolanus contempt for the common people. Although Aufidius and Coriolanus
have a great respect for one another's courage, they are locked into a bitter rivalry, and
Aufidius longs for the opportunity to defeat Coriolanus in combat. When Aufidius and
Coriolanus make an alliance against Rome, Coriolanus is too arrogant to realize that
Aufidius may have ambitions of his own. While Coriolanus is bent on punishing Rome,
Aufidius is motivated by the desire to become more powerful than Coriolanus. Aufidius
is violently angry when Coriolanus betrays him and arranges for him to be killed. He
tramples on Coriolanus' body but is overcome by sorrow and acknowledges that his old
enemy was a man of honour.

Aumerle, The Duke of
A historical figure (c. 1373-1415) and a character in *King Richard II*, Aumerle is a
courtier and one of the flatterers of the King, whom Bolingbroke believes are a corrupt

influence. Aumerle is a hypocrite, who boasts to Richard of the pretended sadness he showed to Bolingbroke when he was banished, when actually he was delighted to see Bolingbroke leave England's shores. Aumerle remains a supporter of the King after Bolingbroke's return to England from exile, offering comfort and advice. After Bolingbroke has deposed the King, Aumerle is accused of having a hand with Richard in the murder of the Duke of Gloucester. He angrily denies the charge but is later punished by being stripped of his dukedom. With the Abbot of Westminster, Aumerle schemes against Bolingbroke, now crowned King, but his plot is discovered. He confesses, but when his mother pleads for his life, he is pardoned by Bolingbroke.

Austria, Limoges, Duke of

A minor character in *King John*, the Duke is referred to as 'Austria'. He is a supporter of King Philip of France against the English King John, and boasts that he killed the former English King, Richard Coeur de Lion. He is mocked and insulted by the Bastard (Richard Coeur de Lion's illegitimate son) who later cuts off his head in battle.

Autolycus

A comic character in *The Winter's Tale*, Autolycus is thoroughly disreputable, a self-confessed rogue, who never lets the opportunity for a bit of petty crime pass him by. He picks the pockets of the poor Old Shepherd's son, stealing the money he has set aside to pay for the sheep-shearing celebrations. There is a chance of more rich pickings for Autolycus at the celebrations, where he sells trinkets, ballads and ribbons to the country people of Bohemia and charms them with his singing. Autolycus sees another way to make money out of the simple Shepherd and his son. He tricks them out of money and the proof of Perdita's identity, terrifying them with stories of the tortures they will endure at Polixene's hands if they cannot prove that Perdita is more than just a simple shepherd girl. When Leontes makes the Old Shepherd and his son 'gentlemen' as their reward for caring for Perdita, Autolycus hopes there may be more opportunities to make his fortune out of them.

Auvergne, Countess of

A minor character in *King Henry VI, Part One*, the French Countess plans to take Talbot prisoner. Pretending that she simply wants to meet a military hero, the Countess invites him to her castle, but Talbot is suspicious of her and comes with a band of soldiers. Her plan foiled, the Countess declares herself honoured to have Talbot in her house, and asks him to dine with her anyway.

Bb

Bacon, Francis (1561–1626)
A philosopher, essayist and lawyer, Bacon became a member of parliament in 1584 and held office as Lord Chancellor in 1618. Accused of accepting bribes, he was briefly imprisoned in the TOWER OF LONDON and banished from parliament and James I's court. He was eventually pardoned but he never re-entered public life and died in debt in London. Some scholars have tried to prove that Bacon was the real author of the 'Stratford Peasant's' [i.e. Shakespeare's] plays. This theory, the BACONIAN THEORY, was conceived by an American namesake Delia Bacon, among others, in 1857, but she produced no convincing evidence for it.

'bad' quartos
See QUARTO.

Bagot, Sir John (William)
A historical figure (d. c. 1400) and a minor character in *King Richard II*, Bagot is one of the King's close advisers, a favourite and one of the flatterers whom Bolingbroke describes as parasites. When Bolingbroke returns from exile, Bagot flees to Ireland to join King Richard but he is captured by Bolingbroke. Bagot accuses Aumerle of being involved in the death of Bolingbroke's father, Gloucester; Bagot then disappears from the play.

Balthasar[1]
A minor character in *The Comedy of Errors*, Balthasar is a friend of Ephesus Antipholus. Antipholus invites him to dine at his house but finds that they have been locked out. Balthasar persuades him not to break down the door as such disorderly behaviour would be bad for his reputation.

Balthasar[2]
A minor character in *Much Ado About Nothing*, Balthasar is a singer in Don Pedro's retinue. He is modest about his voice but sings the song 'Sigh no more ladies' for his master. He is put in charge of organizing the music for Hero's wedding.

Balthasar[3]
A minor character in *Romeo and Juliet*, Balthasar is Romeo's faithful servant who brings the fateful, if mistaken, news of Juliet's death to his master in Mantua. He accompanies Romeo to the Capulet's tomb where he is ordered to leave Romeo alone on pain of death. Concerned for his master's safety, Balthasar waits in the churchyard but he can do nothing to prevent the tragic outcome.

Balthazar
A minor character in *The Merchant of Venice*, Balthazar is Portia's servant who is sent to fetch the male clothing that she and Nerissa use to disguise themselves.

BALTHAZAR is also the name Portia uses when she is pretending to be a young doctor from Rome in the court scene.

Bandits

Three minor characters in *Timon of Athens*, the Bandits hear that Timon, in his self-imposed exile in the woods, has found gold. They intend to rob Timon, but are startled to discover that he wants to give them gold as part of his plan to corrupt humanity. He praises them because they are more honest in their criminal way of life than those members of society who make a pretence of being virtuous.

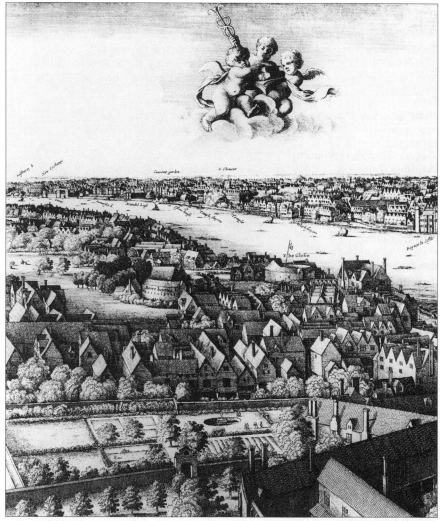

Bankside, London   © *Guildhall Library, London*

Bankside or Bank Side

A district of south London in Shakespeare's time, part of the present Southwark, extending for about half a mile along the south bank of the River Thames west of London Bridge and outside the limits of the City of London. Within this area of marshy ground where the houses were built on a raised dyke, there were prisons, bull rings, and bear pits such as the famous Beargarden, as well as several Elizabethan playhouses including the GLOBE and the ROSE. The theatre manager Philip Henslowe and the actor Edward Alleyn lived in Bankside and so possibly did Shakespeare between 1596 and 1599. The NATIONAL THEATRE now stands on the South Bank not far from the Bankside area. *See illustration on page 24 and the map of London in the supplement.*

Banquo

A character in *Macbeth*, Banquo is a Scottish nobleman and the father of Fleance. He is an honourable man and a courageous soldier who has fought alongside Macbeth with distinction, quelling a rebellion against King Duncan of Scotland. Returning from battle, Banquo and Macbeth encounter the three Witches who prophesy that Banquo's heirs shall become kings of Scotland. Banquo has premonitions of evil and after King Duncan's death, he becomes suspicious of Macbeth; before he can act, Macbeth arranges for him to be murdered too. Banquo's ghost returns to haunt Macbeth; it appears at a banquet and terrifies Macbeth who is the only person who sees the apparition. *See also* GHOSTS.

Baptista Minola

A character in *The Taming of the Shrew*, Baptista Minola is a rich citizen of Padua and father to Katherina (Kate) and her younger sister Bianca. Baptista is anxious to find a husband for Kate, whose shrewish [sharp-tempered] behaviour is making this very difficult, and he insists that until Kate is married Bianca must remain single. He is extremely relieved when Petruchio takes his difficult daughter off his hands and amazed at Petruchio's success in taming the 'shrew'. He is a sociable man and a good-natured father who does the best, as he sees it, for his daughters, but he has no real authority over two strong-minded young women.

Barbary[1]

A minor, non-speaking character in *The Two Noble Kinsmen*, Barbary is one of the Morris dancers. *See* COUNTRYWOMEN.

Barbary[2]

The name of King Richard's horse in *King Richard II* which Bolingbroke rides in the coronation procession when he is crowned King Henry IV. A 'Barbary' was the name for an Arab horse. *See* GROOM OF THE STABLE.

Barbican Theatre, The

The London home of the ROYAL SHAKESPEARE COMPANY since 1982. THE PIT, a smaller theatre converted from a rehearsal room, is housed in the Barbican centre.

bard

An old-fashioned word meaning poet. Shakespeare is sometimes referred to as 'The Bard' or the 'Bard of Avon'. The word BARDOLATORY, coined to describe an extreme reverence for the words of Shakespeare, is a combination of the words 'bard' and 'idolatory'.

Bardolph

A comic character in *King Henry IV, Parts One and Two*, *King Henry V* and *The Merry Wives of Windsor*, Bardolph is one of Falstaff's disreputable drinking companions, famous for his crimson complexion and in particular for his bright red nose which Falstaff says shines like a beacon in the dark. In *Henry IV, Part One*, Bardolph takes part in the highway robbery at Gad's Hill. In *Part Two*, he helps Falstaff to recruit villagers for the army and then pockets bribes from two of them to arrange their release.

In *The Merry Wives of Windsor*, Bardolph's role is a minor one. He works as a tapster [a server of ale] at the Garter Inn and brings Falstaff a quart of sack [sherry] to warm him up after his misadventure in a muddy ditch.

In *King Henry V*, Bardolph is a soldier in the King's army fighting in France. Lawless as ever (the Boy, Falstaff's Page, comments that he will steal anything), Bardolph robs a church but his crime is discovered and he is sentenced to be hanged.

Bardolph, Lord

A historical figure (1368-1408) and a minor character in *King Henry IV, Part Two*, Lord Bardolph is one of the nobles rebelling against the King. Lord Bardolph mistakenly brings Northumberland news that the rebels have been victorious when in fact they have been defeated. He is referred to throughout the play as 'Lord Bardolph', presumably so that he will not be confused with the fictional character of 'Bardolph' above.

Barnadine

A minor comic character in *Measure for Measure*, Barnadine is a long-serving prisoner who has been in the same gaol as Claudio. During the relaxed regime of the Duke of Vienna he came and went as he liked, and was often drunk for days at a time. On the day of his execution, Barnadine cheerfully refuses to cooperate with the executioner because he says he drank too much the night before, and is therefore unprepared to meet his death. In the reconciliation at the end of the play, the Duke pardons Barnadine.

Barnado

See BERNARDO.

Bartholomew

The name of the Page in *The Taming of the Shrew* who appears in the Induction; *see* PAGE.

Bassanio

A central character in *The Merchant of Venice*, Bassanio is Antonio's friend. He loves the wealthy Portia but cannot afford to woo her in the style befitting an heiress. Antonio suggests that Bassanio borrows money from Shylock, using his name as security on the loan; in doing so, Bassanio unwittingly endangers his friend's life. With money in his pocket Bassanio pays court to Portia. Put to the test of choosing the right casket of three, he chooses the least outwardly valuable because he knows how deceptive mere outward beauty can be, and wins Portia's hand in marriage. When news comes that Antonio's life is threatened by Shylock because the loan has not been repaid, Bassanio hurries to his side. In the courtroom he says he would sacrifice even his wife to save his friend, unaware that Portia is present, disguised as the lawyer. In the happy resolution to the play, Bassanio learns of Portia's role in saving Antonio's life.

Bassano, Emilia (1570-1654)

A member of a family of Italian musicians at Queen Elizabeth's court who had an affair with Lord Hunsdon, The Lord Chamberlain and patron of the LORD CHAMBERLAIN'S MEN, by whom she bore a child. While she was pregnant she married Alphonse LANIER, another royal musician. It is possible that Emilia Bassano may have known Shakespeare through her connection with the Lord Chamberlain's Men and she is one of the suggested candidates for the DARK LADY OF THE SONNETS.

Basset

A minor character in *Henry VI, Part One*, Basset is one of Somerset's followers and a supporter of the red rose faction of Lancaster who quarrels with one of the Duke of York's supporters. *See* LANCASTER, HOUSE OF.

Bassianus

A minor character in *Titus Andronicus*, Bassianus is a general in the Roman army. He loves Lavinia and when she is promised in marriage to his brother the Emperor Saturnius, Bassianus immediately snatches her away, helped by Titus' sons, and they marry. During a hunting party, Bassianus and Lavinia discover the adulterous Tamora in an illicit meeting with her lover the Moor Aaron. Bassianus is killed by Tamora's two sons so that he cannot tell Saturnius of his wife's infidelity. As part of Aaron's wicked scheme, Titus' sons Martius and Quintus are later framed for his murder.

Bastard, Philip the

A historical figure (d. c. 1228) and a character in *King John*, Philip is a half brother to Robert Faulconbridge. In a family dispute, Robert claims that Philip is a illegitimate and that he is not therefore entitled to inherit the Faulconbridge lands. When his mother, Lady Faulconbridge, confesses that Philip is indeed a bastard and the son of Richard Coeur de Lion [Lionheart], he becomes King John's protégé and is given the title of Sir Richard Lionheart. However, the Bastard still feels that he has been robbed of his birthright and is keenly aware of his poverty. Ambitious and greedy, he climbs the social ladder. A cynical but humorous character, he insults the King's enemies and mocks the nobility but he is one of the few nobles who remains loyal to the English cause. When King John is dead, the Bastard acknowledges Prince Henry as England's new King and ends the play with a speech of fervent patriotism.

Bastard of Orleans

A minor character in *King Henry VI, Part One*, the Bastard is one of the commanders of the French army who introduces La Pucelle, Joan of Arc, as the saviour of France to the Dauphin Charles.

Bates, John

A minor character in *King Henry V*, Bates is a soldier in the English army and one of the men to whom the disguised King talks on the eve of the Battle of Agincourt. He wishes he did not have to go into battle but nonetheless vows to fight bravely for his country.

Bavian

A minor, non-speaking part in *The Two Noble Kinsmen*, an 'actor playing a Bavian' appears in the cast list. The Bavian, an ape-like figure with a long tail, is a character in the Morris dance performed for Duke Theseus. See COUNTRYMEN.

Bawd
A minor comic character in *Pericles*, the Bawd (the word 'bawd' means pimp) runs the brothel with her husband the Pandar (another word for pimp) where Marina is sold into prostitution. She is a coarse, cold-hearted business woman, who regards her workforce as marketable assets rather than human beings. She tries to teach Marina the tricks of her new trade and becomes extremely angry when the virtuous Marina reforms her clients, and says she must either be raped, and lose her virginity, or be killed.

bawdy
Comic language crudely referring to sex; Mercutio's speeches in *Romeo and Juliet* are full of bawdy; for example he likens the lovesick Romeo to a jester 'that runs lolling up and down to hide his bauble in a hole [have intercourse]'.

Baylis, Lilian
See OLD VIC, THE

Beadle
One of several minor characters appearing in *King Henry IV, Part Two* and *King Henry VI, Part Two*; a beadle is a parish official whose job is to punish petty criminals. In *Henry IV*, Beadles are sent to punish Hostess Quickly and Doll Tearsheet because it is said they have been involved in murder. The women jeer at the First Beadle because he is so thin. In *Henry VI*, a Beadle is instructed to whip the imposter Simpcox.

Beatrice
The heroine of *Much Ado About Nothing*, Beatrice is Leonato's niece. She is a witty young woman with an acid tongue who scorns the very idea of love. However, her first words in the play reveal that flames of an old passion for Benedick still burn. Beatrice treats him with disdain, but when Hero and her companions trick her into believing that Benedick is in love with her, Beatrice gradually swallows her pride, and admits to herself that she returns his love. Her prickliness is a facade; at heart she is loving and loyal. When Hero is cruelly accused of infidelity, Beatrice remains convinced of her innocence, despite the evidence against her, and asks for Benedick's support. United by a common cause, Beatrice and Benedick's romance blossoms. They marry alongside Hero and Claudio, and Benedick stops Beatrice's final witticism with a kiss.

Beaufort, Cardinal
See WINCHESTER, BISHOP OF.

Beaumont, Francis (c. 1584–1616)
A dramatist and poet, Beaumont was a friend of Ben JONSON who, from about 1606 to 1616, collaborated with John FLETCHER in writing plays. Among these were *Philaster* (1610) and *The Maid's Tragedy* (1611); Beaumont is thought to have been the sole author of the comedy *The Knight of The Burning Pestle* (1609). In 1613 he married a wealthy woman and from then on ceased writing for the theatre.

Bedford, Duke of
A historical figure (1389-1435) and a minor character in *King Henry V* and King *Henry VI, Part One*; in *Henry V*, Bedford is King Henry's brother who is present at Agincourt. In *Henry VI*, Bedford is the young King's uncle and the Regent who rules in France. A brave soldier, Bedford mourns the loss of King Henry V at the beginning of the play and

fights for England at Orleans. At Rouen, Bedford is ill and appears in a chair but he is determined to cheer his men on to the fight and dies happily after the English are victorious. The Duke of Bedford is the same historical figure who appears in *King Henry IV, Parts One and Two,* where is he known as PRINCE JOHN.

Beeston, Christopher (d. 1638)
An actor and member of a company of actors, the LORD CHAMBERLAIN'S MEN, for about four years from 1598. Thereafter, he acted with and managed a number of smaller companies, eventually forming his own company of boy actors popularly known as 'Beeston's Boys'. His son, WILLIAM BEESTON, who was also an actor, provided biographical information about Shakespeare for John AUBREY'S *Brief Lives*.

Belarius
A character in *Cymbeline,* Belarius, a Lord, was wrongly accused of treason and banished by Cymbeline before the beginning of the play. In revenge for this injustice, Belarius snatched the King's two young sons, Arviragus and Guiderius, and took them with him to live in exile in Wales. Disguised as 'Morgan', the white-haired Belarius enjoys the simple life they have led for twenty years, which he says is more honest than life at court. He is a good old man who shows kindness to the disguised Imogen and insists that Cloten is given a decent burial. Despite his age, Belarius fights with such vigour against the Roman enemy that he is knighted by Cymbeline after the battle. When Guiderius is condemned to death for killing Cloten, Belarius is forced to reveal his identity and confess to his crime in order to save his adopted son's life. In the reconciliation that ends the play Belarius is forgiven by Cymbeline.

Belch, Sir Toby
A comic character in *Twelfth Night,* Sir Toby is Olivia's uncle who, as his names implies, indulges an immoderate appetite for food and drink. A man with a zest for life who enjoys a practical joke, Sir Toby encourages Maria to make a fool of his old adversary, the PURITAN Malvolio. However, Sir Toby is not altogether good-natured. A deception that began innocently turns cruel when he proposes that as a joke, Malvolio should be imprisoned and treated as a madman. There is mischief in Sir Toby's less than kind manipulation of his friend Sir Andrew Aguecheek, whom he persuades to fight a duel with the disguised Viola. He describes Viola as a fearless fencer, knowing full well that Sir Andrew will be terrified. When the joke rebounds and they are both beaten over the head by Sebastian, Sir Toby turns petulantly on his friend calling him a fool. In the happy resolution to the play, Sir Toby is reported as marrying Maria.

Bellario
In *The Merchant of Venice,* Bellario is mentioned but does not appear. He is a relation of Portia and a learned doctor of Padua who provides the men's clothing for Portia and Nerissa's disguise. When Portia arrives for the trial between Shylock and Antonio she announces herself as being sent by Dr Bellario who has sent a letter praising her ability as the young lawyer from Rome.

Belleforest, François de (1530–1583)
A French author whose work, particularly a collection of stories entitled *Histoires Tragiques,* published in English in 1566, may have provided the sources for some of Shakespeare's plays such as *Hamlet, Titus Andronicus,* and *Twelfth Night.*

Benedick
The hero of *Much Ado About Nothing*, Benedick is a young soldier who is just returned from war. A humorous and light-hearted young man, he enjoys the company of women, but scorns the idea of love and repeatedly vows never to marry. Benedick's relationship with the prickly Beatrice is combative but he clearly enjoys their witty exchanges. Tricked by Claudio and his companions into believing that Beatrice loves him, Benedick admits to himself that he returns her love, although his attempts to woo her with his inept poetry are a dismal failure. When Beatrice calls on Benedick to defend Hero's honour, Benedick obliges, agreeing to fight a duel with Claudio, although it means making an enemy of an old friend. Joined with Beatrice in a common cause, Benedick declares his love; he rejects his earlier opinions of marriage, sealing his love for her with a kiss.

Benfield, Robert (d. c. 1650)
One of the 26 principal actors listed in the First FOLIO edition of Shakespeare's plays in 1623. He joined the KING'S MEN, probably in 1614 and remained with the company until 1642.

Benvolio
A character in *Romeo and Juliet*, Benvolio is a friend of Romeo and Mercutio, and Montague's nephew. His name means 'good will' and his role in the play is a conciliatory one. He first appears trying to make peace between the brawling servants of the Montague and Capulet households. Later he attempts to dissuade Mercutio from fighting with Tybalt and, after the fateful duel between them, he gives a fair account of events to the Prince. Thereafter, he plays no further part in the action of the play.

Berkeley
A minor character in *King Richard III*, Berkeley is Lady Anne's silent attendant.

Berkeley, Lord
A historical figure (d. 1416) and a minor character in *King Richard II*, Lord Berkeley greets the exiled Bolingbroke on his return to England and asks him, on behalf of the Duke of York, Governor of England, the reason for his invasion.

Bernardo (Barnado)
A minor character in *Hamlet*, Bernardo is one of the sentries who has seen the Ghost of Hamlet's Father before the beginning of the play.

Bernhardt, Sarah (1845–1923)
A French actress and tragedienne, Sarah Bernhardt played Lady Macbeth and Cordelia in *King Lear* in French translations and also took the part of Hamlet in Paris, London and New York. She repeated her success in this role in a silent film of *Hamlet* (1900), the first film of the play ever to be made.

Berowne (Biron)
The hero of *Love's Labour's Lost*, the witty Berowne is a young nobleman at the court of Navarre where the King and his companions have sworn to renounce the company of women for a period of three years and to devote their time to learning. Berowne, a realist, doubts that they will be able to keep their vow and he is proved right when the

French Princess and her companions arrive from France, and he immediately falls in love with Rosaline. Torn between love and scholarship, Berowne secretly courts Rosaline, justifying himself by claiming that women are the source of all learning. Berowne and his companions abandon their vows and, absurdly disguised as Russians, woo the young ladies with high-flown speeches. The women mock them and Berowne realizes that plain speaking rather than extravagant language is the way to win them round. At the end of the play, Rosaline demands that Berowne proves his love by spending a year caring for the sick.

Berry, Duke of
A minor character in *King Henry V*, the Duke of Berry is named in the cast list but his role is a silent one.

Bertram, Count of Rossillion (Rousillon)
The hero of *All's Well that Ends Well*, Bertram is an arrogant young nobleman. Despite his protestations, he is forced by the King of France into marrying Helena, whom he despises because her social rank is so far beneath his own. Disgusted, Bertram leaves for the war in Italy in a sulk, vowing never to sleep with his wife until she fulfils two seemingly impossible conditions. In Italy, Bertram sets out to seduce a virgin, Diana, but fails to notice in the darkness that Helena has taken her place. His response to news of Helena's supposed death is casual to say the least, and his treatment of Diana, as he tries to lie his way out of trouble, marks a further moral decline. Shameful though Bertram's behaviour is, he is partly excused because of his youth, and the obvious influence of Parolles. In the happy resolution to the play, Bertram is reunited with his loving and constant wife.

Bess, Good Queen
See GOOD QUEEN BESS.

Betterton, Thomas (1635–1710)
A leading actor and member of the company of actors managed by William DAVENANT (who claimed to be Shakespeare's illegitimate son), Betterton was acclaimed in the roles of Hamlet, Macbeth and Othello. He wrote an adaptation of *Henry IV, Parts One and Two*, which was immensely popular in his lifetime.

Bevis, George
A minor character in *King Henry VI, Part Two*, Bevis is one of the rebel Jack Cade's followers. It is believed that the name 'George Bevis' may have belonged to the actor who originally played the part of the character, who otherwise had been given no name.

Bianca[1]
A character in *Othello*, Bianca is a courtesan and Cassio's adoring but quick-tempered mistress who is made wildly jealous when she mistakenly thinks Cassio has given her a handkerchief belonging to another woman. When she finds Cassio lying wounded in the street, Bianca is genuinely distressed and although Emilia calls her a 'strumpet' [prostitute] she says her life is an honest one.

Bianca[2]
A central character in *The Taming of the Shrew*, Bianca is Katherina's beautiful and apparently demure younger sister, who suffers from her sister's violent outbursts of

temper. She has a string of suitors, but her father insists that she remains single until Katherina has found a husband. Bianca obediently agrees to devote her time to study, but when the disguised Lucentio woos Bianca under the pretence of teaching her Latin, she becomes much less serious about her lessons. With an unexpected show of strong-mindedness, she marries Lucentio in secret and without her father's consent. At a banquet held to celebrate Bianca's and Katherina's marriages, their husbands make a bet on which of the two sisters is the most obedient. Bianca refuses to obey her husband just because he wants to win his bet, and ironically shows herself to be more independent than her reformed sister.

Bigot, The Lord
A minor character in *King John*, Bigot is a noble who rebels against King John after the death of Arthur and joins the French forces.

Biondello
A minor character in *The Taming of the Shrew*, Biondello is Lucentio's servant. When Lucentio's other servant, Tranio, disguises himself as their master, Biondello enters into the deception with great enthusiasm. He describes Petruchio's journey to his wedding dressed in shabby old clothes and riding a broken-down old horse.

Birnam Wood
A forest in *Macbeth,* close to Dunsinane castle. The three Witches prophesy that Macbeth will be safe until Birnam Wood moves to Dunsinane. This seemingly impossible prediction comes true when Malcolm's army camouflaged with branches cut from the woods marches on Macbeth at Dunsinane, and he is killed.

Biron
See BEROWNE.

Birthplace, The
The house in HENLEY STREET in Stratford-on-Avon where Shakespeare was almost certainly born. The house has changed little since the 16th century, and it can be visited today.

Bishop of Ely
See ELY, BISHOP OF.

Bishop of Lincoln
See LINCOLN, BISHOP OF.

Bishop of Winchester
See WINCHESTER, BISHOP OF.

Bishops
Minor characters in *King Richard III*, the Bishops are employed by Richard to help give an impression that he is a pious man when he meets the Mayor. In fact, neither clergyman is a bishop; one is a doctor, Dr Shaa, and the other is a humble friar, Friar Penker.

black characters
Africans were regarded as exotic in Shakespeare's England and were popular on the stage; in Love's Labour's Lost, for example, 'Blackamoors' are featured in the

MASQUE. However, there are only two central black characters in Shakespeare's plays. One is Othello, a Moor and the tragic hero of the play of that name, whom Shakespeare portrays as a noble man and a courageous soldier. Iago, the villain of the play, crudely associates Othello's colour with bestial sexuality, but only he and Desdemona's angry father, Brabantio, make Othello feel that race is an issue in the play. Shakespeare may have created his character after a visit to London by the Moorish ambassador from the King of Barbary in 1600.

Shakespeare's other central black character is Aaron, the villain of Titus Andronicus who describes himself as have a soul as black as his face, and speaks of his infant child as a 'thick-lipped slave'. Aaron's colour distinguishes him from the other characters, but in a play in which the white hero Titus is also capable of horrific cruelty, Shakespeare does not connect evil with the colour of a character's skin.

Some postcolonial [a critical term referring to the impact of European and Western culture on another existing culture] interpretations of Shakespeare's plays regard the character of Caliban, Prospero's slave in The Tempest, as having racial implications, although Shakespeare makes no reference to Caliban's colour. The French Caribbean playwright Aimé Césaire (1913-) portrays Caliban as a black slave and Prospero as a white colonialist in his reworking of The Tempest, *Une Tempête* (1969). *See also* ALDRIDGE, IRA, ROBESON, PAUL.

Blackfriars
A district in the City of London, close to St Paul's Cathedral, which in Shakespeare's time was a fashionable residential area. See the map of London at the back of the book.

Blackfriars Theatre
An Elizabethan playhouse in Blackfriars in London; designed by James BURBAGE, who bought the lease in 1596, it was converted from another theatre which had been erected earlier by Richard FARRANT on the site of a 13th-century Dominican priory. It was originally planned as a public theatre, but local residents feared having rowdy audiences in their neighbourhood and insisted that the theatre should continue to accommodate BOY COMPANIES only. It therefore became a rather exclusive and expensive private theatre. The CHILDREN OF THE CHAPEL played there from 1600 to 1608 when Shakespeare's company the LORD CHAMBERLAIN'S MEN (later the King's Men) acquired the lease. Many of his later plays were performed here, particularly during the winter months because, unlike the GLOBE, it had a roof which protected audiences from bad weather. The building was pulled down in 1655. See PLAYHOUSES.

Blanche
A historical figure (d. 1254) and a minor character in *King John*, Blanche of Spain is King John's niece who marries the French Dauphin, Lewis. When war breaks out between England and France, Blanche has conflicting loyalties and is concerned for the safety of both her husband and her uncle.

blank verse
A form of unrhymed verse, usually written in lines with a regular arrangement of five stressed and five unstressed syllables known as IAMBIC PENTAMETER. For example:

> If music be the food of love, play on,
>
> Give me excess of it, that, surfeiting,
>
> The appetite may sicken, and so die.

Blank verse was first used in England by the Earl of Surrey in his translation of *The Aeneid* (1540) and by the time Shakespeare was writing, it had become the standard medium for dramatic verse.

Blunt, Sir James
A historical figure (d. 1493) and a minor character in *King Richard III*, Blunt is a member of Richmond's victorious army at the Battle of BOSWORTH.

Blunt, Sir John
A historical figure (d. 1418) and a minor character in *King Henry IV, Part Two*, Blunt is one of King Henry's supporters who is ordered to guard the rebel Coleville.

Blunt, Sir Walter
A historical figure (d. 1403) and a minor character in *King Henry IV, Part One*, Blunt is one of King Henry's supporters. He distinguishes himself on the field of battle when, disguised as the King, he fights to the death in single combat with Douglas who believes him to be Henry.

Boatswain
A minor character in *The Tempest*, the Boatswain is one of the crew of the ship that is driven onto Prospero's island in the storm. An old hand, used to storms at sea, he is infuriated when Antonio and Sebastian give advice on how best to manage the boat and orders them to return to their cabins. In the magical resolution to the play, the Boatswain expresses his amazement at finding the ship has miraculously been repaired.

Bolingbroke, Henry; Duke of Hereford (Herford) and later King Henry IV of England
A historical figure (1366-1413)and a character in *King Richard II*, Bolingbroke is the son of John of Gaunt and King Richard's cousin. He is a forceful young man, unlike the weak and changeable Richard. Bolingbroke is banished by Richard for treason but, when his father dies and Richard seizes the family wealth and titles that should rightfully be his, Bolingbroke returns to England and demands the restitution of his inheritance. While Richard is pondering on his best course of action, Bolingbroke raises a rebellion against him. When Richard eventually capitulates and agrees to the return of Bolingbroke's possessions, it is too late to appease Bolingbroke who has the ineffectual king thrown in prison. Richard is later murdered, and Bolingbroke is crowned King HENRY IV. Later, Bolingbroke suffers pangs of guilt and vows to go on a pilgrimage to the Holy Land to seek forgiveness.

Bolingbroke, Roger
A minor character in *King Henry VI, Part Two*, Bolingbroke is a conjurer. He pretends to summon up spirits so that the Duchess of Gloucester can question them about the future and ask them about the chances of her making a successful bid for power.

Bona
A minor character in *King Henry VI, Part Three*, Bona is the French King's sister-in-law. A political marriage is proposed between Bona and King Edward but when Edward disregards the arrangement and marries someone else instead, she calls for revenge.

book
The script of a play, used as the acting version by a company of actors. In Shakespeare's time, the hand-written book, prepared with notes and stage directions by the BOOK-KEEPER, had to be submitted to the MASTER OF THE REVELS for licensing before the play could be performed in public.

book-keeper or book-holder
A member of an Elizabethan theatre company who was responsible for the safe-keeping of the hand-written play scripts (known as books) and for submitting them to the MASTER OF THE REVELS for permission to perform a play. He prepared the text with notes about STAGE DIRECTIONS, and copied out individual parts on rolls of paper (from which the word ROLE may derive), as well as performing the duties of the PROMPTER. He also would have written out the plot of a play with notes about PROPS and stage directions, etc., and hung it at the back of the stage to help actors who had to learn new plays all the time; this was called the PLATT. The character of Quince in *A Midsummer Night's Dream* is a caricature of a book-keeper.

Borachio
A minor character in *Much Ado About Nothing*, Borachio is one of Don John's followers. He is paid by Don John to blacken Hero's name and so prevent her marriage to Claudio from going ahead. Borachio arranges a night-time assignation with Hero's maid Margaret, and makes it appear as if it is Hero who is flirting with another man. Borachio is overheard by the night watchmen boasting of his deception to Conrade and is arrested by Dogberry. Borachio, believing that Hero has died of shame, confesses and repents.

Bosworth
The site of the Battle of Bosworth (1485), in the English Midlands, where King Richard III was defeated by the Earl of Richmond, later to become King Henry VII. In Shakespeare's play, *King Richard III*, Richard famously loses his horse in the battle. The battle of Bosworth is of particular significance in English history as it marked the end of the WARS OF THE ROSES and the beginning of the TUDOR Dynasty.

Bottom, Nick
A comic character, a CLOWN, in *A Midsummer Night's Dream*, Bottom is a weaver and one of the Athenian workmen who enacts the MASQUE of *Pyramus and Thisbe* before Duke Theseus. His name may derive from the ball of thread or yarn which was known as a 'bottom'. Bottom is an ambitious amateur actor who takes acting very seriously. Cast in the main role of Pyramus, he is worried about the kind of beard the hero would wear, and when it comes to the scene of Pyramus' death he gives a sensational performance. Bottom enjoys the sound of his own voice, although he frequently and comically misuses words, but he is at heart a good-natured and courteous man. The victim of Puck's mischief and with his head transformed into an ass's head he is adored

by Titania and enjoys the attentions of her fairies. When the spell is removed, Bottom reflects with wonder on the experiences of his 'dream'.

The character of Bottom may have been a parody of Edward ALLEYN, an actor in the ADMIRAL'S MEN, the rival group of actors to Shakespeare's company the LORD CHAMBERLAIN'S MEN.

Boult
A comic character in *Pericles*, Boult is a servant at the brothel run by the Pandar and the Bawd who is put in charge of advertising Marina's charms in the market-place. When Marina's innocence and virtue has the effect of driving away custom from the brothel, Boult tells her she must either lose her virginity or be killed, because she is letting down the profession of the prostitute. Boult, however, has a streak of decency, unlike his employers, and he is persuaded by Marina to find her somewhere else to live among honest women. He rather doubts that he will be able to persuade the Bawd and the Pandar to free Marina, but a bigger problem he says is that he has very few honest acquaintances.

Bourbon, Duke of
A minor character in *King Henry V*, the Duke of Bourbon urges his fellow French nobles to follow him and fight the English to the death at Agincourt. He is later mentioned as one of the French soldiers killed in the battle.

Bourchier, The Lord Cardinal
See CARDINAL, LORD BOURCHIER.

Bowdler, Thomas (1754–1825)
The editor of the *Family Shakespeare* (1818), a radically expurgated edition of the plays which excluded any of the passages that Bowdler thought were offensive or indecent, and which was very popular with Victorian readers. The term 'bowdlerize', meaning to censor and cut text, derives from his name.

Boy
A minor character appearing in the cast list of several of Shakespeare's plays, a Boy is often a servant, for example Falstaff' PAGE in *King Henry V*, Mariana's Boy in *Measure for Measure*, who sings the song 'Take, O take those lips away' to her. In *The Two Noble Kinsmen*, a Boy in a white robe takes part in the wedding procession of Theseus and Hippolyta, singing and strewing flowers.

Sometimes the Boy is a child character, for example Macduff's son who is murdered in *Macbeth*, or King Richard's nephew who is imprisoned in *King Richard III*. Such a part would have been played by an apprenticed boy actor belonging to an adult company of players, such as Shakespeare's LORD CHAMBERLAIN'S MEN, or by a younger child actor from one of the BOY COMPANIES (*see below*). Today, the part of a 'Boy' is often played by a woman.

boy companies or boy players
Companies of boy actors, such as the CHILDREN OF THE CHAPEL and the CHILDREN OF ST PAUL'S, who were recruited from schools or the chapels of the royal household, where acting and the art of RHETORIC formed part of their education. The boys were trained by scholars and musicians to act, often in Latin, and to sing and dance. Boy

companies were serious rivals to adult companies. They performed plays written for adults and with adult characters in them regularly for the Elizabethan court and at the private BLACKFRIARS THEATRE, though never in the less exclusive public playhouses. By the 1580s, their popularity had waned, but under the patronage of James I, who came to the throne in 1603, new children's companies were established, including the CHILDREN OF THE KING'S REVELS in 1606. The CHILDREN OF THE QUEEN'S REVELS, an earlier company which had failed, was re-established under the patronage of King James's wife, Queen Anne in 1610. The popularity of boy actors continued into the next decade, but by the 1630s children's companies had died out. Boy actors often went on to join companies of adult players when their voices broke, becoming apprenticed for two or three years to an established actor who would instruct and maintain them.

When actors visit Elsinore in *Hamlet*, Rosencrantz describes boy players as 'an eyrie [nest] of children, little eyases [noisy young hawks]', a direct reference to the Children of the Chapel. See ACTORS AND ACTING; COMPANIES OF ACTORS; CHILDREN OF THE KING'S REVELS.

Boyet
A minor character in *Love's Labour's Lost*, Boyet is a witty and elegant nobleman in the entourage of the Princess of France. He is smooth-tongued and something of a ladies' man, according to Berowne who takes a strong dislike to him. Boyet is highly amused when he overhears the King and his young companions plan to court the French ladies in disguise as Russians and warns the Princess of their intentions.

Brabantio
A minor character in *Othello*, Brabantio is Desdemona's father who cannot forgive his daughter for marrying Othello in secret.

He abuses Othello and accuses him of bewitching his daughter and drugging her with magic herbs. Ironically, he warns Othello that Desdemona may deceive him as she has deceived her own father. Brabantio is reported as dying from grief.

Bradley, A. C. (Andrew Cecil) (1851–1935)
A literary critic and scholar, Bradley is best known for his psychological character analyses, entitled *Shakespearean Tragedy* (1904). *See* SHAKESPEAREAN CRITICISM.

Brakenbury, Sir Robert
A historical figure (d. 1485) and character in *King Richard III*, Brakenbury is Lieutenant of the TOWER OF LONDON and gaoler of the young princes murdered there. He arrests Clarence on Richard's instructions, and prevents Queen Elizabeth, the Duchess of York and Lady Anne from visiting the princes. Though not complicit in Richard's villainy, Brakenbury chooses not to ask questions. He remains loyal and dies fighting for Richard on the battle field of Bosworth.

Brandon
A minor character in *King Henry VIII*, Brandon arrests the Duke of Buckingham and Lord Abergavenny for treason. They are to be taken to the TOWER OF LONDON, and Brandon says he is sorry to see them denied their freedom.

Brandon, Sir William

A historical figure and a minor character in *King Richard III*, Brandon is one of
Richmond's followers who is killed at the Battle of Bosworth.

Bretagne (Britain, Brittany), Duke of

A minor character in *King Henry V*, the Duke of Bretagne is one of the French nobles
who expresses his surprise at the fighting ability of the English.

Brook

The name that the disguised Ford uses in *The Merry Wives of Windsor*; see FORD,
FRANK.

Brooke, Arthur (d. 1563)

A poet and translator, Brooke wrote *The Tragicall Historye of Romeus and Juliet*
(1562), a long and rather leaden verse version of a French prose story from *Histoires
Tragiques* (1559), by the French writer BELLEFOREST. It was almost certainly the source
of Shakespeare's *Romeo and Juliet*.

Brother

A minor character in *The Two Noble Kinsmen*, the Jailer's Brother brings his deranged
niece, the Jailer's Daughter, back home after she has been found wandering.

Brutus, Junius

A character in *Coriolanus*, Brutus is created a tribune [representative of the people] with
Sicinius after rioting over corn shortages has disrupted the city. Brutus is ageing, bald,
sly and insincere and he allows Sicinius to do most of the talking. The tribunes condemn
the aristocratic Coriolanus for his arrogance and after he has been proposed as a Consul,
they incite the crowd to riot. Brutus has Coriolanus arrested and suggests throwing him
off a rock to his death but he is overruled. Brutus and Sicinius, in manipulating the
volatile populace, are responsible for Coriolanus' banishment and his subsequent march
on Rome but they put the blame on the ruling Senators.

Brutus, Marcus

A historical figure (c. 79-42 BC) and a character in *Julius Caesar*, Brutus is a member
of the Senate, the ruling council in Rome, who is growing ill with worry about Caesar's
abuse of power. A thinker and a man of conscience, he decides that Caesar's life may
have to be sacrificed to free Rome from his tyranny, and he is persuaded by Cassius to
lead a conspiracy against their leader. After the assassination, Brutus reassures the
people of Rome that he is not seeking power for himself, and although the crowd call
for him to be their leader, he quietly walks away. However, Brutus can be almost as
high-handed as Caesar, and his refusal to take advice leads him to make serious errors of
judgement. He underestimates Antony, allowing him to make his influential funeral
oration, and he makes a disastrous tactical mistake at Philippi. Brutus kills himself in
order to avoid the capture and dishonour he most dreads. Beyond the world of politics,
Brutus is a kind man, held in great affection not only by his wife, but by his friends and
even his servants, and respected by his enemies.

Buckingham, Duke of[1]

A historical figure (1402-55) and character in *King Henry VI, Part Two and father of the
Buckingham in King Richard III* (see below), Buckingham conspires with Somerset and

Suffolk to discredit the Duke of Gloucester. Buckingham sees himself as a possible successor to Gloucester's position as Protector. He is sent by the King to offer pardons to Jack Cade's followers and confronts the rebellious Duke of York on the King's behalf.

Buckingham, Duke of[2]

A historical figure (1455-83) and character in *King Richard III*, Buckingham is Richard's chief ally and spokesman whom Shakespeare describes in a rare stage direction as wearing rusty armour, indicating his corrupt nature. Buckingham is well aware of Richard's murderous villainy and plays an active role in his conspiracies and, like Richard, openly admits that he is two-faced. However, when Richard proposes to murder the little Princes in the TOWER OF LONDON, Buckingham has misgivings and raises forces against the King. He is captured and executed. Buckingham's ghost appears to haunt Richard on the eve of the Battle of Bosworth.

Buckingham, Duke of[3]

A historical figure (1478-1521), and a character in *King Henry VIII*, Buckingham is outspoken, and angry about Cardinal Wolsey's abuse of power. He senses that Wolsey is planning his downfall, and his suspicions are proved correct. The first of Wolsey's victims, Buckingham is arrested for treason and condemned on the false evidence of his surveyor [manager of his estates]. On the way to his execution, the Duke makes a farewell speech, proclaiming his innocence and forgiving his enemies. Buckingham had been held in high esteem by King Henry, and it is a sign of Wolsey's influence over the King that he does not intervene to prevent Buckingham's arrest. Buckingham is the son of the Duke of Buckingham in *King Richard III* and grandson of the Buckingham in *King Henry IV, Part Two* (*see above*).

Bullcalf, Peter

A minor comic character in *King Henry IV, Part Two*, Bullcalf is a villager recruited by Falstaff to join the King's army. His name suggests that he is a strongly-built young man but he claims that he is too sickly to fight. He pays Bardolph a considerable amount of money for his release.

Bullen, Anne

See ANNE BOLEYN (BULLEN).

Bum

Surname of Pompey, a comic character in *Measure for Measure*. It is slang for an idle fellow.

Burbage, Cuthbert (c. 1566–1636)

An Elizabethan theatre manager, Burbage was involved with his brother, the actor Richard Burbage, in building the GLOBE THEATRE, using timbers from an old playhouse, the THEATRE, which had been built by his father James Burbage. He raised capital for the enterprise by devising the system, adopted later by other companies, in which a group of SHARERS invested in the theatre company and took a percentage of its profits.

Burbage, James (c. 1530–1597)

An Elizabethan actor, Burbage began his career as a carpenter before becoming a leading player with the QUEEN'S MEN and LEICESTER'S MEN. He was responsible for building the first purpose-built English theatre, the THEATRE, in Shoreditch in London in 1576-77, and designed the BLACKFRIARS THEATRE in 1596. He was the father of the actor Richard Burbage and his brother Cuthbert, the theatre manager.

Burbage, Richard (c. 1567–1619)
A leading actor in Shakespeare's time, Burbage performed first with the ADMIRAL'S MEN and later with the LORD CHAMBERLAIN'S MEN. Known especially for playing tragic heroes, Burbage was probably the first actor to take the parts of Hamlet, Lear and Othello and he was the proprietor of the BLACKFRIARS THEATRE and the GLOBE. Burbage was also an accomplished painter, and is believed by some to have painted a portrait of Shakespeare, the CHANDOS PORTRAIT, which hangs in the National Portrait Gallery in London. In his will, Shakespeare left a sum of money to Burbage to buy a memorial ring.

Burgundy, Duke of[1]
A minor character in *King Henry V*, the Duke of Burgundy urges King Henry and King Charles of France to make peace following the Battle of Agincourt and speaks of the horrors of war. He jokes with Henry about his wooing of Katherine.

Burgundy, Duke of[2]
A minor character in *King Henry VI, Part One*, the Duke of Burgundy is an ally of the English at the beginning of the play, fighting for them at Orleans and Rouen. When he meets the French forces in order to discuss terms he is persuaded by La Pucelle, Joan of Arc, to join the French side.

Burgundy, Duke of[3]
A minor character in *King Lear*, Burgundy is a candidate for the hand of Lear's youngest daughter, Cordelia, in marriage. He refuses to marry her because she has been disinherited by her father and has no dowry.

burlesque
A type of comedy which imitates the form of a serious work but in an absurd manner. Burlesque has a particular appeal for a contemporaneous audience who can appreciate the references to current affairs, figures, or fashions. An example of burlesque is the 'most lamentable comedy' of Pyramus and Thisbe in *A Midsummer Night's Dream*. Compare SATIRE.

Bushy, Sir John
A minor character in *King Henry II*, Bushy is one of the Kings's close advisers and a royal favourite. He is one of the parasites, along with Bagot and Greene, whom Bolingbroke condemns for having a bad influence on the King and sentences to death. Bushy's style of speaking is high-flown and courtly to an extreme.

Butts, Dr
A minor character in *King Henry VIII*, Dr Butts is the King's physician. He tells Henry that Archbishop Cranmer is not being treated with sufficient respect, because he has been left waiting in a corridor, in the company of mere servants, before he is admitted to the council to be questioned about heresy. Sir William Butts was a historical figure (d.1545) and a highly regarded physician, whose portrait was painted by Hans Holbein (1497-1543) and hangs in the Court Room of the Barber-Surgeons' Hall in the City of London.

Cc

Cade, Jack
A historical figure (d. 1450) and a character in *King Henry VI, Part Two*, Cade is the leader of the peasant rebellion against the King who is secretly backed by the Duke of York. He pretends to be of noble blood but he is an ambitious rogue with more brawn than brains; he promises his followers social equality and cheaper beer when he is in power. First, he plans to destroy the TOWER OF LONDON and then kill all the lawyers, and in fact anyone who is educated. Cade and his men are beaten and Cade flees to his home county of Kent where he takes refuge in the garden of Alexander Iden, a gentleman. When Iden finds Cade he kills him and proudly takes his severed head to London to present it to King Henry.

Cadwal
In *Cymbeline*, Cadwal is the name Belarius gives to ARVIRAGUS, Cymbeline's son whom he snatched as a young child.

Caesar, Julius
The central character in *Julius Caesar*; *see* JULIUS CAESAR.

Caesar, Octavius
A historical figure (63 BC-AD 14) and a character in *Julius Caesar* and *Antony and Cleopatra*, Octavius Caesar is Julius Caesar's adopted son and an ambitious politician.

In *Julius Caesar*, Octavius Caesar is referred to throughout as OCTAVIUS. He is a young man whom Cassius calls a mere schoolboy, but despite his inexperience he proves an able leader; clear-headed and less impulsive than his ally Antony. After his father's assassination, Octavius forms a triumvirate [rule of three] together with Antony and Lepidus, to govern the Roman Empire. They eradicate their political enemies to strengthen their position and confront Caesar's assassins, Cassius and Brutus, in battle at Philippi. Octavius vows to avenge his father's death but when he discovers Brutus has committed suicide, he shows his dead enemy respect and orders him to be buried with honour.

In *Antony and Cleopatra*, Octavius Caesar is known as CAESAR. He is personally ambitious and Antony is now his rival rather than an ally. Caesar condemns Antony's conduct in Egypt and accuses him of collaborating in Fulvia's rebellion but in a vain attempt to strengthen their alliance, Caesar agrees to the marriage of his sister Octavia to Antony. With cool efficiency, Caesar disposes of his fellow ruler, Lepidus, and sets about acquiring more power. When Antony deserts Octavia to return to Cleopatra, Caesar leads his forces in victory against Antony but it is with sorrow rather than triumph that he laments the death of his former friend. Caesar remains the controlled and unemotional character of *Julius Caesar*; in command of his feelings at all times, he expresses strong disapproval of the excessive drinking at Pompey's banquet.

caesura

An emphatic pause in a line of verse. It usually occurs after the third FOOT but in BLANK verse it can be varied to imitate the patterns of normal speech without disrupting the rhythm of the verse. In SCANSION a caesura is usually shown by the symbol //. For example:

> She sat like Patience on a monument,
>
> Smiling at grief. // Was not this love indeed?

Caius

A minor character in *Titus Andronicus*, Caius is a kinsman [relative] of Titus Andronicus. His name appears in the cast list but apart from being present when Titus shoots arrows to the gods and at the capture of Chiron and Demetrius, he takes no part in the action.

Caius, Doctor

A comic character in *The Merry Wives of Windsor*, Dr Caius is a French doctor of medicine. The hot-tempered and flamboyant Doctor is in love with Anne Page and when he discovers that Evans is also in love with her, Caius challenges him to a duel. The Host of the Garter Inn tricks the two out of fighting and Caius and Evans plan their revenge on the Host by tricking him out of three of his horses. Anne's mother favours Dr Caius' suit of her daughter and their marriage is secretly arranged, but when the time comes for the couple to elope, Anne has already married her lover Fenton. Caius discovers to his horror that Anne has been substituted by a boy in disguise. Dr Caius' heavy French accent and his maltreatment of the English language are a rich source of comedy.

Caius Lucius

A character in *Cymbeline*; *see* LUCIUS, CAIUS.

Caius Martius (Marcius)

The hero of *Coriolanus*; Caius Martius was renamed CORIOLANUS after his victory over the Volscians at Corioli.

Calchas (Calchus)

A minor character in *Troilus and Cressida*, Calchas is Cressida's father who has deserted the Trojan side and joined the Greeks. At his suggestion, the Greeks make the crucial exchange with the Trojans in which Antenor, whom they have recently captured from Troy, is returned while Cressida is sent to join her father.

Caliban

A central character in *The Tempest*, Caliban is a deformed, half-human savage, son of the witch Sycorax. He was the original owner of the island and its only inhabitant, apart from the spirit Ariel, before Prospero's arrival. Prospero and Miranda needed Caliban's help in order to survive, and in return Prospero tried to educate Caliban. However, although Caliban acquired some human skills, he never learned any moral principles and when Miranda grew older, Caliban tried to rape her. For this crime, Prospero enslaved Caliban who now serves Prospero with a deep resentment. When the drunken Stephano and Trinculo are shipwrecked on Prospero's island, Caliban is eager to help them to in their attempt to kill Prospero and take over the island. Despite his brutishness, Caliban has a poetic sense of beauty and he develops some insight by the end of the play, recognizing that he was a fool to be taken in by Stephano. In the happy resolution to the play, Prospero leaves Caliban on the island, free to live life as he will.

The name Caliban is an anagram of 'cannibal', which was spelt 'canibal' in Elizabethan English. A modern interpretation of the play often portrays Caliban as an example of a native inhabitant oppressed by the presence of a colonising power in the form of Prospero. *See also* BLACK CHARACTERS

Calpurnia (Calphurnia)
A historical figure (active 59-44 BC) and a character in *Julius Caesar*, Calpurnia is Caesar's devoted wife. She is unable to have children and Caesar's lack of an heir makes his position vulnerable. Calpurnia fears for her husband's safety. She believes that recent dire omens and a vivid and terrifying nightmare foretell his death and tries, unsuccessfully, to persuade him to pretend that he is too ill to attend the Senate.

Cambio
In *The Taming of the Shrew*, the name that LUCENTIO adopts when he disguises himself as a schoolmaster (*cambio* means 'change' in Italian).

Cambridge, Richard Earl of
A historical figure (1376-1415) and a minor character in *King Henry V*, Cambridge is one of the conspirators against King Henry who is motivated by promises of gold from Henry's enemies in France. A hypocrite, Cambridge flatters the King and pretends to be loyal to him but Henry is aware of his treacherous intentions and sentences him to death.

Camillo
A character in *The Winter's Tale*, Camillo is a Lord of Sicilia. King Leontes orders Camillo to poison King Polixenes whom he mistakenly suspects of having an affair with his wife. Unwilling to commit murder, the good Camillo warns Polixenes and flees with him to Bohemia where he remains as his loyal friend. Some years later, when Polixenes' son Florizel is courting Perdita, Camillo helps the young couple to elope to Sicilia. He, too, returns to his home country and is reconciled with Leontes, who suggests that he should marry Paulina.

Campeius, Cardinal
A historical figure (1472-1539) and a minor character in *King Henry VIII*, Cardinal Campeius is the Pope's envoy sent from Rome to discuss the proposed annulment of Queen Katherine's marriage to the King. Campeius is irritated by the Queen's stubborn refusal to cooperate; he suggests that her trial be adjourned and fails to give the King the decision he so badly wants. Before Campeius returns to Rome, he warns Wolsey that there is gossip about his ruthless ambition.

Canidius
A historical figure (d. 30 BC) and a minor character in *Antony and Cleopatra*, Canidius is a lieutenant-general in Antony's army. He is convinced that it would be better to fight Caesar on land and tries to persuade Antony not to engage in a battle at sea. Concerned, and angry too, that his leader is led by a woman, Canidius is proved doubly right; he surrenders to Caesar after the disastrous sea battle at Actium when Cleopatra's ships flee.

canon

In literature, a list of the recognized works of a writer, or an accepted body of 'major' literature. The canon of Shakespeare's works consists of 37 plays, two narrative poems 'The Rape of Lucrece' and 'Venus and Adonis', the poem 'The Phoenix and the Turtle', and 154 sonnets. Many scholars believe that the play *The Two Noble Kinsmen* (c. 1613), probably written by Shakespeare in collaboration with John FLETCHER, and perhaps *The Reign of King Edward III* (c. 1596), a play whose authorship is uncertain, should be included in the canon.

Canterbury, Archbishop of

A historical figure (1362-1443) and a minor character in *King Henry V*, the Archbishop praises the King for his transformation from a wild young Prince (the Prince HAL of the *King Henry IV* plays) to a just and responsible King. He urges Henry to go to war with France to take the French crown and lands which the Archbishop says are rightfully his by law. The Archbishop is at least partly motivated by the fact the King's involvement overseas will take his mind off a contemplated seizure of Church property.

Caphis

A minor character in *Timon of Athens*, Caphis is a servant of one of the Senators of Athens. He is sent on an unsuccessful mission to recover the money owed to his master by Timon along with servants of Timon's other creditors.

Capilet (Capulet), Widow

A minor character in *All's Well That Ends Well*; *see* WIDOW CAPILET.

Captain

One of several minor characters who appear in Shakespeare's plays, commanding either on land or sea. In many cases, a Captain acts as a bearer of information and his function is to move the plot forward. Sometimes a Captain will describe an event that occurred OFF-STAGE, or make a comment on a particular situation.

In *Hamlet*, for example, the Captain, a soldier in Fortinbras' army, tells Hamlet that Fortinbras is on his way to conquer part of Poland. In *King Richard II*, the Captain of the Welsh army announces that his troops have deserted the battlefield because they have not seen the King for days, and tells of strange omens surrounding rumours of the King's death.

In *Twelfth Night*, the Captain's actions have a small bearing on events. He gives Viola, shipwrecked on the shores of Illyria, hope that her brother Sebastian is alive and helps her to disguise herself as a boy.

Capuchius, Lord

A minor character in *King Henry VIII*, Capuchius is an Ambassador from the Emperor Charles V, Katherine of Aragon's nephew. King Henry sends Capuchius to visit the sick and frail Queen Katherine after her divorce with a message of good will, which Katherine says comes too late to comfort her. She sends a return message to Henry asking him to care foremost for their daughter, and then for her servants. She also hopes to be given a burial befitting a queen and the daughter of a king.

Capulet
A character in *Romeo and Juliet*, Capulet is Juliet's overbearing father and head of the Capulet family in Verona. He dotes on his daughter, who represents all his hopes for future generations. At first he is anxious to protect her from too early a marriage with Paris but after Tybalt's death, he insists she marries Paris and demands her total obedience. When Juliet defies him, Capulet is furious and threatens to disinherit her. Although he is involved in the vendetta against the Montagues, Capulet dissuades his nephew Tybalt from fighting with his enemy Romeo at the masked ball, and he is reconciled with the Montagues after Juliet's death.

Capulet, Cousin
A minor character in *Romeo and Juliet*, Cousin Capulet is an old friend and relative of Capulet who makes a brief appearance at the masked ball.

Capulet, Lady
A minor character in *Romeo and Juliet*, Lady Capulet is Juliet's unsentimental mother who has a rather formal relationship with her daughter whom she would like to see married to Paris. Lady Capulet is a generation younger than her husband.

Cardenio
The title of a play, now lost, which some scholars believe may have been written by Shakespeare. The play was based on the story of Cardenio, a character in *Don Quixote* by Miguel de Cervantes (1547-1616) which had appeared in an English translation in 1612. In 1613, Shakespeare's company of players, the KING'S MEN, is recorded as performing a play called *Cardenno* or *Cardenna* and some fifty years on, a publisher claimed that this was indeed a play written by Shakespeare in collaboration with John FLETCHER. No firm evidence has ever been brought forward since then to support the claim and the play was not included in the 1623 First FOLIO edition of Shakespeare's plays.

Cardinal Beaufort, Bishop of Winchester
A character in *King Henry VI, Part Two*, *see* WINCHESTER, BISHOP OF.

Cardinal, Lord Bourchier
A historical figure (c. 1404-1486) and minor character in *King Richard III*, the Cardinal is the Archbishop of Canterbury who is easily persuaded by Buckingham to take the young Duke of York, one of the little princes, from his place of sanctuary in the TOWER OF LONDON.

Carlisle, Bishop of
A historical figure (d. 1409) and a minor character in *King Richard II*, the Bishop of Carlisle remains loyal to King Richard after Bolingbroke's seizure of his crown. He formally condemns Bolingbroke for a crime against the King and against God (see DIVINE RIGHT OF KINGS), and predicts civil war in England as a consequence. The Bishop is arrested for treason, but once Bolingbroke is crowned King, he pardons the Bishop because he admires his integrity.

Carpenter
A minor character in *Julius Caesar*, the Carpenter is a Roman workman. As the play opens, he is among the crowd that have gathered to greet Caesar on his triumphal return to Rome.

Casca (Caska)

A historical figure (d. 42 BC) and a character in *Julius Caesar*, Casca is one of the conspirators against Caesar. As storms ravage the city of Rome, Casca is troubled by strange omens which he believes warn of future disaster. Cassius exploits this superstitious tendency, persuading Casca to join in the conspiracy to kill Caesar. When the conspirators are plotting Caesar's assassination, Casca appears indecisive, one moment agreeing that Cicero should be included in their plans, and the next minute suggesting they should leave Cicero out. Casca proves himself resolute enough in the end. He is the first of the conspirators to stab Caesar, but after the murder he disappears from the play.

Cassandra

A legendary figure and a minor character in *Troilus and Cressida*, Cassandra is the Trojan King Priam's daughter who has prophetic powers. She prophesies that Troy will be destroyed unless the Greeks return Helen but, although her brother Hector listens to her, Troilus says she is mad. Cassandra nightly dreams of Hector's death and begs him not to fight, but he ignores her warning and is killed.

Cassio

A character in *Othello*, Cassio is a professional soldier and Othello's loyal lieutenant. His promotion in the army has ignited Iago's jealousy and Iago schemes to discredit him. Iago exploits Cassio's weak head, plying him with wine that he really does not want, until Cassio becomes drunkenly violent. He gets into a fight and is dismissed from his post by an angry Othello. Iago then makes it look as if Cassio is having an affair with Othello's wife Desdemona. He plants Desdemona's handkerchief, supposedly evidence, on Cassio to provide proof of his guilt. Cassio, like Othello, is easily taken in by Iago, whom he describes as an 'honest' man and his friend. He exposes Iago in the end, but too late to prevent Desdemona and Othello's deaths. Cassio is given command of the army on Othello's death.

Cassius, Caius

A historical figure (d. 42 BC) and a character in *Julius Caesar*, Cassius is described by Caesar as thin and hungry-looking. He is the prime mover in the conspiracy to assassinate Caesar, but unlike Brutus, Cassius is motivated as much by personal hatred of Caesar as concern for the fate of Rome. He is manipulative and devious rather than confrontational. He persuades Brutus to lead the conspiracy, exploiting Brutus' sense of honour, and he plays on Caska's superstitious nature to persuade him to join their cause. Clever though he is, Cassius lacks resolve and this leads him to make mistakes that contribute to his downfall. Most disastrously, he agrees to let Antony address the crowd after Caesar's death and at the battle of Philippi he lets himself be overruled by Brutus who makes a fatal tactical error. Cassius kills himself in order to avoid capture and dishonour.

Catesby

A historical figure (d. 1485) and a minor character in *King Richard III*, Catesby is one of Richard's unscrupulous followers. He is involved in the deaths of Clarence and Hastings as well as the murder of the little princes in the TOWER OF LONDON.

catharsis
Derived from the Greek word for purging, catharsis is the purifying effect of the emotions of compassion or fear, and the subsequent sense of relief, experienced by the audience of a tragedy. ARISTOTLE first described the cathartic effect of tragedy in his treatise *Poetics* in which he wrote: 'raising pity and fear purges the mind of these passions'. *See also* ARISTOTLE.

Cathness
A minor, unspeaking, character in *Macbeth*, Cathness is a Scottish nobleman who joins forces with Prince Malcolm against Macbeth.

Catling, Simon
A minor character in *Romeo and Juliet*, Catling is one of the MUSICIANS hired to play at Juliet's wedding. A 'catling' is a cat-gut string for a small lute.

Cato, Young
A minor character in *Julius Caesar*, Young Cato is an officer in Cassius and Brutus's army, whose sister Portia is married to Brutus and whose father was Marcus Cato a sworn enemy of Caesar. He fights bravely at the battle of Philippi but he is killed.

Celia
A character in *As You Like It*, Celia is Duke Frederick's daughter, and Rosalind's cousin. The cousins are such devoted friends that when Rosalind's father Duke Senior is banished, Rosalind remains behind with Celia; and when Rosalind is eventually banished too, Celia goes with her into exile. Celia is a strong-minded young woman; she defies her father, and willingly exchanges a comfortable life at court for one of rustic simplicity in the Forest of ARDEN, in disguise as 'Aliena'. Celia's chief role in Arden is to listen patiently to her friend's expressions of love for Orlando. At the end of the play, Celia's reward is marriage to the reformed Oliver.

cellarage or cellar
A space beneath the stage in Elizabethan PLAYHOUSES, which may have been used for storing PROPS and from which characters, such as the Ghost of Hamlet's father, had access to and from the stage through a trap door. In *Antony and Cleopatra*, the cellarage is used as a hidden space for musicians. There is a stage direction, 'Music of the hautboys [oboes] is under the stage' and the eerie sound of music coming apparently from under the earth terrifies soldiers on the eve of a battle.

censorship
In spite of Queen Elizabeth's enthusiasm for the theatre and the royal patronage she exercised over it, 16th-century governments imposed strict censorship on Elizabethan players and playwrights as one method of forestalling civil disorder. Under an act of 1574 all public performances were regulated, and from 1581 the MASTER OF THE REVELS, acting as a licensing authority whose permission had to be sought before a play could be performed, scanned all play scripts for obscenity, blasphemy and possible sedition. After 1606, his powers were extended to the printing and publication of play scripts. Performances were forbidden on Sundays, during Lent, and during outbreaks of the PLAGUE (as well as on Thursdays which was a day set aside for bear-baiting). Under a second act of 1574, permission to perform a play within the limits of the City of

London had to be granted by the largely puritan City Fathers, an authority with whom theatre companies were in frequent conflict. The City Fathers feared the spread of disease and, believing that violent or profane dramas would brutalize and corrupt audiences, were always apprehensive that lawlessness might erupt where crowds gathered together.

London theatres were accordingly under constant threat of closure and were regularly shut down for one reason or another. In 1597 they were shut for a few months after *The Isle of Dogs*, a play by Thomas NASHE written in collaboration with Ben Jonson and deemed treasonable by the authorities, was performed at the SWAN Theatre. After the uprising masterminded by the Earl of ESSEX in 1601, plays that recounted recent English history such as *King Richard II* (the play that Essex's followers had requested the LORD CHAMBERLAIN'S MEN to perform as a preliminary to his rebellion) were banned.

The puritanical sections of society thoroughly disapproved of drama and play books, deemed unworthy of academic study, were banned from the shelves of such august institutions as the Bodleian Library at Oxford University. Despite this opposition and all the restrictions censorship imposed, the theatre flourished. Actors, practised in the art of extemporizing, could foil the Office of the Revels by slipping in a topical or subversive comment during performances which had not previously appeared in the approved text. It was in order to escape the prohibitions of censorship that theatre managers began to build their theatres beyond the City limits, for example on BANKSIDE, outside the jurisdiction of the City Fathers.

centre stage
A position in the middle of the stage which an actor may take up when the character he plays is dominating the action of the play. *See* DOWNSTAGE; UPSTAGE.

Ceres
Ceres is one of the deities appearing in the MASQUE performed for Miranda and Ferdinand in *The Tempest*. *See* SPIRITS.

Cerimon
A character in *Pericles*, Cerimon is a benevolent nobleman and a renowned physician who is known not only for his skill as a doctor but for his goodness to the people of Ephesus. His generosity is demonstrated when he gives shelter to two strangers lost in a storm. The chest containing the unconscious body of Thaisa, half drowned in a storm, is brought to Cerimon who revives her and cares for her. When she is recovered, Cerimon accompanies Thaisa to Diana's temple and ensures that she has with her the jewels and a letter that were in her coffin and with which she is afterwards able to identify herself. Cerimon confirms Thaisa's story when she later meets Pericles.

Cesario
In *Twelfth Night*, Cesario is the name that the character Viola adopts when she is in disguise as a young man.

Chamberlain's Men
See LORD CHAMBERLAIN'S MEN, THE

Chancellor, Lord

A minor character in *King Henry VIII*, the Lord Chancellor presides over the meeting of the Council that accuses Cranmer of heresy, and commits him to the TOWER OF LONDON. When King Henry intervenes to stop Cranmer's imprisonment, the Chancellor maintains that the council was simply providing Cranmer with an opportunity to defend his position.

The office of Lord Chancellor originated in the 12th century, when its holders were churchmen, who also acted as the King's secretary. The office still exists in Britain today, but is no longer connected to the Church. Today's Lord Chancellor is the head of the legal system in England.

Chandos Portrait

A portrait, named after its owners the Dukes of Chandos, which was said to be a picture of Shakespeare painted from life by the actor Richard BURBAGE. Modern scholars have cast doubt on the identity both of the artist and the subject. *See also* DROESHOUT, MARTIN.

Changeling

A character in *A Midsummer Night's Dream* who is referred to in the play but who does not appear in the cast list or speak. A changeling was a mortal child stolen by the fairies. In the play Titania has adopted a young Indian boy, a changeling stolen from an Indian King according to one of the fairies. Titania adores the child, but Oberon, King of the fairies and her husband, is jealous and wants the child to be his page.

character

Someone who is represented in a play by an actor and whose personality is evident from their behaviour during the action of the play, from their dialogue, and from what other characters may say about them. In Shakespearean COMEDY, a character's nature usually remains unchanged; in TRAGEDY, a character may undergo some moral or emotional alteration as a result of what he or she has experienced during the course of the drama. Often an audience may have to discover for itself the essential nature of a character: sometimes a character reveals his true self by confiding in the audience. An example is King Richard III who says he is 'determined to prove a villain' at the outset.

Charles

A minor character in *As You Like It*, Charles is a wrestler in Duke Frederick's entourage, whose strength is such that few of his challengers emerge from the ring without broken bones or worse. Hearing that Orlando plans to challenge Charles, the scheming Oliver tells the wrestler that Orlando is a villain who deserves to die, and hints that Charles will be rewarded if Orlando is killed. In fact, Charles is soundly beaten by Orlando.

Charles the Sixth, the French King

A historical figure (1368-1422) and a character in *King Henry V*, in real life Charles suffered from bouts of mental illness. In Shakespeare's play, the King is a formal, and rather ineffectual character. He reminds the French courtiers of past battles lost to the English and orders defensive measures to be taken against further English invasion. After the battle of Agincourt, King Charles accepts the terms of peace with England in which Henry is to become King of France and agrees to let Henry marry his daughter Katherine.

Charles, Dauphin and afterward King of France

A historical figure (1403-1461) and a character in *King Henry VI, Part One*, Charles is King Charles VII of France but he is referred to throughout as 'Dauphin' (sometimes Dolphin), a title given to the French heir to the throne but not to the King. The English did not recognize Charles as the rightful King of France because they claimed the French throne for themselves following the victories of HENRY V.

When Charles is introduced to Joan La Pucelle, he tests her by challenging her to single combat; Joan wins, convincing Charles of her miraculous powers. He is inspired by her but when things go badly for the French he turns on Joan, calling her a deceiver. Charles does not lose all confidence in Joan, however, and he uses her powers of persuasion to win the Duke of Burgundy over to join the French cause. Despite this extra support for the French, the English triumph and Charles is forced to agree to a peace treaty.

Charmian

A character in *Antony and Cleopatra*, Charmian is one of Cleopatra's attendants and her companion. A vivacious and good-natured young woman, she jokes with Iras and Cleopatra about the Soothsayer's predictions that she will live longer than her mistress. She says her ambition is to marry three kings in one morning and outlive them all. She is fiercely loyal to Cleopatra right to the end, and when Cleopatra dies, she lovingly rearranges her crown. Proudly declaring that her queen's death was a fitting one, Charmian kills herself with the asp (a poisonous snake) and dies alongside her mistress.

Chatillon

A minor character in *King John*, Chatillon is the French ambassador who tells King John of the King of France's intention to go to war to fight for Prince Arthur's right to be King of England.

Chief Justice

A character in *King Henry IV, Part Two*; *see* LORD CHIEF JUSTICE.

Children of the chapel

The foremost company of boy actors whose members were choir boys from the Chapel Royal and who were specially trained to act. They regularly performed at court and at the BLACKFRIARS THEATRE and in 1610, under the patronage of James I's wife, Queen Anne, they became known as the Children of the Queen's Revels. See BOY COMPANIES.

Children of St Paul's

A company of specially trained boy actors, whose members were choir boys from St Paul's Cathedral in London and who performed frequently at court and at the BLACKFRIARS THEATRE. *See* BOY COMPANIES.

Children of the King's Revels

A company of boy actors founded in 1606 under the patronage of King James I. It is possible that this company was the CHILDREN OF ST PAUL'S renamed. The Children of the King's Revels was part-owned by the playwright Michael DRAYTON and performed at the newly founded WHITEFRIARS THEATRE. *See* BOY COMPANIES.

Children of the Queen's Revels
A company of boy actors first established in 1603 under the patronage of King James I's wife, Queen Anne. The company did not flourish and was renamed the Children of the Revels, and later, the Children of Blackfriars. In 1608 the company reformed under new management, and as the Children of Whitefriars they performed at the newly established WHITEFRIARS THEATRE. In 1610, their original title, Children of the Queen's Revels, was restored to them. *See* BOY COMPANIES

Chiron
A character in *Titus Andronicus*, the bloodthirsty Chiron is the youngest son of the Goth Queen Tamora. When Tamora and her sons are captured by Titus and brought to Rome and her eldest son Alabarbus is hacked to death, Chiron comments on the brutality of the Romans. Thereafter, he and Demetrius go on a campaign of sadistic violence and murder. Rivals in lust for the possession of Titus' daughter Lavinia the brothers quarrel but eventually agree to share her. They kill her fiance, Bassianus, rape and horribly mutilate Lavinia and pin the blame for Bassianus' murder on Titus' sons. When Titus discovers that it was Chiron and Demetrius who violated Lavinia he kills them and as a peculiarly terrible revenge he bakes them in a pie which he serves up to their mother.

chorus
In ancient Greek drama, the chorus was a group of actors representing ordinary people who commented on the action of the play but took no part in it. In Shakespeare's plays, the chorus performs a similar function, but is a single actor who may describe the background to the forthcoming action in a PROLOGUE at the beginning of a play or comment on its resolution in an EPILOGUE. A Chorus introduces *King Henry V* for example and, as the character of Time, announces the passage of sixteen years between Acts III and IV in *The Winter's Tale*.

Chorus[1]
In *King Henry V*, the Chorus (see above) is a narrator who introduces each of the five acts of the play with a flourish of stylized poetry. At the beginning, he apologizes for the inadequacy of the theatre, 'this wooden O' of the GLOBE, as the setting for the momentous events of the play and asks the audience to imagine that the stage is in turn a castle, or a battlefield. He rounds off the play with an EPILOGUE in which he looks forward to the exploits of the future King Henry VI.

Chorus[2]
In *Romeo and Juliet*, the Chorus (*see* CHORUS *above*) introduces the play and describes the long-established quarrel between the Montagues and Capulets, the two families of Romeo and Juliet. Before Act II, he relates that Romeo and Juliet have met and fallen in love. Both the Chorus's speeches are in the form of a SONNET.

chronicle play
A drama portraying historical events and reflecting national pride that were extremely popular in 16th-century England, particularly following England's triumphant defeat of the Spanish Armada in 1588. They were often performed in INN-YARDS and provided excitement and theatrical spectacle rather than an accurate description of events or characters. Chronicle plays were based on the historical accounts of Edward HALLE and

HOLINSHED'S *Chronicles*, the same source material that Shakespeare used for his
HISTORY PLAYS.

Cibber, Colley (1671–1757)

An actor, playwright, and poet, Cibber was made Poet Laureate in 1730. He is best
remembered now for his adaptation of Shakespeare's *King Richard III* which he staged
in 1700, taking the title role himself. It was a shortened and crude version of the original
and though it was popular with audiences until the end of the 19th century, Cibber's
rewriting is now regarded as an act of literary vandalism. A frequently quoted line from
the adapted play is: 'Off with his head. So much for Buckingham'. Cibber's version
remained the standard text until well into the 19th century and Laurence OLIVIER
included parts of it in his film version of *King Richard III* (1955). Cibber also wrote a
popular version of *King Lear* which GARRICK performed in 1773. Fanny Burney
(1752-1840) the writer and diarist wrote of Cibber's *Lear*: 'To my ears every line of
Cibber's is feeble and paltry.'

Cicero

A historical figure (106-43 BC) and a minor character in *Julius Caesar*, Cicero is a
silver-haired elder statesman and a Roman senator [member of the ruling council].
Caska reports that Cicero spoke at the games in Greek which he for one could not
understand. The conspirators against Caesar discuss whether or not they should include
Cicero in their plot but Brutus rejects the idea because he says Cicero is unlikely to enter
into any scheme that others have originated. He is said to be one of the senators that
Antony and Octavius put to death after Caesar's assassination.

Cimber, Metellus

A character in *Julius Caesar*, *see* METELLUS CIMBER.

Cinna

A historical figure (d. 44 BC) and a minor character in *Julius Caesar*, Cinna is one of
the conspirators against Caesar. He is given the task of leaving anonymous,
inflammatory letters around, where Brutus will see them, in order to persuade him to
join Cassius's assassination plot. He takes part in the planning and the murder and, as
Caesar is stabbed, Cinna cries out, 'Tyranny is dead'.

Cinna the Poet

A minor character in *Julius Caesar*, Cinna the poet is the victim of mob violence after
the assassination of Caesar. The crowds run riot, and simply because Cinna the poet
bears the same name as Cinna the conspirator, they kill him although he protests his
innocence.

Citizens

Minor characters in several of Shakespeare's plays, Citizens respond to, and comment
on events rather like a CHORUS.

   In *Coriolanus*, the Citizens of Rome (see also PLEBEIANS) have a significant role to
play in a play which has class-conflict at its core. The ordinary people of Rome feel
oppressed by their aristocratic rulers and regard the arrogant Coriolanus as their chief
enemy. Described as a 'many-headed multitude' by one of their number, the Citizens

are a fickle, wavering, body of opinion, who shift from supporting Coriolanus to demanding his death and back again.

In *King Richard III*, the Citizens are the frightened people of Shakespeare's own England who express unease at the sinister events surrounding the crown. They hope for better things, but when Richard proclaims himself King, the Citizens of London greet him in a silence that speaks for itself.

In *Romeo and Juliet*, the Citizens are the townspeople of Verona who try to prevent the fighting between the Capulet and Montague families. They represent order in a disordered world. *See also* PLEBEIANS in *Julius Caesar*.

City Fathers, The

The largely PURITAN licensing authorities in London with whom Elizabethan theatre companies were frequently in conflict. *See* CENSORSHIP.

Clarence, George Duke of

A historical figure (1449-1478) and a character in *King Richard III*, Clarence is Richard's brother and in line to succeed to the throne of England. Clarence's first name is George and there is a superstition that someone whose name begins with 'G' will murder the King's heirs. As part of his plan to seize the throne for himself, Richard turns his elder brother, King Edward, against Clarence who is arrested and thrown into the TOWER OF LONDON. There, he has a nightmare in which he drowns, and meets the ghosts of those he has killed. His conscience awakened, Clarence is in anguish but he still trusts Richard. However, Richard has arranged for his death; two men stab Clarence and stuff his body into a barrel of malmsey [wine]. Although Clarence's role is a minor one, his murder demonstrates the lengths to which Richard is prepared to go to achieve his goal. (The account of Clarence's death is not historically accurate; see RICHARD III.)

The character of the Duke of Clarence also appears in *King Henry VI, Part Three*, where he is known as 'GEORGE' before he is given the title of 'Duke'.

Clarence, Thomas Duke of

A historical figure (1388-1421) and a minor character in *King Henry IV, Part Two* and *King Henry V*, Clarence is King Henry IV's son and Prince Hal's brother. In *Henry IV*, the King tells Clarence to be loyal to his brother Prince Hal when he becomes King and to keep the peace between the royal brothers. In *Henry V*, the Duke of Clarence is a silent character.

Claudio[1] (Claudius)

A minor character in *Julius Caesar*, Claudio is a soldier in Cassius and Brutus's army. Brutus asks Claudio and Varrus to sleep in his tent before the battle Phillipi in case he needs them to take messages to Cassius during the night. When Brutus wakes after Caesar's ghost has visited him, Claudio says he saw nothing.

Claudio[2]

A character in *Measure for Measure*, Claudio is Isabella's brother. He loves Juliet whom he plans to marry but the wedding has been delayed because of difficulties with her family over a dowry. Under Angelo's strict regime, Claudio is arrested for having made Juliet pregnant and is summarily sentenced to death. He begs his sister to help him but when Isabella pleads with Angelo to show mercy to her brother, he agrees only on the condition that she sleeps with him. Claudio is an uncomplicated character and warm-hearted by nature, and as Isabella's refusal means certain death for him, he finds it hard to understand her uncompromising attitude. Angelo demands that Claudio's head is brought to him after the execution, but the disguised Duke arranges for the substitution of the head of another prisoner who died that day. In the happy resolution of the play, the Duke pardons Claudio who is free to marry Juliet.

Claudio[3]

A character in *Much Ado About Nothing*, Claudio is a friend of Benedick. He is a conventional, rather shallow, young man, who is described as having the courage of a lion combined with the gentleness of a lamb. Returned from the war, Claudio visits Leonato's house and falls immediately in love with Leonato's daughter, Hero. Happy to be in love himself, Claudio takes part in tricking Benedick into believing that Beatrice loves him and enjoys the joke. Before his wedding can take place, Claudio is persuaded by the wicked Don John into believing that Hero has been unfaithful to him. Claudio does not hesitate to believe the worst of Hero, and his angry rejection is swift and uncompromising. When he hears that Hero is not only innocent but that she has died of shame, he is full of remorse and agrees to marry someone, supposedly Leonato's niece, whom Leonato chooses for him. The 'niece' turns out to be Hero, and the young lovers are reunited.

Claudius

A character in *Hamlet*, Claudius is King of Denmark and Hamlet's uncle and step-father. He has acquired the throne by killing the old King (Hamlet's father) and has married Hamlet's widowed mother Gertrude. He presides over a corrupt court where there is heavy drinking. Hamlet has been told of Claudius' crime by his Father's Ghost, and hopes to prompt Claudius into an admission of guilt when the visiting actors perform a play about the murder of a king before the court. Although Claudius is a self-confessed villain, he feels guilty about his crimes. He tries to pray for forgiveness but cannot make a full and sincere repentance. He plots with Rosencrantz and Guildenstern to rid himself of Hamlet's disturbing presence at court, and when that plot fails he uses Laertes in another murderous plan to kill Hamlet with a poisoned sword. The plot backfires on Claudius and he is killed by Hamlet with the same deadly weapon.

Cleomenes

A minor character in *The Winter's Tale*, Cleomenes is a lord of Sicilia who is sent by Leontes to consult the oracle.

Cleon

A character in *Pericles*, Cleon is Dionyza's weak husband and the Governor of Tharsus. He owes a debt of gratitude to Pericles who has helped to relieve Tharsus from starvation. Pericles asks Cleon and Dionyza to repay the debt by bringing up his baby daughter Marina, but Marina grows up to be more beautiful than their own daughter. The jealous Dionyza plots to have Marina murdered but Cleon refuses to be involved. Gower, the Chorus, relates in the Epilogue that Dion and Dionyza are burned in their palace by the citizens of Tharsus enraged at the supposed murder of the innocent Marina.

Cleopatra

A historical figure (68-30 BC) and the tragic heroine of *Antony and Cleopatra*, Cleopatra is the Queen of Egypt whose beauty is legendary. She has already had a love affair with Julius Caesar, before ensnaring another powerful Roman, Antony, in her web of charms. Cleopatra is exotic and volatile and her court is opulent and luxurious. Under her influence Antony neglects his political duties and when he is recalled to Rome, Cleopatra uses all her seductive wiles to try persuade him to stay. She is genuinely hurt at the news of Antony's diplomatic marriage to Octavia, but comforted to hear that Octavia does not in any way rival her beauty. Although Cleopatra loves Antony passionately, her selfishness destroys him in the end. Her flight at the Battle of Actium marks the start of his downfall, and his death is the result of a cruel deception - her pretended suicide. Preferring death to dishonour, Cleopatra kills herself with an asp [poisonous snake]. Enobarbus describes Cleopatra most aptly as a woman of infinite variety whom age can never destroy.

In Shakespeare's time the part of Cleopatra would, like all other female roles, have been played by a boy actor. Shakespeare cleverly ensures that as an older woman, the character is never shown in a love scene with Antony that might make her look ridiculous.

Clerk of Chatham

A minor character in *King Henry VI, Part Two*, the Clerk is ruthlessly killed by Jack Cade's rebels purely on the grounds that his education makes him their natural enemy.

Clifford, Lord[1]

A minor character in *King Henry VI, Part Two*, Clifford and his son YOUNG CLIFFORD are supporters of King Henry. Clifford is sent by the King to offer a pardon to Jack Cade and his rebels. He fights bravely at the Battle of St Albans on the King's side but is killed by the Duke of York. Young Clifford swears to avenge his father's death.

Clifford, Lord[2]

A minor character in *King Henry VI, Part Three*, Lord Clifford is the YOUNG CLIFFORD of *Part Two* (*see above*) who, bent of avenging his father's death, kills the Duke of York. His revenge extends to Rutland, the Duke of York's youngest son, whom he savagely kills in spite of the child's pleas for mercy.

Clitus

A minor character in *Julius Caesar*, Clitus is a soldier in Brutus and Cassius's army. After the battle of Philippi, Brutus asks Clitus to help him to commit suicide, but Clitus refuses saying that he would rather kill himself.

Cloten

A character in *Cymbeline*, Cloten is the ambitious Queen's son and Cymbeline's step-son. He is dim-witted and quarrelsome, a luckless lout whom his mother would like to see married to Imogen. Cloten's clumsy attempts to woo Imogen fail, and he is cut to the quick when she tells him that even the shabbiest of Posthumus' clothes are more precious to her than Cloten. He vows to be revenged, and when Imogen flees to Wales he hatches a plan to pursue and rape her, wearing Posthumus' clothes as he does so, and then to kill Posthumus. His plan is foiled by Imogen's brother Guiderius who kills and beheads the wretched Cloten.

clown

A comic stage character appearing in a variety of guises, but usually a servant or a rustic figure, such as Launce in *Two Gentlemen of Verona* and Bottom in *A Midsummer Night's Dream*; in the tragedies, the Porter in *Macbeth* and the Gravedigger in *Hamlet*, are clowns who provide interludes of comic relief. The broad comedy of Shakespeare's clowns, which may sometimes seem laboured to modern audiences, was played notably in Shakespeare's day by Will KEMP and can overlap with the more subtle and intellectual characterization of the FOOL.

Clown

One of various minor comic characters (*see above*) appearing in several of Shakespeare's plays. In *Antony and Cleopatra* the Clown is a fig seller who supplies Cleopatra with the asp she uses to kill herself. He solemnly warns Cleopatra that poisonous snakes are dangerous and not to be trusted and provides comic irony at a moment of high tension in the play.

In *Othello*, the Clown is Othello's servant and a jester and in *Titus Andronicus* the Clown is a dim-witted rustic character appearing in a brief interlude of comic relief carrying two pigeons in a basket. Titus pays him to deliver the pigeons to the Emperor Saturnius together with a knife wrapped up in a threatening letter. The contents of the letter make Saturnius so angry that he has the poor Clown hanged. The Clown is yet another innocent victim in the cycle of revenge.

In *The Winter's Tale*, the Clown is the son of the Old Shepherd who adopts Perdita in Bohemia. He tells his father how Antigonus and a sailor have been attacked and killed by a bear and relates the story with gory relish. In love with Mopsa, the good-natured Clown is easy prey to the cunning Autolycus who robs him of the money he intended to use to buy food for the sheep-shearing festival. At the end of the play King Leontes rewards the Clown and his father for their care of his daughter Perdita. They are given a sharp rise in social status and the Clown boasts of having become a 'gentleman'.

The Clown is also a central character in *Twelfth Night* (see FESTE) and a comic character in *All's Well That Ends Well* (*see* LAVATCH).

Cobbler

A minor character in *Julius Caesar*, the Cobbler is a workmen who is one of the crowd that has gathered to cheer Caesar as he makes his triumphal return to Rome. The Cobbler jokes with the tribunes [civil officers] who are trying to disperse the crowd.

Cobham, Eleanor

A character in *King Henry VI, Part Two*; *See* GLOUCESTER, DUCHESS OF.

Cobweb

A minor character in *A Midsummer Night's Dream*, Cobweb is one of the fairies in Titania's retinue. While the bewitched and deluded Titania is in love with Bottom with his asses head, Cobweb waits on Bottom and gathers honey for him. The part of Cobweb was probably played in Shakespeare's time by a child actor from one of the royal choir schools. *See* BOY COMPANIES.

Coleville, Sir John
A minor character in *King Henry IV, Part Two*, Coleville is one of the rebels fighting
against King Henry who agrees to a peace treaty only to discover that it is a treacherous
plot devised by Prince John. In the fight, Coleville gives himself to Falstaff, who
pretends that he has captured Coleville only after a hard struggle.

comedy
A type of drama that is amusing and which has a happy resolution; it the opposite of
TRAGEDY. Comedy includes works of SATIRE and BURLESQUE, which use dialogue to
mock people or institutions, as well as plays such as *The Merry Wives of Windsor* in
which the humour arises out of the circumstances of the plot and series of
misunderstandings. Shakespeare's comedies are concerned with the lives of ordinary
people rather than with statesmen or kings. They are sometimes romantic stories in
which a rather idealized hero and heroine overcome external, rather than psychological,
difficulties and are finally united in love.

 High comedy is exemplified by the kind of witty and sophisticated dialogue that occurs
in plays like *Much Ado About Nothing,* and low comedy by the BAWDY exchanges of
the Nurse in *Romeo and Juliet* or the farcical exchanges of the rustics in *A Midsummer
Night's Dream*. In comic dialogue the humour often arises out of punning (see PUN), in
which words that sound the same but have entirely different meanings are deliberately
used to make a joke, or out of the unintended misuse of words that sound similar (see
MALAPROPISM). Many of Shakespeare's puns are lost to modern audiences because the
pronunciation of words has altered in modern times.

 The tradition of comic drama has its roots in ancient Greece with the rural musical
festivals of DIONYSUS, the god of wine and fruitfulness. It developed in England with
medieval MIRACLE plays and later MORALITY PLAYS which, though often serious,
included strong elements of comedy. Dramatic comedy as we recognize it first appeared
in the 16th century in two plays, *Ralph Roister Doister* (c. 1553) by Nicholas UDALL
and the anonymous *Gammer Gurton's Needle* (1566). Gradually, concerns of morality
in comedy were replaced by elements of romance, borrowed from French and Italian
literature.

 Shakespeare's comedies, sixteen in all, were first categorized as such in the 1623 First
FOLIO edition of his plays. *See the table of Shakespeare's plays in the supplement.*

Comedy of Errors, The
One of Shakespeare's early comedies and his shortest play, *The Comedy of Errors* was
written around 1593-94 and first published in the First FOLIO edition of his plays in
1623. The play's first recorded performance was in December 1594 at Gray's Inn, one
of the London law schools (see INNS OF COURT). The main source for the plot were two
plays by the Roman dramatist Plautus (c. 254-184 BC), *Menaechmi* (an English
translation was published in 1595) and *Amphitruo*. These were comedies about twins,
mistaken identities and the double master-servant story. The play, written mostly in
verse, some of it in rhyming couplets, is romantic and fantastical, fast-moving and often
farcical (*see* FARCE). The plot hinges on mistaken identities and the play examines the
power of forgiveness and reconciliation to restore order in a chaotic world, an idea that
is often present in Shakespeare's plays. The action takes place in Ephesus within the

space of twenty-four hours and unlike Shakespeare's other plays, *The Comedy of Errors* adheres to the principle of the three unities.

SYNOPSIS: Thirty-three years before the play, a Merchant from Syracuse, Egeon, and his wife Emilia adopted twin boys (both called Dromio) to be servants to their twin sons (both called Antipholus). The family was shipwrecked and separated; Emilia with one Antipholus and one of the Dromio twins landed in Ephesus and believing that she had lost the rest of her family she entered a convent there. Egeon, with the other Antipholus and Dromio, returned to Syracuse and eighteen years later began a desperate search for his lost son which eventually took him to Ephesus, at which point the play opens. Unknown to Egeon, Emilia's Antipholus is living in Ephesus with his Dromio. He has grown into a respected and prosperous citizen, happily married to Adriana. By pure chance, Egeon's Antipholus from Syracuse arrives in Ephesus at the same time as his father, together with his servant Dromio. From then on a comedy of errors is unleashed as both sets of twins are repeatedly mistaken for each other. Both Dromios are increasingly bewildered as the Antipholuses, unable to tell them apart, seem to be giving contradictory orders all the time. Likewise, both Antipholuses are confused by the apparently strange behaviour of their servants. Ephesus Antipholus is threatened with arrest for debt and his wife has him declared a lunatic by a magician, Dr Pinch, from whom he only just manages to escape. Syracuse Antipholus, convinced by now that everyone else is quite mad, seeks refuge in a nearby convent. The Abbess of the convent, who is of course the twins' mother Emila, arrives in time to shed light on affairs. Finally, identities are unravelled and parents, twins, husbands and wives are happily reunited.

comic relief
An comic interlude in a serious work that provides a dramatic contrast in mood and a lightening of tension. An example is the drunken Porter's speech in *Macbeth*. Dr JOHNSON praised Shakespeare for mixing tragedy and comedy in this way.

Cominius
A character in *Coriolanus*, Cominius is a Roman general who leads the army against the Volscians, with Coriolanus as his second-in-command. Cominius, naturally more cautious that Coriolanus, is persuaded by him to follow up victory at Corioli with another attack on the Volscians because, he says, he can never deny Coriolanus' requests. It is Cominius who rewards Coriolanus' courage at Corioli by giving him the name 'Coriolanus'. A simple soldier and a good man, Cominius is a genuine patriot, in contrast to Coriolanus who is ambitious for personal glory. When Coriolanus is made Consul, Cominius does his best to persuade him to show humility to the crowd but even after the people of Rome have turned on Coriolanus, Cominius remains loyal and promises to follow him into exile. Cominius tries to persuade Coriolanus not to invade Rome, but Coriolanus is deaf to his old friend's advice.

Commedia dell'Arte
A form of comedy performed in 16th- and 17th-century Europe by touring groups of professional Italian actors. The dialogue was usually improvised around a 'scenario' or set situation involving a series of masked and easily recognizable STOCK CHARACTERS such as PANTALOON, an old father who tries to oppose the young lovers, and

HARLEQUIN, a cunning servant. Elizabethan dramatists were greatly influenced by the Commedia dell'Arte.

companies of actors or companies of players
During the Middle Ages, troupes of strolling players, acrobats and musicians travelled the country performing in the halls of great houses or on village greens, using anything from carts to purpose-built staging on which to act their plays. By the 16th century, numerous restrictions had been put on the performances of plays in public and an act of 1572 classified actors as 'vagabonds' [someone with no fixed address]. They could only avoid imprisonment for 'vagrancy' [wandering like a vagabond] by banding together to form companies of players under the patronage of a nobleman. Thus legitimized, actors were provided with a livery or a badge by their patron but not with a regular wage; they had to make their living from audience takings.

Companies continued touring the provinces and some of them performed as far afield as Europe, but increasingly players began to stay in one place for longer. Many played regularly in INN-YARDS which provided them with accommodation as well as with semi-permanent theatres. Some companies ceased travelling altogether and based themselves in London where by 1576 purpose-built theatres were appearing. Some rented theatres from entrepreneurs like Philip HENSLOWE, while others such as the LORD CHAMBERLAIN'S MEN at the GLOBE built their own (*see* HOUSEKEEPERS).

Once formed, companies stayed together as a group over many years. They consisted of around 30 members of whom about ten, known as sharers, took on the expenses of theatre maintenance and of mounting productions. One of the major expenses of the 'SHARERS' was acquiring new material from dramatists. Plays were bought for about £6 on average and became the property of the company. Profits too were shared and large profits could be made in good times, but when outbreaks of plague forced London theatres to close companies would have a lean time and be forced to travel the country again in order to survive. The sharers employed other actors, 'HIRELINGS' who were paid a weekly wage of about six shillings, and apprenticed boys who played the female roles. Other members of the company included the musicians, the BOOK-KEEPER who looked after the play texts, the TIREMAN who was responsible for the costumes and the PROPS, and the STAGE-KEEPER who swept and tidied the stage and theatre.

In Shakespeare's lifetime there were about eleven companies of adult players performing regularly in London on a frequently changing REPERTORY system despite the problems of CENSORSHIP and outbreaks of plague. Of these the most notable was the LORD CHAMBERLAIN'S MEN, for whom Shakespeare wrote and acted for over sixteen years, and its main rival the ADMIRAL'S MEN. Queen Elizabeth had her own company the QUEEN'S MEN from 1583 to 1594. *See also* ACTORS AND ACTING; BOY COMPANIES.

conceit
A figure of speech in which two unalike things are juxtaposed in a striking and unexpected parallel. A conceit is a device which was often employed in 16th-century poetry, particularly in love poems. Shakespeare parodies this in Sonnet 130: 'My mistress' eyes are nothing like the sun; Coral is far more red than her lips' red: If snow be white, why then her breasts are dun; If hairs be wires, black wires grow on her head'.

Condell, Henry (d. 1627)

A principal actor with Shakespeare's company of players the LORD CHAMBERLAIN'S MEN, a HOUSEKEEPER [part-owner] of the Blackfriars Theatre and a SHARER in the Globe Theatre. Together with fellow actor, JOHN HEMING (C. 1556-1630), Condell edited the First FOLIO edition of Shakespeare's plays, not in order to make a profit but 'only to keep the memory of so worthy a Friend and Fellow alive, as was our Shakespeare'. In his will, Shakespeare bequeathed the sum of twenty-six shillings and eightpence each to Condell and Heming to buy a memorial ring.

confidant

A character in a play in whom the hero or heroine confides their intimate feelings. A confidant is often a minor figure, such as a servant or a trusted friend like Horatio in *Hamlet*, who may act as a medium through which characters can reveal their intentions to the audience.

Conrade

A character in *Much Ado About Nothing*, Conrade is a follower of the wicked Don John. He takes part with Borachio in the scheme to make it appear as if Hero has been unfaithful to her fiance Claudio. Conrade and Borachio are arrested by the Night Watchmen who have overheard a discussion about the plot. Conrade is infuriated by Dogberry, who questions him, and loses his temper.

Conspirators

Minor characters in *Coriolanus*; jealous of Coriolanus and furious at his betrayal, the Volscian leader Aufidius arranges for conspirators to kill his old enemy. The Conspirators stir up the crowd's anger against Coriolanus before the murder.

Constable of France, Charles Delabreth

A minor character in *King Henry V*, the Constable of France is contemptuous of the English but warns the Dauphin that he may have underestimated the English King Henry V. The Constable nonetheless believes that the French will easily defeat the English at Agincourt, but his confidence is misplaced, and he is reported as being killed in battle.

Constance

A historical figure (d. 1201) and a character in *King John*, Constance is the widow of King John's brother and mother of his nephew young Arthur. Constance believes that her son, and not John, is the rightful King of England. When a diplomatic marriage is made between the French Dauphin [heir to the French throne] and King John's niece Blanche, Constance is furiously angry that lands belonging to England are being returned to France. She feels betrayed by the French King Philip who had previously given her cause his support and rages against his treachery. After young Arthur's death, Constance is hysterical with grief. She speaks touchingly of how she will miss her son in a speech which some scholars believe reflects Shakespeare's response to the death of his own son Hamnet who died at about the time the play was written.

copyright

See ELIZABETHAN DRAMATISTS.

Cordelia

A character in *King Lear*, Cordelia is Lear's youngest daughter, a determined woman who knows her own mind. Lear demands that Cordelia makes a public declaration of her total love for him in exchange for which he will give her a share of his kingdom. Cordelia refuses because she is honest enough to realize the impossibility of such a promise. Lear disinherits her, furious at her obstinacy, and she leaves England to marry the King of France who, unlike her father, recognizes her natural goodness. When she hears of Lear's suffering at the hands of her vindictive sisters, Goneril and Regan, Cordelia raises an army and returns to England in defence of her father. In the battle that follows Cordelia is defeated by her enemy Edmund and imprisoned with Lear. She is briefly reconciled with her father before she is hanged. Lear, grief-stricken, refuses to believe she is dead and cradles her body in his arms before he dies of a broken heart.

Corin

A character in *As You Like It*, Corin is a shepherd in the Forest of ARDEN, and a kindly old man who does his best to advise the lovesick Silvius in his courting of Phebe; he admits that his heart was often broken in his youth. Corin is something of a philosopher who is content with his life, although he describes the life of a shepherd whose master is neglectful, as a hard one. When Celia and Rosalind meet Corin in Arden, he arranges for them to buy his master's cottage and flock of sheep. They promise to pay him better wages, and Corin promises to serve them faithfully.

Coriolanus (Caius Martius)

A legendary warrior and the hero of *Coriolanus*, Caius Martius is a Roman aristocrat. He is dominated by his powerful mother, Volumnia, who has brought him up to be a fearless soldier and to despise the common people of Rome. Sent to subdue a local a tribe, the Volscians (who live in Corioles), Martius returns to Rome triumphant, proudly displaying his battle scars, and is given the name Coriolanus in honour of his victory. He is made Consul, and custom requires him to beg the people for their support. Coriolanus is a man of action not words and unable to make compromises; true humility is abhorrent to him and he addresses the crowd in arrogant tones. The crowd turn against Coriolanus and he is banished. Bent on revenge, Coriolanus allies himself to his old enemy Aufidius, the leader of the Volscians and together they march on Rome. Coriolanus' mother makes an impassioned appeal to her son and persuades him not to conquer the city but Aufidius, furious at Coriolanus' betrayal, arranges for him to be killed.

Coriolanus

One of Shakespeare's Roman plays and a late TRAGEDY which was written around 1607-08 and first published in the first FOLIO edition of 1623. There are no recorded performances of the play in Shakespeare's lifetime but it presumably was performed.

The main source for the play was a 16th century translation into English of *Lives of the Greeks and Romans* by PLUTARCH. *Coriolanus* is a political drama set in Ancient Rome in about 490 BC. Like Shakespeare's history plays, it examines the problem of deposing a bad ruler and the consequent civil unrest. It explores themes of pride and revenge and class hatred.

SYNOPSIS: There is unrest among the ordinary people of Rome who are growing hungry while there are plentiful supplies of corn stored in the houses of the rich.

Martius, a celebrated soldier and an aristocrat (not yet known as Coriolanus), addresses the crowd. He has no sympathy for their plight but says that Brutus and Sicinius, tribunes [elected representatives of the people], have been appointed to deal with their grievances. The Volscians, a neighbouring warrior tribe living in Corioli, are reported as marching on Rome led by Aufidius, an old enemy of Martius. Martius, second in command to the Roman general Cominius, leads an army in victory over the Volscians, sustaining terrible wounds. He is welcomed home as a hero and given the name of Coriolanus because of his courage at Corioli. He is further honoured by being nominated as Consul, the highest political office in Rome. Tradition requires that be speaks to the people and asks for their support in all humility but Coriolanus is typically arrogant as he addresses the citizens whom he openly despises. The tribunes, aware that they will lose their authority if Coriolanus is given too much power stir up feeling against him. There is open rebellion and Coriolanus is seized and sentenced to death. His few supporters plead for his life and Coriolanus is banished. Bent on revenge, he joins forces with his old enemy Aufidius and leads the Volscians against Rome. As they reach the city, the panicking people now say they were wrong to banish Coriolanus. His old friends and allies beg him to spare Rome but Coriolanus is unmoved until his mother makes an impassioned plea. Coriolanus makes peace with the Volscians but enraged at his betrayal Aufidius organizes his assassination.

Corioles (Corioli)

Corioles is an ancient city near Rome, home of the warlike tribe of the Volscians, and the setting for scenes in Corialanus. The Volscians defend the town of Corioles against the Roman army, and the Roman soldier, Caius Martius, displays such courage in the battle that he is afterwards given the name of 'Coriolanus' in recognition of his heroism.

Corioli

See CORIOLES

Cornelius[1]

A minor character in *Cymbeline*; Cornelius is the Queen's physician. She asks him to supply a poison with which she intends to kill Imogen although she tells Cornelius that she is only going to use it on animals. The honest physician is suspicious of her and substitutes a harmless potion which will only induce a deep sleep, but which will make the victim appear dead. At the end of the play, Cornelius brings news that the Queen has died and has made a full confession on her deathbed.

Cornelius[2]

A minor character in *Hamlet*, Cornelius is sent as a messenger to the King of Norway by Claudius. Together with Voltemand he delivers Claudius' demand that Fortinbras, Prince of Norway, must be prevented from invading Denmark. Cornelius and Voltemand return with a message of friendship from Norway.

Cornwall, Duke of

A character in *King Lear*, Cornwall is Regan's husband who is as villainous as his wife is vindictive. His part in the play is a small one but he embodies the atmosphere of evil that pervades the play. He threatens to execute the innocent Edgar and puts Kent, Lear's faithful follower, into the stocks. Cornwall's cruelty escalates, and at the pinnacle of horror he brutally puts out the eyes of Gloucester, Lear's loyal old friend. One of his servants is so appalled at Cornwall's crime that he kills his master. Cornwall's death is POETIC JUSTICE.

Costard

A comic character in *Love's Labour's Lost*, Costard is the quick-witted servant of Don Armado who is arrested for flirting with the country girl, Jaquenetta. Armado, who is also in love with Jaquenetta, offers Costard his freedom if he will deliver a letter to her. At the same time, Berowne asks Costard to deliver a love poem to Rosaline. Costard delivers the letters to the wrong women with the result that Berowne is forced to admit that he has broken his vow to renounce the company of women. It is Costard who brings the news that Jaquenetta is pregnant and urges Armado to make an honest woman of her. He takes part in the court entertainment of the Nine Worthies playing Pompey the Great but he makes a mess of his lines. He sympathizes with Nathaniel the Curate who also fails to make his mark on the stage.

costume

In the Elizabethan theatre, most plays would have been costumed in contemporary 16th-century clothes, although it is probable that some attempt was made by Elizabethan theatre companies to provide historical dress where appropriate. For example, Roman togas were possibly used in plays such as *Julius Caesar*, although in that play, Caesar is referred to as wearing a doublet, an Elizabethan garment. Cleopatra's costume, for example, would probably have resembled one of Queen Elizabeth I's rich gowns.

A member of the company, known as the TIREMAN, was in charge of the wardrobe and although leading actors would probably have provided their own costumes (see PHILLIPS, AUGUSTINE for example), the company would have costumed the hired actors (see HIRELINGS) and the boy actors. Large sums of money were spent on the costumes and actors were lavishly and elaborately dressed in rich satins and velvets, costing as much as £1 a yard, with lace and gold and silver trimmings. Indeed, costumes represented such an expensive investment for theatre managers that they would fine any actor who was found wearing his costume outside the theatre. Sometimes costumes were acquired second-hand; when noblemen died they would often leave their clothes to their servants and since such dress was usually unsuitable for everyday wear it was often sold by the beneficiaries to theatre companies.

Some MAKE-UP was probably used; white for ghosts, red noses for drunkards, and black for characters such as the Moor, Othello.

Countrymen

Minor characters in *The Two Noble Kinsmen*, a group of cheerful Countrymen, overheard by Arcite, joke bawdily, and discuss their May Day celebrations. They tell Arcite about the forthcoming games which are to include various trials of strength. Five Countrymen or villagers, named as Arcas, Rycas and Sennois, a Taborer [drummer], and the Bavian [character dressed as an ape] together with five Countrywomen (*see below*) perform a Morris dance for Duke Theseus. The Duke rewards them with money to buy paint for their maypole. (The Morris dance was traditionally performed by pairs of dancers representing the characters from the Robin Hood legend.)

Countrywomen
Minor characters in *The Two Noble Kinsmen*, five Countrywomen, named as Barbary (Barbara), Friz (short for 'Francis'), Luce (Lucy), Maudlin (short for 'Magdelen'), and Nell, join the Countrymen (*see above*) in their Morris dance. The Schoolmaster, who is conducting the dance, instructs the Countrywomen to dance nimbly and sweetly. A sixth dancer, Cicely, angers the Schoolmaster by failing to turn up.

coup de théâtre
A sudden and often surprising happening in a play which has the effect of dramatically altering the action and bringing about a resolution. An example is the apparent bringing to life of Hermione's statue in *The Winter's Tale*.

couplet
Two lines of rhymed verse with a similar or identical METRE in an a-a-b-b-c-c pattern. They often occur at the end of a poem and may contain a moral. Shakespearean sonnets end with a rhyming couplet.

Court, Alexander
A minor character in *King Henry V*, Court is a soldier in the English army. King Henry, disguised as an ordinary soldier, talks briefly to Court when visiting his troops on the eve of the Battle of Agincourt.

Courtesan
A minor character in *The Comedy of Errors*, the pretty and witty Courtesan [prostitute] is entertained by Ephesus Antipholus in a tavern (off-stage) after he has been barred from his home by his wife, Adriana. Antipholus promises to give the Courtesan the gold chain he has had made for Adriana; later the Courtesan demands the chain or the return of a gold ring she had given him. However, she approaches the wrong Antipholus whose bewildered behaviour convinces her that he has gone quite mad. The Courtesan tells Adriana what has happened and accompanies her when Ephesus Antipholus, once again mistaken for his twin, is declared insane by Dr Pinch.

Crab
The name of the dog belonging to Launce, a comic character in *The Two Gentlemen of Verona*. His master describes him as the 'sourest-natured dog that lives'.

Cranmer, Thomas
A historical figure (1489-1556) and a character in *King Henry VIII*, Cranmer opposes the pro-Catholic Wolsey, supporting Henry in his determination to divorce Katharine of Aragon. An advisor to the King, Cranmer is created Archbishop of Canterbury (in defiance of the Pope), and crowns Anne Bullen (Boleyn) Queen of England. Cranmer fears his political enemies are laying a trap for him but Henry, who holds Cranmer in the highest regard, promises that he will always have the King's backing; Cranmer is moved to tears by Henry's kind words. Wolsey's successors charge Cranmer with heresy and threaten him with imprisonment in the TOWER OF LONDON, but Henry intervenes to save his loyal friend. Godfather to Princess Elizabeth, he gives an oration at her christening prophesying her future greatness. Cranmer, a Protestant, is presented in the play as the most virtuous of figures while, Wolsey, representative of the Catholic Church, is portrayed in a bad light.

Cressida

A legendary figure and the heroine of *Troilus and Cressida*, Cressida is attracted to the Trojan Prince Troilus. Her Uncle Pandarus arranges for them to meet and although at first Cressida professes not to care for him, they fall in love and swear to be faithful to one another. The Trojans exchange Cressida for one of their soldiers held prisoner by the Greeks and the lovers are tragically parted. When Cressida arrives at the Greek camp she is greeted with a kiss of welcome from each of the commanders. She responds playfully but although she is obviously an object of sexual desire, only Ulysses brands her as prostitute. Cressida still loves Troilus, but she is in the care of Diomedes who tries to seduce her. She has to survive as best she can, and her promise of fidelity to Troilus now seems very fragile. Cressida is won over by Diomedes and gives him a keepsake that Troilus had given to her. Troilus is secretly watching and is heartbroken by her infidelity.

criticism

See LITERARY CRITICISM.

Cromwell

A historical figure (Thomas Cromwell c. 1485-1540) and a character in *King Henry VIII*, Cromwell is Cardinal Wolsey's loyal servant. When Wolsey falls from grace, Cromwell is genuinely saddened; however, soon after the Cardinal's death, his career advances. He is given a court appointment, and becomes the King's secretary. Cromwell is secretary of the council that tries Cranmer for heresy; he defends Cranmer and is himself accused by the pro-Catholic Gardiner of sympathy with the Protestant cause. Cromwell changes his allegiance from the Pope to King Henry, head of the newly established Church of England; in Shakespeare's view, this was a change of position from wrong to right.

cue

A sign to an actor that it is his turn to speak or move. A cue may be a sound or gesture, or a fellow actor's line of dialogue.

Curan

A minor character in *King Lear*, Curan is a courtier who tells Edmund that the Dukes of Cornwall and Albany are quarrelling.

Curio

A minor character in *Twelfth Night*, Curio is an elegant and witty gentleman at Duke Orsino's court.

curtain

The practice of drawing a curtain across the front of the stage to signal the end of an act or a performance was not established in public PLAYHOUSES in Shakespeare's time. There is controversy as to exactly when a curtain was first used in this way in the theatre, but it was probably not common practice until the arrival of the PROSCENIUM ARCH in theatres during the 17th century. In Elizabethan playhouses, a painted curtain might sometimes be hung at the back of the stage as a piece of minimal SCENERY. *See* PLAY PRODUCTION AND PERFORMANCE.

Curtain, The
A public playhouse in Shoreditch, the second purpose-built theatre in London, built in 1576 beyond the city limits and managed by Richard BURBAGE. Little is known of the companies who played at the Curtain but in 1598 it was leased for a while to the LORD CHAMBERLAIN'S MEN and Shakespeare himself may have acted here. *See* PLAYHOUSES.

Curtis
A minor character in *The Taming of the Shrew*, Curtis is Petruchio's chief servant in his country house. He has made everything ready for the arrival of his master and his new mistress Katherina and pumps Gremio, Petruchio's personal servant, for information.

Cymbeline
A historical figure (d. c. AD 40) and the title character of *Cymbeline*, Cymbeline was the historical King of Ancient Celtic Britain at a time of the Roman invasion. In the play, the authoritarian Cymbeline is furious with his daughter, Imogen, when she marries Posthumus against his wishes. He is a rather weak husband to the ambitious Queen, blind to her scheming and ultimately murderous intentions towards his daughter. His poor judgement of others is also evident in his treatment of Belarius whom he wrongly accused of treachery and banished, with the result that he lost his two sons. Through good fortune, rather than learned wisdom, Cymbeline is finally reunited with his children and his position on the throne is secured after a battle with the Romans.

Cymbeline
One of Shakespeare's later plays, a ROMANCE, *Cymbeline* was written sometime between 1606 and 1610 and first published in the first FOLIO of 1623. It may have had its first performance at the GLOBE in 1611.

A main source for the battle between the Romans and the Britons was HOLINSHED'S *Chronicles* and the plot of Posthumus' bet was based on a story from the *Decameron*, a collection of stories by the Italian writer Giovanni Boccaccio (1313-75). The play, set in Ancient Britain, has a complicated plot and explores themes of trust and infidelity, truth and pretence, love and reconciliation.

SYNOPSIS: King Cymbeline has three children. His sons, Guiderius and Arviragus were snatched away as babies by Belarius in revenge for wrong done to him by the King. His daughter, Imogen, has angered Cymbeline by marrying Posthumus against his wishes and Posthumus is banished. Posthumus rashly bets a friend that Imogen will always remain faithful to him, but he is tricked into believing that she has slept with another man, and is so angry that he plans to kill her. Imogen flees to Wales disguised as a boy. She finds shelter in a cave which unknown to her is the home of Belarius and her long-lost brothers who are living as outlaws. Imogen is pursued by Cloten, the oafish son of her wicked step-mother the Queen. He is jealous of Posthumus and has come, wearing Posthumus' clothes, to take Imogen for himself. Imogen's brothers kill Cloten and cut off his head, unknown to Imogen who has fallen ill and is unconscious. Her brothers, believing that Imogen is dead sorrowfully lay her body beside the decapitated Cloten. When Imogen recovers and sees a headless corpse wearing her husband's clothes, she is heartbroken, assuming that it is Posthumus. At home Cymbeline is confronting a Roman invasion. Belarius and Imogen's brothers join the army and fight valiantly against the Romans while

Posthumus, filled with remorse at the way he has treated Imogen, also fights for Britain on another part of the battlefield. Cymbeline is captured by the Romans but rescued in the nick of time by Belarius, Imogen's brothers and Posthumus. Anxious to thank those who saved his life, Cymbeline calls for his rescuers to be brought before him. In a final scene of explanation, reconciliation and reunion, the identities of Cymbeline's long-lost sons are revealed and Cymbeline blesses Imogen and Posthumus' marriage.

Dd

dactyl
A metrical FOOT consisting of a stressed syllable followed by two unstressed ones, as in 'Romeo'.

Dardanius
A minor character in *Julius Caesar*, Dardanius is a soldier in Cassius' and Brutus' army. At the battle of Philippi, Brutus asks Dardanius to help him commit suicide, but Dardanius says he cannot bring himself to do such a thing.

Dark Lady of the Sonnets, The
A faithless, dark-haired woman with 'raven black' eyes to whom Shakespeare addressed the later SONNETS (127 to 154) and who, despite scholarly conjecture, has remained unidentified. She may have been a composite invention of the poet or a real person; it has even been proposed that the Dark Lady may have been a young man and the object of Shakespeare's homosexual love. There has been speculation that she was Penelope Rich, sister of the Earl of ESSEX, a London prostitute known as Lucy Negro, or an innkeeper's wife with whom Shakespeare was alleged to have had an affair (see DAVENANT). She may have been Mary Fitton, a maid of honour to Queen Elizabeth who bore an illegitimate child by William Herbert, Earl of PEMBROKE or Emilia BASSANO (later Lanier), a brunette and the mistress of Lord Hunsdon the Lord Chamberlain (the patron of Shakespeare's company of players) who belonged to a family of Italian musicians at the court: we know from the sonnets that the Dark Lady played a musical instrument. The only other personal details that can be gleaned from the poems are that she was married and that she had an adulterous relationship with the poet, among other men, that was marked by bitterness and feelings of guilt.
See also W H, MR.

Daughter
A character in *The Two Noble Kinsmen*, the eighteen-year-old Jailer's Daughter cares for Palamon and Arcite when they are prisoners of war. She falls in love with Palamon, and helps him to escape, but afterwards she goes mad with grief at losing Palamon and anxiety that he may die. She throws herself into a lake, but is rescued by her Wooer who is out fishing, and eventually she is brought home by a friend of her father's. A Doctor is called in to cure the Daughter and suggests that the Wooer disguises himself as Palamon and makes love to her in a darkened room. The Wooer patiently undertakes the task, and the Daughter is reported later as cured and about to be married.

Daughter, of Antiochus
A minor character in *Pericles*, she is the daughter of King Antiochus. Pericles visits Antiochus in his search for a wife but before he can win the Daughter's hand he has to solve a riddle set by her father. To his horror, Pericles discovers that the answer to the

riddle reveals an incestuous relationship between the King and his Daughter and he flees Antiochus in disgust. The King and his Daughter are later reported as having been consumed in a fire sent down from the heavens by the angry gods.

Dauphin
The title which Shakespeare gives to King CHARLES VII of France in *King Henry VI, Part One*. Dauphin (sometimes Dolphin), is in fact a title given to the French heir to the throne but not to the King.

Dauphin, Lewis the
A character in *King John*; *see* LEWIS.

Dauphin, Louis the
A historical figure (1396-1415) and a character in *King Henry V*, the Dauphin is the son of King Charles VI of France and heir to the French throne. He is an arrogant young man who is full of contempt for England and the English. He scorns King Henry to whom he sends a barrel of tennis balls with a message saying that he considers Henry is only fit for playing games and is not man enough to fight battles. On the eve of the Battle of Agincourt the Dauphin, untroubled by the prospect of fighting the next day, discusses the merits of horses and mistresses with his companions and bets on who of them will take the greatest number of English prisoners. He is confident that the French will win the battle and when the French are beaten he threatens to kill himself.

Davenant or D'Avenant, William (1606–68)
Shakespeare's supposed illegitimate son, William Davenant was a playwright and theatrical entrepreneur after the restoration of the monarchy in England in 1660. He was responsible for several extremely popular adaptations of Shakespeare's plays; some of his revisions were radical ones and included the addition of completely new characters and situations. A fervent royalist, he fought for King Charles I during the English Civil War (1642-48) and was knighted for bravery.

Davenant always claimed to be Shakespeare's natural son, as well as the poet's godson, and traded on his claim. His story, first documented by John AUBREY, was that Shakespeare who frequently stayed at an Oxford inn en route between London and Stratford had an affair with the inn-keeper's wife. She bore him a son, christened William after his father, of whom it was said the poet became extremely fond. No evidence has ever been found to support Davenant's claim.

Davy
A minor comic character in *King Henry IV, Part Two*, Davy is a countryman and Justice Shallow's servant whose responsibilities include paying his master's bills and waiting at table.

Decius Brutus
A historical figure (d. 43 BC) and a minor character in *Julius Caesar*, Decius Brutus is one of the conspirators against Caesar who is present when the assassination is planned. He says he will be responsible for making sure that Caesar goes to the Capitol, where he is to be killed. When Caesar is persuaded by his wife Calpurnia not to leave the house because she is afraid for his life, Decius crucially manages to convince him to go to the Senate after all.

Decretas (Dercetas)

A historical figure (active 30 BC) and a minor character in *Antony and Cleopatra*, Decretas is one of Antony's followers. He arrives as Antony has stabbed himself and decides that this is the moment to defect to Caesar. Decretas believes that if he takes Antony's sword to Caesar he will find favour with him as the person who brings the news of Antony's death. He speaks of Antony as a man of honour who has courageously chosen to take his own life.

Deiphobus

A minor character in *Troilus and Cressida*, Deiphobus is a Trojan warrior and one of King Priam's sons.

Dekker, Thomas (c. 1570-1632)

A playwright and contemporary of Shakespeare, Dekker collaborated with other dramatists and wrote several plays for the theatre manager Philip HENSLOWE. His best known play is the comedy *The Shoemaker's holiday* (1600). He also wrote a pamphlet entitled *The Gull's Hornbook* instructing fashionable young men on how to behave themselves correctly in a theatre. Dekker spent his life in poverty and debt but nonetheless was spoken of as a man with a cheerful disposition although he was involved in a long-running literary squabble with Ben JONSON.

Delabreth, Charles, the Constable of France

A minor character in *King Henry V*; *see* CONSTABLE OF FRANCE.

Demetrius[1]

A minor character in *Antony and Cleopatra*, Demetrius is one of Antony's followers. He has heard the rumours surrounding Antony, and his relationship with Cleopatra, and regrets that Antony has aroused Caesar's disapproval.

Demetrius[2]

A central character in *A Midsummer Night's Dream*, Demetrius is the young Athenian in love with Hermia. Hermia's father has chosen Demetrius as his daughter's future husband but Hermia, who loves Lysander, resolutely refuses to marry him. Demetrius is alerted to the proposed elopement of Hermia and Lysander by Helena, a friend of the runaway couple, who is hopelessly in love with him. Demetrius is greatly irritated to find Helena tagging along as he goes in pursuit of Lysander and Hermia but despite his rudeness to her, he is unable to shake her off. Demetrius, bewitched by Puck's magic spells, is made to fall in love with Helena, whose first reaction after his earlier harshness is disbelief and anger. Demetrius, unsure whether he is yet awake or dreaming, vows to love her and the happy couple are married.

Demetrius[3]

A character in *Titus Andronicus*, Demetrius is the son of Tamora, Queen of the Goths. As cruel and bloodthirsty as his mother and his brother Chiron, Demetrius is central to the cycle of violence and revenge in the play. Demetrius and Chiron quarrel over Lavinia, Titus' daughter, whom they both desire. Agreeing that the best thing would be to share her, they kill her fiance Bassianus and rape and horribly mutilate Lavinia. The brothers pin the blame for Bassianus' murder on Titus' sons but in time Lavinia is able to indicate that Demetrius and Chiron were responsible for the murder and rape. In a macabre and peculiarly terrible revenge, Titus kills Demetrius and Chiron, bakes them in a pie and serves it up to their mother Tamora at a banquet.

Dennis
A minor character in *As You Like It*, Dennis is one of Oliver's servants, who announces the arrival of the wrestler Charles.

Denny, Sir Anthony
A minor character in *King Henry VIII*, Denny is a courtier who escorts Archbishop Cranmer to a late night meeting with the King.

dénouement
The unravelling of a plot which is usually the final and sometimes dramatic climax of a play when conflicts are resolved and mysteries explained.

Derby's Men
The original name of the company of actors known as STRANGE'S MEN. It is possible that Shakespeare may have acted with the company between 1593 and 1594.

Dercetas
See DECRETAS.

Desdemona
The heroine of *Othello*, Desdemona is the devoted wife of Othello, the Moor. She has married Othello against her father's wishes and she shows maturity and courage in the face of her father's prejudice and anger. A happy young bride, she gladly accompanies her husband to Cyprus when he is put in command of the Venetian army. There, Desdemona becomes the pawn in Iago's plot to discredit Cassio and ruin Othello. Iago lays a trap using a handkerchief, which Othello had given to Desdemona as a token of his love, as evidence of her supposed infidelity. The victim of Iago's villainy, Desdemona is bewildered by Othello's subsequent accusations of faithlessness. She swears her love for him is unchanged and unconditional and helplessly protests her innocence, but Othello's jealousy is so far out of control that he smothers and kills her.

deus ex machina
A Latin phrase meaning literally 'a god appearing from a machine'. In drama, it can describe any kind of contrived or artificial device, such as the sudden arrival of a long-lost relative or the discovery of a vital letter, which contributes to the resolution of a play. In *Cymbeline*, the Roman god Jupiter literally appears from some kind of machinery, lowered from above the stage, and promises the hero, Posthumus, that all will be well. *Compare* COUP DE THÉÂTRE.

De Witt, Johannes (born c. 1576)
A Dutch student who visited London in 1596 and wrote about his experiences in *Observationes Londinienses*, which contained a sketch and a description of the SWAN THEATRE. The original of the now famous sketch was lost but a friend of De Witt's made a copy of it which still survives.

dialogue
Lines spoken by two or more characters in a play; 'internal dialogue' is an actor's speech when he debates with himself. *Compare* MONOLOGUE.

Diana[1]

A character in *All's Well that Ends Well*, Diana is Widow Capilet's daughter. Bertram is making advances to Diana but although she admires him she knows he is married. When Helena, Bertram's wife, seeks her help in the plan to trick her husband, Diana gladly agrees to let Helena take her place in bed but first she asks Bertram to give her his ring as a sign of trust. When Bertram returns to France, Diana follows him to the court and confronts him. She maintains that Bertram has not fulfilled a promise to marry her and produces his ring as proof. She is about to be put in prison when Helena makes her surprise appearance and explains everything. In the play's happy resolution, the King offers to provide a dowry for Diana as a reward for her part in saving Helena and Bertram's marriage.

Diana[2]

A minor character in *Pericles*, in legend Diana was an ancient pagan goddess of chastity and a virgin huntress. In *Pericles*, Thaisa, believing that her husband and son and have drowned in a shipwreck, vows to remain chaste for ever and goes to join Diana's temple in Ephesus. Diana appears to Pericles in a dream and instructs him to go to Ephesus where is he united with Thaisa.

Dick the Butcher

A minor character in *King Henry VI, Part Two*, Dick is one of the rebel Jack Cade's followers. His ambition is to kill all the lawyers in England.

Diomedes[1]

A minor character in *Antony and Cleopatra*, Diomedes is one of Cleopatra's attendants. Cleopatra sends Diomedes to tell Antony that she has misled him and that she is, after all, alive and has not committed suicide as was reported. Diomedes arrives with the news too late; Antony is already dying.

Diomedes[2]

A legendary figure and a character in *Troilus and Cressida*, Diomedes is a Greek warrior who is sent to Troy to bring Cressida to Greece. He charms Cressida and succeeds in seducing her. She gives him a sleeve, a keepsake that Troilus had given her, and Diomedes wears it in his helmet on the battlefield. Troilus challenges him to fight but is overpowered by Diomedes who sends Troilus' horse to Cressida as proof that he is victorious.

Dion

A minor character in *The Winter's Tale*, Dion is a Lord of Sicilia who is sent by Leontes to consult the Oracle.

Dionyza

A character in *Pericles*, the evil Dionyza is the wife of Cleon, Governor of Tharsus. When Pericles places his daughter, Marina, in Dionyza and Cleon's care, they promise to bring her up as their own. However, as Marina grows up into a beautiful young girl who is more attractive and gifted than their own daughter Philoten, they become jealous of her. Dionyza persuades her servant Leonine to murder Marina and although he fails to kill her he tells Dionyza that she is dead. Like Lady Macbeth, Dionyza thinks her husband is too soft-hearted: she, in contrast, is without pity and poisons Leonine, the one witness who might be able to expose her wickedness.

director
In the modern theatre or in films, the person whose job it is to interpret the text of a play and to guide and direct the actors both artistically and technically in their performance.

disclosure
The revelation of something that is crucial to the outcome of a play, which may bring about a tragic resolution or a happy reconciliation. An example is Emilia's disclosure that Desdemona is innocent in *Othello*.

dithyramb
A usually short speech or hymn of ecstatic praise.

Divine Right of Kings, The
A political and religious doctrine, widely held in the medieval world and in Shakespeare's time, was that a Christian King was divinely anointed by God and responsible not to his government or people but to God alone. This belief meant that the king's authority was total; a crime against the monarchy was a crime against God. Characters in Shakespeare's HISTORY PLAYS frequently face a dilemma over the problem of remaining loyal to an inadequate or corrupt king.

Doctor
A minor character in *The Two Noble Kinsmen*, the Doctor is called in to cure the Jailer's Daughter. She has gone mad with grief and anxiety after helping Palamon, whom she loves, to escape from jail. A kindly, but wordy man, the Doctor proposes that the Wooer, who loves the Daughter, should pretend to be Palamon and make love to her in a darkened room. His treatment is surprisingly successful.

Doctor Caius
A character in *The Merry Wives of Windsor*; see CAIUS, DOCTOR.

Doctors
Minor characters in two plays; in *Macbeth* a Scottish Doctor witnesses Lady Macbeth's sleepwalking and an English Doctor tells of the English King's power to cure the sick with a touch.

In *King Lear*, the Doctor is a servant to Cordelia. He assures her that Lear can regain his sanity and his kindness contrasts with the cruelty in the play.

Dogberry
A comic character, a CLOWN, in *Much Ado About Nothing*, Dogberry is the dim-witted but enthusiastic local policeman in charge of the nightwatchmen. He instructs his men on how to do their job but his instructions are as confused as his vocabulary. Wordy and pompous, he misuses language sensationally as he interrogates his prisoners and he drives Leonato to distraction with his lengthy and rambling account of Borachio and Conrade's villainy. However, his part in affairs is a crucial one, because it is Dogberry and his men who provide the proof of Hero's innocence.

It is probable that William KEMP first took the part of Dogberry.

Dolabella

A minor character in *Antony and Cleopatra*, Dolabella is one of Caesar's followers who is sent to guard Cleopatra after the queen's surrender to Caesar. As Cleopatra sings Antony's praises, Dolabella finds it hard to get a word in edgeways. He is kind to Cleopatra and warns her that she has only three more days to remain in Egypt before Caesar sends for her to parade her through the streets of Rome.

Doll Tearsheet

A character in *King Henry IV, Part Two* and *King Henry V*. *See* TEARSHEET, DOLL.

Domitius Enobarbus

A character in *Antony and Cleopatra*, *see* ENOBARBUS, DOMITIUS.

Donaldbain

A historical figure (c. 1033-1099) and a minor character in *Macbeth*, Donaldbain is the younger son of King Duncan. After King Duncan's murder, Donalbain fears that suspicion for his father's death may fall on him and his brother Malcolm. He flees to Ireland and takes no further part in the action.

Don Adriano de Armado

See ARMADO.

Don John

A character in *Much Ado About Nothing*, Don John is the bastard brother of Don Pedro, the Prince of Aragon. Don John, who has quarrelled with his brother, openly admits that he is a thorough-going villain. Motivated purely by his jealousy, Don John is determined to prevent the marriage between Hero and Claudio and pays his companion, Borachio, to make it look as if Hero has been unfaithful to Claudio. When his plot is uncovered, Don John flees but in a slightly dark note at the end of the play it is reported that he has been captured and is being brought back to Messina. Benedick declares that he will be punished.

Donne, John (c. 1571–1631)

A poet and writer, Donne was brought up as a Roman Catholic but became a priest in the Anglican Church in 1615 and was appointed Dean of St Paul's in 1621. He is regarded as the greatest exponent of Metaphysical poetry which is characterized by its dramatic form, striking imagery, and witty conceits. *See* CONCEIT, METAPHYSICAL.

Don Pedro

A character in *Much Ado About Nothing*, Don Pedro is the Prince of Aragon who has recently returned from a victorious campaign. He trades witty exchanges with Benedick but he is also something of a romantic who encourages his friends in their complicated love affairs. He offers to woo Hero on Claudio's behalf at the masked ball and, with Claudio's help, he tricks Benedick into believing that Beatrice has fallen in love with him. Don Pedro is quick to condemn Hero, when he is wrongly informed that she has been unfaithful to Claudio by his scheming brother, Don John. However, unlike Don John, Don Pedro is well-intentioned by nature. When he learns that Hero is completely innocent he is sorry to have misjudged her and delighted to discover that she is, after all, alive.

Dorcas
A minor comic character in *The Winter's Tale*, Dorcas is a lively country bumpkin who appears with her friend Mopsa at the sheep shearing-feast and sings with Autolycus.

Doricles
In *The Winter's Tale*, the name adopted by Prince Florizel when he appears in disguise to woo Perdita.

Dorset, The Marquess of
A historical figure (1451-1501) and a minor character in *King Richard III*, Dorset is Queen Elizabeth's elder son. When the Queen hears that Richard has seized the crown, she sends Dorset abroad to join Richmond's rebellion against the King; he makes an appearance at the Battle of Bosworth.

Douglas, Archibald Earl of
A historical figure (1369-1424) and a minor character in *King Henry IV, Part One*, Douglas is a proud Scottish noble who rebels against King Henry. He searches for the King at the Battle of Shrewsbury so that he can kill him. He kills Sir Walter Blunt, whom he mistakes for Henry, and he nearly succeeds in killing Henry but is prevented by Prince Hal. Douglas is captured in the battle but Prince Hal is so impressed with his courage that he sets him free.

downstage
A position at the front of the stage where the actor is closest to the audience. *Compare* CENTRE STAGE; UPSTAGE.

drama
A form of literature, intended for acting out on a stage, in which the narrative is usually conveyed by dialogue that is spoken aloud as actors take on the roles of characters and act out the story on stage.

Drama as we know it has its roots in the Classical theatre of Ancient Greece and Rome where the genres of COMEDY and TRAGEDY were categorized, and where plays were performed in purpose-built theatres, by professional actors wearing masks. After the Classical period, the theatrical tradition in Europe was kept alive by troupes of travelling acrobats, musicians and storytellers. During the Middle Ages in England, drama began to develop out of the liturgy of the Christian Church and pageants about the life of Christ were acted out in Latin by priests in churches. Gradually laymen began to take the place of priests and performances, in the vernacular [day-to-day English language], were given outside churches on specially built wooden stages. Productions became increasingly complex and the contemporary costumes were lavish. Stories from the Old Testament were enacted and comedy was introduced in the form of comic characters such as Noah's wife (*see* MIRACLE PLAYS; MORALITY PLAYS).

As the influence of the RENAISSANCE was felt in Elizabethan England, drama underwent a further change and secular plays were increasingly performed. Plays, in Latin and in English, were written for and presented by boys and young men in schools and universities and at the INNS OF COURT. Most of these dramas were serious, moralizing and often allegorical (*see* ALLEGORY) but some comedies were specially written too (*see* UDALL). Companies of boy actors and professional adult players were

formed for whom dramatists were commissioned to write plays and drama was given
the ultimate seal of approval with the royal patronage of Queen Elizabeth I. *See*
ELIZABETHAN DRAMA.

dramatic criticism
See DRYDEN; LITERARY CRITICISM; SHAKESPEAREAN CRITICISM.

dramatic irony
A state in a narrative when the reader or audience are better informed about what is
really happening in the play than the characters. The audience is aware that a character
is behaving in an inappropriate way given the true circumstances of his situation and
such knowledge can increase tension or heighten humour. An example of the way in
which tragedy can be intensified by dramatic irony is in the final act of *Romeo and
Juliet* when the audience, who know that Juliet is not really dead but simply drugged,
witness Romeo's grief and suicide on his discovery of her unconscious and apparently
dead body. *See* IRONY; TRAGIC IRONY.

dramatis personae
A list of all the characters who appear in a play, which is given at the beginning of the
text. No dramatis personae appeared in the QUARTO editions of Shakespeare's plays,
and in the First FOLIO of 1623 the list of the characters and the names of the actors who
played them was given at the end of the playscript.

dramaturgy
The art or the theory of dramatic production.

Drawer
One of several minor comic character's in *King Henry IV, Parts One and Two*; a drawer
is one of the servants at the Boar's Head, a tavern that Falstaff frequents. In *Part Two*,
Prince Hal and Poins disguise themselves as Drawers to play a trick on Falstaff. *See also*
FRANCIS, A DRAWER.

Drayton, Michael (1563–1631)
A prolific poet and author of numerous odes and satires, Drayton knew Shakespeare,
and it is thought possible that he may have contributed some verse to his plays. Drayton
collaborated on some twenty plays for the theatre manager Philip HENSLOWE and one of
them, *Sir John Oldcastle*, was printed in 1619 with the name of Shakespeare incorrectly
given as its author. However, he is best remembered for a series of pastoral poems
entitled '*Idea, The Shepherd's Garland*' (1593) and a collection of historical poems
'*The Baron's Ward*' (1603). There is an unconfirmed story that Shakespeare died of a
fever contracted after a 'merry meeting' in Stratford with Drayton and Ben JONSON.

Droeshout, Martin (c. 1601-50)
A Flemish painter whose portrait of Shakespeare, the DROESHOUT ENGRAVING,
APPEARED IN THE FIRST FOLIO edition of the plays. It was considered by Ben JONSON to
be an excellent likeness of the poet. Since Droeshout was a mere fifteen years old when
Shakespeare died, it is more likely that the portrait was copied from another picture
rather than drawn from life. *See the portrait at* SHAKESPEARE

Dromio of Ephesus
A comic character in *The Comedy of Errors*, Dromio of Ephesus is the identical twin brother of SYRACUSE DROMIO *(see below)*. The Dromio twins had been adopted by Egeon and Emilia in infancy to be servants to their infant sons, the Antipholus twins, but the family was shipwrecked and the two sets of twins were separated. Ephesus Dromio and one of the Antipholus twins were washed ashore in Ephesus where they are living at the time of the play. Unknown to Ephesus Dromio, his twin, Syracuse Dromio, and the other Antipholus are visiting the city. Comic scenes of mistaken identity follow as both Dromios (and both Antipholuses) are repeatedly confused with their twins. Ephesus Dromio is beaten and abused for apparently getting things wrong but fortunately he is a tough character, ironic and witty, and a survivor. He is happily reunited with his twin at the end of the play.

Dromio of Syracuse
A comic character in *The Comedy of Errors*, Dromio is the identical twin brother of EPHESUS DROMIO *(see above)*. In the shipwreck, Syracuse Dromio and one Antipholus twin, were washed ashore in Syracuse. Syracuse Antipholus, in search of his lost twin brother, travels to Ephesus with Dromio where, unknown to them, the other Dromio and Antipholus are living. A comedy of errors follows as both sets of twins are repeatedly mistaken for one another. Syracuse Dromio is given several beatings as he does his best to respond to what seem to be increasingly confused orders. Syracuse Dromio and his master have a companionable relationship. A happy-go-lucky character, a CLOWN, Dromio is described by Antipholus as his FOOL who cheers him up when his spirits are low. Dromio is reunited with his twin brother at the end of the play and jokes with him as to who of them is the eldest.

Dryden, John (1631–1700)
A poet, critic and prolific playwright, Dryden's best known plays are *Marriage-a-la-Mode* (1673) and *All for Love* (1678). In 1668, Dryden launched the tradition of dramatic criticism with his 'Essay of Dramatick Poesie' which included an appraisal of the works of Shakespeare. This was followed by a *Preface to Troilus and Cressida* (1679), a play which Dryden adapted as he regarded the work as crude. He wrote that Shakespeare '...of all modern and perhaps ancient poets had the largest and most comprehensive soul'. *See* SHAKESPEAREAN CRITICISM.

Dudley's men
The first organized company of professional actors in England, which was founded under the patronage of Robert Dudley, Queen Elizabeth's favourite, in 1559. Their name changed to LEICESTER'S MEN when Dudley received the title of Earl of Leicester in 1564.

Duke (Vincentio)
A central character in *Measure for Measure*, the Duke, named Vincentio in the cast list, is always referred to as the Duke. The Duke is concerned that his rule in Vienna has been too permissive and decides to appoint Angelo to rule in his place, believing he is the right man to restore order and discipline. The Duke disguises himself as a travelling friar, Friar Ludowick, so that he can see for himself the results of Angelo's new administration. As a friar, he is trusted by the other characters and he is in a position to influence events. Learning of Angelo's tyrannical new regime, he enlists Isabella and

Mariana's aid in a plan to expose his deputy's hypocrisy. The Duke then makes a grand entrance to the city as himself; the PERSONIFICATION of mercy and forgiveness, he dispenses justice, measure for measure, and asks Isabella to be his wife.

Duke

A minor character in *The Two Gentlemen of Verona*, The Duke of Milan is sometimes referred to as Emperor. The Duke is Silvia's father, who wants his daughter to marry Thurio. When he learns of Silvia's plan to elope with her lover Valentine, he orders Valentine to leave the city on pain of death. In the happy resolution to the play, the Duke forgives Valentine and declares that he is worthy of Silvia's hand in marriage.

Duke Frederick

A character in *As You Like It*, Duke Frederick is Duke Senior's brother. Duke Frederick, the one-dimensional villain of the piece, has seized Duke Senior's lands and sent his brother into exile. He banishes Duke Senior's daughter, Rosalind, from his kingdom, only because she is highly praised by everyone else. His ruthlessness rebounds on him when his own daughter, Celia, deserts him and follows Rosalind to the Forest of ARDEN. Duke Frederick seizes Oliver's lands next, sending him to bring back Orlando, dead or alive. However, Duke Frederick, leading an army into Arden against his brother, meets a religious old man and is miraculously reformed. He returns his brother's lands and retires from the world.

Duke Senior

A character in *As You Like It*, Duke Senior has been banished by his younger brother, Duke Frederick (see above) who has seized all his lands, and now lives in exile in The Forest of ARDEN with his companions. They lead a good life, hunting, feasting and merry-making, and the Duke compares his present carefree existence with the restraints of court life. When Orlando bursts in on him demanding food, Duke Senior receives him with great courtesy and invites him to join them at dinner. The Duke fails to recognise his daughter Rosalind in her disguise as the youth 'Ganymede', although he does notice that Ganymede bears some sort of resemblance to her. He blesses Rosalind's marriage to Orlando in the end, and when his dukedom is returned by the reformed Duke Frederick, he prepares to resume life as a responsible ruler, after one last celebration in Arden.

Dull, Anthony

A minor comic character in *Love's Labour's Lost*, Dull is a dim-witted constable who arrests Costard for flirting with Jaquenetta. His role is that of the straight man for the comic characters of Holofernes and Nathaniel whose pedantic language is often quite incomprehensible. Dull himself has difficulty with language and misuses words but when things become too confusing for him, he simply resorts to silence. Dull is aptly named, but when the entertainment of the Nine Worthies is being planned, he rather surprisingly offers to dance or play the tabor [a small drum].

Dumaine[1]

The name of two minor characters in *All's Well that Ends Well*; see LORDS.

Dumaine[2]

A character in *Love's Labour's Lost*, Dumaine is an elegant young nobleman. He is one of the lords at the court of Navarre who has taken an oath to lead an almost monastic life of scholarship and celibacy for three years. When the French Princess visits Navarre, Dumaine immediately falls in love with Katherine, one of the Princess's ladies-in-waiting. He abandons learning and sends her gifts of poetry (rather bad poetry), and a pair of gloves and, dressed as a Russian from Moscow, he sets out to woo her. Katherine, who remarks on his smooth, unbearded face, responds coolly to his overtures and says she will give him as much love as she is able to in a year's time, while he promises to remain faithful and true to her in the meanwhile.

dumb-show
A mimed summary of the action of a play, often accompanied by music, which introduced some early Elizabethan plays. The play-within-a-play in *Hamlet* is preceded by a dumb-show. In *Pericles*, the Chorus introduces three dumb-shows in which the characters silently enact parts of the narrative that have occurred between the ending of the last act and the beginning of the next.

Duncan
A historical figure (d. 1040) and a character in *Macbeth*, Duncan is the elderly King of Scotland who confers the title of Thane of Cawdor on Macbeth as a reward for his courage in battle. When Duncan visits Macbeth's castle, he is ruthlessly murdered by Macbeth who claims his crown.

The historical Duncan, King of Scotland, was Macbeth's cousin and probably younger than Shakespeare's Duncan. He was killed during a civil war in Scotland and Macbeth took the throne.

Dunsinane
A castle on a hill in *Macbeth*, close to BIRNAM WOOD, which is the setting for the play's bloody climax.

Ee

Edgar

A character in *King Lear*, Edgar is Gloucester's elder son, who is falsely accused by his half-brother Edmund of plotting against their father's life. Gloucester threatens to kill his son and Edgar is forced to flee. He disguises himself as a lunatic beggar, calls himself 'Poor Tom,' and wanders on the heath, where he meets the deranged King Lear, and later his father who has been cruelly blinded. Edmund shows compassion, caring for a father who has misjudged him. He takes the suicidal Gloucester to the edge of Dover Cliffs and tricks him into believing that he has survived a leap from the cliffs. Edgar is an agent of goodness and humanity in a play with evil and cruelty at its heart. Like Cordelia, Edgar is wronged by a father to whom, like her, he remains loyal. He saves his father's life and after Lear's death, he is poised to save Britain from the darkness and chaos into which it has fallen.

Edmund

A character in *King Lear*, Edmund is the ruthless and deceitful illegitimate son of the Duke of Gloucester; Edgar's younger half-brother, and the stereotypical villain of the piece.

Edmund convinces Gloucester that he is a devoted son, but that Edgar is wickedly plotting against their father. Edmund is actually ambitious for power himself and confides his real intentions in the audience. Edmund then betrays his father to Lear's daughter Regan, whose husband gouges out the poor old man's eyes. As part of his plan to become king, Edmund pretends to make love to Regan, and then in turn to Goneril, Lear's other daughter, with the result that the sisters quarrel over him. Edmund leads the army against Cordelia's forces; he captures Cordelia and Lear and orders them to be killed, before he is mortally wounded in single combat by his brother Edgar.

Edmund, Earl of Rutland

A character in *King Henry VI, Part Three*; *see* RUTLAND, EARL OF.

Edward III

A HISTORY PLAY by an unknown author, first published in 1596. The play was ascribed to Shakespeare in the 17th century, but was subsequently thought to have been written by another writer. Recent scholarship, particularly that of Dr Eric Sams in *Shakespeare's Edward III* (1996), makes a strong case for concluding that the play probably was written by Shakespeare, in collaboration with another dramatist. Certainly one line in the play: 'Lilies that fester smell far worse than weeds' also appears in one of Shakespeare's sonnets (number 94).

The Reign of King Edward III was probably written around 1592-93, when Shakespeare was in his late twenties; it recounts the years of fighting between England and France during Edward's reign (1327-1377) and the passionate but unrequited love of Edward for the Countess of Salisbury.

Edward, Earl of March and later King Edward IV

A historical figure (1442-1483) and a character who appears in three history plays, *King Henry VI, Parts Two and Three,* and *King Richard III*

In *Henry VI, Part Two* Edward, the Duke of York's elder son, is called upon by his father to support the Yorkist claim to the throne. (*See* YORK, HOUSE OF.)

In *Part Three*, Edward makes his own bid to become King. When his father is killed, Edward raises an army and after a hard-won victory, orders King Henry to be imprisoned in the TOWER OF LONDON. The Earl of Warwick is dispatched to France to arrange a diplomatic marriage but in the meantime, Edward has fallen in love with and married the widowed Lady Elizabeth Grey. This hasty and self-indulgent union angers not only the French but also Warwick, who turns against Edward and vows to dethrone him. Edward is briefly overcome by Warwick's forces but ultimately he triumphs. He declares himself King again, banishes Henry's Queen Margaret and stabs their son the young Edward, Prince of Wales to death. When his even more ruthless brother Richard (the future King Richard III) murders King Henry, Edward's seat on the throne is secured.

In *King Richard III*, Edward appears briefly as a sick and saintly old man, whose death opens the way for his brother Richard to seize the crown. His character is quite different from the unscrupulous Edward that Shakespeare depicts in *King Henry VI, Part Three.*

Edward, Prince of Wales

A historical figure (1453-71) and a character in *King Henry VI, Part Three*, Edward is the son of King Henry VI and Queen Margaret and heir to the throne of England. He is a courageous young man who criticizes his father for his weakness as King. When Edward, Earl of March, seizes the throne the young Prince Edward, who stands in his way, is ruthlessly stabbed to death.

Edward, Prince (Prince of Wales, and declared King Edward V)

A historical figure (1470-c. 1483) and a character in *King Richard III*, Edward is the elder son of King Edward IV. He is thirteen years old at the time of the play, a bold and lively boy. Arriving in London on the death of his father, he is declared King of England although never actually crowned. Richard, driven by ambition to become King himself, has Edward, together with his younger brother the Duke of York, imprisoned in the TOWER OF LONDON and arranges for them to be murdered there. Edward's ghost haunts Richard on the eve of the Battle of BOSWORTH.

Shakespeare's SOURCES for the plot of *King Richard III*, led him to believe that Richard was responsible for the deaths of Edward and his brother in the Tower, but there is no historical evidence whatsoever to confirm this.

Egeon (Aegeon)

A character in *The Comedy of Errors*, Egeon is a merchant from Syracuse, and father of the twin Antipholuses. He is searching for his long-lost son when he arrives in Ephesus, where he is told that he must pay a ransom or face death. Egeon tells the Duke of Ephesus the tragic story of his family's shipwreck, and the loss of his wife and son. The

Duke is sufficiently moved by Egeon's account to allow him twenty-four hours to raise the money. When the time is up, and Egeon is still unable to pay, he is taken to his execution close to a priory where, as luck will have it, he finds both his sons and his long-lost wife Emilia, and his life is spared. Egeon plays little part in the action, but his presence at the beginning and the end of the play frames the story.

Egeus
A minor character in *A Midsummer Night's Dream*, Egeus is Hermia's authoritarian father who believes that he has the right to dispose of his daughter's hand in marriage as he thinks fit. He has chosen a prospective husband for her, but Hermia, who loves Lysander, is refusing to cooperate. Egeus asks Theseus, Duke of Athens, to mediate, and he rules in Egeus' favour. However, the Duke softens towards the young lovers after their midsummer night's adventures in the woods, and overrules Egeus, who is greatly annoyed.

Eglamour
A minor character in *The Two Gentlemen of Verona*, Eglamour is the chivalrous old knight who helps Silvia to find her lover, the banished Valentine. Silvia has great faith in Eglamour, believing him to be wise and honourable, but when she is captured by Outlaws, Eglamour abandons her and makes a cowardly escape.

Elbow
A comic character in *Measure for Measure*, Elbow is a simple-minded and self-important constable who does his best to police the criminal underworld of Vienna. He brings Mistress Overdone and the pimp Pompey before Angelo and Escalus on charges of procuring prostitutes, but his wild misuse of language (*see* MALAPROPISM) makes him hard to understand. Elbow also tries to imprison Froth, whom he accuses of some vague wrong to his pregnant wife. His determination to observe the letter of the law makes him a kind of comic parallel to Angelo.

Eleanor
See GLOUCESTER, DUCHESS OF IN KING HENRY VI, PART TWO

Eleanor, Queen
A historical figure (1122-1204) and a minor character in *King John*, Eleanor is King John's mother and the young Arthur's Grandmother. Eleanor is a forceful character, strong in her defence of her son. She quarrels angrily with Constance over a will which she says proves Arthur has no right to the throne. John hears news of Eleanor's death before the French invade England and is grief-stricken.

elision
The joining together of two syllables in a word by omitting a vowel sound; for example 'speak'st' for speakest; 'cam'st' for camest, or 'flow'r' for flower. Elision is sometimes used in verse in order to accommodate a word into a line of particular metric length.

Elizabeth I (1533–1603)
Elizabeth I was Queen of England for 45 years from 1558, and therefore for most of Shakespeare's lifetime. Elizabeth was the only surviving child of the TUDOR King Henry VIII and Anne Boleyn. Henry had divorced his first wife, Katharine of Aragon,

because of her failure to provide a male heir and in order to marry Anne, and for this reason some doubted the legitimacy of Elizabeth's birth and so her right to accede to the throne. As a result, and despite her personal popularity, there were plots against her life throughout her reign.

Brought up as a Protestant, following her father's break with the Church of Rome, Elizabeth formally established the Anglican Church in England. This brought her into conflict with both English and Scottish Roman Catholics, in spite of her own personal religious tolerance. Tension increased when in 1568 her Roman Catholic cousin Mary Queen of Scots, who was regarded as the rightful queen of England by English Catholics, was forced to flee Scotland and came to England. Fearing Mary's presence might be a catalyst for further Catholic uprisings, Elizabeth held her captive for nearly 20 years; she was eventually executed with Elizabeth's reluctant approval in 1587 following the discovery of yet another conspiracy.

Elizabeth, or the Virgin Queen as she was sometimes called, chose not to marry, fearing that an alliance with a foreign prince might jeopardize the security of her position on the throne. She had her favourites at court, however, most notably Robert Dudley, the Earl of LEICESTER, whom she would have liked to marry and who may have been her lover, and the Earl of ESSEX. Strong-minded, though not always physically strong, the red-headed queen (who wore a red wig in later years) sometimes displayed a volcanic temper but she deployed her feminine appeal and intelligent diplomacy to manipulate and control the nobles at court. She was a highly educated woman with an remarkable and versatile intellect who was fluent in Latin and Greek besides several other languages. She dressed extravagantly in bejewelled gowns (a French envoy reported that she had 3,000 dresses in her wardrobe) and must have appeared a truly regal figure in spite of her blackened teeth, caused by eating too many sweets. She loved hunting and dancing and was a skilled player of the virginals [a keyboard instrument like a small harpsichord, named after her].

The Queen took a lively interest in literature and drama. During the summer months when her court progressed round the country visiting both royal and private establishments, plays and MASQUES would be performed especially for her pleasure. In 1553 she became patron of her own company of actors, QUEEN ELIZABETH'S MEN or the QUEEN'S MEN; Shakespeare himself may have been a member of the company in 1587. Her patronage ensured that the theatre flourished despite the fervent opposition of the Puritans. Seventeenth-century tradition had it that FALSTAFF was a favourite character of the Queen and that *The Merry Wives of Windsor* was written as the result of her request to prolong the character's life and to show him in love.

In Shakespeare's *King Henry VIII*, the birth of Queen ELizabeth is announced to Henry. Archbishop Cranmer, gives a eulogy to the newborn Princess and looks forward to the many blessings she will bring to England.

Elizabeth, Queen

A historical figure (1437-1492) and character in *King Richard III*, Elizabeth is King Edward IV's Queen and Lord Rivers' sister who is suspicious of Richard from the outset. Richard despises her because she is a commoner who had been married before she became Queen (*see* LADY ELIZABETH GREY). The old Queen Margaret, a Lancastrian Queen and an old enemy of the House of YORK, prophesies that the Yorkist Queen Elizabeth's sons will die and that she will be widowed. The prophecies are

Elizabeth I, *artist: Nicholas Hilliard*

By courtesy of the National Portrait Gallery, London

fulfilled when King Edward dies and Richard has her two young sons, Prince Edward and the Duke of York, murdered in the TOWER OF LONDON. Elizabeth curses Richard and tries to prevent him from marrying her daughter, but like many before her, Elizabeth succumbs to his magnetic charm and agrees to the marriage.

Elizabethan Age, The
The period in English history from 1558 to 1603 during which time Elizabeth I was queen. Under Elizabeth's firm rule, and despite simmering conflict between Roman Catholics and the newly established Protestant Church, England prospered, becoming a world maritime and trading power with a formidable navy and navigators such as Francis Drake (c. 1540-96) and Martin Frobisher (c. 1535-94) making important voyages of exploration.

 The Elizabethan Age was characterized by the growth of HUMANISM and by the English RENAISSANCE with its flowering of the arts, in particular literature, and the birth of the professional theatre in England. It witnessed the emergence of poets such as DRAYTON, SIDNEY, and SPENSER; of essayists such as RALEIGH and BACON, and of dramatists such as MARLOWE and Shakespeare. There was a desire to learn, and newly founded grammar schools provided free education. It was a time of intense national pride, particularly after the defeat of the Spanish Armada in 1588, something that was reflected in much contemporary drama.

Elizabethan drama

The Elizabethan age was a time of great popular enthusiasm for drama, although it was not regarded as an art form and was not given the academic consideration it receives today. Plays were performed in private houses and at court, and there were more theatres in London than in any other European capital city. The demand for new plays was huge; they appeared at an astonishing rate and the turnover of new material was so fast that each play only ran for an average of ten performances. During one three-year period the ADMIRAL'S MEN performed on average eighteen new plays each year, and the Elizabethan appetite for drama was such that during the winter of 1607-08 a ship owner even organized performances of *Hamlet* and *King Richard II* for the sailors on one of his merchant ships, the *Dragon*.

The forerunners of Elizabethan drama were the early Medieval miracle plays, dramatizations of bible stories in Latin, enacted by the clergy, and often performed in church. The later Medieval MYSTERY PLAYS, grew out of this tradition; they were written in English and performed on carts, moveable stages, in the open air. They were dramatizations of religious themes which were related to the lives of ordinary people, and were often comic, sometimes even bawdy. Closer to Shakespeare's theatre, were MORALITY PLAYS, allegorical dramas (*see* ALLEGORY) about the conflict between personified figures of 'Good' and 'Evil'. In the 15th and 16th centuries, another kind of drama developed in interludes, short plays or MASQUES which were performed by professional actors at court, in private houses, or in the law schools of the INNS OF COURT.

By the middle of the 16th century, other, outside, influences were being brought to bear on drama as, increasingly, people travelled abroad. Travellers to Italy brought back ideas from performances by the COMMEDIA DELL'ARTE and Elizabethan dramatists added to them new elements of characterization and verbal, rather than SLAPSTICK humour. Although students at Oxford and Cambridge Universities were still writing and acting in plays written in Latin, more and more drama was being written in English. At the same time, the English language itself was rapidly becoming more complex, enriched and vitalized by additions from French and Italian.

The first BLANK verse play ever written in English was a tragedy by two lawyers, Thomas Sackville and Thomas Norton, *GORBODUC* (1565). The earliest English comedies were *Ralph Roister Doister* (1563) by Nicholas UDALL and an anonymous rustic farce, *Gammer Gurton's Needle* (1566). Elizabethan national pride and interest in recent history was reflected in CHRONICLE PLAYS, and exceedingly bloodthirsty and somewhat crude REVENGE PLAYS were particularly popular with audiences. The first of these was *Spanish Tragedy* (c. 1585) by Thomas Kydd. *See also* ACTORS AND ACTING; BOY COMPANIES; CENSORSHIP; COMPANIES OF ACTORS; DRAMA; PLAY PRODUCTION AND PERFORMANCE, AND PLAYHOUSES.

Elizabethan dramatists

The voracious appetite of Elizabethan audiences for new plays meant that there was a constant demand for the work of dramatists like DEKKER, JONSON, MARLOWE and WEBSTER. Some playwrights, like Shakespeare, wrote for one company of actors in which they had a financial share, while others were commissioned by various companies to write new plays. It was common for Elizabethan dramatists to collaborate with one another, and as many as four or five writers might join forces to write a play.

There was no copyright law [the protection of ownership in a literary work] in Shakespeare's time. The only protection for a dramatist was an assumption in common law that ownership of unpublished material belonged to its author. A body called the STATIONERS' COMPANY to some extent protected the rights of publishers to print works, but an author could do little to prevent PIRATED EDITIONS of his plays being printed. When a play was written, the author would sell it for a lump sum (the theatre manager Philip HENSLOWE paid on average about £6 for a play) to the company of actors, whose joint property it became, and who might amend it to suit their financial resources and actors' abilities. The dramatist would earn no royalties thereafter and generally would make considerably less money than the actors. Nevertheless, outstanding writers such as Shakespeare did make a good living from their work.

Elsinore
A sea port in Denmark and the setting for *Hamlet*.

Ely, Bishop of
A historical figure (d. 1435) and a minor character in *King Henry V*, the Bishop of Ely urges the King to follow in the footsteps of his ancestors and to make war on France. (Not to be confused with the Bishop of Ely *below.*)

Ely, Bishop of (John Morton)
A historical figure (c. 1420-1500) and a minor character in *King Richard III*, the Bishop of Ely is at first one of Richard's supporters but he is later reported as joining forces with the rebel Richmond. The character is notable mainly because he responds to Richard's request for some strawberries from his garden. (Not to be confused with the Bishop of Ely *above*.)

Emilia[1]
A minor character in *The Comedy of Errors*, wife to Egeon. *See* AEMILIA.

Emilia[2]
A character in *Othello*, Emilia is Iago's wife, and Desdemona's lady-in-waiting and confidante. Emilia is unaware of Iago's plot to discredit Desdemona, but she unwittingly participates in it when she provides him with Desdemona's handkerchief, the supposed evidence of Desdemona's infidelity. Emilia is straightforward, and not afraid to speak her mind; she is an unsentimental wife with a low opinion of men and marriage. Where Desdemona demonstrates total love and trust for her husband, Emilia, who has to endure Iago's snubs, says she would commit adultery if the reward was great enough. She heaps abuse on Othello for misjudging Desdemona, defending her mistress's name to the last, and when Iago is exposed for the villain he is, Emilia turns on him. She is fatally stabbed by Iago and dies by her mistress's side.

Emilia[3]
The heroine of *The Two Noble Kinsmen*, Emilia is the unconscious destroyer of the kinsmen's friendship. Her beauty is such that when Palamon and Arcite first glimpse her from their prison window, they both fall instantly and passionately in love. Emilia recalls a childhood friendship with Flavina, that was so complete she is sure she could never love a man as much. However, when she meets Arcite at the May Day games, she falls for his manly beauty. Emilia faces a terrible dilemma choosing between the two

young men who love her. When it is decided that they will fight a duel, she pores over pictures of her suitors, itemizing their virtues, and imploring Diana, goddess of chastity, for help. Emilia, knowing that one of them must die for her sake, waits in an agony until the duel is won by Arcite. She accepts Arcite as her husband. sharing his grief when Palamon is condemned to be executed under the terms of the duel. When Arcite is almost immediately killed, falling from a horse that Emilia had given him, she sheds tears for him, but with quiet acceptance prepares to marry Palamon, who has been reprieved.

Emilia[4]
A minor character in *The Winter's Tale*, Emilia is Hermione's lady-in-waiting who accompanies her mistress to prison.

Emilius
See AEMILIUS.

empathy
A feeling of identification with, and an understanding sympathy for someone, that may be experienced by a reader or an audience.

end rhyme
See RHYME.

end-stopped
The end of a line of poetry when there is either a full stop (period) or a natural pause or break in a phrase. Shakespeare's dramatic verse developed from the end-stopped BLANK verse of his early plays to the more flowing run-on style of his later work. An example from *Love's Labour's Lost* is:

> Pardon me, sir, this jewel did she wear;
>
> And Lord Berowne, I thank him, is my dear.
>
> What, will you have me, or your pearl again?

Compare ENJAMBEMENT.

enjambement
The continuation of a line of poetry into the next line, seemingly without a pause. Enjambement is the opposite of END-STOPPED. An example from *Twelfth Night* is:

> There is no woman's sides
>
> Can bide the beating of so strong a passion
>
> As love doth give my heart; no woman's heart
>
> So big, to hold so much.

Enobarbus, Domitius
A character in *Antony and Cleopatra*, Enobarbus is Antony's friend and advisor. A plain-speaking man, he is an astute observer of affairs. Enobarbus witnesses the first meeting of Antony and Cleopatra, and describes Cleopatra's legendary beauty at length; he recognizes the hold she has over Antony. Enobarbus is a realist with no illusions about the honesty of politicians, and he recognizes the hypocrisy of Caesar and Lepidus.

Foreseeing disaster, Enobarbus tries to persuade Antony to fight his battle with Caesar on land and not at sea. When, as he predicted, Antony is beaten in a sea battle, he blames Cleopatra for his defeat. As Antony's passion begins to cloud his judgement, Enobarbus's loyalty is strained to breaking point. He cannot bear to see Antony in decline and he deserts his friend for Caesar. He is subsequently overcome with remorse and dies heart-broken.

Ephesus, Solinus Duke of
A minor character in *The Comedy of Errors*, the Duke is the ruler of Ephesus and an upholder of its laws. The Duke tells Egeon on his arrival in Ephesus that he must pay a ransom or be killed. When Egeon recounts the tragic tale of the loss of his wife and son in a shipwreck, the Duke is sufficiently moved to allow Egeon time to raise the money. When Egeon is still unable to pay, the Duke takes him to be executed but becomes caught up in the confusions of mistaken identity and thinks that everyone has gone mad. When all the mistakes have been unravelled, the Duke pardons Egeon and joins the celebrations.

epigram
A short poem with a witty ending, or a short witty saying. Shakespeare's sonnets end with an epigram, in two lines of rhyming verse. An example is:

> O, learn to read what silent love hath writ.

> To hear with eyes belongs to love's fine wit.

epilogue
A speech that comes at the end of a play in which a central character or CHORUS addresses the audience directly commenting on the play as a whole, or on its ending. An example is Rosalind's prose speech at the end of *As You Like It*.

The EPILOGUE at the end of *The Two Noble Kinsmen*, expresses the hope that the audience have enjoyed the play in rhyming couplets.

epithet
An adjective, or adjectival phrase, which describes a particular quality in a person or thing. An example is the description of the hot-tempered Tybalt in *Romeo and Juliet* as 'The fiery Tybalt'.

eponymous
A word describing the hero or heroine of a book or play whose name is the same as that of the title. For example, Hamlet is the eponymous hero of *Hamlet*.

Eros
A minor character in *Antony and Cleopatra*, Eros is Antony's faithful servant whom Antony earlier freed from slavery. Believing that Cleopatra has committed suicide, Antony orders Eros to kill him with his sword, but Eros cannot bear to kill his master and instead kills himself.

Erpingham, Sir Thomas
A minor character in *King Henry V*, Sir Thomas Erpingham is an officer in the King's army. He is a much-respected soldier, an honourable old man, who lends his cloak to the King so that he can visit his troops in disguise before the Battle of Agincourt.

Escalus

A character in *Measure for Measure*, Escalus is a respected elder statesman. When the
Duke appoints Angelo as his deputy in Vienna during his absence, he instructs Escalus
to be Angelo's second-in-command. Escalus disagrees with Angelo's rigid insistence on
the letter of the law, and is more inclined to show the kind of leniency to wrongdoers
that characterized the Duke's rule. When the pimp, Pompey, is brought before him on
charges of procuring prostitutes, Escalus lets him go with a half-hearted warning. He
appeals to Angelo to show mercy to Claudio but his weak protestations are ignored. A
fundamentally good man who tries to do his best, Escalus is astonished to learn of
Angelo's villainy.

Escalus, Prince

A character in *Romeo and Juliet*, Escalus is Prince of Verona. A formal figure, who
represents law and order, he tries in vain to mediate in the feud between the Montagues
and the Capulets. Escalus banishes Romeo to Mantua after Tybalt has been killed and
sets the tragic train of events in motion.

Escanus (Escanes)

A minor character in *Pericles*, Escanus is a loyal and trusted lord of Tyre and second in
the chain of command to Helicanus. Gower, the CHORUS, relates that Escanus is left to
govern Tyre when Pericles and Helicanus leave for Tharsus to see Marina.

Essex, Earl of

A minor character in *King John*, Essex is briefly involved in the dispute between Robert
Faulconbridge and his brother Philip the Bastard.

Essex, 2nd Earl of (1566–1601)

The title of Robert Devereux, a soldier, courtier and cousin of Queen Elizabeth, and her
sometime favourite. Their relationship was punctuated with quarrels and reconciliations
and he may even have been her lover, although she was thirty-three years his senior.
Essex was the stepson of another of the Queen's favourites, the Earl of LEICESTER, who
helped to advance the young man's position at court. As Essex's influence grew he was
given command of several, not always successful, expeditions against England's old
adversary, Spain. He held office in Ireland in 1599 as Lord Lieutenant, where he was
sent by the Queen to quell a rebellion. He mismanaged affairs and as a result of his
failure to subdue the Irish rebels, he was discredited and forbidden to return to court. He
subsequently raised an army of supporters, including Shakespeare's patron
SOUTHAMPTON, with the intention of removing the Queen's advisers and surrounding
her with his own men. He tried to gain the support of the City of London, but was
captured almost immediately, accused of treason and executed.

As a preliminary to his rebellion, Essex's supporters requested that the LORD
CHAMBERLAIN'S MEN should put on a special performance of *King Richard II*,
apparently believing that a play which describes how an ineffectual monarch was
deposed would persuade audiences to rally to his cause.

Euriphile

The name of Cymbeline's sons' nurse; Euriphile has died before the beginning of the
play and takes no part in the action. When Belarius kidnapped the two boys, Guiderius
and Arviragus, from Cymbeline, he snatched Euriphile too and later married her.

Euphronius
See AMBASSADOR.

Evans, Sir Hugh
A comic character in *The Merry Wives of Windsor*, Evans is an eccentric Welshman with a strong Welsh accent and unique style of speaking. Evans, a clergyman and a schoolmaster, is a good-natured man who remains good-humoured even when he is challenged to a duel by the equally eccentric Dr Caius because of their rivalry for the hand of Anne Page. When the Host urges the two combatants to make peace with one another, they feel they have been made fools of and plan their revenge on the Host in which they trick him out of three of his horses. In the scene of Falstaff's final humiliation in Windsor Park, Evans joins in tormenting Falstaff. Falstaff says that Evans makes 'fritters' of the English language, and in a comic scene full of puns, when Evans tests the young boy William Page on his knowledge of Latin grammar, he massacres both English and Latin.

Executioner
A minor, non-speaking role in *The Two Noble Kinsmen*, the Executioner is poised to decapitate Palamon when news comes that Arcite is dying, and the execution is halted.

Exeter, Duke of[1]
A minor character in *King Henry V* and *King Henry VI, Part One*; In *Henry V*, Exeter is a supporter of King Henry and he arrests the nobles who are conspiring against the King's life.

In *Henry VI, Part One*, The Duke of Exeter is the young King Henry's great uncle, and his tutor, who fears that quarrelling among the English nobles will harm the nation. (The Duke of Exeter is not the same character as the Duke of Exeter who appears in *King Henry VI, Part Three* below.)

Exeter, Duke of[2]
A minor character in *King Henry VI, Part Three*, Exeter is a loyal supporter of King Henry against the Duke of York's claim to the throne.

exeunt
The plural form of exit; used as a stage direction when more than one character is instructed to leave the stage.

exeunt omnes
A stage direction instructing all the actors to leave the stage.

exit
A stage direction when one character is instructed to leave the stage.

exposition
The opening section of a play which sets the scene and mood and gives the background to the characters and the forthcoming action. An example is the opening scene of *Romeo and Juliet* in which essential information about the ancient feud between the Capulets and Montagues is given and an atmosphere of tension and antagonism is created.

extemporize

To improvise; *see* IMPROVISATION.

Exton, Sir Piers

A minor character in *King Richard II*, Sir Piers Exton overhears part of a conversation in which he believes Bolingbroke to say that he wants King Richard killed. Exton and his men hurry to Pontefract Castle where Richard is being held, and kill him there. Exton is tormented with feelings of guilt at the murder, but nonetheless presents Richard's body to Bolingbroke in the hope of being rewarded. Bolingbroke denies wanting Richard to be killed and ignores Exton.

Ff

f., plural ff.
An abbreviation for FOLIO.

F
An abbreviation for the First FOLIO edition of Shakespeare's plays printed in 1623.

Fabian
A character in *Twelfth Night*, Fabian is a member of Olivia's household and a drinking companion of Sir Toby Belch and Sir Andrew Aguecheek. Fabian enjoys bear-baiting, and he has quarrelled with the PURITAN steward Malvolio who has banned the sport. In retaliation, Fabian takes pleasure in baiting Malvolio, and plays along with Sir Toby in Malvolio's downfall. At the end of the play Fabian defends his involvement in the plot against Malvolio but makes light of any cruelty, saying that the whole thing was a laughing matter rather than a vengeful one.

Fairies
Fairies appear in two of Shakespeare's comedies, and the parts were almost certainly played by child actors from the royal choir schools. *See* BOY COMPANIES.

 In *The Merry Wives of Windsor*, the wives dress up a group of children as Fairies as part of their plot to frighten Falstaff into a confession. The Fairies pounce on Falstaff as he waits for Mistress Ford at midnight in Windsor Forest, and pinch him, and burn him with their candles.

 In *A Midsummer Night's Dream*, Oberon and Titania are King and Queen of the fairies. Titania's retinue of fairies sing her to sleep, and four of them are given names: COBWEB, MOTH, MUSTARDSEED and PEASEBLOSSOM. When Titania is bewitched by Oberon to fall in love with Bottom with his ass's head, she orders her fairies to attend to his every need.

Falconbridge, Lord
A minor character in *King Richard VI, Part Three*, Falconbridge is a supporter of King Edward and the Yorkist cause. *See* YORK, HOUSE OF.

False Folio
An edition of ten of Shakespeare's plays in unreliable and pirated texts which was produced by the London printer W JAGGARD in 1619. *See* FOLIO; PIRATED EDITIONS.

Falstaff, Sir John[1]
A central comic character in *King Henry IV, Parts One and Two* and *The Merry Wives of Windsor* whose death is described in *King Henry V*. It is said that Queen Elizabeth I enjoyed the character of Falstaff so much in the *Henry IV* plays that she particularly asked for the character to appear in another play in which he fell in love. Sir John

Falstaff is an overweight, hard-drinking rogue with a huge appetite for life, whose existence centres on the Boar's Head Tavern, and who is as cowardly as he is boastful.

In *King Henry IV, Part One* Falstaff, a drinking companion of the young Prince Hal, is self-indulgent and wholly irresponsible. He pockets the money that he has been given to raise an army; he brags about the number of thieves he fought off at Gad's Hill, when in fact he fled from the fight, and he tries to take the credit for the death of Hotspur who was actually killed by Prince Hal. Falstaff, whose instinct is for self-preservation, maintains that honour is an overvalued virtue. His shares his riotous lifestyle with the young Prince Hal, although Hal will reform when he becomes king in *Part Two*.

In *Part Two*, Falstaff's vitality is undiminished although he refers to his age and ill-health. Following the robbery at Gad's Hill in *Part One*, Falstaff is in trouble with the law. He is also in trouble with Mistress Quickly, who claims Falstaff has gone back on his promise of marriage. Falstaff manages to wriggle out of all his obligations, and even to squeeze a further loan out of the poor woman, adding to a string of unpaid debts. He selects recruits for the King's army with an eye to their ability to pay him a bribe for their freedom. When Prince Hal is proclaimed King, Falstaff is confident that his old friend Hal will welcome him as a favourite and hopes for advancement, but the new King sternly reproves him for his dissipated life. The law finally catches up with Falstaff and he is sent to FLEET PRISON.

In *The Merry Wives of Windsor*, the plot revolves around Falstaff's attempts to court two women at once. The wives, Mistress Ford and Mistress Page, are furious and are determined to be revenged. They set up a series of assignations with Falstaff, and at the same time tip off Mistress Ford's jealous husband. On each occasion, Master Ford bursts in on the supposed lovers and Falstaff is forced to make a hasty and undignified exit. Falstaff's humiliation reaches a comic climax in Windsor Forest where he is terrified by a group of children, dressed as fairies and goblins. Falstaff realizes that he has been made a fool of and confesses everything. In the happy resolution of the play he is forgiven.

In *King Henry V*, Mistress Quickly speaks fondly of Falstaff and describes his death to his old friends Nym, Bardoph and Pistol.

The character of Falstaff was originally named SIR JOHN OLDCASTLE but the real Oldcastle family were appalled that such a dissolute character bore their name and demanded that Shakespeare should change it.

Falstaff, Sir John[2]

(Not to be confused with SIR JOHN FALSTAFF *above.)*

A character in *King Henry VI, Part One*, Falstaff is named as FASTOLFE in some editions of the play. Falstaff is soldier, but a coward, and his failure to stand his ground after the Siege of Orleans results in the heroic Talbot being taken captive. He flees from battle again at Rouen, after which Talbot tears the Order of the Garter from Falstaff's leg and he is banished by King Henry.

Fang

A minor comic character in *King Henry IV, Part Two*, Fang with his assistant Snare, is an ineffectual constable who tries, unsuccessfully, to arrest Falstaff for debt.

farce
A form of COMEDY that is characterized by a complicated and fast-moving plot in which the characters find themselves in compromising situations, which often involves mistaken identity, and which relies on physical rather than verbal humour. *The Merry Wives of Windsor* is a farce.

Farrant, Richard (d. 1580)
A court musician and composer, and director of The Children of Windsor, a boys choir who performed for Queen Elizabeth. Farrant was also a theatrical entrepreneur and founder of the first theatre to be established on the site of the Blackfriars Priory. *See* BLACKFRIARS THEATRE.

fate
The inescapable chain of events and their consequences which are outside the control of a character and which play a part in shaping his or her destiny; an element which may occur in TRAGEDY. For example, in *Romeo and Juliet*, an accident of fate determines that a vital letter, informing Romeo that Juliet is going to take a sleeping drug, fails to reach him. As a result, when he discovers Juliet unconscious he assumes her to be dead and kills himself.

Father that has killed his son
A minor character in *King Henry VI, Part Three*, the Father has tragically mistaken his son's identity in the heat of battle and killed him. King Henry witnesses the father's sorrow and grieves himself for the terrible loss of life the civil war has caused.

Faulconbridge, Lady
A minor character in *King John* and the mother of Robert Faulconbridge and Philip the Bastard. When Robert claims that his brother is illegitimate, Lady Faulconbridge is forced to admit that Philip the Bastard was the product of an adulterous relationship with Richard Coeur de Lion.

Faulconbridge, Robert
A character in *King John*; *see* ROBERT.

Feeble, Francis
A minor comic character in *King Henry IV, Part Two*, Feeble is a woman's tailor and one of the villagers who Falstaff recruits for the army. Falstaff says Feeble will be a real asset to the army because he will be quick to run in the event of a retreat.

feminine ending
The concluding sound of a line of verse when it ends with an extra unstressed syllable. For example: 'And, darkly bright, are bright in dark direc*ted*'. *Compare* MASCULINE ENDING; *see* STRESS.

feminine rhyme
See RHYME.

Fenton
A character in *The Merry Wives of Windsor*, Fenton is a romantic young gentleman who loves Anne Page. Anne's father thinks that because his social ranking is higher than

theirs, and because he has been keeping company with the delinquent Prince Hal, (*See* KING HENRY IV, PART ONE) Fenton is not a fit suitor. Fenton admits that he was first attracted to Anne because of her father's wealth, but says now he truly loves her. Fenton takes matters into his own hands and, against her father's wishes, marries Anne in secret. In the play's happy resolution, Fenton and Anne are forgiven by her parents.

Ferdinand

A character in *The Tempest*, Ferdinand is the son of Alonso, King of Naples. Ferdinand is shipwrecked on Prospero's magic island and separated in the storm from the rest of the survivors. He swims ashore and is led by Ariel's mysterious music to Prospero's cell where he finds Miranda and falls immediately in love with her. Prospero tests Ferdinand's love. by enslaving him and forcing him to chop logs. When Ferdinand has proved himself by his patience (unlike the resentful slave Caliban), Prospero gives his blessing to a marriage with his daughter, but insists that they remain chaste until the wedding rites have been performed. Ferdinand, in contrast to his wicked father, represents an ideal of goodness and nobility and, with Miranda, symbolizes the healing power of love.

Feste

A character in *Twelfth Night*, Feste is Olivia's jester, of whom the PURITAN Malvolio thoroughly disapproves. Feste takes part in the plot to discredit Malvolio and gets his revenge. He masquerades as Sir Topas the Curate, and torments his old enemy by treating him as a witless lunatic. Feste may appear frivolous and superficial with his light-hearted quibbling, but his songs about life and death, and the transience of youth and love, reveal a serious side to his nature, and introduce a sombre note into the comedy. He sings a tragi-comical, anti-romantic EPILOGUE at the end of the play, and returns the audience to reality with his closing promise that the actors will 'strive to please you every day'.

Feste is more FOOL than CLOWN, although his character appears as 'Clown' in the cast list. The part was first played by Robert ARMIN.

Fidele

The name that the IMOGEN, the heroine of *Cymbeline*, takes when she disguises herself as a boy.

Field, Nathan (1587–1620)

One of the 26 'Principall Actors' listed in the First FOLIO edition of Shakespeare's plays in 1623. Although his father was a PURITAN who thoroughly disapproved of the theatre, Field was recruited from St Paul's school in London to join the CHILDREN OF THE CHAPEL a company of boy actors and singers. As an adult actor, he was a member of the KING'S MEN from 1615 and appeared in the plays of Ben JONSON, who greatly admired his acting ability.

Fiends

In *King Henry VI, Part One*, Joan La Pucelle calls up Fiends from under the earth and offers them her body and her soul in exchange for help in defeating the English forces. Joan's incantations are not powerful enough to influence the Fiends. They depart in silence and immediately after Joan is captured by the Duke of York.

figurative language

Language that is used in an imaginative, ornate or poetic way. Figurative language makes use of figures of speech. For example:

> Full many a glorious morning I have seen
>
> Flatter the mountain tops with sovereign eye,
>
> Kissing with golden face the meadows green.

figure of speech

A word or expression which is used in a sense other than its literal meaning in order to create a particular effect or to make a comparison. Examples of figures of speech are: METAPHOR, PERSONIFICATION and SIMILE.

First Folio

See FOLIO.

First Player

A minor character in *Hamlet,* the First Player is the leading actor in a troupe of players visiting the court, who probably takes the part of the Player King in THE MURDER OF GONZAGO which the company performs. Hamlet gives him advice on acting techniques.

Fishermen

Minor comic characters in *Pericles*, the Fishermen express their sympathy for those whom fate decrees are lost at sea. When Pericles is shipwrecked at Tharsus, they tell him about King Simonides' beautiful daughter, Thaisa, who is looking for a husband and they guide him to the king's court.

Fitton, Mary (c. 1578–1647)

One of Queen Elizabeth's Maids of Honour who has been proposed as a possible candidate for the mysterious DARK LADY of Shakespeare's sonnets. Two portraits of Mary Fitton, however, show her to have been light-haired. She was the mistress of William Herbert, Earl of PEMBROKE (who may have been 'Mr W H', the unknown dedicatee of the sonnets) who was dismissed from the court and imprisoned when he refused to marry her.

Fitzwater, Lord

A minor character in *King Richard II*, Lord Fitzwater supports Bagot when he accuses the Duke of Aumerle of murdering the Duke of Gloucester. Fitzwater challenges Aumerle to single combat and is in turn challenged by the Duke of Surrey, who says he is lying. After Richard's death, when Bolingbroke is crowned King Henry IV, Bolingbroke promises to reward Fitzwater for his loyalty.

Flaminius

A minor character in *Timon of Athens*, Flaminius is one of Timon's faithful servants whose loyalty contrasts with the hypocrisy of the flattering lords. He is sent by Timon to ask for a loan from Lucullus, who is under the impression that Flaminius has come to give him a present from Timon. When Lucullus realizes he is being asked for money he refuses to help and tries to bribe Flaminius to say that he never saw Lucullus. Flaminius angrily throws the money back in Lucullus' face and curses him.

flat

In a modern theatre, a flat is a piece of stage scenery. It is a large canvas-covered frame, which is painted to depict the background of a scene, such as a distant view of a castle or forest, and hung at the back of the SET. Sets in Elizabethan PLAYHOUSES would have been bare of such scenery; the only equivalent would have been hangings at the back of the stage.

Flavius[1]

A minor character in *Julius Caesar*, Flavius is one of the tribunes [civil officer] of the people. At the opening of the play Flavius and his fellow tribune Murellus rebuke the Roman citizens who have taken a day off work to cheer Caesar. The tribunes criticize the crowd for neglecting their old hero Pompey, in favour of a new one. After they have dispersed the crowd, the tribunes remove the decorations put up in Caesar's honour. They are reported later as having been 'put to silence' for doing so.

Flavius[2]

A character in *Timon of Athens*, Flavius is the name of Timon's steward. *See* STEWARD.

Fleance

A minor character in *Macbeth*, Fleance is Banquo's son who escapes when his father is murdered.

Fleet Prison

A famous prison in London in Shakespeare's time, named after the city's River Fleet and near to the Fleet Street of modern times. It was built in the 12th century and used to house a variety of prisoners, from political ones to criminals and debtors, until it was pulled down in 1844. In *King Henry IV, Part Two*, the disgraced Falstaff is sent to the Fleet Prison.

Fletcher, John (1579–1625)

A dramatist, Fletcher came from a family of churchmen. He often collaborated with other playwrights, in particular with MASSINGER and his friend BEAUMONT, but he was the sole author of over sixteen plays including *Philaster* (c. 1610) and *The Wild Goose Chase* (1621). He wrote plays for the BOY COMPANIES, and after Shakespeare's death he became the leading dramatist for the KING'S MEN. It is highly likely that Fletcher was the co-author with Shakespeare of *King Henry VIII* and *The Two Noble Kinsmen*.

flies

Machinery in a modern theatre, high above a stage and hidden from an audience, from which scenery can be raised or lowered by a system of pulleys and ropes or counterweights. In Elizabethan PLAYHOUSES, there would have been some kind of device for lowering characters on to the stage; for example, the god JUPITER who is lowered from the heavens above in *Cymbeline*.

Florence, Duke of

A minor character in *All's Well that Ends Well*, the Duke of Florence is fighting with the French against Siena. Bertram joins his army and is appointed general in charge of the horses.

Florizel

A character in *The Winter's Tale*, Florizel is a Prince of Bohemia and King Polixenes' son and a stereotypical romantic hero. He is courting Perdita in a humble disguise as 'Doricles' because he believes that she is just a poor shepherd girl (in fact, she is the long-lost daughter of King Leontes). Florizel's father, Polixenes, forbids his son to marry Perdita because he believes she is not a suitable wife for a future king. The lovers elope to Sicilia, where Perdita's true identity is revealed, and their marriage is blessed by both their fathers in a scene of reconciliation. Florizel's unwavering love for Perdita is part of the pattern of redemption by love in the play.

Fluellen, Captain

A character in *King Henry V*, Fluellen, an officer in the English army fighting in France, is a professional soldier whose fighting skills and passion for military discipline are respected by the King. A Welshman with a strong accent, Fluellen is fiercely proud of his nationality and wears a leek in his cap as an emblem of his country. He congratulates King Henry on having Welsh blood in his veins. Argumentative by nature, Fluellen quarrels with Pistol who jeers at his Welshness. Fluellen gets his revenge by forcing Pistol to eat his leek.

Flute, Francis

A comic character in *A Midsummer Night's Dream*, Flute is an Athenian workmen, a bellows-mender, and one of the amateur actors in the MASQUE of *Pyramus and Thisbe* which is performed for Duke Theseus at his wedding. His name, which is suitable for of man of his profession, may also suggest that he has a flute-like, high-pitched voice. Flute is clearly a smooth-faced and rather self-conscious youth who is annoyed to be given the part of the heroine, Thisbe, because he maintains he has a beard coming.

folio

A sheet of paper which is folded in two to make four pages; or a very large-format book which is made up of folio sheets bound together.

The FIRST FOLIO, the earliest one-volume collection of Shakespeare's plays, was printed and bound in this way in 1623 by Jaggards, printers of London, seven years after the poet's death. About 1,000 copies were printed and were probably sold for about £1 each. The First Folio contained the DROESHOUT portrait of Shakespeare, poems by Ben JONSON, an epistle written by the editors, dedications to the Earls of Pembroke and Montgomery and a list of the principal actors who had appeared in the plays. The thirty-six plays (*Pericles* was not included in this collection) were categorized for the first time as comedies, histories and tragedies and edited by Henry CONDELL and John HEMING, members of Shakespeare's company of actors, the Lord Chamberlain's Men. They used the dramatist's own manuscripts, acting versions of the plays, and the printed QUARTO editions. Some stage directions and scene changes were incorporated and a number of oaths were cut; mistakes found their way in to the texts, which differ in some instances from the quarto editions. The second folio, which contained further corrections, the third folio which included *Pericles* and seven other plays almost certainly not by Shakespeare, and the fourth folio editions, appeared between 1632 and 1685. *See* FOUL PAPERS; PRINCIPALL ACTORS; QUARTO; ROWE

fool

A comedian, the fool derives from the jester, a professional entertainer at the court whose job was to amuse king and courtiers with his clowning. Jesters and fools traditionally wore 'motley', a particoloured costume with a fool's cap, or hood, with ass's ears and bells, and carried a 'bauble', a mock sceptre or staff of office. In Elizabethan cast lists, comic characters can be named as either 'clown' or 'fool'. Although the role of the fool may overlap with the CLOWN, they are quite different character types. (In *Twelfth Night*, the character of Feste appears in the cast list as 'clown', but in fact his role is much more that of 'fool'.)

In Shakespeare's comedies, the character and function of the fool is more complex than that of a simple entertainer. Whereas the humour of the clown arises from the broad comedy of SLAPSTICK or BAWDY, or the unintentional misuse of words (for example the character of Dogberry in *Much Ado About Nothing*), the wit of the fool is more abstract. His comedy may be anarchic, but his use of words is deliberate; his punning and riddling sharp and witty. Traditionally melancholic, the fool rarely intervenes in events. He usually remains emotionally disengaged from the other characters and his detachment allows him to comment on their actions rather like a CHORUS. Olivia in *Twelfth Night* says of Feste, her fool: "There is no slander in an allowed [licensed] fool". The character of Touchstone in *As You Like It*, is a fool, and in the same play, the melancholy Jaques says he wishes he could wear 'motley' so that he could ridicule the world like the fool.

In the tragedies, the fool often provides COMIC relief but again his function is complex and even symbolic. Free from the conventional restrictions of the master/servant relationship, he may provide a distorted but illuminating reflection of the behaviour of the hero. An example is the Fool in *King Lear*, a kind of alter ego who acts as his master's conscience, mirroring Lear's 'reason in madness' with his PARADOXES and puns. When Hamlet is 'mad' he takes on some of the traits of the fool with his absurd flights of fancy, punning and black humour.

Fool

A complex character in *King Lear*, the Fool is the King's jester, and Lear's companion in his deranged wanderings. He acts as a kind of conscience for his old master, and often opens his eyes to his follies. The Fool's comments on life, and his songs and riddles, have a black humour and provide COMIC RELIEF. The Fool disappears before the climax of the play, possibly dying of cold and grief; his last words are: 'And I'll go to bed at noon'. The Fool is like Cordelia in his devotion to Lear, whom he calls his 'Nuncle' [uncle], and it has been suggested that in Shakespeare's time, the same actor who played Cordelia took the part of the Fool as well. *See also* FOOL *above*.

Fool, A

A minor comic character in *Timon of Athens*, the Fool makes only a brief appearance in the play. He is a friend of Apemantus who exchanges jokes and puns with the servants of Timon's creditors who have come to claim the money owed to their masters.

foot

A group of two or more syllables in a metric line of verse, one of which is more strongly emphasized or stressed than the others, that forms the basis of the RHYTHM. In SCANSION, the stressed syllable is shown with ‾ over the top and the unstressed syllable

is marked ˘, as in 'To be, or not to be'. The most common foot in English verse is the
IAMB, consisting of a short unstressed syllable followed by a stressed one as in the word
'Macbeth'. Other feet include ANAPAEST, with its pattern of two unstressed syllables
followed a stressed one as in 'Much ado'; DACTYL, a stressed syllable followed by two
unstressed ones as in 'Romeo'; SPONDEE, a foot of two equally stressed syllables:
'Adam'; TROCHEE, a stressed syllable followed by an unstressed one as in 'Hamlet'. *See*
IAMBIC PENTAMETER; METRE.

footlights
A row of lights at the front of the stage. There would have been no artificial lighting in
Elizabethan public PLAYHOUSES, although in private theatres, such as the BLACKFRIARS
THEATRE, the stage would have been lit by candles.

Ford, Master Frank
A character in *The Merry Wives of Windsor*, Master Ford is a citizen of Windsor and
Alice Ford's jealous husband. The 'merry wives', Mistress Ford and Mistress Page, bent
on tricking Falstaff, play a joke on Ford as well, using Falstaff as the bait. Ford is told
that his wife and Falstaff are meeting secretly but when he bursts in on them, in disguise
as a 'Mr Brook', Falstaff is nowhere to be found. On one occasion, Falstaff has been
smuggled out in a laundry basket; on another, Falstaff is disguised as the old woman of
Brainford, an old enemy of Ford's, who Ford beats black and blue. When Ford learns
that his wife has been faithful to him all along, husband and wife are happily reconciled
and Ford forgives a chastened Falstaff.

Ford, Mistress Alice
A character in *The Merry Wives of Windsor*, Mistress Ford is one of the 'merry wives'
who is the object of Falstaff's desire. When she, and her friend Mistress Page, receive
identical love letters from Falstaff they are determined to be revenged and at the same
time play a trick on her jealous husband. The wives delight in devising Falstaff's
downfall. They invite Falstaff to Mistress Ford's house and alert Master Ford to the
fact that his wife is entertaining another man. Falstaff is forced into making two
undignified exits and Mistress Ford can congratulate herself on teaching both her
husband, and Falstaff, a lesson. She cheerfully joins in Falstaff's final undoing in
Windsor Park.

Ford, John (c. 1585–c. 1640)
A dramatist and poet, Ford collaborated with DEKKER on some of his plays. His best
known play, *'Tis Pity She's A Whore'* (c. 1626), is about the incestuous relationship
between a brother and a sister.

foreshadowing
See PREFIGURE.

Forester
A minor character in *Love's Labour's Lost*, the Forester is present during the royal
hunting party and shows the Princess of France the best place to stand in order to make
the 'fairest shot' at deer. She teases him, pretending to interpret his advice as an insult to
her fair beauty and insists that he praises her looks.

form

The structure and shape of a work as defined by the sequence of events and, in the case of a play, by the number of acts and scenes. The word form is also used to describe a literary GENRE, such as verse form.

Fortinbras

A character in *Hamlet*, Fortinbras is the Prince of Norway whose father was killed by Hamlet's father during war between Denmark and Norway. Fortinbras is a hot-blooded young man; like Hamlet, Fortinbras must avenge his father's death, but he is much more resolute by nature. Hearing that Fortinbras is undertaking an invasion of Poland, Hamlet realizes for himself the contrast between his own hesitancy and Fortinbras' commitment to action. Hamlet proclaims Fortinbras as the next King of Denmark, believing that will be able to restore order to the Kingdom of Denmark.

Fortune Theatre

A public playhouse built in London in Golden Lane, Cripplegate, in 1600 by Philip HENSLOWE and Edward ALLEYN as a rival to the GLOBE. The Fortune was a typical wooden playhouse with a large stage measuring about 13m x 8m. It was unusual only in that its roof was tiled rather than thatched, and it was square in design, perhaps copying the layout of the INN-YARDS that were formerly used to stage plays. It became the permanent home of the ADMIRAL'S MEN but was burned down in 1613; it was rebuilt in brick and in the more usual circular design ten years later.

foul papers

In Elizabethan English, a first complete hand-written draft of a play, with subsequent corrections and any stage directions marked on it. It is probable that the QUARTO editions of Shakespeare's plays were printed from his foul papers.

France, King of[1]

A character in *All's Well that Ends Well*, the King of France is incurably ill. Helena restores the King to health, using a remedy of her physician father's, and as a reward he sanctions her marriage to the husband of her choice, Bertram. The King, knew Bertram's father and hopes the young man will grow up to resemble him. He is angry when Bertram treats Helena with contempt, and reproves him for valuing social rank more highly than natural virtue. A wise and just ruler, the King eventually forgives Bertram for his treatment of Helena, on the grounds that it was just the folly of youth. He insists that justice shall be done to Diana, who has saved Bertram and Helena's marriage, and generously offers to provide her dowry. He rounds off the play with his hope that the bitter past is behind them and that all has ended well.

France, King of[2]

A minor character in *King Lear*, the King of France marries Cordelia even though she has no dowry. He recognizes the natural goodness and honesty in Cordelia that her own father has failed to see.

Francis

A minor comic character in *King Henry IV, Parts One and Two*, Francis is a simple-minded DRAWER, one of the servants at the Boars Head, a tavern frequented by Falstaff. In *Part One*, the easily confused Francis is teased by Prince Hal and Poins in a scene of SLAPSTICK comedy. In *Part Two*, Francis seems to have gone up in the world and is giving orders to the other drawers.

Francis, Friar

A minor character in *Much Ado About Nothing*, Friar Francis is about to conduct marry Hero and Claudio, when Claudio accuses his bride of infidelity and stops the wedding. Friar Francis believes in Hero's innocence and persuades her father that she has been wronged. He suggests that news of Hero's death from shame should be announced in the hope that grief will prompt Claudio into loving her again. In the end, when all the misunderstandings have been explained, the Friar marries Hero and Claudio together with Beatrice and Benedick.

Francisca (Francesca)

A minor character in *Measure for Measure*, Francisca is a nun in the convent which Isabella is about to join. She makes a brief appearance when she tells Isabella about the rules of the order. She listens to Isabella's comments about the rules, which Isabella thinks are too free and easy.

Francisco[1]

A minor character in *Hamlet*, Francisco is a sentry on the walls of Elsinore castle who is relieved from duty at the beginning of the play.

Francisco[2]

A minor character in *The Tempest*; *see* ADRIAN AND FRANCISCO.

Frederick, Duke

See DUKE FREDERICK.

Frenchman

A minor character in *Cymbeline*, the Frenchman is a friend of Philario, Posthumus' host in Italy. His memory of an earlier meeting with Posthumus, whom he recalls fighting a duel with over the faithfulness or otherwise of women, prompts Posthumus into making the disastrous bet with Iachimo over Imogen's fidelity.

French Sergeant

A minor character in *King Henry VI, Part One*, the Sergeant orders the French sentries to guard the walls at Orleans.

Friar Francis

See FRANCIS, FRIAR.

Friar John

See JOHN, FRIAR.

Friar Laurence

See LAURENCE, FRIAR.

Friar Peter

A minor character in *Measure for Measure*, named 'Thomas' in the stage directions of one scene, and 'Peter' in a later scene. *See* THOMAS, FRIAR

Friends, Two

Minor characters in *The Two Noble Kinsmen*, one of the Jailer's Friends reassures him that he is not going to be punished by Duke Theseus for allowing Palamon to escape from jail. Another Friend sympathizes with the Jailer when he hears that his Daughter has gone mad.

Froth

A minor comic character in *Measure for Measure*, Froth is described in the cast list as a 'foolish Gentleman'. He is arrested by the constable, Elbow, for insulting his pregnant wife, but Froth's only crime seems to have been eating some prunes that Elbow's pregnant wife was craving for. He is dismissed with a caution not to consort with servingmen who draw ale, and Froth jokes that he only enters a bar when he is 'drawn in'.

Friz

A minor, non-speaking part in *The Two Noble Kinsmen*, Friz is one of the villagers who perform a Morris dance for Duke Theseus. *See* COUNTRYWOMEN.

Fulvia

In *Antony and Cleopatra*, Fulvia is Antony's wife who is described as having a shrill tongue. Not appearing in the play itself, Fulvia is reported stirring up a rebellion against Caesar while Antony is away in Egypt. News of her death is given to Antony by a messenger.

Gg

Gadshill
A minor character in *King Henry IV, Part One*, Gadshill is a professional highway robber and a friend of Falstaff and Prince Hal. Gadshill, together with Falstaff and a gang of thieves, rob a group of travellers, but are themselves robbed of their spoils by Prince Hal and Poins. The robbery take place at GAD'S HILL.

Gad's Hill
A hill in Kent in south east England that was notorious for highway robberies in Shakespeare's time, and from which the character of Gadshill (see above) in *King Henry IV, Part One* gets his name.

gallery
In Elizabethan PLAYHOUSES galleries were built round three sides of the theatre, in three tiers, and near enough to the stage to give an excellent view. Gallery seating was, therefore, fairly expensive but the most exclusive seats in the theatre were in a part of the gallery that was partitioned to create private rooms, similar to boxes in a modern theatre.

 In modern theatres, the gallery is the highest balcony in a theatre, and as they are furthest from the stage, gallery seats are the cheapest.

Gallus
A minor character in *Antony and Cleopatra*, Gallus is one of Caesar's followers. When Cleopatra is captured by Caesar, Gallus commands the soldiers who are sent to guard her.

Ganymede
The name that Rosalind in *As You Like It* adopts when, disguised as a boy, she is living in the Forest of Arden. Shakespeare may have chosen the name 'Ganymede' for his heroine because it was one associated with beauty: the original Ganymede was a legendary figure, who was such a beautiful young man that he was carried off by the gods to live among them.

Gaoler
A minor character in *The Winter's Tale*, the Gaoler guards the wronged Hermione in prison. He is sympathetic to her plight, but he is afraid of the consequences of breaking the law if he helps her. However, he does allow Paulina to visit Hermione and to take the infant Perdita from the prison.

Gaolers, Two
Two minor comic characters in *Cymbeline*, the Gaolers talk to Posthumus in his condemned cell on the eve of his execution. They discuss the advantages of being

hanged, which include freedom from further anxieties, from tavern bills and from toothache, but are still surprised that Posthumus is so eager to die.

Gardener and his Man
Minor characters in *King Richard II*, the head Gardener has an allegorical function (see ALLEGORY). He talks to his Man about the disordered state of the nation, which he says is like an overgrown garden choked by weeds. He discusses the capture of King Richard by the rebel Bolingbroke while, unknown to him, Queen Isabel can overhear. When she learns the bad news about her husband, she turns angrily on the Gardener who is sympathetic to her grief and lays flowers on the ground in remembrance of her tears.

Gardiner
A historical figure (Stephen Gardiner c. 1483-1555) and a character in *King Henry VIII*, Gardiner is the King's secretary, who is promoted to become Bishop of Winchester. He is pro-Catholic, an unscrupulous ally of Cardinal Wolsey, and a mortal enemy of Cranmer, the Archbishop of Canterbury. Gardiner is instrumental in bringing accusations of heresy against Cranmer. When King Henry intervenes to prevent both Cranmer's imprisonment and the advance of Gardiner's ambitions, Gardiner professes his loyalty to the King in a speech oozing with insincerity. Henry recognizes Gardiner's cruel nature, and is unimpressed. He commands Gardiner to embrace his former enemy Cranmer, and Gardiner does so with an astonishingly quick change of heart, and a pretence of good grace.

Gargrave, Sir Thomas
A minor character in *King Henry VI, Part One*, Gargrave is killed with Salisbury at the Siege of Orleans.

Garrick, David (1717–79)
An actor and manager of the Drury Lane Theatre in London, Garrick made his name originally in a production of *King Richard III* in 1741. He continued to dominate the stage as the greatest Shakespearean actor of his time. His acting, unlike that of 16th-century actors, was naturalistic, and his theatrical innovations included the use of concealed lighting in stage productions. An intimate friend of Dr JOHNSON, Garrick was a tyrannical director with a violent temper. In 1769, he inaugurated the first Shakespeare celebration at Stratford-on-Avon, which lasted for three days with dancing, speeches, and fireworks. Surprisingly, none of Shakespeare's plays were performed during the festival.

Garter King-at-Arms
A minor character in *King Henry VIII*, Garter King-at-Arms is a senior official in King Henry's court, who is present at the coronation of Anne Bullen and at the christening of the Princess Elizabeth, and who is also part of the pageantry in the play. Garter King-at-Arms is the title still given to one of the most senior officers of the Order of the Garter, an order of English knighthood founded in the 14th century. The Garter King-at-Arms still attends important state occasions such as the opening of the British Parliament.

gatherers
Members of a company of actors in Shakespeare's time, also known as box-holders, who were responsible for collecting entrance money to the theatre. Half the amount collected was paid to the HOUSEKEEPERS, who owned the theatre, to pay for the rent. The rest was kept by the company, but it was often said that the gatherers took some of the money for themselves. The name of the 'box-office' in a modern theatre derives from the fact that the gatherers collected the money in boxes.

Gaunt, John of, Duke of Lancaster
A historical figure (1340-99) and a character in *King Richard II*, John of Gaunt is King Richard's uncle and Henry Bolingbroke's father, and a respected elder statesman. Before the action of the play, Gaunt's brother, the Duke of Gloucester, was murdered in France. Now, Gaunt suspects that Richard may have had a hand in his brother's death, but he feels bound to remain loyal to his King whom he believes has a DIVINE RIGHT to rule. Gaunt is a man of honour who urges his son, Bolingbroke, to be obedient to King Richard, and a man of peace who tells his brother's widow that he will have no part in avenging Gloucester's death. When the patriotic Gaunt knows death is approaching, he grieves for the state of the England he loves which has been ruined and plunged into debt by the King. He warns Richard that he is unpopular because of his bad management of the country, and finally accuses him of murdering his brother before he is carried off to die.

General of the French Forces in Bordeaux
A minor character in *King Henry VI, Part One*, the General refuses to surrender to Talbot.

genre
A type of literary form which conforms to particular conventions; in drama, and in Shakespeare's plays in particular, the genres are TRAGEDY, COMEDY and HISTORY PLAYS.

Gentleman
The character of a 'Gentleman', appears in cast lists of several of Shakespeare's plays. In most cases, the Gentleman is a minor character, who often acts as a bearer of news; his function is simply to move the plot forward. Sometimes a Gentleman gives a vivid description of an event which occurred OFF-STAGE, or acts as a commentator on events, establishing a particular point of view for the audience.

In *King Henry VIII*, Gentlemen at Henry's court discuss the fall of the Duke of Buckingham and the national anger it has aroused, and a rumour that the King and Queen Katherine are to separate. Their conversations plant the idea in the audience's mind that Buckingham and Katherine are victims of Cardinal Wolsey's political manoeuvering. Later, three Gentlemen talk about the coronation of Anne Boleyn, describing her angelic beauty, and the rapturous response of the people to their new queen, and so establish her as worthy of being the mother of the future Queen of England.

In *King Lear*, a Gentleman touchingly describes how Cordelia wept when she heard the news of her father's desperate situation. In *King Richard III*, a Gentleman takes a small, but more active, part in affairs when he tries unsuccessfully to prevent Richard from

interrupting King Henry's funeral procession. In *Measure for Measure*, two Gentlemen joke about venereal disease in front of Mistress Overdone, the brothel-keeper, and establish the existence of a corrupt underworld in the play.
See also TWO GENTLEMEN OF VERONA.

Gentlewoman
A minor character in *Macbeth*, the Gentlewoman attends Lady Macbeth and witnesses her sleep-walking.

George, afterwards Duke of Clarence
A historical figure (1449-1478) and a character in *King Henry VI, Part Three*, George is the Duke of York's son and Edward's brother. George supports Edward, who has designs on the throne, but thinks that his brother has made a bad mistake in marrying the commoner Lady Grey, instead of making a useful diplomatic marriage elsewhere. George is so angry, in fact, that he changes sides and joins King Henry fighting against Edward. In another swift change of loyalties, George is persuaded by his younger brother, Richard, to return to Edward's cause. Later he plays a part in the killing of Henry's son, the young Prince of Wales. When Edward is proclaimed King Edward IV, George is given the title of DUKE OF CLARENCE. He is sometimes referred to as 'Clarence' by other characters in the play, and he is the same Duke of Clarence who appears in *King Richard III*.

Gerald
See SCHOOLMASTER.

Gertrude
A character in *Hamlet*, Gertrude is Queen of Denmark and Hamlet's mother who has recently married Claudius, her late husband's brother. Claudius is also her late husband's murderer. Gertrude is not implicated in the old King's murder and it is not clear how much, if anything, she knows about his death. Distressed at the haste of her second marriage, and disgusted by a union he considers incestuous, Hamlet confronts his mother and accuses her of adultery with Claudius before the old King died. Gertrude believes Hamlet is mad at first, but eventually admits her guilt. She does not have the courage to stand up to Claudius, or to change anything; she can only promise not to alert him to Hamlet's plans. Gertrude dies when she mistakenly drinks the poison that Claudius intends for Hamlet. She tries to warn her son about the danger, but her single maternal action comes too late.

Although Gertrude is a passive character, she is pivotal to the play because Hamlet's revulsion at her adultery leads him to a wider mistrust of love, and a loathing of sex in women, including Ophelia.

ghosts
An element in particular of the REVENGE tragedies of the Elizabethan theatre, ghosts often appear in order to prick consciences and spur characters into action, or to promise vengeance. Their supernatural visitations may also serve to create an atmosphere of pervasive evil, or to represent a character's psychological state. Ghosts feature in five of Shakespeare's plays.

Ghosts, or APPARITIONS, appear to Posthumus, the hero of *Cymbeline*, as he lies in a prison cell longing for death. His family visit Posthumus in a dream and as they gather round him singing, they call on the god Jupiter to help him. Jupiter himself appears and promises that Posthumus' fortunes will be restored and that he will be reunited with his wife Imogen. When the ghostly apparitions vanish and Posthumus awakes, he takes some comfort from his vision.

In *Julius Caesar*, Caesar's Ghost appears briefly to Brutus on the eve of battle to announce that he will see Brutus again at Philippi. Brutus is not sure if the Ghost is angel or devil and the Ghost says he is Brutus' 'evil spirit'. On the point of suicide, Brutus tells Volumnius that he has had two other visitations from the Ghost of Caesar and that he knows his 'hour is come'.

In *Macbeth*, the Ghost of the murdered Banquo makes several appearances. The first is at the banquet held following Banquo's bloody death when it sits, silent, in Macbeth's place. It vanishes, only to make another brief appearance moments later. Macbeth is horror-stricken but as it does not speak, nor is it seen by any one else, it may be that this apparition is a hallucination like the dagger: a symbolic embodiment of his state of mind. The Ghost appears again when Macbeth visits the witches. The weird sisters first summon up three apparitions, an armed head, a bloody child and a crowned child with a tree in his hand, who warn Macbeth against Macduff. The witches then call on a ghostly procession of eight kings, followed by Banquo's Ghost, to appear.

In *Richard III* the vengeful Ghosts of those whom Richard has killed appear to him in a troubling dream on the eve of the battle of Bosworth. They include the Ghosts of the little Princes murdered in the tower. Each Ghost tells him that in remembrance of his crimes, they will sit heavy on his soul and charge him to 'despair and die'. When he awakes, the King, who has hitherto seemed without remorse, speaks of his 'coward conscience' and fears that his dead enemies will be revenged on him.

In *Hamlet*, the Ghost of Hamlet's father is a character with a pivotal role in the play. (It is thought that Shakespeare may have played the part himself.) He is an awe-inspiring, armoured figure who first appears, silently stalking the shadows on the castle battlements. The Ghost vanishes before anyone can speak to it, but Horatio believes it is a portent of evil. When Hamlet confronts the Ghost of his father, it accuses Claudius as his murderer and makes Hamlet swear to avenge his death. As dawn breaks, the Ghost leaves. Speaking from beneath the stage as from the underworld (see CELLARAGE), the Ghost demands that his visitation is kept a secret. When Hamlet confronts Gertrude with her guilt, the ghost appears briefly once more to sharpen Hamlet's 'blunted purpose'. The Queen cannot see anything and thinks Hamlet's behaviour is proof of his madness.

Although the Ghost of Hamlet's father has died without the last rites being observed, he never asks for prayers for the repose of his soul. Like some hellish demon, he appears only at night and vanishes before sunrise, demanding only revenge.

Giraldo
See SCHOOLMASTER.

Girl
A historical figure (Margaret Plantagenet 1473-1541) and a minor character in *King Richard III*, the Girl is Clarence's daughter and Richard's niece who mourns her father after his death. Fearful that the Girl might have a claim to the throne, Richard marries her off to a commoner. The character is never given a name by Shakespeare, and appears in the cast list and stage directions simply as 'Girl'.

Glansdale, Sir William
A minor character in *King Henry VI, Part One*, Glansdale is a soldier at the siege of Orleans, who is present when Salisbury is killed.

Glendower, Owen
A historical figure (c. 1359-c. 1416) and a character in *King Henry IV, Part One*, Glendower is a Welshman and one of the rebel nobles fighting against King Henry. When Glendower and Hotspur meet with the other nobles to plan their military campaign, Glendower boasts of his supernatural powers. Hotspur is thoroughly irritated and they quarrel, although Glendower tries several times to make peace. Glendower's nature is a superstitious one. Influenced by certain prophecies, he decides to stay away from the crucial battle of Shrewsbury, disastrously weakening the rebel forces. Glendower, who acts as an interpreter for his Welsh-speaking daughter, demonstrates a love of music which was thought typical of the Welsh. His daughter marries MORTIMER (see MORTIMER, LADY)

Globe Theatre
The largest and best known of the Elizabethan public PLAYHOUSES in Bankside, near London Bridge, outside the City of London (*see* CENSORSHIP; *see also the illustration at* BANKSIDE). It was founded in 1599 by Cuthbert and Richard BURBAGE, Shakespeare and Will KEMP for the LORD CHAMBERLAIN'S MEN company of actors, who had acquired the site the previous year. Shakespeare had a fifth share in its profits and was also liable for a proportion of the running expenses. The first recorded performance of one of Shakespeare's plays at the Globe was of *Julius Caesar* in 1599.

It cost £600 (in Elizabethan currency) to build and was constructed partly from timbers taken from the THEATRE, which had recently been pulled down. The Globe was a typical Elizabethan playhouse and was said to accommodate an audience of 2000. Open-roofed, it was used only during the months when dry weather could most reasonably be relied upon; after 1613 the company used the roofed BLACKFRIARS THEATRE during the winter. The Globe was burnt to the ground in a matter of hours in 1613 when a sound-effect canon set fire to the thatch during a performance of *King Henry VIII*. No one was injured, but it was reported that one man's breeches were set alight and had to be extinguished with ale. The theatre was rebuilt a year later with a tiled roof. It was closed in 1642 when all London theatres were shut down by the PURITANS, and demolished two years later. The Globe is referred to as 'this wooden O' by the Chorus in the Prologue to *King Henry V*.

Globe: Shakespeare's Globe Theatre
A historically accurate reconstruction of the Elizabethan GLOBE THEATRE built near to the original site in London, which opened in 1996. *See* WANAMAKER, SAM. *See also illustration on page 110.*

Gloucester, Duchess of
A historical figure (d. 1399) and a minor character in *King Richard II*, the Duchess of Gloucester is the widow of the Duke of Gloucester, who has been murdered before the action of the play. She is grieving for the loss of her husband and passionately urges her brother-in-law, John of Gaunt, to avenge his death. The Duchess returns to the family home where she says she will die of her grief and her death is later reported to the Duke of York.

Gloucester, Eleanor Duchess of

A historical figure (d. c. 1446) and a character in *King Henry VI, Part Two*, Eleanor, affectionately known as Nell, is the Duke of Gloucester's wife. Eleanor is ambitious for Gloucester and consults witches to look into the future for her. Unknown to Eleanor, the witches have been hired by her husband's enemies in a plan to trap her into exposing her ambitions, and to disgrace him. She is arrested for witchcraft, insulted by Queen Margaret and sentenced to public penance and banishment. As she walks through the streets in her penitent's clothes, a once proud women now publicly humiliated, her husband expresses his sympathy for her.

Gloucester, Humphrey, Duke of

A historical figure (1390-1447) and a character in *King Henry IV, Part Two, King Henry V* and *King Henry VI, Parts One and Two*, Gloucester is the youngest of King Henry IV's sons.

In *Henry IV, Part Two*, Gloucester greets his brother, Prince Hal, when he arrives at their father's deathbed.

In *Henry V*, Gloucester's role is again a minor one, fighting alongside the King in France.

photo: Richard Kalina

Shakespeare's Globe Theatre

In *Henry VI, Parts One and Two*, Gloucester is sometimes referred to as Duke Humphrey. In *Part One*, he is Protector of the Kingdom of England during his nephew King Henry's infancy. He is involved in a long-running and vicious quarrel with the Bishop of Winchester, whom he accuses of being irreligious. Gloucester opposes Henry's marriage to Margaret of Anjou, believing that a union with the Earl of Armagnac's daughter would be a wiser political move

In *Part Two*, Gloucester is still Protector of the Kingdom and continues to be opposed to Henry's marriage; his ancient quarrel with Winchester, newly made Cardinal, still simmers. Gloucester's wife, Eleanor, wants him to make a bid for power but the good Duke, though a proud man, is not an ambitious one and remains loyal to the King. Gloucester stands in the way of other nobles vying for power; Suffolk, for one, is determined to be rid of him and hatches a plot in which the innocent Duke is accused of collaborating in his wife's treachery. Henry believes the old man is not guilty but Gloucester is murdered by Suffolk's men before he is able to prove his innocence.

Gloucester, Earl of

A character in *King Lear*, the Earl of Gloucester is Edgar and Edmund's father. Gloucester, persuaded by the scheming Edmund to believe that Edgar is hatching a plot to kill him, threatens to kill his elder son. Gloucester remains loyal to Lear but he is cruelly punished by Regan for his loyalty, and his eyes are gouged out. Blinded and suicidal, he is thrown out into the wilderness of the heath. There he meets Edgar (who he does not recognize in his disguise as 'Poor Tom', a lunatic beggar) who guides him towards Dover and, pretending to take him to the very edge of the cliffs, tricks Gloucester out of suicide. Reunited with Edgar at the last, Gloucester dies but he has gained insight from his sufferings, which largely parallel Lear's tragic experiences. Like Lear, he has been blind to the innate goodness of one of his children and taken in by another, with tragic consequences.

Gobbo, Launcelot

A comic character in *The Merchant of Venice*, Launcelot Gobbo appears as a CLOWN in the cast list, but he has many of the qualities of the FOOL with his punning and quick-witted comments on life. Launcelot is Shylock's servant but he later joins Bassanio's household. Launcelot makes his dislike of Shylock clear, describing him as a miser, and exhibiting a strong prejudice against Shylock because he is a Jew. He plays a cruel trick on his father, Old Gobbo, who is blind, by pretending to be a stranger and telling Old Gobbo that Launcelot his son is dead.

Gobbo, Old

A minor comic character in *The Merchant of Venice*, Old Gobbo is Launcelot Gobbo's father (see above). Old Gobbo is blind and not recognizing his son when they meet, he asks him the way. Launcelot plays a trick on him and tells Gobbo his son has died.

Goneril

A central character in *King Lear*, Goneril is Lear's villainous daughter and wife to the Duke of Albany. In order to gain a portion of Lear's kingdom, Goneril pretends to love her father extravagantly. In fact she is intent on acquiring control of the whole kingdom for herself. Her sister Regan's rival for power, Goneril humiliates her father and quarrels with him. She finally turns him out of her house, oblivious of his fate in the storm that rages. She is contemptuous of her husband Albany, who is a decent man, and allies herself with the ruthless and ambitious Edmund with whom she has an affair. Goneril finds herself again in deadly competition with her sister Regan, who also loves Edmund. When her scheming is finally exposed, Goneril poisons Regan and kills herself.

Gonzalo

A character in *The Tempest*, Gonzalo is an honest old councillor and the one of the people shipwrecked on Prospero's island. Before the time of the play, Prospero's Dukedom in Milan was seized by his treacherous brother Antonio who cast Prospero and Miranda adrift in a small boat. Gonzalo, loyal to Prospero, made sure that Prospero had some of his books and that there were sufficient provisions on board to keep them alive. On Prospero's island, Gonzalo's concern is for others and he tries to console Alonso who fears that his son Ferdinand is drowned. Gonzalo is brought before Prospero by Ariel's magic and greeted with affection. He is overjoyed to see that Ferdinand has survived and blesses his marriage with Miranda. Gonzalo is a talkative but kindly old man; the object of young men's scorn, he always remains good-humoured. By nature an optimist, he sees the potential of the island to become a utopia, a kind of earthly paradise.

Good Queen Bess

An affectionate name given to Queen Elizabeth I.

Goodfellow, Robin

Another name for the character PUCK in *A Midsummer Night's Dream*.

Gorboduc

Ferrex and Porrex, otherwise known as *Gorboduc*, is considered the first blank verse tragedy in English. It was written in 1565, one year after the birth of Shakespeare, by two lawyers, Thomas Sackville and Thomas Norton. *Gorboduc* was a HISTORY PLAY with little action and a great deal of static dialogue; it was written for performance by the authors' fellow law students in the INNS OF COURT (a London law school).

Goths

Minor characters in *Titus Andronicus*; historically the Goths were a barbarian tribe of Northern Europeans who were often in conflict with the Romans. At the beginning of the play, Titus has just returned from conquering the Goths and has captured their queen, Tamora, and her four sons. When Titus decides to depose Saturnius and restore order in Rome which has become chaotic largely due to the scheming of Tamora, he turns to the warrior Goths for military support. Led by Titus's son Lucius, they march on Rome and one of the Goths discovers Aaron and his baby hiding behind a wall.

Governor of Harfleur

A minor character in *King Henry V*, the Governor surrenders Harfleur to the English when he realizes that the town can no longer defend itself.

Governor of Paris

A minor character in *King Henry VI, Part One*, the Governor is present when King Henry is crowned king of France.

Gower[1]

A minor character in *King Henry IV, Part Two*, Gower is a supporter of the King and a messenger.

Gower[2]

A character in *Pericles*, Gower is the CHORUS in the play. He introduces each of the five acts with a PROLOGUE and a dumb-show and, at the end of the play, he speaks an EPILOGUE. The character of Gower was based on an English poet, John Gower (c. 1330-1408) who was a contemporary of Geoffrey Chaucer. A 16th- century edition of Gower's *Confessio Amantis* provided a source for the story of Pericles, and Gower's old-fashioned style of speaking in the play imitates the style of the real Gower's poetry.

Gower, Captain

A character in *King Henry V*, Captain Gower is one of the officers in King Henry's army. A courageous and honourable soldier, he oversees the digging of trenches and tunnels at the siege of Harfleur, and fights at Agincourt. He despises amateur soldiers such as the cowardly and dishonest Pistol; he angrily reproaches Pistol for mocking Fluellen, a professional soldier and a brave Welshman who wears a leek in his cap as an ancient tradition.

Grandpré, Earl of Grandpré

A minor character in *King Henry V*, the Earl of Grandpré is one of the overconfident French nobles who holds England and the English in contempt. On the eve of the Battle of Agincourt he is impatient for the fighting to begin but he is reported later as having been killed.

Granville Barker, Harley (1877–1946)

An actor, critic, playwright and revolutionary director of Shakespeare's plays, whose revival of *Twelfth Night* in 1912 was hailed for its pace and vitality. Granville Barker used unabridged texts and sets that were unusually simple for that time. He wrote a series of scholarly *Prefaces* to Shakespeare between 1927 and 1945. His best-remembered play is *The Voysey Inheritance* (1905).

Gratiano[1]

A character in *The Merchant of Venice*, Gratiano is a Venetian gentleman and a friend of Antonio and Bassanio who is in love with Portia's lady-in-waiting, Nerissa. He is a light-hearted, rather wild character who enjoys life and whom Bassanio describes as talking a lot of nonsense. However, when Shylock's case against Antonio is being heard before the court, Gratiano shows an unpleasant side to his nature when he baits Shylock and triumphs over his defeat. He is tricked by Nerissa, who is disguised in men's clothing as a lawyer's clerk, into parting with a ring which she had earlier given him as a keepsake. Later, Nerissa scolds him for having given the ring away to another woman but when everything is finally revealed Gratiano and Nerissa are united in love.

Gratiano[2]

A minor character in *Othello*, Gratiano is Desdemona's uncle. He arrives in Cyprus from Venice, with news that Desdemona's father has died of grief at the marriage of his daughter to the Moor Othello.

Gravedigger

A minor character in *Hamlet* who digs Ophelia's grave and jokes about life and death in a comic interlude. He presents Hamlet with the skull of YORICK, the late court jester.

Greene, Robert (1558–92)

A writer and dramatist, Greene was notorious for his quarrelsome nature. Following a misspent youth, he wrote a number of tracts and pamphlets including *Greene's Groatsworth of Wit* (1592), an extraordinary outburst written in the last weeks of his life and published after his death. In it, he singled out the young Shakespeare for angry comment, referring to him as 'an upstart crow ... [who] supposes he is as well able to bombast out blanke verse as the best of you ... in his own conceit the only Shake-scene in a countrey'. It has been suggested that Greene may have had a hand in writing *King Henry VI, Parts One and Two*, *Titus Andronicus* and *The Two Gentlemen of Verona*. Tradition holds that he died after surfeiting on pickled herrings and Rhenish wine.

Greene (Green), Sir Henry

A historical figure (d. 1399) and a minor character in *King Richard II*, Greene is one of Richard's close advisers whom Bolingbroke regards as a parasite and bad influence on the King. When Bolingbroke lands in England with his rebel forces Greene flees to Bristol. He is captured by Bolingbroke along with two other of the King's advisers, Bagot and Bushy, and sentenced to death.

Gregory

A minor character in *Romeo and Juliet*, Gregory is a servant in the Capulet household. He fights with the servants of the Montague family at the beginning of the play in a scene which establishes the long-running feud between the two families.

Gremio

A comic character in *The Taming of the Shrew*, Gremio is a rich old man who is described as a PANTALOON (the stock character of the greedy old man in the COMMEDIA DELL'ARTE) in the stage directions. He is in love with the beautiful and sweet Bianca and foolish enough to believe that money is the key to unlock her heart. Gremio boasts of all his possessions from jewels to cattle in order to impress Bianca's father, who has promised his daughter to the richest suitor, but he is outdone by Lucentio's clever servant Tranio in disguise as his master. Ironically, it is Gremio who introduces Bianca's future husband to her when he unwittingly hires Lucentio in his guise as a teacher to be Bianca's tutor. *(Do not confuse with* GRUMIO IN THE SAME PLAY*).*

Grey, Lady Elizabeth, afterwards Queen to Edward IV

A historical figure (1437–92) and a character in *King Henry VI, Part Three*, Lady Grey is a widow and a commoner with whom Edward suddenly falls in love. When she refuses to become his mistress, Edward marries her, to the anger of his supporters, in particular the Earl of Warwick who defects to King Henry's cause. Lady Grey finds herself at the centre of a political turmoil which erupts into war and she is concerned for the safety of her unborn child.

  Lady Grey is the Queen Elizabeth of *King Richard III* whose children, the little princes, are murdered by Richard in the TOWER OF LONDON.

Grey, Lord

A historical figure (really Sir Richard Grey, d. 1483) and a minor character in *King Richard III*, Lord Grey is Queen Elizabeth's younger son. Richard has Grey executed at Pontefract, simply because he stands in the way of Richard's ambitions for the crown.

Grey's ghost appears before Richard in a dream on the eve of the Battle of Bosworth and prophesies the King's downfall.

Grey, Sir Thomas
A historical figure (d. 1415) and a minor character in *King Henry V*, Sir Thomas Grey is one of the conspirators against the King who was bribed by the promise of French gold. The King sentences him to death, and although Grey asks for mercy he acknowledges that the sentence is a just one.

Griffith
A minor character in *King Henry VIII*, Griffith is a Gentleman-Usher in attendance on the sick Queen Katherine in her exile in Kimbolton. Griffith tells the Queen that Wolsey has died, and when Katherine speaks bitterly of her old enemy, Griffith gently suggests that no man is wholly evil and describes some of his virtues. Katherine thanks Griffith for his more generous view of Wolsey, which she says has helped to lay her hatred of him to rest.

Groom of the Stable to King Richard
A minor character in *King Richard II*, the Groom visits Richard in his prison just before his death. He tells his master that Bolingbroke rode Barbary, Richard's horse which the Groom had personally looked after, in his coronation procession. The Groom who wishes that the horse had stumbled and killed Bolingbroke, is one of the few people who remains loyal to the King.

Grooms of the Chamber
An honorary title conferred on the royal players of Queen Elizabeth and King James as members of the royal household. When Shakespeare's company, the KING'S MEN, were sworn in as grooms in 1604, each actor was provided with four and a half yards of scarlet cloth for his livery; the grooms formed part of King James I's coronation procession.

groundlings
Members of the audience in Elizabethan PLAYHOUSES who paid one penny to stand in the 'ground' or PIT. Hamlet refers to the groundlings' preference for 'dumb-shows and noise' and for over-acting rather than for more subtle or sophisticated entertainment.

Grumio
A comic character in *The Taming of the Shrew*, Grumio is Petruchio's trusted personal servant. He is a shrewd character who recognizes that his master's initial interest in Katherina is because she is a rich man's daughter. He attends Petruchio at his wedding to Katherina, dressed like his master in a bizarre outfit of tattered clothing, and he is responsible for preparing for the arrival of Katherina and her husband at Petruchio's country house. When Katherina has been denied food as part of Petruchio's taming technique, Grumio tantalizes her by describing various dishes and then saying that none of them would be suitable for her. (Do not confuse with GREMIO in the same play).

Guiderius
A character in *Cymbeline*, Guiderius is Cymbeline's son who, along with his younger brother Arviragus, was snatched as a young child by Belarius in revenge for an injustice.

For twenty years, Belarius has brought up the boys in exile in Wales and has given Guiderius the name of 'Polydore'. In spite of their simple upbringing, the two princes display the nobleness of nature and the courage befitting a king's sons. Guiderius and his brother show great kindness to the boy 'Fidele' (actually their long-lost sister Imogen) who lands in their midst; Guiderius kills the luckless Cloten (who tries to attack Imogen), with great efficiency, cutting off his head. The princes' bravery in battle is instrumental in saving the British army from defeat and they are honoured by their father with whom they are reconciled in the fairy tale resolution to the play.

Guildenstern
See ROSENCRANTZ AND GUILDENSTERN

Guilford, Sir Henry
A minor character in *King Henry VIII*, Guilford acts as the master of ceremonies at Wolsey's banquet, welcoming the Cardinal's guests to what he hopes will be a merry occasion.

Gull's Hornbook, The
See DEKKER, THOMAS.

Gunpowder Plot, the
A failed Roman Catholic plot, in 1605, to blow up KING JAMES I and his ministers at the opening of Parliament in London. After an anonymous tip-off, Guy Fawkes (1570-1606), and other fellow conspirators, were discovered in the cellars beneath the Houses of Parliament with barrels of gunpowder that had been smuggled into the building. They were arrested and executed. As a result of the Gunpowder Plot, King James' popularity in England rose considerably.

Gurney, James
A minor character in *King John*, Gurney is Lady Faulconbridge's servant.

Hh

Haberdasher
A minor character in *The Taming of the Shrew*, *see* TAILOR.

Hal, Prince
The name given to the Prince in *King Henry IV*; *see* HENRY, PRINCE.

Halberdier
A minor character in *King Richard III*, the Halberdier is a soldier armed with a halberd [a combined spear and battleaxe] who guards the coffin of King Henry VI and stops Richard from halting the funeral procession.

Hall, Elizabeth (1608–1670)
The only daughter of Susanna HALL (Shakespeare's elder daughter; see below) and John Hall; she was married twice; to THOMAS NASH in 1626 who died twenty-one years later, and to John Bernard in 1649. The last of Shakespeare's direct descendants, she died without children.

Hall, Susanna (1583–1649)
Shakespeare's elder daughter who was born six months after his marriage to Anne HATHAWAY. Aged twenty-four, Susanna married John Hall (1575-1635), a renowned Stratford physician who may very likely have attended Shakespeare in his last illness. They lived in Hall's Croft in Stratford (which can still be visited today) where their only child, ELIZABETH (*see above*), was born. In 1613, Susanna was touched by scandal. She brought a successful legal action against one John Lane who had publicly accused her of adultery with a Stratford hatter. This event is recounted in a play, *The Herbal Bed* by Peter Whelan, premiered by the RSC in Stratford in 1996.

When her father died, Susanna and her husband moved to grander premises at New Place, Shakespeare's house which Elizabeth in due course inherited. Susanna's gravestone, which bears an epitaph describing her as 'Witty above her sex', can be seen alongside Shakespeare's grave in Holy Trinity Church at Stratford-on-Avon.

Hall, William
See W H, MR.

Halle, (Hall) Edward (c. 1498–1547)
An English politician, lawyer, and historian, Halle was the author of a famous account of English history between 1399 and 1532, which was Shakespeare's main source for his early HISTORY PLAYS. His book, entitled *The Union of the Two Noble and Illustre Families of Lancaster and York*, was published in 1548, a year after his death. It was largely an exercise in propaganda, in which Halle sought to glorify the TUDOR dynasty (Queen Elizabeth I was the last Tudor monarch). A staunch Protestant himself, Halle

admired Henry VIII for his break with the Roman Catholic Church, and his foundation of the Protestant Church of England, and he justified the Tudors' claim to the throne. *See also* HOLINSHED'S *Chronicles.*

Hamlet

The tragic hero of *Hamlet*, Hamlet, Prince of Denmark, an introspective and isolated figure, is grieving for the recent death of his father the King; he is distressed by the hasty remarriage of his mother Gertrude to the old King's brother Claudius. The Ghost of his father appears to Hamlet and describes how he was foully murdered by Claudius, now King, and demands revenge. Hamlet feigns madness as a way of discovering the truth, but his mental distress is real enough. He turns against Ophelia whom he has previously loved, with obscene insults, and angrily confronts Gertrude whose affection for Claudius disgusts him. Hamlet becomes increasingly convinced of Claudius' guilt and plans to kill him, but he is confronted with the dilemma of having to commit a murder in order to avenge one. He agonizes over his position, and contemplates suicide. While he delays, events overtake him. He kills Polonius, Ophelia's father, by mistake and is sent away to England by Claudius who is plotting Hamlet's death. The plot fails, and Hamlet returns to Denmark in a different frame of mind. He is saddened to find that Ophelia has drowned herself, but seems ready to accept whatever destiny has to offer him. Claudius arranges a duel between Hamlet and Ophelia's brother Laertes, but unknown to Hamlet, Laertes weapon is poisoned; in the confusion of the fight both Laertes and Hamlet are killed. Before he dies, Hamlet kills Claudius and finally avenges his father's death.

The character of Hamlet derives from the conventional hero of REVENGE TRAGEDY, but, transformed by Shakespeare, becomes a complex and enigmatic figure. He is the complete RENAISSANCE man, whom Ophelia describes as having a 'noble mind ...The courtier's, soldier's, scholar's eye, tongue, sword'. This princely figure is faced with a crisis which forces him to question the reality of the world he inhabits, the nature of responsibility, and ultimately the meaning of life and death itself.

Hamlet

A TRAGEDY by Shakespeare, written between 1599 and 1601, in the mature brilliance of his mid-career, *Hamlet* has received more critical attention, and attracted more outstanding theatrical performances than any other of Shakespeare's plays. It was first published in a QUARTO edition in 1603. It was probably first performed in 1602. The source for the play was most likely a lost anonymous REVENGE play called *Hamlet* (perhaps by Thomas KYD), often referred to as the *Ur-Hamlet*. Set in Elsinore in Denmark, *Hamlet* explores themes of revenge, madness, and political and moral corruption. It is concerned with the dual nature of man, and with the dilemma of righting a wrong by committing another wrong. At the centre of the play is HAMLET himself. Many of Shakespeare's concerns are woven into the play, including the relationship between real life and the theatre. It is hard not to see Shakespeare himself in the character of Hamlet, instructing the players how to act.

SYNOPSIS : Prince Hamlet is the son of the King of Denmark, who has recently died. Hamlet is disgusted because his mother, Queen Gertrude, has married her dead husband's brother, Claudius, with what Hamlet sees as indecent haste. His father's ghost appears to Hamlet, reveals that he was murdered by Claudius, and demands that Hamlet avenge his death, but to spare his mother. Greatly distressed, Hamlet pretends to be mad as a way of discovering the truth; he is abusive to Ophelia, whom he has loved, and insults her father Polonius. Hamlet arranges for a troupe of travelling players to enact a play which describes a king murdered by his brother, hoping that Claudius's reactions to it will reveal a guilty conscience. The play within a play, referred to as the 'Mousetrap' by Hamlet, is a turning point in the action; a dramatic illusion becomes the trap through which Hamlet can catch the truth and confirm the Ghost's story. An opportunity to kill Claudius presents itself to Hamlet, but he is unable to act, although by now he is confident of Claudius' guilt. He angrily confronts his mother in her chamber where the ghost reappears (seen only by Hamlet) urging him on to revenge. Hearing a noise behind a curtain, Hamlet stabs Polonius who has been secretly observing his behaviour. Polonius's murder gives Claudius a reason to dispatch Hamlet to England, where he narrowly escapes a death planned for him by Claudius. In Hamlet's absence Ophelia goes mad and drowns herself, and her brother Laertes returns from France to avenge his father Polonius's death. When Hamlet returns to Denmark, Claudius sees a way to exploit Laertes in murdering Hamlet. He arranges a fencing competition between them, in which Laertes will used a poisoned weapon. Claudius also prepares a fatal poisoned drink which Gertrude drinks by mistake during the duel. Laertes mortally wounds Hamlet, who immediately deals a fatal blow to Laertes, and then wounds Claudius and forces him to drink the poisoned wine. Hamlet lives long enough to welcome Prince Fortinbras of Norway, whom Hamlet names as his successor to rule Denmark, a kingdom now purged of Claudius' evil.

Harcourt
A minor character in *King Henry IV, Part Two*, Harcourt is a supporter of the King who brings news that the rebels have finally been defeated.

Harlequin
Originally a STOCK CHARACTER from 16th-century Italian comedy, Arlecchino or Arlequin was a cunning servant (see COMMEDIA DELL'ARTE). Adopted into the contemporary English dramatic tradition, Harlequin developed into a mischievous, acrobatic CLOWN, with a costume of diamond-shaped patches, and only later into the mute innocent of early English pantomime who acts out his love for Columbine in mime. The character of Puck in *Midsummer Night's Dream*, with his ability to change his shape, is a kind of harlequin.

Harry Percy
See HOTSPUR.

Hart, Joan (1569–1646)
Shakespeare's younger sister who married a Stratford hatter, William Hart (d. 1616), in about 1600; they seem often to have been in debt. They had four children: WILLIAM (*see below*), the eldest, who eventually became an actor; Thomas (1605-c. 1670); and Mary (1603-07) and Michael (1608-18) who both died in childhood. In his will, Shakespeare left Joan his clothes and stipulated that she should live in his HENLEY STREET house for the rest of her life.

Hart, William (1600-39)

Joan Shakespeare's son (*see* HART, JOAN *above*) and Shakespeare's nephew, William Hart became an actor, and during the 1630s he was a member of the KING'S MEN company of players. He probably did not marry, but it is believed by some that the restoration actor, CHARLES HART (d. 1693), was William's illegitimate son.

Hastings[1] [Lord]

A historical figure (d. 1405) and a minor character in *King Henry IV, Part Two*, Hastings is one of the rebels against King Henry; he is in favour of accepting the peace offered to the rebels by Prince John. When, later, Prince John treacherously disregards the treaty, Hastings is arrested and sentenced to death.

Hastings[2]

A historical figure (c. 1430-83) and a character in *King Henry VI, Part Three* and *King Richard III*; in *Henry VI*, Hastings is a minor character. He is a supporter of King Edward and the Yorkist cause.

 In *Richard III*, Hastings is Richard's loyal supporter whose fortunes rise with Richard's. He turns a blind eye to Richard's villainy, but has misgivings about Richard snatching the throne from the rightful heirs. He expresses his doubts to Buckingham, but although he is confident of Richard's loyalty to him, Hastings pays the penalty for his dissension. Richard frames Hastings, accusing him of treason, and has him summarily executed; his severed head is brought to Richard. His ghost appears to Richard in a dream on the eve of the Battle of Bosworth and prophesies the King's downfall.

Hathaway, Anne (1556–1623)

Shakespeare's wife and the eldest daughter of a prosperous yeoman farmer of Hewlands Farm, on the edge of the forest of ARDEN near Stratford-on-Avon. The Hathaway and Shakespeare families were known to one another before William began to woo Anne, whom he married in November 1582. The wedding seems to have been arranged rather hurriedly, which is not altogether surprising as Anne was already pregnant. She produced their first daughter, Susanna, six months later. Twins, Judith and Hamnet (d. 1595) followed in 1585. Anne was eight years older than William, but she outlived her husband by seven years. Much has been made of the fact that in his will Shakespeare only left her the furniture and their second-best bed, but there is no reason to suppose that this indicates a lack of affection for his wife. Common law entitled her to a share in her husband's estate during her remaining lifetime and while the best bed would have been reserved for visitors to the house, the second-best would have been the marital bed and therefore of sentimental value; Anne Hathaway's family home can still be visited at Shottery, just outside Stratford.

heavens, the

A canopy supported on wooden pillars that formed a covering over the stage of an Elizabethan playhouse and beneath which a painted curtain might sometimes be hung (*see also entry for* CURTAIN). Spectacular effects could be created by raising or lowering actors or PROPS, such as throne or a cloud, through a trap door in the heavens. The underside was probably painted blue and decorated with gold stars. (*See* PLAYHOUSES).

Hecate

A minor character in *Macbeth*, Hecate is a goddess of the Underworld who is furious with the Three Witches for talking to Macbeth without first consulting her.

Hector

A legendary figure and a central character in *Troilus and Cressida*, Hector is the son of Priam, King of Troy. Hector is a military hero, and a man of honour who is admired by both Trojans and Greeks, and whose nobility and courtesy is evident when he visits the Greek camp. Called upon to fight the Greek hero Achilles in single combat, Hector's chivalry proves his undoing; he makes the mistake of sparing Achilles' life. Achilles, who is far less chivalrous, later orders his soldiers to kill Hector while he is unarmed and defenceless. However, Hector is less than perfect himself. He is proud and stubborn, refusing to heed the warnings of his family that he will be killed. His death follows a dishonourable lapse in which he kills a Greek soldier in order to steal his particularly beautiful armour. Hector removes his own armour to try on his spoils, and when Achilles' men find him unprotected and unarmed, they kill him.

Helen[1]

A minor character in *Cymbeline*, Helen is Imogen's lady-in-waiting. She waits on Imogen on the night that Iachimo hides in her mistress's bedroom.

Helen[2]

A legendary figure and a character in *Troilus and Cressida*, Helen is the Greek Menelaus' wife who is at present living happily with Paris in Troy. Her capture from the Greeks by the Trojans was the original cause of the long war now raging between Greece and Troy. Helen is renowned as the most beautiful of all women, but she is empty-headed and flirtatious, and there are those on both sides who are concerned about the number of lives lost on her behalf and wonder whether she is really worth fighting a war over. In Christopher MARLOWE's play *Dr Faustus*, the beautiful Helen is famously described as having 'a face that launched a thousand ships'.

Helena[1]

A character in *All's Well that Ends Well*, Helena is an orphan, a famous physician's daughter, who has fallen in love with the arrogant Bertram. Hearing that the King of France is incurably ill, and confident that a remedy of her father's will make him well, she travels to the court where Bertram is also on a visit. She cures the King, who rewards her with Bertram as her chosen husband. Bertram, disgusted to have a mere doctor's daughter as his wife, cruelly rejects her, vowing never to be a husband to her until she has fulfilled two seemingly impossible tasks. Helena hurt, but undaunted, sets out to win her husband back. Resorting to disguise and trickery, her determination and her belief in Bertram never falter. Supposed dead by Bertram, Helena makes a dramatic appearance in the final scene, and explains how she has fulfilled Bertram's conditions. The two are reconciled and while Helena seems too good for Bertram it is to be supposed that her constancy and love with redeem him.

Helena[2]

A character in *A Midsummer Night's Dream*, Helena, described as tall and blond, adores Demetrius, despite his complete indifference to her. When Helena's great friend Hermia is planning to elope with her lover Lysander, she confides in Helena, who betrays the confidence, telling Demetrius of the proposed elopement. Demetrius loves Hermia, and pursues the fleeing lovers into the woods. Helena annoyingly tags along too. Helena lacks confidence in her charms and when, bewitched by Puck, both Demetrius and Lysander declare their love for her, she is baffled, and believes that they are mocking her. Her frustration increases when Hermia accuses her of stealing Lysander from her. Helped by Oberon's magic, she finally wins Demetrius' love which she says is like finding a jewel.

Helenus

A minor character in *Troilus and Cressida*, Helenus is one of the Trojan King Priam's sons and a priest. Helenus is not convinced that it is worth fighting a long war over the capture of Helen, and suggests returning her to the Greeks and making peace.

Helicanus (Helicane)

A minor character in *Pericles*, Helicanus is a lord of Tyre and an elder statesman whom the Chorus, Gower, describes as an ideal of honesty and loyalty. He is Pericles' second-in-command who governs Tyre in Pericles' absence. While Pericles is away, certain of the nobles suggest that Helicanus should declare himself the permanent ruler of Tyre, but he refuses and sends word to Pericles to return home. Helicanus accompanies Pericles when he travels to reclaim Marina, comforts him when he seems to have lost his daughter, and is present when Marina and Pericles are reunited and later when Pericles discovers Thaisa in Ephesus.

hell mouth

A movable, cave-like structure, representing the entrance to hell, which was sited over a trap door in the stage of an Elizabethan playhouse. The HELL MOUTH was an important feature in morality plays, and theatrical manager Philip HENSLOWE makes frequent mention of a hell mouth in his lists of PROPS.

Heming (or Hemminge), John (d. 1630)

A principal actor with the LORD CHAMBERLAIN'S MEN company of players from 1594, he may also have been their business manager when they became the KING'S MEN. Together with fellow actor Henry CONDELL, Heming edited the First FOLIO edition of Shakespeare's plays in 1623. A father of twelve, and a respected and prosperous man, Heming had a quarter share in the Globe theatre on his death.

Henley Street

A street in Stratford-on-Avon in which is the house where Shakespeare is believed to have been born. John Shakespeare, William's father, acquired the property around 1552 and on his death in 1601 left it to his son. Originally acquired as two separate dwellings, the house was lived in by his sister Joan after Shakespeare's death and passed to his daughter Susanna in 1646. The 'BIRTHPLACE' now belongs to the Shakespeare Birthplace Trust and can be visited by the public today.

Henry, Duke of Richmond

A minor character in *King Henry VI, Part Three*, *see* RICHMOND, DUKE OF.

Henry IV, King of England (1367–1413)

Historical Figure. Henry of Bolingbroke, Duke of Lancaster, become King of England in 1399. In 1398, he had taken a leading part in an unsuccessful revolt against his cousin

RICHARD II, who had enraged British nobles by assuming absolute power in England. Henry was banished by Richard and his lands were seized, but a year later he invaded England and successfully claimed the throne. In becoming King, Henry established the House of LANCASTER as a royal dynasty. His rule eventually brought a new order and stability to English life, but the years of his reign were not without turbulence, and Henry had to deal with a series of uprisings, particularly in the North of England (led by Henry Percy (Harry Hotspur)) and in Wales (led by Owen Glendower). Henry was also plagued by financial problems and he made frequent, if not always successful, demands to Parliament that more money should be raised from taxes. On his death, Henry left England a legacy of national debt. Henry IV is the subject of Shakespeare's two-part play *King Henry IV, Parts One and Two. See table of kings and queens in the supplement.*

Henry IV, King

Title Character. A historical figure (1367-1413 - see above) and the title character of *King Henry IV, Parts One and Two*, Henry also appears as Henry BOLINGBROKE in *King Richard II*, the play in which he deposes the King.

At the beginning of *Henry IV, Part One*, King Henry is uneasy. He is planning to embark on a holy war as a penance for his part in the death of Richard II, when news comes of rebellion in Wales and Scotland. Henry feels that his nobles have let him down and stubbornly refuses to pay a ransom for one of them, Mortimer, who has been captured by the Welsh rebels. (Henry is particularly wary of Mortimer because he was proclaimed heir to the throne by Richard II.) The nobles in turn feel betrayed by Henry and plan a rebellion against him in England; the King tries to make a peace with the rebels but they do not trust him and refuse to agree to it. At the battle of Shrewsbury the King is victorious and Prince Hal saves his father's life.

In *Part Two* Henry, whose position on the throne remains weak, is exhausted by the burden of Kingship. He still longs to go on a crusade to the Holy Land, but as news comes that the rebels have been defeated in the north of England he collapses. The King's last request is to be taken to the Jerusalem Chamber to die. It is a poignant request since the room named the Jerusalem Chamber is the closest King Henry ever gets to the Holy Land he so longs to see.

Henry IV, King, Part One

One of Shakespeare's HISTORY PLAYS, *King Henry IV, Part One* was the second of his historical tetralogy [series of four interrelated plays] from *King Richard II* to *King Henry V*, written around 1596-97. It was first published in a QUARTO edition of 1598 from the original FOUL papers [handwritten play scripts]. *Henry IV, Part One* was probably first performed in 1597. The main sources for the play were HOLINSHED'S *Chronicles* and an anonymous play *The Famous Victories of Henry V* (c. 1594) which provided Shakespeare with the basis for the character of Falstaff (called John OLDCASTLE in the original play). The play, set between 1402 and 1403, explores themes of courage and honour, responsibility and kingship.

SYNOPSIS : The action of the play continues from *King Richard II*, which ended when Henry Bolingbroke deposed King Richard, and moves between the court and low-life London. Bolingbroke is now crowned Henry IV and sits uneasily on the throne. He feels remorse at his part in Richard's death and mistrusts his nobles, who in turn mistrust him, and rebel against him. Owen Glendower leads the rebellion in Wales, and the Percy family from the North, headed by Hotspur and his father the Duke of Northumberland, lead the rebels in England. King Henry despairs of his son, Prince Hal, who is leading a carefree life of idleness in the company of Falstaff and other petty criminals in the taverns of London. Ironically, Henry admires his enemy Hotspur as a man of action, and wishes Hal could be more like him. Hal knows that he will have to reform when he one day becomes King, but for the moment enjoys irresponsibility. Hal and his drinking companions take part in a highway robbery at Gad's Hill, and afterwards Hal and Poins disguise themselves and pretend to attack Falstaff who flees in terror. Later at the Boar's Head tavern, Falstaff boasts of how many men he fought off in hand-to-hand fighting, until the Prince gives a true account. When the King needs his son's support against the rebels, Prince Hal shows a new found maturity; he accepts command and puts Falstaff in charge of a group of foot soldiers. The King's attempts to make peace with the rebels fail and the armies meet at Shrewsbury. In the battle Hal fights courageously, and kills Hotspur in single combat, a death claimed later by the cowardly Falstaff. The rebels are defeated, and the King's position on the throne is for the moment secured.

Henry IV, King, Part Two

One of Shakespeare's HISTORY PLAYS, *King Henry IV, Part Two* was written around 1597-98, the third in his second historical tetralogy [series of four interrelated works] and the sequel to *Part One*. It was published in a QUARTO edition in 1600, and performed several times before 1600. The main sources of the play were HOLINSHED'S *Chronicles* and an anonymous play *The Famous Victories of Henry V* (c. 1594).

The action takes place between 1403 and 1413 and the play, which is full of images of disease, examines the qualities that are needed to be a good king.

SYNOPSIS : In *Part Two* the rebellion which has been simmering in *Part One* continues, and the rebels who were defeated in the North of England regroup, despite the retreat of one of their number, Northumberland, to Scotland. King Henry still sits uneasily on the throne, burdened with problems of state and still hoping to go on a crusade to the Holy Land. Prince John of Lancaster, Prince Hal's younger brother, tricks the rebels into agreeing to a peace treaty. He promises that the King will address their grievances, but in return they must disband their armies. As soon as they are disarmed, the rebel leaders are arrested and sentenced to death. Falstaff is in trouble with the law, first for his part in the highway robbery at Gad's Hill which took place in *Part One*, and then for failing to pay his debts to Hostess Quickly who is soon persuaded to forgive him. He is sent to organize recruitment for the King's army and with the help of a country lawyer, Justice Shallow, he picks out a handful of pitiful and unsuitable men. As the troubled King Henry lies dying, Prince Hal watches him as he sleeps. Believing that his father is dead Hal takes the crown and puts it on his own head and reflects on the heavy duties of kingship that lie ahead of him. When the King wakes he reproaches his son bitterly for anticipating his death, but he believes Hal's explanation and forgives him. Hal promises to abandon his wayward life and to prepare himself for his future responsibilities, and his father gives him his blessing. Hal is proclaimed King Henry V on his father's death. Riding in state, he is stopped by Falstaff who is hopeful of advancement now that his old friend is King, but the newly reformed Hal will have nothing to do with Falstaff, and banishes him. A new order is being established which has no place in it for Falstaff and his tavern companions, who are later arrested by the Lord Chief Justice, when the law finally catches up with them, and temporarily sent to the FLEET PRISON.

Henry V, King of England (1387–1422)

Historical Figure. Son of Henry IV, Henry V was King of England from 1413. As the Prince of Wales (Shakespeare's PRINCE HAL), he had defended his father's throne from the rebels in Wales, led by Owen Glendower, and then in the North of England, led by Henry Percy, Duke of Northumberland. During his reign, Henry sought to conquer France and claim the French crown. He undertook two great expeditions against the French, in 1415, and from 1417 to 1419 when Normandy was secured for England. Among Henry's many notable victories, the Battle of Agincourt stands out as his greatest. On 25 Oct 1415, St Crispin's Day, a small force of English bowmen confronted a much larger army of French knights at Agincourt in Northern France and, despite being outnumbered, the English won. In 1420, Henry married Catherine de Valois, the daughter of the French king, and became officially recognized as heir to the French throne. Before he was able to assume the French crown, Henry contracted dysentery and died.

The wars in France left England again in debt, but Henry V was a strong king, and was held in the English imagination as a glamorous and heroic figure. The historian Holinshed (see HOLINSHED'S *Chronicles*) describes Henry as 'a King of life without spot' and as having great physical strength. Henry V is the subject of Shakespeare's play KING HENRY V. *See the table of kings and queens in the Supplement.*

Henry V, King

Title Character. A historical figure (1387-1422, *see above*) and the title character of *King Henry V*; Henry is the reformed Prince HAL of the *King Henry IV* plays, who has been newly crowned King. Henry's rule is firm, and while he is capable of showing mercy to minor offenders, such as the man who insulted him while drunk, he is swift to condemn those who have conspired against his life, or his kingdom. He replies to the French Dauphin's insolent message and present of tennis balls, that he is not in the mood for games, and issues a stern warning of his intention to invade France. Henry's patriotism is never in doubt. He is determined to make England glorious again and he inspires his men to fight with rousing speeches promising that their exploits will long be remembered. Henry, whose youth was spent passing the time with ordinary people in the tavern, has not lost his common touch now that he is King. However, in his wooing of the French Princess Katherine, Henry displays the awkwardness of a man who is more at home in a soldier's world.

Henry V, King

One of Shakespeare's HISTORY PLAYS, *King Henry V* was the last in his second historical tetralogy [series of four interrelated plays] in which *King Richard II* and *King Henry IV, Parts One and Two* came before. *Henry V* was written around 1598-99 and first published in a QUARTO edition in 1600. Primary sources for the play were HOLINSHED'S *CHRONICLES* and an earlier anonymous play, *The Famous Victories of Henry the Fifth* (c. 1594). The play was made into a notable film by Sir Lawrence

Olivier in 1944 at the end of the Second World War, and has remained particularly popular with English audiences ever since. Set in England and France between 1415 and 1420, *Henry V* justifies the English claim to the French crown, and explores the responsibility of Kingship, as well as themes of courage and patriotism, and social order. In *Henry V*, as in other of Shakespeare's history plays, the French are always made to look arrogant, foolish and incompetent.

SYNOPSIS : The play is introduced by the Chorus who asks the audience to imagine the scenes of battle that are to follow. Henry, newly made King, is urged by the Archbishop of Canterbury to make war on England's old enemy France. A gift of tennis balls arrives at Henry's court from the French Dauphin; the gift is a veiled insult as it carries the implication that the French think Henry is only fit for playing games and not for serious matters. The insult sharpens Henry's resolve to invade France, but before leaving England he discovers that three nobles have been conspiring to assassinate him. Henry condemns them to death. In France, the English army successfully takes the town of Harfleur and marches on towards Calais. En route the English encounter the French army at Agincourt. Although the English are vastly outnumbered by the French they secure a victory, and a peace treaty is drawn up with the French King Charles in which Henry is made heir to the French crown and marries the French Princess Katherine. The play ends with news of the birth of Henry's son, the future King Henry VI, and foretells of his failure to hold onto the French crown his father has just won.

Henry's old drinking companion Falstaff (who featured in the *Henry IV* plays) dies at the beginning of the play but his friends, Bardolph, Nym and Pistol go to France to fight and their exploits provide comic relief in the action. Bardolph and Nym are eventually hanged for stealing but Pistol survives the fighting only to be thrashed by the Welsh Captain Fluellen whom Pistol has continually mocked for wearing a leek, the Welsh national emblem.

Henry VI, King of England (1421–71)
Historical Figure. Son of Henry V and Catherine de Valois of France, and King of England from 1422, Henry became King when he was only nine months old. During his childhood, England was governed by regents, the Duke of Gloucester in England, and the Duke of Bedford in France. As a result of his father's successful claim to the French throne, Henry was also crowned King of France in 1431. During Henry's reign, the French, resentful of rule by a foreign power and later inspired by Joan of Arc at Orleans in 1429, won back all the lands, including Normandy, that the English had taken during the reign of Henry V.

At home, Richard Duke of York mounted an unsuccessful claim to the throne in 1454 and so began the thirty years of dynastic civil war in England known as the WARS OF THE ROSES between the House of YORK and the ruling House of LANCASTER. Henry was eventually deposed and exiled in 1461. The Duke of York's son assumed the crown as King Edward IV, although Henry was temporarily restored to power by the Lancastrians in April of 1471. One month later, Henry was imprisoned and murdered in the TOWER OF LONDON. He was the last Lancastrian King of England. Henry was a gentle, sensitive and deeply religious man and a patron of the arts. He was subject to periods of mental illness and ill-equipped to be a monarch. Henry VI (see below) is the subject of Shakespeare's three-part play *King Henry VI, Parts One, Two and Three*. See the table of kings and queens in the Supplement.

Henry VI, King
Title Character. A historical figure (1421-71 – *see above*) and the title character of *King Henry VI, Parts One, Two and Three*; in *Part One*, the boy King Henry, son of HENRY V, is a minor character. At the outset of the play, he is too young to rule and the Kingdom is governed by a Protector, the Duke of Gloucester. A young man by the end of the play, Henry is surrounded by quarrelling nobles and never really imposes his authority. He is manipulated by the Duke of Suffolk into marriage with Margaret of Anjou.

In *Part Two*, Henry is dominated by his wife Margaret and the scheming Suffolk, who are ambitious for themselves. Henry is weak, a pious young man more given to prayer than to politics. When his old friend Gloucester is murdered by Suffolk, Henry mourns but fails to take strong control as his nobles continue to jostle for power around him. Henry, preferring a quiet life, leaves it to others to put down the peoples' rebellion lead by Jack Cade and plays into the Duke of York's hands by allowing him to command an army in Ireland; an army that York uses in his triumphant victory over the King at the Battle of St Albans.

In *Part Three*, Henry tries to secure his position as King and to make a peace between the factions of York and Lancaster. He agrees that on his death the crown will pass to the Duke of York and his heirs, rather than to his own son the Prince of Wales. Queen Margaret despises Henry for disinheriting their son and takes control of affairs. From then on, Henry increasingly withdraws from decision-making and leadership. He sees his kingdom torn apart by civil war and would prefer to live the life of a simple shepherd rather than be a king. When Edward's position on the throne is secured, Henry is imprisoned in the TOWER OF LONDON where he is murdered by Richard, Duke of Gloucester, the future King Richard III.

In *Richard III*, Henry's ghost appears before Richard on the eve of the Battle of Bosworth.

Henry VI, King, Part One
One of Shakespeare's early HISTORY PLAYS, *King Henry VI, Part One* is the first in his *King Henry VI* to *King Richard III* tetralogy [group of four interrelated works]. *Henry VI, Part One* was written around 1590 and first published in the First FOLIO edition of 1623. The play, possibly written for PEMBROKE'S MEN was most likely first performed in London in 1592. Sources for *Henry VI* were HOLINSHED'S *CHRONICLES* and the historical writing of Edward HALLE, but Shakespeare adapts history to suit his own dramatic purposes. The fate of England is at the heart of the play, rather than any central character, and themes are the security of the crown and the rightness of the English cause against the French. Set during the HUNDRED YEARS WAR between England and France, the action of the play alternates between the two countries. During the 18th and 19th centuries, scholars believed that *Henry VI, Part One* was either a collaboration between Shakespeare and another playwright or that it was written entirely by somebody other than Shakespeare.

SYNOPSIS : The play opens with the funeral of King Henry V, a heroic figure who had conquered most of France for England during his reign. As his son Henry VI is a mere infant, the Duke of Gloucester is Protector of the Kingdom. Enmities break out between factions of ambitious nobles, particularly between the Duke of Gloucester and the powerful Bishop of Winchester. News arrives that the French, inspired by La Pucelle, Joan of Arc, are winning back all the lands they had lost despite the efforts of the English, mostly notably the valiant Lord Talbot. By the end of the play, in which Shakespeare has compressed time, Henry has grown into a young man and marries the French Margaret of Anjou. The marriage, arranged by the devious Duke of Suffolk, cements a peace between England and France but the price paid is the surrender of French territory. Suffolk has fallen in love with Margaret himself and declares his intention to rule over both her and the King. *Henry VI, Part One* ends with a fragile political order; during the play the seeds are sown of the disruptive civil WARS OF THE ROSES, a dispute for the crown which features in *Henry VI, Parts Two and Three*.

Henry VI, King, Part Two

One of Shakespeare's early HISTORY PLAYS, *King Henry VI, Part Two* was written around 1590-91, the second in his *Henry VI* to *Richard III* tetralogy [group of four interrelated works], and first published in a QUARTO edition in 1594. There is no record of its first performance. Sources for the play were HOLINSHED'S *CHRONICLES* and the histories of Edward HALLE, but Shakespeare adapts history to suit his own dramatic purposes. Set in England during the 1450s, the play is concerned with political intrigue and social and moral disorder.

SYNOPSIS : The sequel to *King Henry VI, Part One*, *Part Two* (probably written two years later) begins where *Part One* (*see above*) left off. Henry and Margaret of Anjou are married, but the young King Henry's reign is to be a troubled one; his nobles, in particular the Dukes of Suffolk and York, are vying for power. Suffolk, in league with the Queen, hatches a plot to disgrace Gloucester, the King's loyal ally. He engineers a trap for Gloucester's wife, Eleanor, whose own ambitions for her husband are exposed and when she is banished, the Queen and Suffolk and others of the nobles accuse the old Duke of treason. Although the King believes that Gloucester is innocent, he does nothing to stop Gloucester being arrested, and Suffolk later murders Gloucester. The Duke of York makes his move for power, gaining the support of the Earls of Warwick and Salisbury for his own claim to the throne. Unrest among Henry's poorer subjects erupts into an open rebellion lead by Jack Cade. The rebels pose no serious threat to the King, who weakly retreats from the violence in London leaving others to deal with the revolt. Suffolk, largely in control of affairs now, sends the Duke of York to Ireland to quell another rebellion there. The Duke of York, supported by the Yorkist Earls of Warwick and Salisbury has been planning his own bid for power. Suffolk plays into York's hands in giving him command of an army which he can ultimately use against the King. When Suffolk is killed by Cade's rebels, the Duke of York makes his claim to the throne public. The King flees and the Duke of York triumphs at the Battle of St Albans. The WARS OF THE ROSES have begun.

Henry VI, King, Part Three

One of Shakespeare's early HISTORY PLAYS, *King Henry VI, Part Three* is the third in his *Henry VI* to *Richard III* tetralogy [group of four interrelated works], *King Henry VI,*

Part Three was written in 1590-91 and first published in a shorter version in a BAD QUARTO edition in 1595. It was probably first performed by PEMBROKE'S MEN around 1592. The main source for the play was Edward HALLE'S account of the English history of the period, but Shakespeare was also indebted to HOLINSHED'S *CHRONICLES*; Shakespeare reorganizes events to suit his own dramatic purposes. The play, set in England in the last years of Henry VI's reign, is concerned with the conflict between the Houses of YORK and LANCASTER and explores themes of political disorder and moral chaos, changing alliances, and revenge.

SYNOPSIS : The Duke of York has recently triumphed over King Henry's forces, and claims the throne. Henry, aware that his position as King is weak, names York as his heir providing he is allowed to remain King during his lifetime. Queen Margaret, furious that Henry has disinherited their own son, leads an army of nobles against York and defeats and kills him. After another hard-fought battle, York's son Edward, with the support of the Earl of Warwick, declares himself King Edward IV and Henry is sent to the TOWER OF LONDON. Warwick goes to France to arrange a marriage between Edward and the French King's sister-in-law, Bona. While Warwick is away, Edward falls in love with Lady Elizabeth Grey and marries her instead, to the fury of Warwick and the King of France. Edward's brothers, George and Richard, are also angry; Richard privately plots to take the crown for himself while George joins Warwick, who has also defected from Edward's side, in support of Henry. Edward is beaten and Henry is briefly and reluctantly made King again. Edward rallies his forces, seizes the crown back and returns Henry back to the Tower where he is murdered by Richard. Henry's heir is killed and his Queen is banished to France.

Henry VIII, King of England (1491–1547)

Historical Figure. Henry VIII, King of England from 1509-1547, stands out as one of the most memorable figures in English history. He was a man of huge appetites and, by the end of his life, massive physical stature. Henry's first wife, Katharine of Aragon, failed to produce the male heir that was needed to secure the throne for the next generation of the TUDOR dynasty. Henry's attempts to get this marriage annulled by the Pope, led to conflict with Rome. He dismissed his Lord Chancellor and senior churchman, Cardinal Wolsey, in 1529, and in 1532 broke with the Roman Catholic Church, proclaiming himself head of the new Church of England. In 1537 he licensed the publication of the Bible in the English language, rather than Latin. Thomas Cranmer became the Archbishop of Canterbury and pursued Henry's strongly anti-papal policy. In this religious upheaval, monasteries were disbanded and destroyed, and a great deal of church culture was lost for ever. However, Henry's reign heralded in a new age of economic and cultural growth, and his court became a centre of learning. After his first marriage, Henry married again five more times. Of his six wives, two, Anne Boleyn (*see* ANNE BOLEYN) and Catherine Howard were executed; two more, Katharine of Aragon and Anne of Cleves were divorced, and one, Jane Seymour, died in childbirth. His last wife, Catherine Parr outlived him. His daughter Elizabeth, born to Henry's second wife Anne Boleyn, became Queen ELIZABETH I of England eleven years and two monarchs after Henry's death.

Shakespeare's *King Henry VIII*, subtitled *All is true*, was a piece of political propaganda, presenting Henry as a blameless figure, whose only real fault lay in putting too much trust in the wily and ambitious Cardinal Wolsey. There is no mention in the play of the cruel fate of four of Henry's wives, nor of his huge and wasteful expenditure on foreign wars and personal extravagance.

Henry VIII, King

Title Character. A historical figure (1491-1547 see above) and the title character of *King Henry VIII*, Henry is a regal figure, who neither shows, nor seems to experience, great emotion. His marriage to his brother's widow, Katharine, troubles his conscience, and he fears that in failing to produce an heir to the throne, he is being punished by God. Henry clearly feels affection for Katherine, but nonetheless casts her aside, and marries the younger Anne Bullen in secret. As the play progresses, so Henry's maturity grows. At first, Henry's trust of Wolsey is such that he allows the faithful Buckingham to be falsely accused of treason and executed. He comes to realize the extent of Wolsey's abuse of power, and rids the court of his influence. Henry holds Cranmer in the highest regard and in intervening to protect his loyal friend, Henry is also defending the newly established Protestant Church of England. Henry is rewarded with the birth of a daughter, ELIZABETH, who will continue the Tudor line into the next generation.

Henry VIII, King or All is True

One of Shakespeare's HISTORY PLAYS, and probably the last play he wrote, *King Henry VIII* was written around 1612, very likely in collaboration with the dramatist John FLETCHER. It was first published in the First FOLIO edition of 1623, and first performed in 1613 in the GLOBE THEATRE. In July of that year, a catastrophic fire was started during a performance of the play, ignited by a shot fired during the scene of Wolsey's banquet, burning the Globe to the ground within less than an hour.

Shakespeare's SOURCES for the play were Holinshed's *Chronicles* and Edward HALLE'S history of the Tudor dynasty.

The play is set in England between 1485 and 1540, although like most of Shakespeare's history plays, time is compressed. *Henry VIII*, written at a time when MASQUES had become increasingly elaborate, involves a series of masque-like pageants for which lengthy and precise stage directions are given. It celebrates the TUDOR dynasty, and Henry's achievement in establishing the Protestant Church of England, and looks forward to Queen Elizabeth I's glorious reign. Like other history plays, the fate of England is at the centre of the play, and the King plays a lesser part in events than Cardinal Wolsey, who is presented as the pro-Catholic villain of the piece. In making Wolsey's responsible for events such as Buckingham's execution, Shakespeare excuses the King from blame. *Henry VIII* explores themes of justice and injustice (there are three trials in the play).

SYNOPSIS : The play opens with a discussion among nobles about the glittering pageantry of the 'Field of the Cloth of Gold', the site of a treaty signed in 1520 between the French and Henry VIII. The Dukes of Norfolk and Buckingham go on to criticize Cardinal Wolsey for his abuses of power. The scene is thus set in which Henry is seen as a heroic figure in gilded armour, while Wolsey is described as a 'keech' [lump of lard] and a 'butcher's cur' [dog]. The Duke of Buckingham is summarily arrested and tried for treason on false evidence, and executed. At a grand banquet held by Wolsey for the King, Henry appears in a masque; dressed as a shepherd, he meets and is charmed by the virtuous, and as importantly, Protestant,

Anne Bullen. Manipulated by Wolsey, Henry begins proceedings to annul his first marriage to Queen Katherine, who is tried and humiliated by Wolsey. She retires from court after her divorce, and dies, heartbroken. Henry has secretly married Anne, to the fury of Wolsey; she is crowned Queen by the new Archbishop of Canterbury, Cranmer, and joyfully accepted by the nation as Henry's new wife. Henry learns of Wolsey's abuses of power; he strips the Cardinal of all his offices and dismisses him from court. Wolsey is reformed by his downfall; genuinely penitent, he ends his life in quiet meditation. Wolsey's pro-Catholic successors plot to destroy Cranmer, accusing him of heresy. Henry, who values his old advisor highly, saves him from imprisonment in the TOWER OF LONDON. When a daughter is born to Henry and Anne, a spectacular celebration is held at the princess's christening, and Cranmer looks forward to her reign as the future Queen Elizabeth I of England.

Henry Percy
See NORTHUMBERLAND, EARL OF in *King Richard II.*

Henry, Prince (later King Henry V)
A historical figure (1387-1422) and a character in *King Henry IV, Parts One and Two*, Prince Henry, known as PRINCE HAL, is the King's eldest son and heir to the throne. In *Part One*, the young Prince's carefree life revolves around life at the Boar's Head Tavern and his friends there, particularly the larger-than-life Falstaff. He takes part in the robbery at Gad's Hill when he and Poins disguise themselves and play a trick on Falstaff. The Prince is aware, however, that he will have to abandon his irresponsible way of life one day, and reform. Meanwhile, King Henry has a poor opinion of his son, and compares him unfavourably with his enemy, the energetic Hotspur. In a comic scene which prefigures a serious one with his father, Hal pretends to be the King criticizing the behaviour of his son, while Falstaff takes the part of Hal defending his way of life and choice of companions. The Prince, who respects Hotspur for his courage and honour, finally proves himself a worthy son and a military hero when he kills Hotspur in single combat.

In *Part Two*, Prince Hal's life still moves between the world of the Tavern and the world of the court, but he shows a growing maturity, responding quickly to an urgent summons to Westminster to see his dying father, the King. Hal watches over his sleeping father, and believing him dead, tries on the crown and reflects on the heavy duty of kingship he must now face. When the King wakes, he misinterprets Hal's actions and reproaches him bitterly for his haste in snatching the crown. Hal explains his mistake and begs forgiveness. Hal is proclaimed KING HENRY V, and declares his intention to be a worthy King. Riding in state through Westminster, the new King passes Falstaff, but ignores him; he has renounced his former life and must now part company with his old companions. He grants Falstaff a pension but banishes him on pain of death.

Henry, Prince
A historical figure (1202-72) and a minor character in *King John*, Henry is the King's son who appears at the end of the play when his father is killed. He takes on the mantle of the next King of England (with the name Henry III) and is a symbol of a new order.

Henslowe, Philip (d. 1616)

An Elizabethan theatre impresario, Henslowe built and managed the ROSE and HOPE theatres and subsequently the FORTUNE theatre, which he built in 1600 in partnership with his son-in-law, the actor Edward ALLEYN. Henslowe kept detailed accounts and a diary, both of which have survived and from which theatre historians have been able to learn a great deal about the amounts of money that were paid to playwrights and actors and the expenses involved in mounting productions of plays.

The younger son of a gamekeeper, Henslowe seems to have had little formal education. He began his working life as an apprentice, probably to a dyer, and became involved in the manufacture of starch and in a pawnbroking business. Putting his business acumen to good use, Henslowe acquired a growing number of properties, including theatres, and also established a financial interest in bear-baiting with Alleyn. Around 1592, he was appointed to the royal household as GROOM OF THE CHAMBER. A hard-headed businessman who was ruthless in his financial dealings, Henslowe was not always on the best of terms with the actors and dramatists with whom he worked, as he was often so slow to pay them what he owed that he was once even accused, though never convicted, of embezzlement.

Heralds

Minor characters in *Coriolanus*, *King Henry V*, *King Henry VI, Parts One and Two*, *King Lear*, *King Richard II*, *Othello*, and *The Two Noble Kinsmen*; Heralds are court officials, who make formal proclamations of victories or losses in battle, summon nobles to parliament or officiate in contests of single combat such as the fight in *Richard II* between Bolingbroke and Mowbray.

Herbert, Sir Walter

A minor character in *King Richard III*, a nobleman who fights on Richmond's side at the Battle of Bosworth.

Herbert, William

See PEMBROKE, 3RD EARL OF.

Hereford, (Herford), Duke of

The title of Henry BOLINGBROKE, a historical figure and character in *King Richard II*.

Hermia

A character in *A Midsummer Night's dream*, Hermia is a strong-minded and independent young woman who is in love with Lysander. Her father Egeus is insisting that she marry Demetrius, the man he has chosen for her husband, but Hermia stubbornly refuses. Hermia and Lysander elope, but become lost in the woods outside Athens. They lie down to rest but when Hermia awakes, she finds that her lover has vanished. Unaware that Lysander has fallen a victim to Puck's magic, Hermia reacts violently when she discovers that he is now in love with her old friend Helena, who has followed her into the woods. Hermia is furious, but the next time she awakes from sleep, she is astonished to find that Lysander, again bewitched by Puck, has been restored to her. At the end of the play, Theseus overrules her father's wishes and Hermia and Lysander are married.

Hermia is described as being small, and the part may have been taken by the same boy actor who played Maria in *Twelfth Night*, who is also said to be small. Hermia is also described as being dark, and has been associated with the DARK LADY OF THE SONNETS by some scholars.

Hermione

A character in *The Winter's Tale*, the patient Hermione is King Leontes' wife. Leontes, seized by a sudden and irrational jealousy, accuses Hermione of having an affair with his old friend Polixenes. Wronged though she is, Hermione remains dignified in the face of Leonte's abuse of her, but she is thrown into prison where she gives birth to a daughter, Perdita, who is taken from her. When she hears of the death of her young son Mamillius, Hermione falls unconscious and is expected to die. However, she survives, and is cared for in secret for the next sixteen years by Paulina. In the final scene, Paulina engineers a dramatic reconciliation with Leontes in which Hermione appears as a statue which comes to life. Hermione's forgiveness of Leontes is central to the theme of redemption through love in the play.

Hero

A character in *Much Ado About Nothing*, Hero is Leonato's daughter and a conventional and charming beauty. At a celebration ball given by her father, Hero meets Claudio, a young soldier returned from the war, who is captivated by her. Hero and Claudio fall in love and arrangements are made for their wedding. Hero, happy in love herself and in high spirits, enjoys tricking her friend Beatrice into believing that Benedick loves her. Unknown to Hero, she is at the centre of a plot by the jealous Don John to convince Claudio that she is promiscuous. At her wedding, Claudio denounces her as unfaithful, and Hero faints. On the priest's advice, an announcement of her death from shame is given out, in the hope that remorse will rekindle Claudio's love for her. When her name is eventually cleared, Hero generously forgives Claudio, and they marry in the happy resolution to the play.

hero

The male PROTAGONIST or central character of a play around whom the plot develops. In Elizabethan plays, the hero is a highborn person, a king or nobleman (it was not until much later that playwrights took characters from a lower social class to be their heroes or heroines). Most of Shakespeare's heroes originated in the plots he borrowed from other writers, but he added new dimensions to the characters making them more complex and more recognizably human. In his tragedies, Shakespeare's heroes are brought down by a combination of a flawed nature (jealousy in Othello, ambition in Macbeth) and fate. Tragic heroes evolved from the heroes of Classical Greek drama, demi-gods whose moral frailty reduced them to the level of mortals.

heroine

The female PROTAGONIST or central character of a play. In Shakespeare's plays, the parts of the heroines were played by boys and this may have put limitations on what could be written for them, although it would certainly have made both more convincing and more piquant the plays in which girls pretend to be boys, such as *Twelfth Night*. Shakespearean heroines, who range from the fourteen-year-old Juliet to the mature queen Cleopatra, are notably independent and display a wide range of qualities; beauty and sensuality (CLEOPATRA), independence of thought and sharp intellect (PORTIA), spontaneity and wit (BEATRICE), evil (Lady MACBETH), innocence and gentleness (DESDEMONA). A number of Shakespeare's heroines are orphans and while several of them have relationships with fathers, only three of them have mothers, Juliet, and Perdita in *A Winter's Tale* and Marina in *Pericles* both of whom believe their mothers to be dead.

Minor female roles, whether friends, confidantes, maids, or tavern wenches, also generally appear as being more than mere ciphers or decorative characters. This may reflect the fact that in Shakespeare's time women from noble families were educated, and even women from humbler families enjoyed a greater degree of freedom than they were to possess centuries later in Victorian times. Maria in *Twelfth Night*, for example, is no aristocrat but she can read and write.

Hervey, William
See W H, MR.

Hippolyta[1]
A legendary figure and a minor character in *A Midsummer Night's Dream*, Hippolyta is the Queen of the Amazons who is soon to be married to Theseus. A dignified and gracious figure, she plays little part in the proceedings except to comment on the extraordinary events of the midsummer's night in the woods. She is coolly critical of the performance of *Pyramus and Thisbe* by Bottom and his troupe which is given to celebrate her wedding.

Hippolyta[2]
A character in *The Two Noble Kinsmen*, Hippolyta, is the same legendary figure as the Hippolyta in *A Midsummer Night's Dream* (*see above*). Her wedding to Duke Theseus of Athens is interrupted by the appearance of three tragic Queens who appeal to Theseus for help. Hippolyta listens sympathetically to their story and nobly insists that the wedding must be postponed so that Theseus can go to war on the Queens' behalf. Gracious, but a formal figure who says little, Hippolyta appears at the May Day games and the tournament held to determine which of the two noble kinsmen, Palamon or Arcite, will win her sister Emilia's hand.

hired man
See HIRELING.

hireling
A second-rank member of an Elizabethan theatre company; an actor, musician or stagehand, who was paid a wage, unlike the principal actors, who shared the profits of the company.

history plays
Dramas about historical events, including the CHRONICLE PLAYS which were so popular with Elizabethan audiences, Marlowe's *Edward II*, and Shakespeare's ten history plays (eleven if *KING EDWARD III* is included). *King Richard II*, *King Henry IV, Parts One and Two*, and *King Henry V* form Shakespeare's first historical tetralogy (series of four interconnected works). *King Henry VI, Parts One, Two and Three* and *King Richard III* form a second tetralogy and justify the position of Queen ELIZABETH I and the TUDOR dynasty on the throne of England.

Shakespeare's history plays, first categorized as such in the First FOLIO edition of 1623, generally recount the struggle for the English crown, and end with the establishment of a new political and social order. They reflected the patriotic zeal of the age, but they were also concerned with problems of kingship and statehood. In particular they confront the doctrine of the DIVINE RIGHT OF KINGS, a belief that Kings are the direct descendants of God, and as such are entitled to total obedience from their subjects. This belief poses a problem to those of the king's subjects who do not think a king is fit to rule because rebellion is a crime not only against the monarchy, but more seriously against God. Most of the history plays depict England's old enemies the French as arrogant, foolish and incompetent, and they are often comic figures. History plays were appreciated by contemporary audiences because they described events which were familiar to them, and which in some cases still shaped their lives. The plays are not strictly historically accurate; Shakespeare sometimes compresses time and even changes the order of events for his dramatic purposes, often expressing what the playwright thought the current reigning monarch (Queen Elizabeth I and later James I) would like to hear rather than the truth. His portrait of RICHARD III as a monster of evil, for example, is undoubtedly biased. Such a bias may also owe something to the fact that Shakespeare and his contemporaries had very limited factual source material to work from apart from the writing of the 16th-century historian Edward HALLE and HOLINSHED'S *Chronicles*.

Holinshed's *Chronicles*
The Chronicles of England, Scotlande, and Irelande, by the English historian Raphael Holinshed (c. 1529-c. 1580) in collaboration with other historians, were written in 1577, when Shakespeare was probably at school. The *Chronicles* recorded episodes and aspects of British history, and Shakespeare drew on them as source material for nearly all his HISTORY PLAYS, as well as for *Cymbeline*, *King Lear* and *Macbeth*. *See also* EDWARD HALLE.

Holland, John
A minor character in *King Henry VI, Part Two*, Holland is one of the rebel Jack Cade's followers. The name 'John Holland' belonged to an actor of Shakespeare's time, and it is believed that he played the part of an otherwise unnamed character.

Holofernes
A comic character in *Love's Labour's Lost*, Holofernes is a pompous schoolmaster and an intellectual snob who scatters his speeches with Latin quotes and classical allusions. The tortuous and pedantic style of his speech, particularly when he is talking to the equally pedantic Nathaniel, make him almost incomprehensible. Holofernes is in charge of arranging an entertainment for the court, and he decides to put on a MASQUE celebrating the lives of the Nine Worthies, notable historic figures, for the King. He takes several of the parts himself, but he is heckled and jeered at by his audience and retires from the stage reproaching them for their bad manners.

Hope Theatre, the
An Elizabethan PLAYHOUSE built on Bankside in London in 1613 on the site of the Bear Garden, and managed by Philip HENSLOWE. Its stage was constructed so that it could be removed to accommodate the regular displays of bear-baiting and cock-fighting that

were held there, and it was said that there was a permanently unpleasant smell of
animals in the theatre. The Hope was demolished in 1656.

Horatio
A character in *Hamlet*, Horatio is a student friend of Hamlet, and the only person in whom
the troubled Prince confides. Horatio is present when the Ghost of Hamlet's Father
appears to his son on the castle battlements. Horatio fears there is something sinister about
the apparition and tries to persuade Hamlet from following the ghost. Hamlet makes him
swear to remain silent about what he has seen, but tells Horatio about his intention to feign
madness, and later, of his intention to test Claudius's guilt with the play about the murder
of a king. Horatio exercises a calming influence over Hamlet, who admires his friend for
not being someone who is a slave to his emotions. Hamlet dies in his arms and Horatio
promises to tell the world the truth of Hamlet's story.

Horner, Thomas
A minor character in *King Henry VI, Part Two*, Horner is a maker of armour. He is
accused by his apprentice, Peter, of saying that the Duke of York, one of his customers,
was the rightful heir to the throne, rather than King Henry. Horner denies the charge but
beaten in combat by Peter, he admits his guilt as he lies dying.

Hortensio
A character in *The Taming of the Shrew*, Hortensio is a harmless young gentleman of
Padua who is in love with Bianca. Bianca's father, Baptista Minola, insists that she
remains single and shut away at home with only teachers for company until Katherina is
married. In order to be near to Bianca, Hortensio disguises himself as a music teacher
called LITIO and joins the Minola household. His first task is to teach Katherina the lute,
but she responds to his teaching by breaking the instrument over his head; Hortensio's
nerves, like the lute, are shattered by this experience. Under the guise of the teacher,
Hortensio continues to woo Bianca, but seeing that she is enamoured of Lucentio, he
decides in the end to bow out and to marry a wealthy widow who has been showing
interest in him. He asks Petruchio for hints on how he should tame his widow who turns
out to be nearly as shrewish as Katherina.

Hortensius
A minor character in *Timon of Athens*, Hortensius is a servant to one of the creditors.
He calls on Timon to collect the money that is due to his master, but his heart is not in
his work because he strongly disapproves of his master's ingratitude. In any event, he
does not think that the creditors have any hope of being repaid because Timon is a
madman.

Host of the Garter Inn
A minor comic character in *The Merry Wives of Windsor*, the Host (he is given no
name) is the Landlord of the Garter Inn and Bardolph's employer; a hearty character, he
has a habit of calling everyone 'Bully' as a term of affection. He encourages the two
eccentric foreigners, Dr Caius and Evans, to fight a duel, but then urges them to make
up. Caius and Evans feel they have been made fools of and are revenged on the Host by
taking his horses, pretending that three mysterious Germans were the thieves. The Host
is downcast at his loss, but cheered when Fenton, whom the Host helps to elope with
Anne Page, offers him compensation in cash.

Host
A minor character in *The Two Gentlemen of Verona*, the jovial Host befriends the disguised Julia in her lodgings.

Hostess or Hostess Quickly
A character in *King Henry IV, Parts One and Two* and *King Henry V*; *see* QUICKLY, HOSTESS.

Hostess
A Character in *The Taming of the Shrew* who appears in the INDUCTION to the play. The Hostess is the landlady at the tavern where Christopher Sly has been drinking so heavily that he later falls in a drunken stupor. She is angry with him because he has not paid her for some glasses he has broken.

Hostilius
A minor character in *Timon of Athens*, Hostilius is visiting Athens in the company of two strangers, when he sees Timon's servant asking LUCIUS to lend his master money. *See* STRANGERS.

Hotspur, Henry Percy
A historical figure (1364-1403) and a character in *King Henry IV, Part One* and *King Richard II*, Hotspur is the Earl of Northumberland's son and a member of the Percy family from the North of England. In *Richard II*, a play that recounts events that occurred before those in the *Henry IV plays*, Hotspur is a minor character who is known as HARRY PERCY. Like his father, Henry Percy the Earl of Northumberland, Harry Percy is a supporter of Bolingbroke and his rebellion against King Richard.

 In *Henry IV*, Young Hotspur (as his name implies) is a man of action, hot-headed, energetic and courageous, who is contrasted with Prince Hal whose life is (temporarily) one of indulgence and idleness. At first, Hotspur fights for the King against rebels in Scotland, but when King Henry refuses to ransom a member of the Percy family, Hotspur and his father turn against him. Hotspur's appetite for military action is so keen that Lady Percy observes he even fights battles in his sleep. His daredevil nature is eventually his undoing. Although his forces are outnumbered by the King's at the crucial battle of Shrewsbury, Hotspur regards the disadvantage as an exciting challenge to be overcome and insists on fighting. The rebels are defeated and Hotspur is killed by Prince Henry.

housekeepers
Owners, or part owners, of Elizabethan PLAYHOUSES, who were in some cases actors, and who were responsible for the upkeep of the buildings and received half the takings. *Compare* SHARERS.

Hubert
A character in *King John*, Hubert is a supporter of King John. He first appears as a representative of the people of Angers trying to persuade the French and English Kings not to make war. When, despite his best efforts, war breaks out and the young Arthur, King John's rival, is captured in battle, Hubert is instructed by the King to take Arthur prisoner and to kill him. Hubert is touched by the boy's courage and innocence, and instead of killing him, he responds to the boy's pleas for mercy and lets him live,

although he pretends to John that Arthur is dead. When the nobles react angrily to news of Arthur's death, Hubert tells John that Arthur is really alive, although unknown to him Arthur has actually died attempting to escape from his prison.

humanism

An intellectual movement that placed man, and the importance of individuals, at the centre of ideas, rather than God or religion. Humanism developed during the reign of Henry VIII among certain scholars (the Oxford Reformers), and the Dutch thinker and writer Erasmus (1466-1536) who for a time was a professor of Divinity and Greek at Cambridge University in England. Humanism was concerned with a revival of Classical learning, and with a move away from medieval thinking, which viewed man as fundamentally sinful and corrupt. Hamlet's speech 'What a piece of work is man!' is sometimes thought to exemplify the view of Elizabethan humanism.

Hume, John

A minor character in *King Henry VI, Part Two*, Hume is a double-dealing and greedy priest who is bribed by the promise of a knighthood from the Duke of Suffolk to spy on the Duke of Gloucester's wife Eleanor. At the same time, he takes money from Eleanor to provide magicians and a witch to predict the future for her.

Humphrey

The first name of the character the Duke of GLOUCESTER in *King Henry VI, Part Two*.

Hundred Years War

A conflict between England and France which raged between 1337 and 1453. The background to the war was a claim made by the PLANTAGENET King of England, Edward III, to the French crown. Edward declared war on France in 1337, and captured large tracts of land. Intermittent fighting continued with further English victories at Crecy (1346), Calais (1347), and Poitiers (1356). By the end of the century the tide of the war was turning in favour of the French, and in 1396 RICHARD II negotiated a peace treaty with France. In 1414, war erupted again when HENRY V led English forces in an invasion of France, winning a famous victory at AGINCOURT. When Henry died in 1422, the French rallied, inspired by Joan of Arc (Joan LA PUCELLE), and the English were driven from French soil. The Hundred Years War forms part of the background to *King Henry IV, Part One*, *Henry V* and *Henry VI, Parts One, Two and Three*.

Hunsdon, Henry Carey, 1st Lord (1524-96)

A first cousin to Queen Elizabeth I, Lord Hunsdon was made LORD CHAMBERLAIN in 1585. He became patron of the company of actors, STRANGE'S MEN, when Lord Strange died, and the company was briefly known as HUNSDONS'S MEN before being renamed the LORD CHAMBERLAIN'S MEN. When he died, his son George Carey, 2nd Lord Hunsdon, succeeded him as Lord Chamberlain and took over patronage of the players, until King James I assumed their patronage, renaming them the KING'S MEN.

Huntingdon, Earl of

A minor character in *King Henry V*, Huntingdon is mentioned in the cast list, and appears in one scene with the King, but the role is a silent one.

Huntsmen
Minor characters who appear in the INDUCTION to *The Taming of the Shrew*, the Huntsmen are members of the Lord's hunting party who discuss the good qualities of his various dogs.

Hymen
A minor character in *The Two Noble Kinsmen*, Hymen appears in the wedding procession that opens the play, carrying a burning torch. Hymen was the Roman god of marriage.

hyperbole
Exaggerated or overstated style or language. An example is the way in which the foppish character Osric speaks in *Hamlet*. He describes Laertes, a very ordinary young man, in high-flown fashion as: 'an absolute gentleman, full of most excellent differences, of very soft society and great showing ... the card or calendar of gentry ... the continent of what part a gentleman would see'.

Ii

Iachimo
A character in *Cymbeline*, Iachimo is an acquaintance Posthumus makes when he is banished to Italy. Posthumus, boasting of his wife Imogen's chastity, rashly bets the cynical Iachimo that he would never be able to seduce her. Iachimo sets out to prove Posthumus, wrong but when Imogen fails to succumb, he resorts to trickery. Iachimo is more rogue than villain, although his deception has serious consequences. He hides in Imogen's bedroom and steals a bracelet from her arm as she lies sleeping. Armed with this apparent proof of her infidelity, he returns to Italy triumphant and wins the bet, breaking Posthumus' heart. Iachimo commands the Roman army that later invades Britain. He is defeated by Posthumus in battle and taken prisoner. In the play's happy resolution, Posthumus forgives Iachimo.

Iago
A central character in *Othello*, Iago is a soldier who has been overlooked for advancement in the army, and who is jealous both of his rival for promotion, Cassio, and of his commander Othello. He plots to ruin them both. Smooth-tongued and ingenious, Iago confides in the audience from the outset, boasting of his villainy which he seems to enjoy for its own sake. The other characters, however, believe Iago is the honest friend he claims to be. His first move is to ply the trusting Cassio with far too much wine, exploiting Cassio's weakness for drink in order to disgrace him. He then convinces Othello that Cassio and Desdemona (Othello's wife) are having an affair. He exercises such a powerful influence over the gullible Othello that he needs only to provide the flimsiest of false evidence - a handkerchief - to persuade Othello of Desdemona's guilt. Iago is finally unmasked, but too late to prevent Desdemona and Othello's tragic deaths.

iamb
A metrical FOOT consisting of a short unstressed syllable followed by a stressed one, as in the word 'Macbeth'.

iambic pentameter
A regular pattern of alternating stressed and unstressed syllables (*see* STRESS) in a metric line of verse, in which there are five feet (*see* FOOT). Iambic pentameter resembles the rhythms of normal English speech and its flexibility makes it a particularly suitable medium for dramatic verse. BLANK verse is written in this form. For example: 'If music be the food of love, play on'.

Iden, Alexander
A minor character in *King Henry VI, Part Two*, Iden is a patriotic Kentish landowner who discovers Jack Cade hiding in his garden. Iden recognizes Cade as the rebel leader,

kills him and presents the King with his severed head. He is rewarded with a knighthood.

imagery
Language in which images, or word pictures, are used to create a particular mood or to evoke a particular response. Thematic imagery refers to images that recur throughout a work in a way that reinforces its meaning. An example is the repeated reference to disease and decay in *Hamlet*, which conveys a sense of the corruption pervading the Danish court; or the frequent mentions of darkness and disease in *Macbeth*, a play about ambition and evil.

Imogen
The heroine of *Cymbeline*, Imogen is Cymbeline's daughter. She has married Posthumus against her father's wishes and when he is banished Imogen is grief-stricken. The Queen, her step-mother, would like her loathsome son, Cloten, to marry Imogen but Imogen recoils from his advances and remains utterly loyal to Posthumus. Quite unnecessarily, Posthumus puts Imogen's fidelity to the test, and believing a false report that she has been unfaithful, he plots to kill her. Imogen flees to safety in Wales disguised as a boy 'Fidele', but never loses faith in a husband whom she knows intends to kill her. Brave and resourceful, she survives as best she can, cared for briefly by two young men whom she does not realize are her brothers. She is pursued by Cloten, wrongly led to believe that Posthumus has been killed, and is finally taken prisoner by the Romans when they invade Britain. In the fairy tale end to the play, she is reunited with Posthumus and reconciled with her father.

impersonation
Imitating, or pretending to be, another person. Elizabethan dramatic conventions allowed one character to impersonate another, sometimes wearing a disguise, and often with comic effect. For example, Feste impersonates a priest in order to deceive Malvolio in *Twelfth Night*. Impersonation may give rise to DRAMATIC IRONY. Compare ROLE REVERSAL.

improvisation
Unrehearsed or impromptu acting without a script. Actors, particularly comic actors such as Will KEMP, in Shakespeare's time were expected to be able to improvise or EXTEMPORIZE.

induction
An introductory scene or PROLOGUE that usually takes the form of a dialogue rather than a MONOLOGUE. There is an induction at the beginning of *The Taming of the Shrew*.

inn-yards
In Shakespeare's time, when professional COMPANIES OF ACTORS first began to band together, many players put on plays at inns where they were guaranteed both accommodation and a captive audience. Performances took place in daylight on staging made from trestles while the audience looked on from windows and galleries surrounding the inn-yard. These ready-made theatres often became semi-permanent and a symbiotic relationship grew up between players and inn-keepers who profited from the extra trade drawn to their hostelries by the drama. An act of 1600 prohibited

performances in inns but by that time the first purpose-built theatres, such as the THEATRE and the Fortune theatre had appeared in London. The design of these early theatres owed much to the open-air layout of an inn courtyard, with the stage surrounded on three sides by galleries where the audience sat. *See* PLAYHOUSES.

inner reality
The thought processes that a character may sometimes disclose to the audience, in an ASIDE or SOLILOQUY, but which are not necessarily evident from his or her behaviour on stage.

inner stage
A small, recessed area at the rear of the stage which theatre historians believe may have existed in Elizabethan PLAYHOUSES. It was probably divided from the main stage by a curtain, and would have been used to represent a tomb, an inner chamber, or a tent on a battlefield for example.

Inns of Court
There are four Inns of Court in present-day London; Gray's Inn, the Middle Temple, the Inner Temple and Lincoln's Inn, and they are a kind of university for law students. They date back to the early 14th century, when they were built to house the young men who came to London to learn law. By the 15th century, students at the Inns of Court also learned dancing and music so that, as the name suggests, they would know how behave at court. Later, the Inns became famous for their elaborate MASQUES and plays. Shakespeare's *The Comedy of Errors* was performed in Gray's Inn in 1594 and *Twelfth Night* played at the Middle Temple in 1602.

interlude
From the 14th to the 16th centuries, an interlude was a kind of short, secular, and often comic play, which, as its name suggests, was performed during an interlude in another entertainment, or at a banquet. Many noblemen retained interlude players as part of their households. King HENRY VIII had a company of eight who used to travel to other houses and town halls around the country to perform. Queen Elizabeth I also had eight interlude players in her royal household, but she had a preference for longer plays, rather than interludes, performed by adult or BOY COMPANIES of players.

The performance of *Pyramus and Thisbe* by the Athenian workmen in *A Midsummer Night's Dream*, during the wedding feast of Duke Theseus, is an example of an interlude.

internal rhyme
See RHYME.

Iras
A character in *Antony and Cleopatra*, Iras is one of Cleopatra's attendants and a good-humoured young woman who jokes with her mistress. Iras vows that Cleopatra will never be taken prisoner by the Romans and helps her mistress prepare for her suicide. She dies alongside Cleopatra in the monument.

Iris
Iris is one of the deities appearing in the MASQUE performed for Miranda and Ferdinand in *The Tempest. See* SPIRITS.

irony
A form of expression, often humorous, in which you say the opposite of what you really mean. A *situation* is ironic when it represents the opposite of what you might expect: for example, the irony in *Othello* is that Othello places his trust in Iago, the very man who is plotting his downfall. *See* DRAMATIC IRONY; TRAGIC IRONY.

Irving, Sir Henry (1838–1905)
The stage name of John Henry Brodribb, actor and manager of the Lyceum theatre in London, Irving was regarded as the greatest actor of his time, although he was sometimes accused of overacting by contemporary critics. Irving was noted for his spectacular staging of Shakespeare's plays, in particular for a revival of *Hamlet* in 1874 and a production of *Romeo and Juliet* in 1882 in which he took the leading role with Ellen TERRY as his leading lady. He was the first member of his profession to be rewarded with a knighthood.

Isabel, Queen to King Richard
A minor character in *King Richard II, see* QUEEN.

Isabel, Queen of France
A historical figure (1370-1435) and a minor character in *King Henry V*, Queen Isabel is the wife of King Charles VI of France and Princess Katherine's mother. She is present when peace is made between France and England and gives her blessing to the marriage of Katherine and King Henry.

Isabella
The heroine of *Measure for Measure*, Isabella is Claudio's sister, who is about to enter a convent. She is a serious young woman and her vocation is so strong that she is critical of the convent for not having stricter rules. When Claudio is sentenced to death, Isabella reluctantly leaves the convent to plead with Angelo for mercy. She is appalled when Angelo says he will free Claudio only if she sleeps with him. Isabella, who is about to take her vow of chastity, resolutely refuses, prizing her virginity more highly than her brother's life. Her refusal reveals that she shares certain 'qualities' with Angelo: inflexibility and cold-bloodedness. The plan to substitute Mariana for Isabella in Angelo's bed, enables Claudio's life to be saved without the sacrifice of Isabella's virginity. In the final reconciliation, she begs the Duke to spare Angelo's life. Isabella seems to have learned something of love and she is now ready to embrace life as the Duke's wife.

Isle of Dogs, The
A satirical play by Thomas NASHE, which may have been written in collaboration with Ben JONSON among others; it was performed by PEMBROKE'S MEN in 1597 at the SWAN Theatre. The play which was critical of state and government was swiftly taken off, and the theatre was closed as the CITY FATHERS feared it might provoke the audience to riot. The play has since been lost.

Jj

Jacobean Drama
Drama written during the reign of James I (1603-1625) that was often characterized by violence and improbable plots. Shakespeare's later plays, which are not typical of the period, date from this time, and include four of his great tragedies; *Antony and Cleopatra*, *King Lear*, *Macbeth* and *Othello*. Major Jacobean playwrights include Francis BEAUMONT who collaborated with John FLETCHER on several plays, Thomas DEKKER, John FORD, Philip MASSINGER, and John WEBSTER.

Jaggard, William and Isaac
Printers in London in Shakespeare's time who published an edition of the *Passionate Pilgrim* (a collection of poems by various poets that Jaggard claimed had been written by Shakespeare) in 1599, and QUARTO editions of some of Shakespeare's plays in 1619, as well as the First FOLIO edition of 1623.

Jailer
A minor character in *The Two Noble Kinsmen*, the Jailer is instructed by Duke Theseus to give the best possible care to his prisoners of war, Palamon and Arcite. The Jailer is a kindly man, but he is unaware that his Daughter adores Palamon and has helped his prisoner escape. He only learns that his Daughter has gone mad with grief when the Wooer tells him, but he calls in the Doctor to effect a cure.

James I (1566–1625)
King of England during the last years of Shakespeare's life from 1603, James was the son of Mary Queen of Scots. He succeeded his distant cousin Queen Elizabeth I because she had failed to marry and provide an heir to the English throne. Already crowned as James VI of Scotland, his rule in England brought political union between the two countries. He was a highly educated man, but his ignorance of English customs and politics made him unpopular. In 1605, there was an abortive attempt by English Roman Catholics to blow up the Houses of Parliament by, among others, Guy Fawkes and Robert Catesby who came from Stratford-on-Avon.

Both James and his wife Queen Anne were even greater enthusiasts for the theatre than Queen Elizabeth had been, and he took over patronage of the LORD CHAMBERLAIN'S MEN, which thereafter was known as the KING'S MEN. Shakespeare and his fellow SHARERS in the company formed part of James's coronation procession in 1605 in their official capacity as GROOMS OF THE CHAMBER. It is probable that *Macbeth* was written to please James who had an intense interest in witchcraft; he wrote a study of it, *Daemonologie*, in 1597 that was an extreme condemnation of its practices.

Jamy, Captain
A minor character in *King Henry V*, Jamy is an officer in the King's army fighting in France. He is a Scotsman with a strong Scottish accent whose courage is admired by the Welsh Captain Fluellen.

Jaquenetta

A minor character in *Love's Labour's Lost*, Jaquenetta is a simple country girl. Costard has a soft spot for Jaquenetta, but Armado adores her. Armado writes her a love letter but it is wrongly delivered by Costard, and Jaquenetta receives a letter written by the supposedly celibate Berowne to Rosaline instead. Jaquenetta, who cannot read, asks Nathaniel to read it aloud to her. She is an honest girl, and when she discovers the mistake, she believes it is her duty to hand Berowne's letter to the King. As a result, Berowne has to admit that he has broken his vow to renounce women. At the end of the play, Costard announces that Jaquenetta is pregnant by Armado, who promises to marry her.

Jaques

A character in *As You Like It* (not to be confused with Jaques de Boys below), Jaques (pronounced 'Jaykweez') is a nobleman and a member of the banished Duke Senior's entourage. Jaques likens life to a drama being acted out, with people playing their parts like actors on a stage; he has assigned himself the role of a melancholic observer. He is a wit and a cynic, with a gloomy view of the world, and says he would like to wear 'motley', the multi-coloured dress of a FOOL, so that, like the fool, he could mock the human predicament. Jaques remains aloof from the central action, but he enjoys joining in a song and is happy to be part of a social occasion, so long as it does not involve dancing which he finds a bore. He has a tender streak, and seeing a wounded deer in the Forest of ARDEN, he tearfully reflects on the deer's plight. When Jaques hears that Duke Frederick has reformed, he decides to join him in a life of religious contemplation, and bids his old companions a fond farewell.

Jaques (Jacques) de Boys

A minor character in *As You Like it*, Jaques is Orlando and Oliver's brother. His name may have been pronounced 'Jakes', and should not be confused with the other Jaques (see above) in the play whose name is pronounced differently. Jaques de Boys is mentioned by Orlando as being a student at university at the beginning of the play, but he does not appear until the end. When he does, Jaques brings news of the black-hearted Duke Frederick's conversion to a life of religious devotion.

Jessica

A character in *The Merchant of Venice*, Jessica is the miserly Shylock's romantic young daughter. She is in love with Lorenzo and they plan to marry but Lorenzo is a Christian, and Shylock is a possessive Jewish father, so Jessica elopes with her lover to Portia's house at Belmont under cover of darkness, dressed as a boy. She takes with her money and jewels belonging to Shylock, including a ring his wife had given him, adding insult to injury. Shylock rages against the loss of his daughter, as well as the loss of his money, and her elopement fuels feelings of paranoia. When she marries Lorenzo, Jessica casts off her Jewish heritage and becomes a Christian.

jester

A professional entertainer, originally a minstrel, the jester probably existed in England as far back as Saxon times. The jester's role was that of clown or court fool, who kept the king and his courtiers amused with his antics. The character of the FOOL in Shakespeare's plays derives from the jester.

Jews

Jewish people first came to England in 1066 and many settled there. Because English Christians believed that the Jews had murdered Jesus Christ, there were frequent clashes between Jews and Christians during the following two hundred years. In 1144, riots broke out in the city of Norwich when Jews were accused of cannibalizing a Christian boy at their Passover. At the coronation of King Richard I of England in 1189, a deputation of Jews was attacked, and a rumour that the King had ordered a general massacre of the Jews caused hundreds of deaths. In 1217, Jewish people were made to wear distinctive yellow badges, and Jewish rights were gradually restricted. In 1290 Jews were expelled from England; those who remained were required by law to observe Christian practices, at least outwardly. In 1655, some 40 years after Shakespeare's death, Jews were readmitted to England. See also ANTI-SEMITISM, MERCHANT OF VENICE and SHYLOCK.

jig

A jig was a kind of crude entertainment of music and dance which was often performed at the end of a play in Shakespeare's time. The name derives from the old French word 'gigue', meaning a violin, which came to be used to describe a particular kind of lively dance. See also PLAY PRODUCTION AND PERFORMANCE

Joan of Arc

See JOAN LA PUCELLE *below.*

Joan La Pucelle

A historical figure (c. 1412-1431) and a character in *King Henry VI, Part One*, Joan La Pucelle is JOAN OF ARC, the Maid of Orleans who is sometimes called Joan of Aire. The Joan of history was a saintly figure who believed she heard voices from God advising her. She inspired the French forces and led them to a notable victory at Orleans. When she was captured by the English, she was tried for heresy, convicted and burned at the stake.

  The Joan of Shakespeare's play was mostly drawn from HOLINSHED'S *Chronicles* which were written with an anti-French bias. While the character of Talbot in the play represents all that is good about England, Joan represents all that is bad about the French. A charismatic leader who inspires the French, Joan persuades King Charles of her miraculous powers, overcoming him in single combat, and eloquently wins the Duke of Burgundy over to the French cause. However, more sinisterly she is accused of witchcraft and conjures up hellish Fiends with whom she tries to make a pact. When Joan is captured by the English she tries to escape death by pretending to be of royal blood and disowns her shepherd father. When that ruse fails, she declares she is pregnant, although still maintaining to be a virgin, and she names various fathers. Finally Joan is led off to be burned at the stake cursing England.

John

A minor character in *The Merry Wives of Windsor*, John is one of Mistress Ford's servants. Together with his fellow servant Robert, John is instructed by Mistress Ford to carry out Falstaff in a basket of dirty washing and dump him and it in a muddy ditch as part of the merry wives' trick on Falstaff.

John, Don
A character in *Much Ado About Nothing*; *see* DON JOHN.

John, Friar
A minor character in *Romeo and Juliet*, Friar John is the messenger who is unable to deliver Friar Lawrence's crucial letter to Romeo explaining about Juliet's feigned death because he is quarantined during an outbreak of PLAGUE.

John, King of England (1167–1216)
Historical Figure. King of England from 1199 to 1216, John was also known as John Lackland. He tried to seize the crown while his brother Richard I Lionheart was still King but being held captive in Germany (1193-94). Richard forgave John and even nominated him as his successor, in preference to Arthur who as the son of John's elder brother was the rightful heir to the throne. Arthur made an attempt to snatch the crown from John with the support of the French king, but was captured, and John had Arthur murdered in 1203. An unpopular monarch, John imposed exceptionally heavy taxes on his subjects. This policy, together with the fact that he lost most of the land in France (hence the name 'Lackland') which had been so hard won by Richard I before him, caused the powerful English nobles to rise up against him. As a result John was forced to sign the Magna Carta in 1215 which guaranteed constitutional reform and certain freedoms for individuals; it limited the King's rights to tax his subjects and reaffirmed the rights of the Church. John is portrayed unflatteringly in Shakespeare's *King John*.

John, King
Title character. A historical figure (1167-1216) (see above), and the title character of Shakespeare's play *King John*. John has inherited the crown from his brother the heroic Richard I Coeur de Lion [Lionheart] whose young nephew, Arthur, also has a claim to be King. John is an inadequate king. He angers his already resentful nobles by weakly agreeing to a peace treaty with an old enemy, France, in which territory won earlier by England was returned to the French. The fragile peace is shattered because the Pope, angered by John, demands that France resumes war with England. Because the French support Arthur's cause, John arranges for Arthur to be murdered. The consequences are disastrous; his nobles turn against him and join forces with the French invading England. The English army eventually triumphs but John's position is fundamentally weakened. In a fittingly unheroic death, John is poisoned.

John, Prince; Lord of Lancaster and later Duke of Bedford
A historical figure (1389-1435) and a character in *King Henry IV, Parts One and Two*. (The same person also appears in *King Henry V* and *King Henry VI, Part One* where he is known as the Duke of BEDFORD.) John is King Henry IV's son.

In *Henry IV, Part One* John is referred to as LANCASTER and his role is a very minor one; he appears in a battle at the end of the play and is praised by his elder brother, Prince Hal, for his courage. In *Part Two*, he appears in the cast list as PRINCE JOHN OF LANCASTER. Lancaster promises that the rebels' grievances will be listened to sympathetically by the king and negotiates a peace with them in which he demands that the rebel armies disband. When the rebel leaders are disarmed, Lancaster betrays them; they are arrested and sentenced to death. Lancaster, who is described by Falstaff as sober and humourless is the exact opposite of his wilder elder brother Prince Hal.

Johnson, Dr Samuel (1709–84)
An English writer and literary critic, Dr Johnson was the author of the *Dictionary of the English Language* (1755), the first of its kind. His celebrated *Prefaces to Shakespeare* were published ten years later. In the Prefaces, he praised Shakespeare for not adhering slavishly to the three UNITIES of time, place and action and for mixing comedy with tragedy. Although he criticized what he saw as Shakespeare's lack of moral purpose, he described him as 'a poet who holds up to his readers a faithful mirror of manners and of life' and applauded Shakespeare for creating characters who were true to life.

Jones, Inigo (1573–1652)
A foremost English architect, Inigo Jones also worked closely with Ben JONSON as a stage designer of the elaborate scenery used in the staging of Jonson's MASQUES. A discovery in 1999 of two short plays, or masques, written by Jones in collaboration with Jonson, revealed that he was also a dramatist. The masques entitled *The Fortunate Isles* and *Loves Triumph Through Callipolis* were performed at court in 1626 and 1630. They were discovered at Wilton House, near Salisbury in Wiltshire, where Inigo Jones worked for some time designing a new building. Companies of players regularly visited the house to perform and Shakespeare almost certainly was a visitor there.

Jonson, Ben (1572–1637)
Poet, essayist and prolific dramatist, Jonson received a good education but began his working life as apprentice to a bricklayer and subsequently enlisted with the English army fighting in Flanders. On his return from the continent, he probably became an actor with PEMBROKE'S MEN and began writing plays for them including *Every Man in his Humour* (1598), a comedy in which Shakespeare himself acted. He is best remembered for his later satires, *Volpone* (1606) and *The Alchemist* (1610). Jonson also wrote numerous masques and poems and a tribute to Shakespeare entitled 'To The Memory of My Beloved Master, Mr William Shakespeare, and what He Hath Left Us' (1623). Reputedly a generous if quarrelsome man and a friend of Shakespeare's who was godfather to one of his children, Jonson is said to have joined with Shakespeare and DRAYTON in a drinking bout that supposedly brought on Shakespeare's fatal fever. Jonson is buried in Westminster Abbey in London where his tomb bears the inscription 'O Rare Ben Jonson'.

Joseph
A minor character in *The Taming of the Shrew*, Joseph is one of Petruchio's five servants. *See* SERVANTS AND SERVINGMEN.

Jourdain, Margery
A minor character in *King Henry VI, Part Two*, Margery is a witch hired to summon up the spirit ASNATH for the Duchess of York to question about her future. Margery is arrested with the Duchess and is sentenced to be burned at the stake.

Julia
The heroine of *The Two Gentlemen of Verona*; Julia is loved by Proteus. She pretends to be indifferent to his advances and tears up a love-letter from him, but later she retrieves the torn fragments so she can read it. When Proteus leaves for Milan, Julia rather awkwardly bids him farewell but they exchange rings, and it dawns on her how much she loves Proteus. She decides to follow him secretly but when she catches up with him,

she finds that he has fallen in love with Silvia. Julia, however, remains true to Proteus. Unrecognizable in male disguise as 'Sebastian', she enters Proteus' service as his page and is put in the difficult position of acting as his messenger to Silvia. She follows Proteus in his bid to rescue Silvia from the Outlaws, and when it looks as if she is finally going to lose Proteus, Julia, ever resourceful, stages a faint and cleverly diverts attention from Silvia. When she recovers, she reveals her identity and Proteus realizes that he has really loved her all the time.

Juliet (Julietta)

A character in *Measure for Measure*, Juliet is engaged to be married to Claudio and is pregnant by him when he is arrested for the crime of sleeping with her. About to give birth, she learns of Claudio's imminent execution with horror, and makes a confession to the Duke (in his guise as a friar) and asks for forgiveness. In the reconciliation a the end of the play, Juliet and Claudio are happily reunited.

Juliet

The tragic heroine of *Romeo and Juliet*, Juliet is a member of the Capulet family who has been brought up almost entirely by her Nurse. At fourteen, her parents think she is old enough for marriage and have decided on a husband for her. When Juliet meets Romeo at the ball, she spars wittily with him and he is charmed by her beauty and spontaneity. Romeo and Juliet fall in love, and marry in secret but when Romeo is banished to Mantua, her father, unaware that she is already a wife, arranges for her to marry Paris. Juliet grows from an impetuous girl to resourceful young woman. She defies her father, but with no one to turn to she has to resort to the one weapon at her disposal, deception. She bravely overcomes her terror at spending the night alone in the family tomb and waits for Romeo. Tragically, her premonition that her grave will be her wedding bed is proved to be true. When Romeo arrives at the tomb to find his young wife unconscious and apparently dead, he kills himself. Juliet, expecting to be joyfully reunited with Romeo, wakes to find her husband's body beside her, and, in turn, kills herself, preferring to embrace death rather than a life without Romeo.

Julius Caesar (c. 102–44 BC)

Historical Figure. Julius Caesar was a great soldier and politician. Together with Pompey the Great and Crassus, Caesar formed the first triumvirate [rule of three] to govern the Roman Empire in 60 BC. In 58 BC Caesar invaded Gaul [ancient France] and in 55 BC he invaded Britain. The triumvirate began to collapse when Crassus was killed and both Pompey and Caesar refused to share power. Caesar went to war with Pompey and defeated him in Egypt, where Pompey was later murdered. Caesar remained in Egypt for a while and had an affair with CLEOPATRA who bore him a son. After defeating Pompey's two sons, Caesar returned to Rome where he held absolute power. Although he was undoubtedly a tyrant, Caesar was popular with the people of Rome. The ruling class, however, became increasingly concerned that he had ambitions for greater power. The prime movers in a conspiracy against Caesar were Brutus and Cassius who, together with others, assassinated Caesar who died at the foot of Pompey's statue in the Capitol on the Ides [15th] of March.

Julius Caesar

Title Character. A historical figure (See above) and the title character of *Julius Caesar*, Caesar is married to Calphurnia. He has ruled over the vast Roman Empire as one of a triumvirate [rule of three] but following his defeat of fellow-triumvir, Pompey, Caesar has assumed absolute power. While Caesar is popular with the ordinary people of Rome, some members of Rome's ruling council, the Senate, are increasingly concerned about his tyranny, and fear that he will agree to be made king. Caesar is an epileptic and deaf in one ear, and he seems to be deaf to the criticisms of his senators. He is certainly deaf to the warnings of the Soothsayer who tells him to beware the 'Ides of March', and to his wife who begs him to stay at home that day. Caesar is determined to go to the Capitol where he is assassinated. Although Caesar dies in the middle of the play, his influence is felt right through to the end and his ghost visits Brutus before the battle at Philippi.

Julius Caesar

One of Shakespeare's ROMAN PLAYS, *Julius Caesar* is a TRAGEDY which was probably written around 1599 and may have been the first play performed at the newly built GLOBE THEATRE in that year. It was first published in the First FOLIO of 1623.

The main source of the play was a 16th-century translation into English of *Lives of the Greeks and Romans* by PLUTARCH. The play is a fast-moving political drama. It is full of conflict and superstition and apart from two minor parts, the cast is entirely male. Set in Ancient Rome in 44 BC, it examines the central dilemma of Shakespeare's HISTORY plays which is the consequence of deposing a national leader.

SYNOPSIS : Caesar is on the way to the games held to celebrate a military triumph, when he is stopped by a Soothsayer who warns him to beware of a particular day, the Ides of March (15th March). Although Caesar is popular with the people of Rome, senior members of Rome's ruling council, the Senate, are concerned that he wants more power. Cassius, who is jealous of Caesar, approaches Brutus and persuades him that they must take action against their tyrannical leader. Amid violent storms and strange omens, the conspirators meet to plan Caesar's assassination. Next morning, 15th March, Caesar is preparing to attend the Senate but his wife Calphurnia, who has had a nightmare in which her husband is killed, tries her best to persuade him not to go. Caesar ignores her warning; at the Senate he is stabbed by each one of the eight conspirators. After Caesar's death Brutus and Antony address the waiting crowd in the market place. Brutus speaks with the voice of reason and asks the crowd to understand that although he loved Caesar, he loved Rome more. Antony's funeral oration is far more impassioned and he stirs up the crowd to violence. An innocent passer-by is killed simply because he bears the same name as one of the conspirators. Caesar's adopted son, Octavius, with Mark Antony and an elder statesman called Lepidus form a triumvirate, [rule of three men] over the Roman Empire and join forces against Brutus and Cassius. On the eve of battle, Brutus and Cassius quarrel but they are reconciled and Brutus decides to march on Antony's forces at Philippi rather than wait for the enemy to come to him. It proves to be a tactical disaster; the battle is lost and Cassius and Brutus kill themselves rather than face capture and dishonour.

Junius Brutus

A character in *Coriolanus*; *see* BRUTUS, JUNIUS.

Juno
Juno is one of the deities appearing in the MASQUE performed for Miranda and Ferdinand in *The Tempest*. *See* SPIRITS.

Jupiter
Jupiter is the king of the Roman gods. A minor character in *Cymbeline*, Jupiter is not named in the cast list but he is one of the Apparitions who appear to Posthumus as he languishes in his condemned cell. Jupiter, who lives in a crystal palace in the skies, makes a dramatic entry from above the stage, seated on an eagle and accompanied by thunder and lightning. He promises that good fortune will smile on Posthumus and leaves a riddle which Posthumus is unable to solve, although he finds some comfort in it. Jupiter represents the divine providence, or fate, that governs events in the play. *See* DEUS EX MACHINA.

Justice
A minor character in *Measure for Measure*, the Justice makes a brief appearance and comments that Angelo is a stern observer of the law.

Kk

Katharine

A character in *Love's Labour's Lost*, Katharine is one of the Princess of France's
entourage visiting the King of Navarre. Witty and beautiful like her companions,
Katharine is a rather one-dimensional character. Dumain falls in love with her but she
responds coolly to his advances, and comments on his youthful lack of a beard. She
promises Dumain that if in a year's time she has enough love, she will marry him then.
Katharine has a brief, touching moment when she displays real feeling remembering the
death of her sister from love.

Katherina (Kate)

The heroine of *The Taming of the Shrew*, Katherina is the wealthy Baptista's elder
daughter. Katherina is frequently, and unfavourably, compared to her sister Bianca, who
has a sweet disposition, while Katherina is notoriously shrewish [sharp-tempered]. Her
father is anxious for her to be married, but always waspish and sometimes even violent,
Katherina sends all her suitors packing. Only one, Petruchio, seems oblivious to her
temper. Katherina and Petruchio are married and he sets out to 'tame' her. Petruchio's
technique is to model his own behaviour on Katherina's shrewishness, at the same time
making repeated references to her sweetness and charm, until she is thoroughly
confused and, eventually, 'tamed'. Katherina grows to love her husband and her love for
him enables her to conform to his view of marriage, in which it is the duty of a wife to
serve and obey. However, it is hard to imagine a witty individualist like Katherina being
entirely submissive for the rest of her life.

Katherine, Princess

A historical figure (1401-38) and a character in *King Henry V*, Katherine is the young
daughter of King Charles VI of France. The French King offers his daughter's hand in
marriage to King Henry and when her lady-in-waiting gives her lessons in English,
Katherine proves to be a quick learner. King Henry is charmed by Katherine's beauty
and modesty and, although she has difficulty in understanding him, she finds him
equally attractive.

Katharine, (Katherine) Queen (of Aragon)

A historical figure (1485-1536) and a character in *King Henry VIII*, Queen Katharine
has long been a true and loyal wife to King Henry, but has failed to produce the male
heir to the throne he so badly needs. She is a champion of the people, and criticizes
Wolsey for imposing heavy taxes in King Henry's name. When the king decides to
separate from Katharine, Wolsey tries to persuade her to agree to a divorce. She accuses
Wolsey, with justification, of being her enemy and although she is heartbroken, she
refuses to shed tears and behaves with all the dignity of a queen. Katharine retires from
court, defeated and ill, when, despite her best efforts, her marriage is annulled. Learning
of Wolsey's death, she speaks forgivingly of him, and her dying message to Henry is

one of extraordinary generosity. She asks only that he should care for her servants and that she should be given a burial befitting a queen and daughter to a king.

Shakespeare portrays Katherine as entirely the victim of Wolsey's political ambition. In fact, Henry must be held responsible too for casting aside a wife who had done him no wrong. It seems that Henry did have a real affection for Katharine, and after their divorce he ensured that she lived out the rest of her life with some degree of dignity and comfort.

Kean, Edmund (1787–1833)

An English actor, Kean was famous for his passionate interpretations of Shakespearean roles. The poet Samuel Coleridge (1772-1834) said: 'To watch [Kean] act, is like reading Shakespeare by flashes of lightning'. Small and dark, and with intense eyes, he stands as one of the great Shakespearean actors. Kean was most acclaimed playing tragic villains such Iago, Macbeth, Othello, Richard III and Shylock. He was probably illegitimate, and he came from a poor and mysterious background as a strolling actor. His personal life was turbulent and sometimes scandalous. Kean was known for his hot-temper and, often drunk, he became increasingly unreliable in performance. He collapsed during a performance of *Othello* in the arms of his son, the actor Charles Kean (1811-68), who was playing Iago, and died shortly after.

By courtesy of the National Portrait Gallery, London

Edmund Kean, *artist: James Northcote*

Keeper of the Prison at Pontefract
A minor character in *King Richard II*, the Keeper brings food to the imprisoned King Richard. Richard asks him to try the food (in case it is poisoned) but the Keeper refuses although this has been his usual practice. Richard turns on him angrily.

Keeper of the Tower
A minor character in *King Richard III*, the Keeper looks after Clarence in the TOWER OF LONDON. Clarence tells him of a disturbing dream he has had.

Keepers
Two minor characters in *King Henry VI, Part Three*, the Keepers are hunting when they meet King Henry, disguised and walking alone. One of them recognizes Henry but says that he now owes allegiance to the new King Edward. The Keepers arrest Henry.

Kemble, Fanny (Frances Anne) (1809–93)
An English actress and dramatist, and member of a large theatrical dynasty, Fanny Kemble began her stage career creating a sensation as the young heroine of *Romeo and Juliet* at Covent Garden in London, in 1829. Her success in the role was so great that she saved the theatre, which was managed by her father Charles Kemble (1757-1854) from impending financial ruin. She had further success playing Shakespearean heroines both in England, and in America, where she lived after her marriage in 1834 to a Southern planter. Divorced in 1849, she took back her maiden name and returned to the English stage, giving Shakespearean readings for some twenty-six years.

Kemp or Kempe, Will (d. c. 1603)
A leading actor and a member with Shakespeare of the company of players, the LORD CHAMBERLAIN'S MEN, Kemp was one of the original shareholders in the GLOBE THEATRE. He began his career as an entertainer with the Earl of LEICESTER as a jester, and travelled with the Earl's retinue during the war with the Netherlands (1585-86). Kemp was known as a wit, and for his physically comic performances as a clown, as well as for his improvisations; he was often involved in lively exchanges with the audience. He appeared in plays by Ben JONSON, and it is known that parts were written specially for him by Shakespeare; for example Dogberry in *Much Ado About Nothing*. He excelled as a dancer and after leaving the Lord Chamberlain's Men in 1599, Kemp danced a MORRIS DANCE all the way from London to Norwich in order to win a bet.

Kent, Earl of
A character in *King Lear*, Kent is Lear's faithful follower. He tries to dissuade Lear from banishing Cordelia, and is sent into exile for daring to disagree with the King. Kent assumes the disguise of a poor servant, Caius, and enters Lear's service in order to remain beside the stubborn old man. When Lear is thrown out by his ungrateful elder daughters, Kent does his best to protect Lear, accompanying him on his bewildered wanderings on the heath. Kent patiently endures his undignified punishment in the stocks, where he is put by Regan, angry with him for helping her father. His loyalty is unwavering; he reunites Lear with Cordelia at Dover, but is overwhelmed with grief when father and daughter both die. He speaks of his own imminent death.

King of France
See FRANCE, KING OF.

King Ferdinand of Navarre
A character in *Love's Labour's Lost*, the King is a formal figure; elegant, courteous, and serious-minded. His ambition is to make his court a centre of learning and he and his companions vow to lead a simple monastic life, and renounce the company of women so as to provide a suitable atmosphere for study. When the Princess of France arrives on a diplomatic visit with her entourage, the King finds himself falling in love with her. He secretly woos her with verses but eventually has to confess to his friends that like them, he has broken his vow of celibacy. The King and his lords court the French ladies, but when the Princess departs for France, she says the King must wait for a year before he can marry her, during which time he must live like a hermit.

King John
One of Shakespeare's early HISTORY PLAYS, *King John* was probably written between 1591 and 1596. Its first recorded performance was nearly two hundred years later in 1737, but it was almost certainly performed in Shakespeare's lifetime. *King John* was first published in the First FOLIO edition of 1623 and entitled *The Life and Death of King John*. Sources for the play were HOLINSHED'S *Chronicles* and probably an anonymous play, *The Troublesome Reigne of John, King of England* (1591).

The play is an adaptation of history in which Shakespeare compresses time, and like most of his history plays it is concerned with the legitimacy of the King and his ability to rule competently, and the problem of remaining loyal to a bad ruler. It is set in England, at the beginning of the 13th century (see JOHN, KING OF ENGLAND). At the centre of the play is the King's quarrel with the Pope, which would have resonated with Elizabethan audiences of Protestant England. They who were no longer subject to the authority of the Pope following England's break with the Roman Catholic Church some sixty years earlier.

SYNOPSIS : King John has inherited the throne of England from his brother, the heroic Richard Coeur de Lion [Lionheart]. John resolves a dispute in which Richard's illegitimate son, Philip the Bastard, gives up his right to inherit family lands in return for the title of Sir Richard Plantagenet. The Bastard becomes John's CONFIDANT and in the end his only ally. John, whose position is already insecure, alienates his nobles when he makes a hasty peace treaty with England's old enemy France, in which territory hard won by England in an earlier war is returned to the French. Peace is short-lived; a quarrel with the Pope results in John's excommunication and a new holy war between France and England. The French support a claim to the English throne from Arthur, Richard Coeur de Lion's son and John's young nephew, and when Arthur is captured in battle by John he orders Hubert to take the boy back to England and kill him. Hubert is touched by Arthur's innocence and spares the boy, but Arthur dies attempting to escape from his prison. His nobles suspect John of Arthur's murder, and desert his cause to join the French forces who are invading England. John, fearful of his own people and of the French, promises to make his peace with the Pope and with France. The French refuse to make a treaty, but in a final battle they are defeated, and their armies retreat. John is poisoned and dies an inglorious death, and his son Prince Henry is proclaimed the new King (Henry III) of a reunited England.

King Lear

One of Shakespeare's later tragedies (see TRAGEDY), *King Lear* was written around 1605 and first published in 1608 in a QUARTO edition entitled, 'M William Shak-spear: His True Chronicle Historie of the life and death of King Lear and his three daughters'. It was probably first performed at the GLOBE THEATRE by the KING'S MEN in 1606. Principal sources of the play are an anonymous play entitled *The True Chronicle Historie of King Leir* (1594), in which Lear finally regains the throne and is reunited with his daughter Cordelia, and HOLINSHED'S *CHRONICLES*. During the 17th and 18th centuries, versions of the play with a happy ending (by Nahum TATE among others) proved very popular.

The play, set in Ancient Britain, explores themes of family duty, madness, political power, vision and blindness, and appearance and reality.

SYNOPSIS : LEAR, aged King of a pre-Christian Britain, decides to abdicate, dividing his kingdom among his three daughters. He demands that each of them makes a declaration of love for him in return for her share. Cordelia, his youngest and only honest daughter, says that although she loves him as a father, one day she will love a husband too. Lear angrily disinherits her, and she leaves England to marry the King of France. Lear's two elder daughters, Goneril and Regan, ingratiate themselves with their father by making the avowal of love he insists on, but they know nothing of love and it is mere pretence. Ambitious for power, and as ruthless as each other, the two sisters quarrel with their stubborn old father over the housing of his huge retinue of knights. Lear rages at their ingratitude; heart-broken, he rushes out into a storm, with his Fool as his only companion. Wandering about on a heath, Lear descends into madness, although insanity brings with it, in the end, a new self-knowledge and human compassion. There, he meets the ragged figure of 'Poor Tom'. 'Tom' is in reality Edgar, son of Gloucester, also banished from home. He is also the victim of family treachery after his scheming illegitimate brother Edmund falsely accuses him of plotting to kill their father. Gloucester is Lear's faithful friend, and, finding the old King on the heath, gives him shelter. The wicked Edmund discovers this and betrays his father to Regan, who with her husband, has Gloucester's eyes gouged out in punishment. Like Lear, Gloucester is also thrown out, destitute, onto the storm-ravaged heath. He meets his son Edgar, still disguised as 'Poor Tom', but does not recognize him. In despair, Gloucester asks for Edgar's help to leap from Dover Cliffs, but Edgar tricks his father out of suicide and into a stoical resignation. Cordelia, learning of her father's plight, returns from France with an army to save her father, and in a touching moment of reconciliation, meets him at Dover. The forces of Goneril and Regan defeat Cordelia's army, but evil destroys itself. Both sisters are in love with Edmund, and Goneril poisons Regan, before stabbing herself, while Edmund is killed, unrepentant, by his brother Edgar. This comes too late to save Cordelia, who has been hanged on Edmund's orders. Lear recovers his sanity only to die, overwhelmed with grief, as he cradles Cordelia's body in his arms, believing in a moment of hope that she is still breathing. The survival of Edgar points to the triumph of good over evil, and a restoration of order in the kingdom.

King's Men, The
The name taken by the acting company the LORD CHAMBERLAIN'S MEN in 1603 when King James I became their patron.

Knights[1]
Minor characters in *Pericles*, the five Knights are suitors for Thaisa's hand in marriage. They parade before Thaisa and King Simonides in a ceremonial tournament, displaying their coats of arms and are later entertained by Simonides at a banquet. Thaisa, who has fallen in love with Pericles, rejects them all.

Knights[2]
Minor characters in *Two Noble Kinsmen,* three Knights accompany Arcite, and three others support Palamon at the duel. They are described by Pirithous as majestic figures in magnificent armour. Arcite and his Knights offer up prayers to Mars, the god of war, amid a clanging of armour and a clap of thunder. Palamon's Knights give thanks to Venus, the goddess of love, while music plays and doves flutter about. When Palamon and his Knights are defeated, they are resigned to an honorable death, and give their purses to the Jailer for his sick daughter.

Kyd, Thomas (c. 1558–c. 1594)
An English playwright and a poet, Kyd is best remembered for his REVENGE TRAGEDIES, most notably the blank verse *Spanish Tragedy* (c. 1592) which was particularly popular with Elizabethan audiences. It is possible that Kyd wrote a version of *Hamlet*, UR-HAMLET, about ten years before Shakespeare wrote his play, but it has been lost. In 1593 he was arrested, accused of immorality and atheism, on the strength of some papers found in his rooms. Kyd, who was probably tortured, claimed that the papers belonged not to him but to his friend, the dramatist Christopher MARLOWE. After Marlowe's death, Kyd was released from prison and died in poverty soon afterwards.

Ll

Ladies

Minor characters in Shakespeare's plays, Ladies are usually the ladies-in-waiting who attend a Queen, for example in *King Richard II* and *Cymbeline* (see HELEN). In *Timon of Athens*, Ladies perform a MASQUE to entertain Timon's guests, and in *The Winter's Tale*, Ladies amuse the King and Queen's young son, Mamillius.

Laertes

A character in *Hamlet*, Laertes is Polonius' son and Ophelia's brother. Laertes has doubts that Hamlet's love for Ophelia is true, and before leaving for France, he warns her not to be too trusting. News of his father's death, brings Laertes back to Denmark seeking revenge. He sees for himself how grief has made Ophelia mad, and learns that it was Hamlet who killed Polonius. At Ophelia's funeral, grieving and angry, he assaults Hamlet, wrestling with him in his sister's grave. Claudius, sees a way to rid himself of both Laertes and Hamlet, and exploits Laertes' impulsive and immature nature, persuading him to fight Hamlet with a poisoned weapon. Laertes, unlike Hamlet, does not reflect on the consequences of his actions, but when he is killed in the duel, he confesses his treachery and begs Hamlet's forgiveness. Like Hamlet, Laertes in seeking to avenge his father's death, has become another victim of Claudius' villainy.

Lafew (Lafeu)

A character in *All's Well that Ends Well*, Lafew is an elder statesman, advisor to the King of France, and a family friend of the widowed Countess Rossillion. Lafew admires Helena, and accompanies her to court where he introduces her to the King as 'Dr She'. A vigorous old man with kindly instincts, Lafew is fatherly towards Bertram, advising him to accept marriage to Helena, and protective of Helena, angrily reproaching the young nobles at court who refuse to marry her. When Helena is supposed dead, Lafew is happy for his daughter to become Bertram's second wife until he learns of Bertram's infidelity with Diana, when he says he would rather pick a son-in-law in a fair than chose Bertram. Lafew is too shrewd to be taken in by Bertram's reprobate companion Parolles, but after Parolles' downfall, the benevolent Lafew gives him money because, he says, even a idiot and a knave must eat.

Lamb, Charles (1775–1834)

An English critic and essayist who collaborated with his elder sister, Mary Ann (1764-1847), on *Tales from Shakespeare* (1807), a rewriting of eighteen of Shakespeare's plays in easily understood prose; Charles undertook the tragedies and Mary the comedies. Lamb also wrote several works on Elizabethan literature, including a controversial essay 'On the Tragedies of Shakespeare' (1811) in which he argued that Shakespeare's plays were not suitable for performance on stage.

Lancaster, Duke of
A character in *King Richard II*; *see* GAUNT, JOHN OF.

Lancaster, The House of
A historical English royal family, the House [family] of Lancaster, was a branch of the
PLANTAGENET family. The dynasty was founded in 1267, when Edmund 'Crouchback',
the second son of Henry III, was granted the earldom of Lancaster. The title of earl was
passed down the line, and was eventually converted into a duchy by royal charter. In
1362, John of Gaunt (son of Edward III) inherited the lands and title through his
marriage to Blanche, sole remaining heiress to the Lancastrian estate. Their son Henry
IV seized the crown from Richard II in 1399, and the royal Lancastrian line continued
through his son Henry V, and his grandson Henry VI, the last Lancastrian monarch.
During the reign of Henry VI (1422-61 and 1470-71) the WARS OF THE ROSES began, in
which the House of YORK fought the House of Lancaster for power, and ultimately for
the English throne. See the table of kings and queens in the Supplement.

Lancaster, Prince John of
A character in *King Henry IV, Part Two*; *see* JOHN, PRINCE.

Langley, Edmund of
A character in *King Richard II*; *see* YORK, DUKE OF.

Langley, Francis (1550-1601)
A London goldsmith and financier, who bought land on Bankside in London on which
he erected the SWAN theatre. He leased the theatre to PEMBROKE'S MEN in 1597, but it
was closed that same year following a performance of the seditious play *Isle of Dogs*.
When some members of Pembroke's Men subsequently defected to other companies,
Langley sued them for breach of contract.

Lanier, Emilia
The married name of Emilia BASSANO

La Pucelle
A character in *King Henry VI, Part One*; *see* JOAN LA PUCELLE.

Lartius, Titus
A minor character in *Coriolanus*, Lartius is a courageous Roman general in the army
fighting the Volscians who declares he will fight on crutches if necessary. At one point
in the battle for Corioli, he believes that Coriolanus has been killed and generously
praises his courage.

Launce
A comic character in *The Two Gentlemen of Verona*, Launce is Proteus' servant, who
plays little part in the main action of the play. He is always accompanied by his dog
Crab, whom he describes as the most hard-hearted of creatures. Launce describes how
disgracefully Crab behaved at the Duke's banquet and how, in the past, he has had to
take the blame for Crab's delinquency. When Launce is sent by Proteus to give a little
dog as a present to Silvia, he loses the dog and offers her Crab instead. The clownish
character of Launce (*see* CLOWN) was probably first played by Will Kemp.

Launcelot Gobbo

A comic character in *The Merchant of Venice*; *see* GOBBO, LAUNCELOT.

Laurence, Friar

A character in *Romeo and Juliet*, Friar Laurence marries the young lovers, hoping that their union will unite the two feuding families of Capulet and Montague. Well-intentioned though he may be, the Friar's moral code is questionable. When Romeo is banished from Verona and Juliet is to be married to Paris, Friar Laurence actually advises her to undergo a second, bigamous, marriage. In the end, the Friar provides the drug which will make Juliet appear dead, but his intervention proves disastrous, when his message telling Romeo that Juliet will only be feigning death fails to reach him. At the end of the play the Friar acts as a kind of CHORUS, explaining to the grief-stricken families what has transpired. He holds himself partly responsible for the fate of the lovers.

Lavatch (Lavache)

A comic character in *All's Well that Ends Well*, the name Lavatch appears in the cast list but the character is referred to as the CLOWN in the play. The Clown is the Countess of Rossillion's rather gloomy and cynical jester, who amuses her with his witty quibbles. He ridicules court manners, saying country life is more to his tastes. In a comic echo of the main plot, the Clown tell his mistress that he wants to marry 'Isbel' for the good of his health and because of his lustful nature. Later he tells her he has changed his mind about marrying Isbel because his appetite for sex has been blunted by his exhausting adventures at court.

Lavinia

A character in *Titus Andronicus*, Lavinia is Titus' daughter and the victim of Tamora's vengeful plotting. Lavinia obediently agrees to be married to the Emperor Saturnius, but is snatched away by Bassianus, who claims her as his fiancee. Lavinia is not a victim by nature; she shows some spirit when she discovers the adulterous Tamora and her lover Aaron together, but she is almost immediately silenced for ever. Tamora's sons seize her, urged on by their mother and Aaron. Lavinia begs to die rather than endure the shame of rape, but her pitiless enemies ravish and mutilate her horribly, cutting off both her hands and cutting out her tongue. Unable to speak or write, it is a while before she is able to identify her attackers, with the aid of a copy of Ovid's *Metamorphoses* (see OVID) in which her own story is paralleled. She helps in the killing of Tamora's sons before Titus kills her, to save her from living any longer with her shame.

Lawyer

A minor character in *King Henry VI, Part One*, the Lawyer is present during the quarrel between Somerset and the Duke of York in the Temple Garden.

Lear

The tragic hero of *King Lear*, Lear is a king of Ancient Britain. Ageing and autocratic, Lear decides to abdicate and to divide the kingdom between his three daughters. He disinherits his youngest daughter, Cordelia, who cannot bring herself to make the unqualified promise of love for him that he demands, and rewards her elder sisters Goneril and Regan, who share power. However, Lear is blinded by pride and still wants to be regarded as king, and he quarrels with Goneril and Regan, accusing them of ingratitude. In a passion of fury, he rushes out into a wild stormy night, accompanied by his Fool. Lear goes mad; wandering on the heath he rages against the universe and holds a mock trial for his daughters. Eventually he is reunited with Cordelia; he recovers his sanity, and with it a new humility, but by then the forces of Goneril and Regan are massed against them. Cordelia is killed and Lear, overwhelmed by grief, cradles her body in his arms and dies.

Le Beau
A minor character in *As You Like It*, Le Beau is one of Duke Frederick's courtiers, who tells Celia and Rosalind about the arrival of Charles the wrestler, and describes matches that have already taken place between the fearsome Charles and his challengers. Afterwards he warns Orlando to flee because Oliver is hatching plots against him. Le Beau has an overblown style of speaking and Rosalind and Celia think he is rather ridiculous.

Le Fer, Monsieur
A minor character in *King Henry V*, Monsieur Le Fer is a French soldier who is captured by Pistol before the Battle of Agincourt. The frightened Monsieur Le Fer speaks no English and has to rely on Pistol's page to interpret. He manages eventually to buy his freedom from Pistol.

Leicester, Robert Dudley, Earl of (1532–88)
A favourite of Queen Elizabeth for some thirty years, and nicknamed by her 'Sweet Robin', Robert Dudley was rewarded with the title Earl of Leicester in 1564. Their relationship was surrounded by gossip, but whether they were actually lovers is not known. Certainly the Queen entertained ideas of marrying him, despite his marriage to Amy Robstart (who died under suspicious circumstances), but she put politics before romance when she proposed Leicester as a possible husband for Mary Queen of Scots. The Queen's plan for this royal union did not materialize, and Leicester was married again in 1578 to Lettice Knollys, becoming step-father to her son the Earl of ESSEX. He fell temporarily out of favour but was later given command of an naval expedition against Spain. In his will Leicester left an immense jewel, consisting of three magnificent emeralds, a large diamond and a rope of pearls, to the Queen. During his career at court he was responsible for certain ceremonial duties and he was always a keen patron of drama, forming LEICESTER'S MEN in 1559.

Leicester's Men
The first organized company of professional actors in England which was founded under the patronage of Robert Dudley in 1559. They were known as DUDLEY'S MEN until Dudley received the title of Earl of Leicester in 1564. The company played frequently for Queen Elizabeth, and in 1574 she granted them a licence to perform anywhere in England, even within the City of London. For the next ten years, until the company disbanded, it was the most prominent group of actors in England. There has been speculation that Shakespeare may have acted with Leicester's Men, but there is no evidence for this.

leitmotif
Originally a musical term, a leitmotif or MOTIF is a theme associated with a character or an idea which runs throughout a play, recurring each time the person or thought appears in the action.

Lenox or Lennox
A minor character in *Macbeth*, Lennox is a Scottish nobleman who supports Prince Malcolm against Macbeth.

Leonardo
A minor character in *The Merchant of Venice*, Leonardo is Bassanio's servant.

Leonato
A character in *Much Ado About Nothing*, Leonato is the Governor of Messina, Hero's loving father and Beatrice's fond uncle. A cheerful and hospitable man, he organizes a masked ball to welcome Benedick and his companions' return from the war, and Claudio immediately falls in love with his daughter. Before Hero and Claudio can marry, the wicked Don John manipulates everyone into believing that Hero has been unfaithful to her future husband. Leonato does not seem to have much faith in his daughter's integrity and believes the lies. He is heart-broken, but he goes along with the pretence that Hero is dead. When Hero's name has been cleared, Leonato tricks Claudio into marrying his 'niece' who of course turns out to be Hero.

Leonatus, Posthumus
A character in *Cymbeline*; *see* POSTHUMUS LEONATUS.

Leonine
A minor character in *Pericles*, Leonine is Dionyza's servant. Dionyza orders the ruthless Leonine to murder Marina and he is only prevented from doing so when pirates rush in and snatch Marina away. Dionyza poisons Leonine for his failure to carry out her orders and because he is a witness to her murderous scheme.

Leontes
A character in *The Winter's Tale*, Leontes is King of Sicilia, who is entertaining his childhood friend, King Polixenes, at court. Leontes begs Polixenes to extend the visit, and asks his wife Hermione to persuade him to stay. Observing Hermione and Polixenes together, Leontes is suddenly seized by an intense and irrational jealousy. He accuses Hermione of infidelity and has her imprisoned, and plans to kill Polixenes. He believes that her newborn child is actually Polixenes' daughter and orders the baby be abandoned. Leontes' passion is so overwhelming that he even refuses to believe the Oracle whose opinion on Hermione's guilt or innocence he has sought. It is only when his young son Mamillius dies from grief at his mother's arrest, that Leontes realizes the wrong he has done Hermione. After an interval of sixteen years, during which he suffers terrible remorse, Leontes is miraculously reunited with Hermione and redeemed by her forgiveness, and is brought together with his long-lost daughter Perdita.

Lepidus
A historical figure, Marcus Aemilius Lepidus (d. 13 BC) and a character in *Julius Caesar* and *Antony and Cleopatra*, Lepidus is a Roman statesman.

In *Julius Caesar*, Lepidus is a minor character. After Caesar's assassination, Antony and Octavius Caesar discuss with Lepidus the fate of their political enemies. When Lepidus has left them, Antony describes him to Octavius as a man who does not live in the real world, and who can be led one way or another as easily as his horse.

In *Antony and Cleopatra*, Lepidus is one of the TRIUMVIRS, with Caesar and Antony, who rule the Roman Empire, but he has the least authority of the three men. When Antony returns to Rome from Egypt, Lepidus tries to heal the rift between Caesar and Antony, and suggests a marriage between Antony and Caesar's sister Octavia to cement their reconciliation. In a humiliating episode at the celebratory banquet on board Pompey's ship, Lepidus allows himself to be persuaded into drinking far too much wine, and is carried off the ship. Not long after, Caesar, recognizing that Lepidus is fundamentally weak, accuses him of treason and has him imprisoned.

Lewis the Dauphin
A historical figure (1187-1226) and a character in *King John*, the Dauphin (heir to the throne) Lewis (Louis) is the King of France's son. As part of a peace treaty between France and England, a diplomatic marriage is arranged between Lewis and Blanche, niece of the English King. The peace is short-lived and when war again breaks out between the two countries Lewis, a courageous soldier, leads the army invading England. The French are beaten back and Lewis' supplies are sunk on the Goodwin sands, and he retreats to France.

Lewis the Eleventh, King of France
A historical figure (1423-83) and a minor character in *King Henry VI, Part Three*; King Lewis [Louis] agrees to a marriage between his sister-in-law, Lady Bona, and King Edward in order to cement an alliance between the two countries. When Edward breaks the agreement by marrying someone else, Lewis angrily pledges his support to Edward's enemy, Queen Margaret.

licensing
See ELIZABETHAN THEATRE; CENSORSHIP.

Lictors
Minor characters in *Coriolanus*, the Lictors form part of a procession with the tribunes and Patricians in the Senate.

In Ancient Rome, Lictors held ceremonial bundles of rods and an axe, and carried out the sentences of the Roman magistrates.

Lieutenant of the Tower
A minor character in *King Henry VI, Part Three*, the Lieutenant guards King Henry in the TOWER OF LONDON, and when the King is released he asks the King's forgiveness for having been his jailer.

Ligarius, Caius
A historical figure (d. 44 BC), and minor character in *Julius Caesar*, Ligarius is one of the conspirators against Caesar. He is a sick old man but he eagerly joins in the planned assassination of Caesar, whose tyranny he hates. He tells Brutus that his involvement will make him well again. Ligarius accompanies Caesar to the senate but he does not appear in the assassination scene.

lighting
Plays performed in Elizabethan open air public PLAYHOUSES began at two o'clock in the afternoon and relied solely on daylight for illumination, although productions in

private roofed playhouses, such as the BLACKFRIARS THEATRE, would have been lit by candles. Since there was no artificial way of showing the time of day in a play, the time, like the place, was indicated in the text. For example, Hamlet says: 'Now is the very witching time of night'.

Limoges, Duke of Austria
A minor character in *King John*; *see* AUSTRIA.

Lincoln, Bishop of
A historical figure (John Longland 1473-1547) and a minor character in *King Henry VIII*, the Bishop of Lincoln speaks at the trial of Queen Katharine, confirming that he advised the King to seek a divorce.

line ending
The concluding syllable of a line of rhymed or unrhymed verse. If the line ending is stressed, or emphasized, according to the rhythm of normal speech, it is referred to as 'masculine'. If the syllable is unstressed it is called a feminine ending.
See FEMININE ENDING, MASCULINE ENDING *for examples.*

literary criticism and theory
Literary criticism tries to make an objective, reasoned assessment of a piece of writing or drama; literary theory is concerned with what lies behind this judgement. We may instinctively recognize Shakespeare's plays as 'literature', but what are the criteria we use to reach this opinion? Literary theory includes such questions as 'what is the use of literature?' 'Does it describe the world around us?' 'How does it affect the reader or audience, or it is perhaps only written to entertain us?'

Through the centuries, critics have wrestled with such questions. A very early work of literary criticism was the *Poetics*, written in the 4th century BC by the Greek philosopher ARISTOTLE, which examined the nature and effects of poetry and tragedy. In England, literary criticism may be said to start with Sir Philip SIDNEY'S essay 'The Apologie for Poetrie, or Defence of Poesie' (1595), a work which brings together various RENAISSANCE critical theories in one persuasive argument. Sidney defended literature as more effective than history or philosophy in teaching and delighting the reader. Much of this early criticism was concerned with the broader moral and social aspects of literature. The writings of Dr JOHNSON in the 18th century focused on the text and its effect on the reader, a focus that was to continue through the 19th century. (*See* SHAKESPEAREAN CRITICISM.)

Later Victorian criticism, which became concerned with 'art for art's sake', was followed in the early 20th century by criticism influenced by fields of thought other than literature. The theories of Karl Marx (1818-83), which saw society as being locked in a conflict between workers and capitalists, provided the basis for Marxist criticism. The writings of the psychologist Sigmund Freud (1856-1939) helped create the development of psychoanalytic criticism, which interpreted literature as the workings of the subconscious mind. Although feminist criticism only emerged fully in the 1960s, the growing interest in the roles of women in society produced a variety of criticism which looked at literature in particular from the point of view of women's experience.

Through the 20th century, a series of interlinked schools of criticism followed developments in linguistics, or the study of the way words gain their significance from being placed in a structure, or pattern, of words with different meanings. They became concerned not only with what a text means, but in particular on how it gets its meaning. The 'Russian Formalists' in the 1920s looked at the structural forms behind poetry, folk tales and narratives. They influenced the American 'New Criticism', which examined the text as an object in itself, apart from its author or its historical context. The various schools of 'Structuralism', developed in Europe and America from the 1960s, also looked at the underlying patterns of literary forms. Post-structuralists, on the other hand, while concerned with form, considered that all structures of meaning, whether words or images, or literary genres, are constantly shifting, and deny that there can be any single authoritative interpretation of a text. 'New Historicism' applies this to the study of the context, its historical setting, of a work of literature as well as to the text itself; both literature and history must be constantly redefined. *See* SHAKESPEAREAN CRITICISM.

Litio
In *The Taming of the Shrew*, Litio is the name Hortensio adopts when he disguises himself as a music teacher.

Lodovico
A minor character in *Othello*, Lodovico is a Venetian noble who is sent to Cyprus at the time when Othello is being overwhelmed by his irrational jealousy. Lodovico witnesses Othello hitting Desdemona. After the tragic deaths of Othello and Desdemona, Lodovico produces the letters that are proof of Iago's wicked plot. He orders Iago to be arrested and tortured.

Lodowick, Friar
In *Measure for Measure*, the Duke of Vienna takes the name of 'Lodowick' when he disguises himself as a friar.

London
The London of Shakespeare's day was one of the great cities of Europe with a population of around 250,000. The city was surrounded by ancient walls, and divided into twenty-six sections, or wards, governed by elected Aldermen, the CITY FATHERS, who were under the authority of the Lord Mayor.

The river Thames was the main thoroughfare, with a constant traffic of merchant ships, water taxis and brightly painted barges. It was spanned by London Bridge where the heads of executed criminals were exhibited on spikes. With its nineteen arches, the bridge was wide enough for houses to be built along it on both sides. On the river banks stood (to the west of the city) the Palace of Westminster where the court resided, and (to the east) the TOWER OF LONDON, a royal castle built to defend the city, which housed a menagerie with lions and tigers, as well as important prisoners.

There were open spaces and gardens in the city, but much of London was overcrowded and insanitary, and the warren of narrow streets provided a breeding ground for disease as well as for crime. There were schools where boys were taught to pick pockets or 'cut purses' and there were some eighteen gaols in the city. Plague was rife; in one year, between December 1602 and December 1603, one-sixth of the population of London was wiped out by the disease.

While life for a small proportion of affluent citizens was conducted in luxury and elegance, for most Londoners it was harsh. Much of the social life in all strata of society

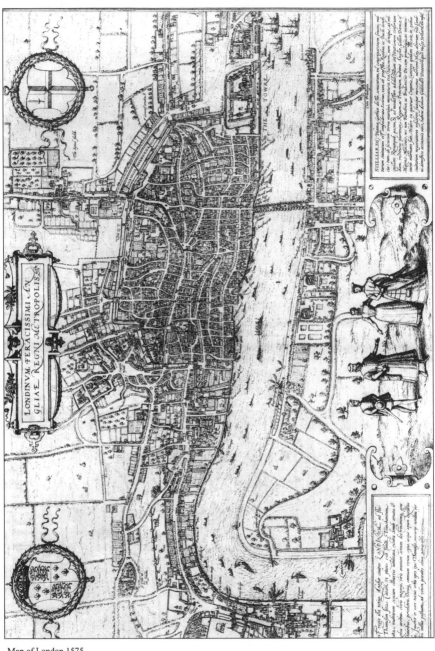

Map of London 1575

was conducted in taverns (as it is in the *King Henry IV* plays), although these were sometimes no more than brothels. Bear- and bull-baiting and cock-fighting were popular entertainments, as were visits to Bedlam (an asylum for the mentally ill) to laugh at its deranged inmates.

Then, as now, London was the theatrical centre of England and contained more theatres (*see* PLAYHOUSES) than any other capital city in Europe. These were concentrated in the area south of the Thames and beyond the limits of the City known as BANKSIDE. (*See* CENSORSHIP)

Longaville

A character in *Love's Labour's Lost*, Longaville is one of the young men who swears an oath to devote three years of his life to celibacy and learning. An undeveloped character, Longaville is described by other characters as merry and witty and tall, as his name suggests. He falls in love with Maria, one of the French ladies visiting Navarre. He woos her with poetry and pearls, and justifies breaking his oath by claiming that as Maria is a goddess he cannot help himself. He agrees to wait for a year before he marries Maria.

Lord

One of several minor characters in Shakespeare's plays, Lords are noblemen at court who may comment on other characters or events. In *King Richard II*, an unnamed noble accuses the Duke of Aumerle of his part in the murder of the Duke of Gloucester and challenges him to a single combat.

In *The Taming of the Shrew*, a Lord appears in the INDUCTION to the play. The Lord finds Sly the tinker in a drunken stupor outside the tavern and decides to play a trick on him. He takes Sly to his country house, has him dressed in fine clothes and attended to by his servants, who pretend that Sly is a noblemen who has been mad for fifteen years. It is a good-natured joke which results in the performance of *The Taming of the Shrew* by a company of travelling actors. *See also* LORDS *below.*

Lord Admiral's Men, The

See ADMIRAL'S MEN, THE.

Lord Chamberlain[1]

A minor character in *King Henry VIII*, the bustling Lord Chamberlain is an officer at Henry's court in charge of entertainment (see below). He oversees the arrangements for Wolsey's banquet held for the King, organizes the seating at dinner, welcomes the masquers, and introduces Anne Bullen to the King. He is later in charge of crowd control at the christening of Princess Elizabeth. Although he is not much involved in affairs of state, the Lord Chamberlain is critical of Wolsey and of the influence he has over the King.

Lord Chamberlain[2]

An important member of Queen Elizabeth I's royal household who supervised the court wardrobe, travel, and accommodation as well as court entertainment, and who appointed the MASTER OF THE REVELS. Until as recently as 1968, the Lord Chamberlain was still responsible for CENSORSHIP in England and for licensing the productions of all plays.

Lord Chamberlain's Men, The

The company of actors for whom Shakespeare wrote exclusively and acted with during the span of his theatrical career (1594-1610). Founded in 1594, under the patronage of Lord HUNSDON, the Lord Chamberlain, it included in its ranks the great tragedian Richard BURBAGE and the comedian Will KEMP (who was replaced by Robert ARMIN in 1599). It was the most successful company of its day, despite the competition of rival companies such as the ADMIRAL'S MEN at the Rose theatre and the CHILDREN OF THE CHAPEL at the Blackfriars Theatre. The Lord Chamberlain's Men performed at NEWINGTON BUTTS and later at the THEATRE before acquiring their own premises, the GLOBE THEATRE, in 1599.

Unlike many other companies, who merely leased the theatres they played in, The Lord Chamberlain's Men owned the Globe. Seven part-owners, or HOUSEKEEPERS, including Shakespeare himself, put up the money for its construction and shared in its profits. The company performed mainly their own playwright Shakespeare's plays, but they also put on works by Ben JONSON. They gave some thirty-two performances at court during Queen Elizabeth I's reign, and were specially requested to put on *Twelfth Night* for the Queen during the Christmas festivities of 1600. After 1603, when King James I became its patron, the success of the company was assured; it became known as the KING'S MEN, and its members were honoured with the official title of GROOMS OF THE CHAMBER. Between 1604 and 1609, the company toured the provinces, but by this time Shakespeare had ceased to act. In 1608 the company acquired the lease of the indoor BLACKFRIARS THEATRE and from then on performed there in the winter months, while continuing to perform in the open-air Globe during the summer.

Lord Chief Justice, The

A character in *King Henry IV, Part Two*, the Lord Chief Justice is the head of the legal system in England. He questions Falstaff about his past crimes and is called upon by Mistress Quickly to arrest Falstaff, who is in debt to her. The Chief Justice, a rather pompous character, is mocked and out-talked by Falstaff who wriggles his way out of trouble, and is let off with a warning. The Chief Justice once imprisoned Prince Hal for a piece of youthful impudence, and when the Prince is proclaimed King he is concerned that Hal may want revenge. He pleads his case and is relieved when Hal praises him for having upheld the law. The Chief Justice finally gets the better of Falstaff; his authority in office now confirmed by the King, he orders Falstaff to be taken off to the Fleet prison.

Lord Howard's Company

See ADMIRAL'S MEN, THE.

Lords

Minor characters in several of Shakespeare's plays; In *All's Well that Ends Well*, four Lords are presented to Helena by the King, so that she can chose a husband from among them. As Helena intends to chose Bertram anyway, she spends little time in speaking to them.

In *Timon of Athens*, the Lords are hypocrites who flatter Timon and take advantage of his generosity, but when Timon is in need of money himself, they all refuse to help him. Timon invites the Lords to a banquet and they attend in the hope of more rich pickings, and pretend to be full of remorse for not lending their benefactor money. Timon pays them back by serving bowls of warm water to his guests, telling them to lap up like dogs.

Two LORDS in *Cymbeline* are companions of the loutish Cloten. The First Lord, who introduces the topic of Iachimo's arrival, is all courtesy to Cloten, while the Second Lord sneers at Cloten behind his back and reflects on Imogen's sad predicament.

In *All's Well that Ends Well*, the two French Lords are brothers, whose names appear in the cast list as Dumaine, but who otherwise appear as FIRST and SECOND Lord. Companions of Bertram in Italy, they play a trick on the cowardly Parolles. They ambush him and, pretending to be the enemy, they blindfold their victim and threaten to kill him, speaking in a fierce-sounding nonsense language. The Lords disapprove of Bertram's behaviour and sympathize with the abandoned Helena, but they believe Parolles is largely to blame for Bertram's moral decline.

Lorenzo
A character in *The Merchant of Venice*, Lorenzo is a stock romantic figure, a Venetian gentleman and Antonio's friend, who is in love with Jessica, Shylock's daughter. Lorenzo and Jessica elope, escaping in a gondola to Portia's country house, Belmont. Portia asks Lorenzo and Jessica to look after her house while she is away in Venice defending Antonio. When he hears Portia is about to return, Lorenzo arranges musicians to entertain them and speaks lyrically about the power of music.

Louis the Dauphin
The son of Charles VI of France in *King Henry V*; *see* DAUPHIN, LOUIS THE.

Lovell, Lord
A historical figure (1454-c. 1487) and a minor character in *King Richard III*, Lord Lovell is one of Richard's supporters. He is involved in Hastings' execution, and brings the severed head to Richard.

Lovell, Sir Thomas
A historical figure (d. 1524) and a minor character in *King Henry VIII*, Sir Thomas Lovell is a courtier and one of Cardinal Wolsey's supporters. Lovell is a conveyor of court gossip who organizes Wolsey's banquet held for the King. He accompanies the condemned Duke of Buckingham on his last journey and asks Buckingham to forgive him.

Lover's Complaint, A
A poem of 47 stanzas in RHYME ROYAL, which may or may not have been an early work by Shakespeare, but whose authorship has never been absolutely determined. It was included in the 1609 edition of the SONNETS. The narrative concerns the encounter of a young woman with a youth who is the perfection of manly beauty. Learning of his earlier promiscuity she resolves to resist his advances, but his pleading is so impassioned that he undermines her resistance. He admits that his reputation for infidelity is deserved, but tells her that in meeting her he is experiencing true love for the first time. The young woman allows herself to be seduced, only to be subsequently abandoned. She expresses regret at falling prey to the young man's charms but acknowledges that she finds him so desirable she might easily succumb another time.

Love's Labour's Lost

One of Shakespeare's early comedies written around 1594-95, *Love's Labour's Lost* was first published in a QUARTO edition in 1598. It may have been written specifically for exclusive private audiences at the BLACKFRIARS THEATRE; certainly it was performed at court for Queen Elizabeth I in the Christmas of 1597. There is no known source for *Love's Labour's Lost*, and unlike Shakespeare's other plays, the plot seems to be entirely the playwright's own invention. A courtly love story, the play is set in the artificial world of Navarre, which seems decidedly English. *Love's Labour's Lost* is full of lyrical rhyming verse and celebrates the triumph of romantic love over sterile scholarship. It revels in elaborate language and makes fun of intellectual pretensions.

SYNOPSIS : The King of Navarre and three lords, Berowne, Longaville and Dumaine, have vowed to devote three years of their lives to study and learning. They undertake to lead a simple, almost monastic life, and to renounce the company of women altogether. Their vows are severely tested when the Princess of France, with three of her ladies, Rosaline, Maria and Katherine, make a diplomatic visit to the Court of Navarre. The young men, catching sight of their beautiful visitors, fall immediately in love with them. Berowne, who all along felt that their promise to be celibate was unrealistic, now argues that they have not broken the spirit of their vow because women are the source of all learning. The young men abandon their vows, but their attempts to woo the French visitors are not altogether successful. Presents and poetry (rather bad poetry), are received coolly, and there is a series of mistakes in which letters are wrongly delivered. Berowne and his friends try another approach. They disguise themselves as Russians from Moscow, hoping that an exotic appearance and high-flown language will melt French hearts. Confusions abound as the young women, who are masked, pretend to be one another. News comes that the French Princess's father has died and she and her friends prepare to leave. Before they go, the young men proclaim the seriousness of their love, but the young ladies insist on putting it to the test. The King and his friends are to resume their studies for a year after which, if their love lasts, the young ladies will return and marry them. A comic sub-plot mimics and intertwines with the courtly love story of the King and his friends. Don Armado, an eccentric Spaniard and Costard, a Clown, are rivals for the hand of Jaquenetta, a country girl, whom Don Armado marries in the end. The play is rounded off with songs about springtime and winter.

Love's Labour's Wonne

The title of a comedy by Shakespeare which may be a lost play, but which is more likely to have been the working title for *All's Well that Ends Well*, or possibly *The Taming of the Shrew*.

Luce[1]

A minor character in *The Comedy of Errors*, Luce is Luciana's maid who refuses to admit Ephesus Antipholus to his own home because she is convinced he is an imposter. Luce may also be the character NELL who is mentioned later in the play. Nell is a fat, greasy, unlovely, kitchen-maid who has set her sights on marrying Syracuse Dromio.

Luce[2]

A minor, non-speaking part in *The Two Noble Kinsmen*; *see* COUNTRYWOMEN.

Lucetta

A minor character in *The Two Gentlemen of Verona*, Lucetta is Julia's maid who helps her to disguise herself as a boy.

Lucentio

A character in *The Taming of the Shrew*, Lucentio is a romantic and eligible young gentleman who has come to Padua to study. The first thing he sees is the beautiful Bianca and he falls immediately in love. He learns that her father keeps her shut away with only her teachers for company, until such time as her elder sister Katherina is married. Determined to win her for himself, Lucentio disguises himself as 'CAMBIO', and becomes her private tutor. Under the pretence of teaching her Latin, Lucentio woos Bianca. Lucentio's disguise is nearly penetrated when first the Pedant, who is Bianca's real teacher, and then his father arrive in Padua, but before his real identity is discovered Lucentio and Bianca elope with the help of his ingenious servant Tranio. Lucentio makes a bet with Petruchio that his wife is more obedient that her shrewish [sharp-tempered] sister Katherina, but he discovers she is not quite so demure as she seems and he loses.

Luciana

A character in *The Comedy of Errors*, Luciana is Adriana's sister, who agrees with the Elizabethan view of marriage that a woman is ruled by her husband. Luciana tries to calm her sister while she awaits her husband Ephesus Antipholus, who is late returning home, and tells her to be patient. When she meets Antipholus later, Luciana scolds him for his neglect of Adriana. As part of the comedy of errors, Luciana has actually been speaking to Antipholus's identical twin brother; she is astounded when the man she believes to be her brother-in-law declares his love for her. Luciana tells Adriana what has happened, making her sister more confused than ever about her husband's apparently lunatic behaviour. When identities are revealed at the end of the play, Syracuse Antipholus says he hopes to marry Luciana.

Lucilius[1]

A minor character in *Julius Caesar*, Lucilius is an officer in Brutus's army. When Brutus and Cassius' forces are defeated at Philippi, Lucilius pretends to be Brutus so that Brutus himself can escape. He is captured by one of Antony's soldiers and Antony is so impressed with Lucilius' courage he orders that his prisoner is to be treated with kindness.

Lucilius[2]

A minor character in *Timon of Athens*, Lucilius is Timon's servant. An Old Athenian complains to Timon that Lucilius, a mere servant, is courting his daughter. Timon promises to make Lucilius rich enough to make him an acceptable son-in-law to the old man.

Lucio

A character in *Measure for Measure*, Lucio, described as a 'fantastic' [a dissolute fop] in the cast list, inhabits that world of lax morals that the Duke would like to see eradicated from Vienna. He is a visitor to Mistress Overdone's brothel and keeps company with Pompey who acts as her pimp, but his friendship does not extend to putting up bail for Pompey when he needs it to avoid going to prison. In conversations with the friar, Lucio mischievously makes up slanderous stories about the absent Duke, not realizing that he is speaking to the Duke in disguise. When the Duke's identity is revealed, Lucio begs him not to make him marry a prostitute as his punishment, which is exactly what the Duke orders him to do. Lucio's redeeming quality is his genuinely warm friendship with Claudio, whom he tries to help.

Lucius[1]

A minor character in *Julius Caesar*, Lucius is Brutus's servant. He admits the conspirators to Brutus's house and then falls asleep while they plan Caesar's murder. Before the battle of Philippi, Lucius waits on his master and sings to him but again he is overcome by sleep. Brutus treats Lucius with kindness and vows that if he lives he will be good to him.

Lucius[2]

A minor character in *Timon of Athens*, Lucius is one of the hypocritical lords who flatter Timon and take advantage of his generosity. To keep in favour with Timon he makes him a present of four white horses with silver harnesses but when Timon himself needs money Lucius refuses to help, although he boasts of being someone who would always help a friend in need. LUCIUS' SERVANT, known by his master's name, is sent to demand the repayment of money owed by Timon to Lucius but comes away empty-handed.

Lucius[3]

A central character in *Titus Andronicus*, Lucius is Titus' eldest son and father of Young Lucius (see below). Lucius is responsible for the first killing of the play, which begins the terrible spiral of revenge that follows. He demands the sacrifice of Alarbus, the most important of the Goth prisoners, to appease the spirits of his brothers who died fighting the Goths. However, in the violent and cruel atmosphere of the play Lucius emerges as a man with relatively noble principles, not as someone who is driven by hate. He cares for his horribly mutilated sister Lavinia, wiping away her tears, and tries to persuade Titus to let him sacrifice his own hand, rather than Titus' hand, to ransom his brothers. He marches on Saturnius only after his father has demanded that his sons swear an oath to right the wrongs done to the family. Lucius is acclaimed Emperor at the end of the play and promises to heal Rome's wounds.

Lucius, Caius

A character in Cymbeline, Caius Lucius is the General commanding the Roman forces. Acting as Augustus Caesar's ambassador from Rome, Lucius courteously informs Cymbeline that Britain must pay a 'tribute' [a kind of tax paid in order to secure peace]. When Cymbeline refuses, Lucius reluctantly declares that war with Rome must follow. In charge of the Roman army in Wales, Lucius comes across 'Fidele', the disguised Imogen, weeping over a dead body which she mistakenly presumes to be that of her lover Posthumus. Lucius shows 'Fidele' great kindness, helping her with the burial of the body and offering employment and protection to the grief-stricken 'boy'. When the Roman army is defeated, Lucius is taken prisoner. Facing death himself, he asks Cymbeline to show mercy to the young boy 'Fidele', and in the final reconciliation in the play, Lucius' own life is spared.

Lucius, Young

A minor character in *Titus Andronicus*, Young Lucius is Lucius' son and Titus' grandson who grieves terribly when Titus is killed. He is a compassionate young boy, concerned for his mutilated aunt Lavinia's suffering, but he is alarmed by the way she follows him around. Trying to escape from her, he drops an armful of books which include a copy of Ovid's *Metamorphoses* (*see* OVID), which Lavinia is crucially able to use to indicate the identity of her attackers.

Lucrece

A narrative poem by Shakespeare, which was later entitled *The Rape of Lucrece*. It was first published in 1594, and dedicated to Henry Wriothsley, Earl of SOUTHAMPTON.

It consists of 265 seven-lined STANZAS in IAMBIC pentameters and has an *a b a b b c c* rhyme scheme. The poem recounts the story of the Roman prince Tarquin's rape of Lucrece and its tragic consequences. The first section explores Tarquin's feelings of guilt and conflict, while the rest is an expression of the distraught Lucrece's grief which, although eloquent, is too formal to inspire real sympathy.

Aroused by his friend Collatine's descriptions of the matchless beauty and virtue of his wife Lucrece, Tarquin becomes obsessed by the idea that he must possess her. He visits the unsuspecting Lucrece, and entertains her with accounts of her husband's military triumphs. As night falls, Tarquin wrestles with his 'frozen conscience and hot burning will', but his lust is overwhelming. He steals into Lucrece's chamber and rapes her. Afterwards, he flees, but Lucrece is condemned to live with the shame that rape has brought on her and on her husband. She begs Collatine to come to her so that she can tell him about her violation. Before she tells him the identity of the perpetrator, she extracts a promise from Collatine that he will take revenge. She reveals Tarquin's name and stabs herself, her self-sacrifice ensuring that Collatine's honour remains unblemished. Lucrece's bleeding body is borne through the streets of Rome, testament to Tarquin's appalling crime, while he is banished for ever.

Lucullus

A minor character in *Timon of Athens*, Lucullus is one of the flattering lords who take advantage of Timon's generosity. He keeps in favour with Timon by giving him a present of a pair of greyhounds. When Timon has lost all his money he sends his servant to Lucullus to ask for a loan. Lucullus, annoyed because he assumed that the servant was bringing him a gift from Timon, refuses, saying that mere friendship is not sufficient grounds for lending money without any security. Later, he tries to cover up his tightfisted response by bribing Timon's servant, Flaminius, to say that he was unable to find Lucullus.

Lucy, Sir William

A minor character in *King Henry VI, Part One*, a soldier who tries to persuade first York and then Somerset to send reinforcements to help Talbot in his final battle. Somerset and York, embroiled in their own quarrel, refuse to help and as a result the battle is lost and Talbot killed.

Lychorida

A minor character in *Pericles*, Lychorida is Marina's devoted nurse. She accompanies Pericles and Thaisa on their voyage to Tyre. When Thaisa gives birth to Marina,

Lychorida hands the newborn baby to Pericles, and tells him that his wife has died in childbirth. When Marina is given to Cleon and Dionyza to bring up as their own child, Lychorida stays with her 'little mistress'.

Lysander

A character in *A Midsummer Night's Dream*, Lysander is an Athenian courtier, and a romantic young man who is in love with Hermia. It is Lysander who makes the famous comment that the course of true love never did run smooth, and his experiences one midsummer's night prove him right. Forbidden to marry Hermia, Lysander suggests that they marry in secret outside Athens and beyond the reach of Athenian law. The lovers meet in a wood but become lost and are forced to spend the night in the open. There Lysander falls victim to Puck's meddling and is bewitched into transferring his affections from Hermia to her friend Helena. When he is finally released from the magic spell, his love for Hermia is restored and the Duke of Athens gives his blessing to their marriage.

Lysimachus

A character in *Pericles*, Lysimachus is the Governor of Mytilene, the city where Marina is sold into prostitution. The Bawd arranges a meeting between Lysimachus and Marina. He assumes that she is a prostitute, but she tells him that she is still a virgin and that she is held in the brothel against her will. Lysimachus is ashamed, and so struck by her purity that he says he will help her. In the end, Lysimachus is instrumental in reuniting Marina with her father. As Governor, he welcomes Pericles to Tyre and when he discovers that Pericles is grief-stricken at the supposed loss of his wife and daughter, he sends Marina to comfort him. Pericles is so grateful to Lysimachus for reuniting him with his daughter that he gives him Marina's hand in marriage, and the couple become the new rulers of Tyre.

Mm

Mab, Queen
A fairy queen, possibly drawn from Irish folklore, who is described in a fantastical speech by Mercutio in *Romeo and Juliet* as a 'midwife' who delivers dreams to those who sleep.

Macbeth
Historical Figure. A historical figure (c. 1005-1057) and the tragic hero of *Macbeth*, Macbeth is a courageous soldier fighting for Duncan, King of Scotland. Returned from battle, he meets three Witches who greet him with the title of Thane [chieftain] of Cawdor and predict that he will become king. When Duncan confers the title of Thane of Cawdor on Macbeth, he is fatally possessed by an ambition to become king himself. Inspired by his ruthless wife Lady Macbeth, who taunts him for being too soft-hearted, he embarks on a series of murders and begins his tragic descent into evil. He kills the King, and dispatches Banquo and the family of his enemy Macduff. Haunted by his crimes, Macbeth turns to the Witches for advice. They promise he will be safe unless two apparently impossible events take place, and Macbeth is temporarily reassured. His confidence is misplaced, and he is killed in battle by Macduff.

Macbeth
One of Shakespeare's later tragedies (*see* TRAGEDY), *Macbeth* was probably written in 1606, the year after the GUNPOWDER PLOT (a failed attempt to blow up Parliament and with it King James I of England), and so would have been especially relevant to contemporary audiences. The play is recorded as being performed at the GLOBE THEATRE in 1611, although it is probable that it was first performed sometime before then. It was not published until the First FOLIO of 1623. As a play about Scottish kingship, it may have been written to please King James who was also James VI of Scotland, and who claimed Duncan as one of his ancestors. James was particularly interested in the evils of witchcraft and himself author of a work on demonology. He was also patron of Shakespeare's company of actors the KING'S MEN.

 The principal source for the play was HOLINSHED'S *Chronicles* and the character of Macbeth was based on a historical figure, the King of Scotland from 1040 to 1057. Like Shakespeare's creation, the real Macbeth seized the crown after murdering Duncan whose family made several unsuccessful attempts to regain the thrown. The play explores themes of evil and witchcraft, suspicion and mistrust, and the supernatural; set in 11th century Scotland, the action is fast-moving and many of the scenes take place in the dark of night. *Macbeth* is sometimes known as the SCOTTISH PLAY, especially by members of the theatrical profession. The play has traditionally been associated with bad luck, and there is a superstition in the theatre that mentioning its real name will bring misfortune.

SYNOPSIS : Macbeth and Banquo have returned from a victorious campaign fought on behalf of Duncan, King of Scotland, and encounter three Witches. They hail Macbeth as Thane [chieftain] of Cawdor (a title he does not yet possess) and predict that he will become King, and that Banquo will father a line of kings. When Duncan rewards his bravery in battle with the title of Thane of Cawdor, the seeds of ambition grow in Macbeth. Possessed by the idea of becoming King and encouraged by his ruthlessly ambitious wife, Lady Macbeth, he commits his first murder, killing the King who is staying with him. Macbeth is crowned King, but begins to fear that Banquo suspects him and arranges for his murder. Macbeth is haunted by Banquo's ghost and, fearful that his crimes will be discovered, he consults the Witches again. They tell him to beware of the old King's general, Macduff, but say that only a man not born of a woman can harm Macbeth and that he will be safe until Birnam Wood moves to Dunsinane. These apparently impossible predictions restore Macbeth's confidence, but when he hears that Macduff has gone to England to join forces with the old King's son, Malcolm, he arranges for the murder of Macduff's wife and her son. Lady Macbeth goes mad and sleepwalks and Macbeth's crimes increasingly prey on his mind. Remembering the Witches' promises, Macbeth is unafraid at Dunsinane as Macduff's army advances, but the soldiers camouflage themselves with branches cut from the trees of Birnam Wood so that it appears as if the woods are moving towards him. Macduff and Macbeth meet and Macduff tells him that his was not a natural birth, so that technically he was not born of a woman. Macbeth knows then that the Witches' predictions have proved true; he is killed in combat by Macduff, and Malcolm is proclaimed king.

Macbeth, Lady
A historical figure (c. 1005-1054) and a character in *Macbeth*, Lady Macbeth is Macbeth's ruthless wife who, like the Witches, exerts an evil influence over her husband. Ambitious for power and inspired by Macbeth's account of the Witches' predictions, she urges him to overcome his scruples and to kill King Duncan. An accomplice in the King's murder, she herself drugs the soldiers guarding the King. Having pushed Macbeth into an abyss of evil, she calls on the powers of Hell to conceal their crime. Steeped in murder, Lady Macbeth finally goes mad, sleepwalking, endlessly washing imagined bloodstains from her hands. Eventually she kills herself.

Macduff
A historical figure (active c. 1054) and a character in *Macbeth*, Macduff is a Scottish nobleman, the Thane [chieftain] of Fife. After the murder of King Duncan, the honourable Macduff grows suspicious of Macbeth and refuses to attend his coronation. Loyal to the old King, he joins forces with Prince Malcolm in England where he hears of the terrible murder by Macbeth of his wife and son. Macduff returns to Scotland and kills Macbeth in battle as an act of personal revenge and displays Macbeth's severed head on a pole. The Witches had earlier warned Macbeth to beware of Macduff but reassured by them that no man born of a woman could harm him, Macbeth had no fear of his enemy. He discovered, too late, that since Macduff's was a caesarian birth [a surgical rather than a natural birth], he was not technically born of a woman.

Macduff, Lady
A minor character in *Macbeth*; Lady Macduff is Macduff's loving wife. When Macduff has left for England to raise an army against Macbeth, she is murdered with her son by Macbeth's hired assassins. Lady Macduff's gentleness as a wife and mother contrasts with Lady Macbeth's villainy.

Macmorris, Captain
A minor character in *King Henry V*, Macmorris is an officer in the English army fighting in France. A hot-tempered Irishman, Macmorris picks a fight with Fluellen, a Welshman who insults the Irish. However, he is impatient to go into battle with their joint enemy, the French, so the quarrel is postponed.

Macready, William Charles (1793–1873)
An actor and theatre manager who was noted as a tragedian and for his spectacular productions of Shakespeare's plays. He did much to restore Shakespeare's texts to their original form following adaptations by dramatists such as Colley CIBBER and Nahum TATE.

madness
The subject of madness is a theme in several of Shakespeare's plays, particularly in the tragedies. In *Hamlet*, the hero feigns madness as a way of discovering the truth, while Ophelia actually goes mad with grief over the death of her father and Hamlet's treatment of her. In *King Lear*, the old King goes mad and loses his grip on reality. In *Macbeth*, Lady Macbeth is driven mad with guilt and kills herself. Madness was a particular characteristic of the avenging hero in Elizabethan REVENGE PLAYS but it was also regarded as a subject for laughter. In Shakespeare's time, the public visited Bethlehem Hospital in London, called Bedlam, to laugh at the lunatics. (In *King Lear*, Edgar in his disguise as 'Poor Tom' calls himself 'Tom-a-Bedlam'). Malvolio in *Twelfth Night* is treated as a lunatic to the great amusement of his tormentors, Sir Toby Belch and Maria.

Maecenas
A historical figure (d. 8 BC) and a minor character in *Antony and Cleopatra*, Maecenas is one of Caesar's followers who tries to make peace between the Roman leaders. He understands the influence that Cleopatra has over Antony and sympathizes with Octavia, Antony's wife, when Antony leaves her. After the Battle of Actium, Maecenas advises Caesar to take advantage of Antony's distraction to advance on him. He comments after Antony's death that Antony possessed virtues and vices in equal measure.

Maid
A minor, non-speaking part, in *The Two Noble Kinsmen*, the Maid attends the Jailer's Daughter while she is recovering from her madness.

make-up
See COSTUME

malapropism
The unintentional and nearly always comic use of words in an incorrect sense. Dogberry, a character in *Much Ado about Nothing*, frequently misuses words in this

way. For example, he says: 'Comparisons are odorous', when what he really means is
that comparisons are 'odious'. The word malapropism derives from Mrs Malaprop, a
character in an 18th-century play, *The Rivals,* by Richard Brinsley Sheridan
(1751-1816), who famously misused words.

Malcolm

A historical figure (d. 1093) and a character in *Macbeth*, Malcolm is the elder son of
King Duncan of Scotland who is named as heir to the throne by his father. Malcolm
escapes to England after his father is murdered by Macbeth and with Macduff's support
he returns to Scotland and reclaims the crown. It is Malcolm who suggests to his
soldiers that they camouflage themselves with branches cut from the trees of Birnam
Wood.

Malvolio

Olivia's steward in *Twelfth Night*; his name means 'ill will'. Self-important,
mean-spirited, and censorious, Malvolio is the scourge of Sir Toby and his fellow
revellers who take their revenge in the comic SUB-PLOT of the play. He is tricked into
believing that Olivia loves him by a forged letter which appeals to his vanity, and
specifically instructs him to call on his mistress wearing ornate yellow stockings and
smiling. He is such a ludicrous figure that Olivia thinks he has lost his senses. This is
the cue for Sir Toby to have him bound and cast into a dark room where he is tormented
and treated as a lunatic. His downfall is POETIC JUSTICE, but Malvolio learns no
humility from his experiences. Unforgiving to the last, he swears revenge on everyone.

  The character of Malvolio may have been intended as a comic satire on a PURITAN
(possibly even on a real recognizable Puritan figure) and as such he would have been a
natural enemy of Shakespeare and his fellow dramatists. This might account for the fact
that Shakespeare creates such an unpleasant character that we can have very little
sympathy for Malvolio even when his fortunes are at their lowest ebb.

Mamillius

A minor character in *The Winter's Tale*, Mamillius is the young son of King Leontes
and Hermione. Like his mother, Mamillius becomes a victim of his father's insane
jealousy but his death from grief at his mother's wrongful arrest is the catalyst for
Leonte's realization that he has misjudged Hermione and for his subsequent remorse.
Mamillius is a playful child who likes to tell stories; he says: "A sad tale's best for
winter".

Marcade (Mercade)

A minor character in *Love's Labour's Lost*, Marcade is a lord in the Princess of France's
entourage. His announcement of the death of the King of France brings the comic
interlude of the NINE WORTHIES to an abrupt end.

Marcellus

A minor character in *Hamlet*, Marcellus is one of the sentries who has seen the Ghost of
Hamlet's Father before the play begins. He is present with Hamlet on the battlements
when the Ghost appears again and tries to dissuade Hamlet from following it.

March, Earl of

A character in *King Henry VI, Part One*; *see* MORTIMER, EDMUND.

Marcus Andronicus
A character in *Titus Andronicus*, Marcus is Titus' humane and straightforward brother and the one character, apart from Lavinia, who is not involved in the appalling cycle of revenge, preferring to be out hunting with his dogs. It is Marcus who discovers Lavinia, mutilated and bleeding, after the rape. He makes a long and formal speech, which some critics have regarded as a heartless response to such a shocking sight, but nevertheless shows concern for her distress. He offers to sacrifice his own hand, rather than Titus', as the ransom for the lives of Quintus and Martius. After Titus' death, Marcus grieves for his brother and justifies Titus' terrible revenge.

Some scholars have questioned the authorship of a scene in which Marcus appears as a man of uncharacteristic violence. He suddenly stabs a fly on his plate because, he says, it reminds him of the wicked Moor, Aaron.

Mardian
A minor character in *Antony and Cleopatra*, Mardian is a eunuch, a musician and entertainer at Cleopatra's court, mocked by his mistress for his sexlessness. Cleopatra sends Mardian to Antony with the false report of her suicide prompting Antony's own tragic death.

Margarelon
A legendary figure and a minor character in *Troilus and Cressida*, Margarelon is the Trojan King Priam's illegitimate son. When he meets Thersites on the battlefield, Margarelon announces himself as a bastard and challenges Thersites to fight but Thersites refuses, saying that he too is a bastard and that one bastard should not fight another.

Margaret
A character in *Much Ado About Nothing*, Margaret is one of Hero's gentlewomen. A cheerful and humorous young woman, she is an innocent pawn in Borachio's scheme to make Hero appear promiscuous. Margaret is persuaded by Borachio, who is pretending to woo her, to dress up in Hero's clothes and to stand at her window one night while Borachio flirts with her from below in hidden in the dark. When Borachio is arrested, he admits his own guilt but swears that Margaret was entirely innocent.

Margaret, (later Queen Margaret)
A historical figure (1430-1482) and a character in *King Henry VI, Parts One, Two and Three* and *King Richard III*: in *Henry VI, Part One*, Margaret's role is a minor one. Daughter of Reignier, the French Duke of Anjou, she is taken as a prisoner of war by the Duke of Suffolk who falls in love with her but woos her on behalf of the young King Henry. When Margaret's marriage with the King is agreed, Suffolk says that Margaret will rule Henry but that he, Suffolk, will rule over them both.

In *Part Two,* Margaret is Queen, but she jeers at King Henry's piety and exploits his weakness to acquire power for herself. She conspires with her old ally Suffolk to bring about the downfall and later the death of the old Duke of Gloucester, the King's advisor and Protector of England. King Henry mourns Gloucester's death but Margaret is exultant. She complains that Henry is so absorbed in his grief that he is neglecting her. When Henry banishes Suffolk for plotting Gloucester's death, Suffolk and Margaret reveal their shared love as they part. Suffolk is killed on his journey into exile and his murderers take his severed head to court where Margaret cradles it in a final gruesome farewell.

In *Part Three*, Margaret snatches the reins of power from the weak King Henry and leads his army against the forces of the Duke of York and his son Edward, Earl of March, the future King Edward IV. Her pitiless nature is evident after the battle of Wakefield when, having captured the Duke of York, she postpones killing him in order to humiliate him first. She puts a paper crown on his head and taunts him about the death of his young son. When it seems that King Henry's cause is lost, Margaret enlists the help of the King of France, but she is finally defeated. She is taken prisoner and her son, the young Prince of Wales, is killed before her eyes before Edward banishes her to France.

In *King Richard III*, Margaret is the Lancastrian King Henry VI's widow (see above). The old Queen is consumed by her hatred of the Yorkist Richard whom she believes killed her husband. (*See* WARS OF THE ROSES.) She curses Queen Elizabeth and Richard, calling for vengeance and rejoicing after the murder of the little Princes (members of the House of York and heirs to the throne) in the TOWER OF LONDON. A French woman, Margaret returns to France before the Battle of Bosworth. Margaret's speeches lament the disruption of the kingdom and the chain of evil and retribution.

Maria[1]

A character in *Love's Labour's Lost*, Maria is one of the ladies-in-waiting who visits the court of Navarre with the French Princess. A witty, if rather one-dimensional character, Maria is wooed by Longaville, whom she promises she to marry after a testing period of twelve months.

Maria[2]

A character in *Twelfth Night*, Maria is Olivia's maid and a feisty and literate young woman who can read and write as well as her mistress. This skill, together with her shrewd assessment of others, are essential elements in the plot against Malvolio. Maria sharply rebukes Sir Toby for keeping late hours, but when Malvolio similarly reprimands Sir Toby and Feste for singing loudly, Maria is outraged and plots her revenge. She forges the letter, supposedly from Olivia, which exploits Malvolio's vanity and brings about his downfall. We hear at the end of the play that she has married Sir Toby.

There are several references in the play to Maria's small size; Sir Toby calls her a little wren. This may originate from the size of the boy player who first took the part.

Mariana[1]

A minor character in *All's Well that Ends Well*, Mariana is a friend of the Widow Capilet in Florence who tells Diana that the Frenchmen are in town, and not to be trusted, particularly Parolles.

Mariana[2]

A character in *Measure for Measure*, Mariana was engaged to be married to Angelo and although he abandoned her when her dowry was lost at sea she loves him still. Mariana agrees to substitute herself for Isabella in Angelo's bed in the scheme to save Claudio's life; she is glad to spare Isabella from shame but with the bed trick she also hopes to win Angelo back for herself. Despite Angelo's lies and hypocrisy, Mariana pleads afterwards with the Duke to spare his life and happily marries him at last. Her forgiveness of Angelo is an important part of the play's final reconciliation.

Marina

A character in *Pericles*, Marina is Pericles and Thaisa's daughter. She is born at sea (her name means 'of the sea') in a storm and it is believed that her mother has died giving birth to her. Pericles gives Marina into the care of the wicked Cleon and Dionyza to be brought up as their own but she grows up to be so much more gifted and charming than their own daughter that her foster parents plan to kill her. She narrowly escapes death but she is snatched by pirates and sold into prostitution. Her innocent virtue has such a profound effect on the men who visit the brothel where she is held that they all become reformed, to the fury of her captors. She is rescued by Lysimachus, who by chance sends Marina to comfort Pericles who is ill with grief, believing that his wife and daughter are both dead. Reunited with his daughter, Pericles is so grateful to Lysimachus that he gives Marina to him in marriage.

Mariner

A minor character in *The Winter's Tale*, the Mariner is a member of the ship's crew that brings Antigonus to the shores of Bohemia where the infant Perdita is abandoned. He warns Antigonus (who is eaten by a bear) that Bohemia is well-known for its wild animals. The Mariner dies in a storm.

Mariners

Minor characters in *The Tempest*, the Mariners are the crew of the ship that is driven by the storm onto Prospero's island. They believe the ship is doomed and resort to prayer.

Mark Antony

A central character in *Antony and Cleopatra* and *Julius Caesar*; *see* ANTONY, MARK.

Marlowe, Christopher (Kit) (1564–93)

A playwright and poet and the son of a shoemaker, Marlowe was educated at Cambridge University. Born in the same year as Shakespeare, he became attached to Edward Alleyn's company of players, the ADMIRAL'S MEN, in 1588 as a dramatist. Marlowe led a debauched life; he was a homosexual and an atheist who expressed such strongly heretical opinions that he was arrested in 1593. Before he could be brought to trial, he was killed during a quarrel in a tavern in Deptford, South London. It has been suggested (though never proved) that he was a government spy and that there may have been a political conspiracy to have him killed.

Had Marlowe lived longer, it is conjectured that he might have become as great a dramatist as Shakespeare. Certainly Marlowe's magnificent verse influenced Shakespeare, who quoted a line from his poem 'Hero and Leander' in *As You Like It* ('Who ever loved that loved not at first sight?'). Marlowe's plays include *Tamburlaine* (c. 1587), one of the first verse dramas to use the medium of BLANK VERSE, *The Jew of Malta* (c. 1588), *Edward II* (c. 1593), and the *Tragedy of Dr Faustus* (probably written around 1588 and published in 1601). It is thought that Marlowe may have been part author of Shakespeare's *Titus Andronicus* and possibly of *King Henry VI*. The theory that he was the author of all of Shakespeare's plays has been discredited.

Marshal, the Lord
A minor character in *King Richard II*, the Lord Marshal is a formal official at the fight between Mowbray and Bolingbroke.

Martext, Sir Oliver
A minor character in *As You Like It*, Sir Oliver Martext is the country curate who is called in to marry Audrey and Touchstone. Jaques has a poor opinion of the curate and interrupts the ceremony, advising Audrey and Touchstone to find a properly qualified priest and to marry in a church. Sir Oliver's name suggests that he might not be able to conduct a marriage properly since he might mar [spoil] the text of the wedding service.

Martius
A character in *Titus Andronicus*, Martius is one of Titus' sons. He helps his brother Mutius and Bassianus snatch Lavinia away before she can be married to Saturnius. As part of the cycle of revenge in the play, Martius with his brother Quintus is framed by the wicked Aaron for the murder of Bassianus. Innocent of the crime, the brothers are led away to their execution as Titus vainly pleads for their lives. Desperate to save his sons, Titus agrees to cut off his hand in exchange for their lives. Titus' hand together with Martius and Quintus' severed heads are returned to him half an hour later, a cruel trick that Aaron relishes. *See also* QUINTUS.

Martius (Marcius), Caius
The name of the hero of *Coriolanus* before he is given the new name of CORIOLANUS in recognition of his great victory at Corioli.

Martius, Young
A minor character in *Coriolanus*, Martius is the young son of Coriolanus and Virgilia. When Virgilia with her mother-in-law Volumnia visit Coriolanus to beg him not to invade Rome, Martius accompanies them and declares that when he is older he will stand and fight, and not run away from danger. Valeria describes Young Martius catching butterflies and tearing them to shreds with his teeth.

Marullus
A minor character in *Julius Caesar*; *see* MURELLUS.

masculine ending
The concluding syllable of a line of verse when it ends with a stressed syllable, for example: 'Shall I compare thee to a summer's *day*'. *Compare* FEMININE ENDING. *See also* STRESS.

masque
Originally a court entertainment in Renaissance Italy, in which masked players performed a short play about mythological characters with interludes of dance and song. Masques were often performed during banquets and the players would mingle with the spectators, asking members of the audience to join in the dance and sometimes presenting them with small gifts. In *King Henry VIII*, the King appears in a masque given at Wolsey's banquet. The King, dressed as a shepherd, asks Anne Boleyn to dance with him. In *Timon of Athens*, a masque is performed at Timon's banquet by the character Cupid with several 'Amazons'; the guests leave the table and each of them

singles out an 'Amazon' to dance with. There are tableau-like masques in *The Tempest*, featuring Prospero's Spirits, which are performed to celebrate Miranda and Ferdinand's betrothal and not only add a spectacular element but also illuminate the story.

In RENAISSANCE England masques developed into extravagant entertainments in which spectacle and music were more important than character and story. They were extremely popular at the courts of Queen Elizabeth I and later of King James I. However, the emphasis on visual effects began eventually to wane, partly because of the enormous costs involved, and dramatists, in particular Ben JONSON, began to be more concerned with the written element.

Unlike actors, masquers were strictly amateur (although occasionally professional actors were hired to take speaking parts) and often members of the court, including women, and children from the Royal choir schools appeared in masques. A troupe of masquers accompany Romeo to the Capulet's ball in *Romeo and Juliet* and the most 'lamentable comedy' of Pyramus and Thisbe in *A Midsummer Night's Dream* is an 'anti-masque', or comic version of a masque.

Massinger, Philip (1583–1640)
An Jacobean dramatist, best known for his satirical comedy, *A New Way To Pay Old Debts* (c. 1625), although much of his work expressed strongly moralistic and Roman Catholic beliefs. From about 1613-15 Massinger wrote plays for the theatre manager Philip HENSLOWE, and collaborated with his fellow dramatists DEKKER and FLETCHER. It is thought by some scholars that he may have had a hand in the writing of Shakespeare's *King Henry VIII* and possibly in *The Two Noble Kinsmen*.

Master of a ship
A minor character in *The Tempest*, the Master is the captain of the ship driven by the storm onto Prospero's magic island. He survives the shipwreck and is amazed to find his ship miraculously restored to its former glory by Prospero's magic at the end of the play.

Master of the Revels
An officer at the court in Shakespeare's time, below the LORD CHAMBERLAIN in rank, whose job was to supervise entertainments for the Queen or King and who was responsible for employing musicians, poets and actors. From 1581 onwards, the OFFICE OF THE REVELS also acted as a licensing authority for plays, censoring those which were thought to contain anything politically subversive, or morally suspect or blasphemous, and to whom companies of players had to apply for permission to perform. In 1606 the powers of the Office were extended to include the publication of plays.

SIR EDMUND TILNEY was Master of the Revels from 1579 until his death in 1610, a time of growing splendour in court entertainment. He was paid a nominal salary for the job, but also made a considerable income from the licensing fees. The Office of the Revels eventually became a theatrical company itself.

Master-Gunner of Orleans, and his Son
A minor character in *King Henry VI, Part One*, the Master-Gunner is a French soldier at the Siege of Orleans. He trains his gun on the English nobles who are spying on the French and his son. fires it, killing the Earl of Salisbury.

Maudlin
A minor, non-speaking part in *The Two Noble Kinsmen*, Maudlin is one of the Morris dancers who perform for Duke Theseus. See COUNTRYWOMEN.

Mayor of London
A minor character in *King Henry VI, Part One*, the Mayor tries to prevent the followers of the Duke of Gloucester and the Bishop of Winchester from fighting and reports outbreaks of disorder on the streets of London.

Mayor of London, Lord
A minor character in *King Richard III*, the mayor is a local politician who is easily persuaded that Hastings' execution was justified.

Mayor of York
A minor character in *King Henry VI, Part Three*, the Mayor is loyal to King Henry. At first he refuses to admit Edward, the King's rival for the throne, to the City of York but he is eventually persuaded to open the city gates.

Measure for Measure
One of Shakespeare's PROBLEM plays, *Measure for Measure* was written around 1603-04 and first published in the First FOLIO edition of 1623. It was first performed on Boxing Day of 1604 by the KING'S MEN.

The primary source for the play was an earlier play, *Promos and Cassandra* (1578) by the English writer George Whetstone (c. 1555-c. 1587). Set in Vienna, *Measure for Measure* explores themes of justice and mercy, chastity and permissiveness.

SYNOPSIS : The Duke of Vienna is concerned that his rule has been too permissive and that as a result Vienna has become an immoral place. He decides to disappear for a while and to hand over power to a deputy, Angelo, whom he believes will restore discipline. Disguised as a friar, he watches what happens under Angelo's sterner regime. Angelo loses no time in enforcing the letter of law. He revives ancient legislation and sentences Claudio to death for making his fiancee Juliet pregnant. Claudio asks his sister, Isabella, to plead with Angelo for his life. Isabella is about to enter a convent and when Angelo agrees to free Claudio only if she will sleep with him, she is appalled and refuses to do so, adamant that she cannot break her vow of chastity even if it means her brother's death. The Duke, who as the Friar has been observing events, suggests a plan to substitute Angelo's ex-fiancee Mariana (whom Angelo abandoned because of problems over her dowry) for Isabella in Angelo's bed. Angelo is fooled and sends instructions to the prison to pardon Claudio, but secretly he orders Claudio's execution to go ahead and demands his head be brought to him. The Duke foils Angelo by arranging for the head of another prisoner who has just died to be taken to Angelo instead and Claudio is saved. The Duke returns to Vienna as himself and, pretending to be ignorant of everything that has happened, listens to the cases that Isabella and Juliet have brought against Angelo. In the end he admits to having been disguised as the Friar, and to knowing the whole truth. Angelo is sentenced to death, but the Duke orders him to marry Mariana before being executed. Isabella and Mariana plead for Angelo's life to be spared, and in the final reconciliation Angelo makes a full repentance, Claudio and Juliet are reunited, and the Duke asks Isabella to be his wife.

Mecaenas
See MAECENAS.

medial stop
A stop (.) or a pause (:) in the middle of a line of verse. *See* CAESURA *for an example.*

melodrama
Literally drama with music; although the term only originated in the late 18th century, it is often used to describe a play in which there is clearly defined morality, heightened emotion, fast-moving action and stereotypical heroes, heroines and villains. Shakespeare's character Richard III is sometimes described as a 'melodramatic villain'.

Melun
A minor character in *King John*, Melun is a French noble who, dying on the field of battle, warns the English nobles Pembroke and Salisbury that the treacherous French Dauphin is going to kill them.

Menas
A minor character in *Antony and Cleopatra*, Menas is one of the notorious and bloodthirsty pirates fighting for Pompey against Caesar. When Pompey makes his peace treaty with Caesar, Menas thinks he has made a mistake. During the drunken feast held aboard Pompey's ship to celebrate the peace, Menas, a cynical opportunist, suggests that Pompey should cut the throats of the Roman leaders and seize power for himself. When Pompey refuses, Menas decides to seek his fortunes elsewhere.

Menecrates
A minor character in *Antony and Cleopatra*, Menecrates, with Menas, is one of the notorious pirates who fights for Pompey in his rebellion against Caesar.

Menelaus
A figure from Greek legend, and a minor character in *Troilus and Cressida*, Menelaus is one of the Greek leaders and Agamemnon's brother who was married to Helen before her capture by the Trojans. Menelaus is ridiculed by his fellow Greeks because he is a cuckold [the husband of a wife who has committed adultery].

Menenius Agrippa
A legendary figure and a character in *Coriolanus*, Menenius is Coriolanus' loyal friend. He is an ageing Roman aristocrat who tries to mediate between the ordinary Citizens of Rome and its rulers. He tells the discontented crowd the fable of the belly and its members [limbs] to explain the relationship in society between the unthinking masses and their responsible rulers. He tries to prevent the riot that breaks out after Coriolanus has addressed the people, asking them to understand that Coriolanus is a warrior and a man of action not of words. When Coriolanus threatens to conquer Rome, Menenius tries once more to make peace. Thoughtfully, he waits until after Coriolanus has dined before he speaks, but his words fall on deaf ears.

Menteth or Menteith
A minor character in *Macbeth*, Menteth a Scottish nobleman who joins forces with Prince Malcolm against Macbeth.

Mercade
See MARCADE.

Merchant, First and Second
Two minor characters in *The Comedy of Errors*; the First Merchant warns Syracuse
Antipholus on his arrival in Ephesus of the law which condemns strangers to death
unless they can pay a ransom.

The Second Merchant is owed money by Angelo the goldsmith who cannot pay
because he in turn is owed money by Ephesus Antipholus for a gold chain. In a violent
rage, the Second Merchant has Antipholus and Angelo arrested, but when he is told that
Antipholus is mad he hastily withdraws.

Merchant of Venice, The
Written between 1596-98, *The Merchant of Venice* was first published, as a comedy, in
a QUARTO edition in 1600. The play's first recorded performance was in at King
James's court in 1605 when it played twice in one week, but there were certainly
unrecorded performances before then. During the 19th century, *The Merchant of Venice*
was particularly popular in England, the role of Shylock made famous by actors such as
Edmund KEAN and Sir Henry IRVING. Nineteenth century stage directors produced
increasingly elaborate sets and amazing special effects for the play set in Venice, with
bridges and gondolas.

The main sources for the play were a story, *Il Pecorone* (1558) by Ser Giovanni and
other, older, traditional stories of the bond [promise to repay borrowed money] for flesh
and the caskets. It is possible, too, that Shakespeare's play may have been indebted to
some extent to *The Jew Of Malta* (1589) by Christopher MARLOWE. Set mostly in
Venice, *The Merchant of Venice* explores themes of greed, and love and forgiveness,
and anti-semitism, a prejudice that flourished in Elizabethan England. Jews had been
mostly expelled from England three hundred years earlier; those remaining in London in
Shakespeare's time were required by law to conform, outwardly at least, to Christianity.
Many Elizabethans would have relied on borrowing money from Jewish moneylenders,
but nonetheless usury [lending money at extortionate rates of interest], practised by the
Jews, was disapproved of. The fact that a Jewish man had been condemned to death for
treason only a few years before the play was written, may have added to a
well-established prejudice.

SYNOPSIS : Bassanio loves the beautiful heiress Portia, but lacks the money to
court her. His friend Antonio is keen to help but since all his money is tied up in a
fleet of merchant ships, Bassanio has to raise a loan from the miserly Jewish
moneylender Shylock. Antonio cheerfully signs an agreement guaranteeing that if
the debt is not repaid within three months when his ships return to Venice, Shylock
can take a pound of flesh instead. Bassanio, courting the heiress Portia, is required
by the terms of her father's will, to chose one of three caskets (one is gold, one
silver and one lead) in order to win her hand. Bassanio, faced with the test, chooses
the lead casket reasoning that external worth and beauty are less important than
what lies inside; his choice is the right one and Portia lovingly accepts him as her
husband. Their happiness is interrupted by news that Shylock has called in
Bassanio's debt and, as all his ships have been lost at sea, Antonio has no money to
pay. Shylock is demanding his pound of flesh and Antonio has been arrested.

Bassanio leaves to help Antonio and Portia implements her own plan to help her
lover and his friend. Disguised as a young lawyer she arrives in the courtroom but
despite her eloquent plea for mercy, Shylock refuses to make any kind of
compromise and sharpens his knife. His daughter, Jessica, has recently eloped with
a Christian nobleman, Lorenzo, and her defection has fuelled Shylock's hatred of
the Christians who abuse and insult him. Portia agrees that he can take his pound of
flesh but says under the terms of his agreement with Antonio he cannot shed one
single drop of blood. Shylock is defeated and stripped of his wealth, Antonio is
freed, and there is a happy reunion of lovers and friends. See also anti-semitism,
Jews

Mercutio

A character in *Romeo and Juliet*, Mercutio is Romeo's carefree and witty friend, a
mercurial character, as his name implies. Mercutio, who makes light of everything, is
cynical about love (his speeches are full of sexual innuendoes) and he teases Romeo
about his youthful passion for Rosaline and then about his more mature love for Juliet.
Reckless and impulsive, Mercutio becomes involved in a quarrel with Tybalt, Juliet's
cousin, which escalates into a fight; he is killed, another victim of the feud between the
Capulets and Montagues. Mercutio dies with a pun on his lips but his death sparks the
chain of events that leads to the tragic deaths of Romeo and Juliet.

It has been suggested that the character of Mercutio was based on Shakespeare's
contemporary, the playwright Christopher MARLOWE. *See also* MAB.

Merry Wives of Windsor, The

One of Shakespeare's comedies, *The Merry Wives of Windsor* was written around
1596-97. There is a tradition that Shakespeare wrote the play in response to a request
from Queen Elizabeth I who particularly liked the character of Falstaff and wanted to
see a play in which the fat knight fell in love. *The Merry Wives of Windsor* was probably
first performed in 1597, and first published in a QUARTO edition in 1602.

The plot of *The Merry Wives of Windsor* is largely Shakespeare's own invention but the
basic story of an unfaithful wife hiding her lover from a jealous husband was an old one
even in Shakespeare's time. The play is unusual for being written in prose, except for
the love scenes between Anne and Fenton, and also because the prime movers in the
plot are women. It is a fast-moving FARCE, set in a bourgeois world, that hinges on
intrigue and disguise with a cast of easily identifiable and often wildly eccentric comic
characters.

SYNOPSIS : Falstaff is courting Mistress Ford and Mistress Page at the same time.
The two Merry Wives are outraged at the insult to their honour as respectable
married women, and furious that he is adding insult to injury by courting them
simultaneously. They plan to teach him a lesson and as Mistress Ford is weary of
her husband's pathological jealousy, their plot involves making a fool of him at the
same time. The Wives invite Falstaff to visit Mistress Ford at her house at a time
when Mr Ford is going to be out. Mr Ford, meanwhile, has got wind of the
proposed meeting between Falstaff and his wife. The Wives arrange things so that
Mr Ford (who has disguised himself as a Mr Brook to catch his wife out), bursts in
during the meeting. They bundle Falstaff into a basket of dirty washing which is
carried off and dumped unceremoniously in a muddy ditch. They repeat the trick,

but on the second occasion they disguise Falstaff as an old lady for whom Ford has a passionate hatred. Ford chases Falstaff and beats him black and blue. When Ford discovers that he has been fooled but that his wife is entirely faithful, they plan Falstaff's final humiliation, which reaches a climax at midnight in Windsor Park, when a group of children dressed as fairies, pursue and torment him. In a SUB-PLOT, the beautiful young Anne Page has three suitors; the dim-witted Slender, the flamboyant French Doctor Caius and the romantic young nobleman Fenton. Her parents disapprove of Fenton; her father arranges for her to marry Slender while her mother arranges her elopement with Dr Caius. Anne foils them by marrying Fenton in secret and Slender and Dr Caius are each tricked into eloping with a boy in women's clothes. In the happy resolution at the end of the play, all wrongdoing is forgiven and everyone is reconciled.

Messala
A historical figure (64 BC-AD 8) and a minor character in *Julius Caesar*, Messala is a supporter of Brutus and Cassius and a soldier in their army. After Caesar's death, Messala brings news to Cassius and Brutus that Octavius and Antony have put a hundred senators, including Cicero, to death and confirms that Portia has died. Messala fights at the battle of Philippi and is reporting to Titinius that Brutus's army has triumphed over Octavius when he discovers the body of Cassius. Messala himself is captured by Octavius and Antony.

Messengers
Minor characters in *The Two Noble Kinsmen*, a Messenger announces the arrival of Arcite and Palamon at the tournament and describes in detail the magnificence of the Knights. After the duel and Palamon's defeat, a Messenger rushes on to halt Palamon's execution because Arcite has been thrown from his horse and killed.

Metamorphoses
See OVID.

metaphor
A way of using language to describe a person, thing or action by likening it to something else that it resembles. The likeness is not intended to be literal but to emphasize a particular quality. For example, the villainous, hunchback King Richard III of Shakespeare's play is referred to as 'that bottled spider ... this pois'nous bunch-back'd toad'. *Compare* IMAGERY; SIMILE; SYMBOL; ALLEGORY.

metaphysical
The word 'metaphysics' (a branch of philosophy concerned with the nature of reality) was first used in a literary connection by the poet and critic John Dryden to describe John Donne's poetry in his *Discourse of Satire* (1693). The term 'metaphysical' was later extended by the 18th-century writer Dr Johnson to describe the group of 17th-century poets, including Donne, whose work is characterized by a dramatic style of writing, full of startling images, parallels and FIGURES OF SPEECH, in contrast to the elegant and idealized love poetry of many Elizabethan poets. Some passages of Shakespeare's poetry foreshadow the metaphysical style.

Metellus Cimber

A historical figure (d. 44 BC) and a character in *Julius Caesar*; Metellus is one of the conspirators against Caesar who is present when the assassination is planned. Metellus' brother has been ordered into exile by Caesar and, as part of the assassination plot, Metellus stops Caesar as he is approaching the Capitol and begs him to allow his brother to return to Rome. The Conspirators are confident that Caesar will say 'no' to Metellus' request, as he has done before, and his refusal is to be the signal for them to crowd round Caesar and stab him.

metonymy

A word or phrase that is associated with somebody or something, and which can be used to represent that thing. For example, the monarchy is commonly referred to as 'the crown'. *Compare* SYNECDOCHE.

metre

Metre is the regular pattern of syllables, stressed and unstressed, that is found in most forms of poetry. In verse, units of syllables known as feet (*see* FOOT) are often arranged in a particular pattern so as to create a regularly repeated rhythm. A verse line structured in this way is known as a METRIC LINE. Lines may be of different lengths, with anything from one to six feet per line; Shakespeare's verse mostly consists of a pentameter line containing five feet (*see* IAMBIC PENTAMETER). The most common metre in English verse is the IAMBIC METRE in which a weak syllable (marked ˘) is followed by a strong one (marked ˉ): 'To be or not to be'.

Michael

A minor character in *King Henry VI, Part Two*, Michael is one of the rebel Jack Cade's followers.

Michael, Sir

A minor character in *King Henry IV, Part One*, Sir Michael is a friend of Richard Scroop, the Archbishop of York and a supporter of the rebel cause against King Henry.

Middleton, Thomas (1580-1627)

An Elizabethan playwright who wrote for the theatre manager Philip HENSLOWE, Middleton collaborated with his fellow dramatist Thomas DEKKER. He wrote a number of comedies for the boy actors of the CHILDREN OF ST PAUL'S but he is probably best remembered now for his tragedy *The Changeling* (1623). For a time during the middle of the 17th century it was thought that some of Middleton's work had been written by Shakespeare.

Midsummer Night's Dream, A

One of Shakespeare's best-known comedies written around 1594-96, *A Midsummer Night's Dream*, was first published in a QUARTO edition in 1600. The play's first recorded performance was at court in 1604, but it may originally have been written as part of the wedding celebrations for the Earl of Derby's marriage in 1595. It was certainly performed publicly several times before 1604. Main sources for the play were Ovid's *Metamorphoses* (*see* OVID), the *Knight's Tale* by Geoffrey Chaucer (c. 1345-1400), and stories from English folklore. The play, set in Athens in ancient Greece, is a fairy story which explores themes of love and marriage, jealousy, and magic.

SYNOPSIS : Hermia's father wants her to marry Demetrius but Hermia loves Lysander; together they decide to run away and marry in secret. Before fleeing to the woods beyond Athens, Hermia tells her friend Helena of the proposed elopement, but Helena, who is hopelessly in love with Demetrius, betrays her confidence and tells Demetrius, who sets off in pursuit of the lovers. He is pursued by the doting Helena. In the woods, the invisible King and Queen of the fairies, Oberon and Titania, are quarrelling. Oberon bewitches Titania as she sleeps so that she will fall in love with the first thing she sets eyes on when she wakes. Oberon has been observing the mortal lovers and feels particularly sorry for Helena. He instructs Puck to use some of the same magic on Demetrius so that he will love Helena. By mistake, Puck casts the spell on Lysander who falls out of love with Hermia and in love with Helena; later Oberon enchants Demetrius who falls for Helena too. Hermia, whom nobody now loves, is furious and quarrels violently with Helena while Lysander and Demetrius plan to fight a duel. Puck leads the confused lovers a merry dance through the wood until they fall into an exhausted sleep, and he can remove the spells. While these events are unfolding, Bottom and his troupe of Athenian workmen are holding rehearsals in another part of the wood for the tragedy of *Pyramus and Thisbe* which they are going to perform at court. Puck, mischievously changes Bottom's head into an ass's head, and makes sure that this is the first sight that greets the waking Titania. She falls passionately in love with Bottom, until Oberon releases her from his charm and Bottom becomes fully human again. The worlds of the fairies and the mortals are restored to harmony. Lysander and Hermia are reunited, and Demetrius now loves Helena. They celebrate their weddings with Theseus, Duke of Athens and his new wife, Hippolyta, entertained by a performance of *Pyramus and Thisbe*.

Milan, Duke of
A minor character in *The Two Gentlemen of Verona*; *see* DUKE.

miracle plays
Early dramatizations of the lives of saints and martyrs, originally written in Latin and performed in churches by priests, miracle plays were the forerunners of 14th century MYSTERY plays.

Miranda
The heroine of *The Tempest*, Miranda is Prospero's daughter and the only woman on his enchanted island. When Miranda was only three years old, she and her father were cast adrift in a small boat by Prospero's wicked brother Antonio and washed up on the uninhabited island's shores. At the time of the play, they have lived there for twelve years and Miranda has never seen any man other than her father. When Ferdinand, who is the son of Prospero's old enemy Alonso, is shipwrecked on the island, Miranda assumes at first that he must be a spirit like Ariel because he seems too noble to be a mere mortal. Miranda and Ferdinand fall in love and, eventually, Prospero gives his blessing to their marriage. In the happy resolution to the play Miranda is joyfully accepted by Alonso as his daughter-in-law. Miranda represents an ideal of innocence, goodness and beauty; her name, which was invented by Shakespeare for his heroine, means 'worthy of admiration'.

Mistress Quickly
A character in *King Henry IV, Parts One and Two*, *King Henry V* and *The Merry Wives of Windsor*; *see* QUICKLY, MISTRESS.

monologue
A monologue is a speech, sometimes a long one, written to be spoken by one person, and usually addressed to the audience rather than to another character on stage. It may be in the form of a PROLOGUE or an EPILOGUE, in which the actor comments on the play, or a SOLILOQUY in which the character may reveal his inner thoughts.

monosyllable
A word which consists of only one syllable. *Compare* POLYSYLLABIC.

Montague
A minor character in *Romeo and Juliet*, Montague is Romeo's father and head of the family feuding with the Capulets in Verona. In the reconciliation at the end of the play, he promises to put up a memorial statue of Juliet, his former enemy's daughter.

Montague, Lady,
A minor character in *Romeo and Juliet*, Lady Montague is Romeo's mother. She is a shadowy figure who appears briefly only twice in the play.

Montague, Marquess of
A historical figure (c. 1428-1471) and a minor character in *King Henry VI, Part Three*, Montague is a supporter of the Duke of York and of Edward. When Edward marries Lady Grey instead of making a diplomatic marriage with the French King's sister-in-law, Montague is furious and abandons the Yorkist cause to fight for the Earl of Warwick and King Henry.

Montaigne, Michel de (1533–1592)
A French writer, Montaigne is regarded as the innovator of the 'essay', a short prose composition which discusses a particular point of view in matters of philosophy, or politics, or religion, in an informal and intimate way. Montaigne, a nobleman and frequent visitor to the Royal court in Paris, trained first as a lawyer. He retired to his country estate in 1568 and devoted his time to writing. His Essays, first published in 1580, were known to Shakespeare in an English translation of 1603 by John Florio (1553-1625), and the essay 'Of Cannibals', in which he describes an ideal community in the newly-discovered America, undoubtedly influenced Shakespeare's writing of *The Tempest*.

Montano
A minor character in *Othello*, Montano is the Governor of Cyprus before Othello's appointment. He is persuaded by Iago that Cassio is a drunkard: this is part of Iago's treacherous plan to discredit Cassio and Othello. When he tries to prevent Cassio from becoming involved in a fight, Montano is wounded. At the end of the play, he captures Iago when he tries to flee from the consequences of his villainy.

Montgomery, Sir John
A historical figure (c. 1430-1495) and a minor character in *King Henry VI, Part Three*, Montgomery is a supporter of Edward and the Yorkist claim to the throne against King Henry.

Montjoy, the French Herald

A minor character in *King Henry V*, Montjoy visits King Henry's court in England to deliver a defiant message from the French King; nonetheless he is received with great courtesy. Before the Battle of Agincourt, when the French are confident of victory, Montjoy comes from the Constable of France asking the English King what ransom he will offer when he is defeated. The French herald's confidence is short-lived; the French are beaten at AGINCOURT and Montjoy asks King Henry for permission to bury the French dead.

The Moor

The name sometimes given to OTHELLO, the Moor of Venice, and the title character of Othello.

Mopsa

A minor character in *The Winter's Tale*, Mopsa is a shepherdess in Bohemia who sings and dances at the sheep-shearing feast.

morality plays

Medieval allegorical (see ALLEGORY) dramas containing a strong Christian moral in which abstracts such as Virtue and Vice were personified. Scenes often included devils dressed in red and black, herding the damned into a HELL MOUTH. Morality plays developed from earlier miracle plays, and were acted in the open air by amateur players. Their influence is evident in much Elizabethan drama; *King Richard III*, for example, derives to some extent from such conventions with its personification of evil in Richard. The best-remembered of the morality plays today is the late 15th-century *Everyman*.

Morgan

In *Cymbeline*, Morgan is the name that the banished BELARIUS takes while he is living in exile.

Morocco, Prince of

A minor character in *The Merchant of Venice*, the Prince of Morocco is one of Portia's unsuccessful suitors who must chose one of three caskets in order to win Portia's hand in marriage. He chooses the golden casket on the basis that it is the most valuable and desirable of the three but discovers that 'all that glisters is not gold'. Portia is glad to be rid of him.

morris dance

A traditional English folk dance, possibly of Moorish origins, which is still performed today. The morris dance is particularly associated with May Day celebrations and frequently represents characters from the legend of Robin Hood. A hobby-horse is sometimes featured and the dancers have ribbons and bells attached to their clothes.

Mortimer, Edmund, Earl of March[1]

A historical figure (1376- c. 1409), uncle to Mortimer, Earl of March (see below) and a minor character in *King Henry IV, Part One*. Mortimer, a supporter of King Henry, fights for the King and is captured in battle by Glendower. When King Henry hears that Mortimer has married his enemy Glendower's daughter (*see* MORTIMER, LADY *below*), he refuses to ransom him. This provokes a disagreement between the King and Hotspur, who is married to Mortimer's sister. When the nobles rebel against the King, Mortimer joins their cause.

Mortimer, Edmund, Earl of March[2]
A historical figure (1391-1424) who died of the PLAGUE aged 33, and a minor character in *King Henry VI, Part One*. Both Shakespeare and his source, *HOLINSHED'S CHRONICLES* confused this Earl of March with his uncle the Earl of March (*see above*). Shakespeare's character is a sick old man who has been imprisoned in the TOWER OF LONDON where he is visited by Richard Plantagenet, Duke of York. Mortimer, a Yorkist, recounts how he was put in prison as a young man during the struggle for the English throne between the Houses of LANCASTER and YORK when the Lancastrian Henry IV came to the throne. As he lies dying, Mortimer names Richard, rather than Henry, as rightful heir to the crown and so establishes the bid for the throne which Richard makes in *Henry VI, Parts Two and Three*.

Mortimer, Sir Hugh and Sir John
Historical figures (who both died in 1460) and minor characters in *King Henry VI, Part Three*, Hugh and John are brothers, and uncles to the Yorkist Edward whose claim to the throne they support. They both die for the cause in battle at Wakefield.

Mortimer, Lady
A historical figure (active 1403-1409) and a minor character in *King Henry IV, Part One*, Lady Mortimer is the daughter of Owen Glendower, married to Sir Edmund Mortimer (*see above*). Lady Mortimer speaks no English and as her husband speaks no Welsh her father has to act as their interpreter. She loves her husband and demonstrates the Welsh fondness for music by singing to him. It is thought that Shakespeare may have written the part of Lady Mortimer for a particular Welsh-speaking actor.

Morton
A minor character in *King Henry IV, Part Two*, Morton is a follower of the Earl of Northumberland in his rebellion against King Henry. Morton brings the news of Harry Hotspur's death to his father Northumberland and persuades him, despite his despair at losing his son, that he should continue with the rebellion.

Moth[1]
A minor comic character in *Love's Labour's Lost*, Moth is a young boy and Don Armado's quick-witted page. Moth is lively and sophisticated; he makes fun of his eccentric master behind his back and advises him on the art of love. Moth is described as being small, and after he forgets his lines in the entertainment of the Nine Worthies, he is given the part of the infant Hercules because of his size.

Moth[2]
A minor character in *A Midsummer Night's Dream*, Moth is one of the fairies in the retinue of Titania, Queen of the fairies. While Titania is bewitched, besotted with Bottom and his ass's head, Moth is ordered to wait on Bottom. In Shakespeare's time, the part of Moth would probably have been played by a child actor from one of the royal choir schools. *See* BOY COMPANIES.

Mother
A minor character in *Cymbeline*, Posthumus' Mother appears to her son in a dream while he languishes in his condemned cell. She is described in the stage directions as an 'Ancient matron'.

motif
A significant recurring theme, or subject, which runs through a work and holds some deeper meaning. For example, in *Romeo and Juliet* the characters' frequent references to light and dark, night and day, reinforce the contrast between the happiness of their love and the tragedy of their deaths.

Mouldy, Ralph (Rafe)
A minor comic character in *King Henry IV, Part Two*, Mouldy is one of the villagers Falstaff recruits for the army although he tells Falstaff that his wife will be unable to cope if he is sent to war. Falstaff jokes about his name and says it is time he saw some action, but Mouldy buys his freedom by bribing Bardolph.

Mousetrap, The
See MURDER OF GONZAGO, THE

Mowbray, Lord
A historical figure (1386-1405) and a minor character in *King Henry IV, Part Two*, Lord Mowbray is a supporter of the Earl of Northumberland in his rebellion against King Henry. He does not think that the rebels should accept the promise of peace made by Prince John of Lancaster. He is right to be cautious; Prince John betrays the rebels and Mowbray, along with the others, is arrested and sentenced to death.

Mowbray, Thomas, Duke of Norfolk
A historical figure (c. 1365-1400) and a minor character in *King Richard II*, Mowbray is accused by Bolingbroke of two crimes of treason. Firstly he stands accused of embezzling money which should have been paid to the army, and secondly, and more seriously, he is charged with the murder of the King's uncle, the Duke of Gloucester. Mowbray stoutly denies the charges but Bolingbroke challenges him to single combat. King Richard, presumably anxious to be rid of someone who might betray his part in Gloucester's death, intervenes in the proceedings and sends Mowbray into lifelong exile.

MS. or ms.
An abbreviation for manuscript. (Note the plural is MSS. OR mss.)

Much Ado About Nothing
One of Shakespeare's romantic comedies (*see* COMEDY), written around 1598 and first published in a QUARTO edition in 1600. *Much Ado About Nothing* was performed several times before its publication, though the date of its first performance is uncertain.

One of the sources for the play is a epic poem, *Orlando Furioso* by an Italian poet Ludovico Ariosto (1474-1533) which was translated into English in 1591. The story of Beatrice and Benedick seems to have been Shakespeare's own invention. *Much Ado About Nothing* is set in Messina in Italy and explores themes of love, and trust and faithfulness.

SYNOPSIS : Benedick, together with his companions Claudio and Don Pedro and Don John, are returning from war. They visit the home of Leonato where a masked ball is held to celebrate their return. Claudio falls in love with Leonato's daughter Hero, while Benedick is getting reacquainted with Hero's cousin Beatrice with whom he had an earlier relationship. Both the prickly Beatrice, and Benedick, a confirmed bachelor, scorn the idea of love and vow that neither of them will every marry. Claudio and Hero are betrothed and plans for the wedding are going ahead, but the jealous Don John is determined to prevent the marriage from taking place. He pays his friend Borachio to make it look as if Hero is unfaithful and at the wedding, Claudio refuses to marry her. Hero faints and the story is put about that she has died of shame and grief. Borachio is arrested by Dogberry's men, and confesses that he engineered the plot to make Hero look guilty. Claudio is appalled at having misjudged her and agrees to marry someone of Leonato's choice, a 'niece'. At the wedding, the veiled bride turns out to be Hero, who forgives Claudio and the two are reunited. All this time, Beatrice and Benedick have been engaged in a duel of witticisms, until they are tricked into love. Benedick's and Beatrice's friends arrange for them each to overhear conversations in which they pretend to discuss how much Benedick loves Beatrice and how deeply she loves him. Ironically, Don John's plot to blacken Hero's name results in bringing Beatrice and Benedick closer together, when Beatrice asks Benedick to challenge Claudio to a fight in defence of Hero. They realize they do love one another and they are married alongside Hero and Claudio. Don John is captured and Benedick vows that he will be punished.

Murder of Gonzago, The
The play within a play in *Hamlet*, which Hamlet arranges to be performed for Claudius. The play, which Hamlet calls *The Mousetrap,* tells a story of murder and seduction which resembles the actual murder of Hamlet's father by Claudius and with which Hamlet hopes to trap Claudius into revealing his guilt.

Murderers
Minor characters in *King Richard III*, the two murderers are hired by Richard to kill his brother Clarence in the TOWER OF LONDON. They stab Clarence and put his body in a barrel of Malmsey [wine]. The First Murderer is ruthless in his task but the Second Murderer has a twinge of conscience when Clarence begs for his life. Their comic dialogue is a contrast to the grisly crime they are about to commit.

Murellus (Marullus)
A historical figure (active 44 BC) and a minor character in *Julius Caesar*, Murellus is one of the tribunes [civil officers] of the people. As the play opens Murellus and his fellow tribune Flavius rebuke the Roman citizens who have taken a day off work to cheer Caesar. The tribunes criticize the crowd for forgetting their former hero Pompey whom Caesar has defeated in a civil war. After they have dispersed the crowd, the tribunes remove the decorations put up in Caesar's honour. They are later reported as having been 'put to silence' for doing so.

music
During Shakespeare's lifetime a vast amount of secular music was written and performed, particularly vocal music. Not only the Queen but also most noble families would have retained bands of musicians to entertain members of their households.

In the theatre, music was used in plays before and during performances; a fanfare of trumpets announced the beginning of a play or the appearance of a king or queen on stage while drums provided a background to battle scenes, and horns to a hunting scene. Songs in plays were used dramatically to illustrate the state of mind of a character, for example Ophelia's distress in *Hamlet*. In a comedy such as *Twelfth Night* music is woven into the action of the play. It even introduces the play with Orsino's opening words 'If music be the food of love, play on', providing entertainment for both Orsino and Sir Toby and his companions as well as an EPILOGUE to the play in the Clown's song. Music is used to create an atmosphere of unease in *Antony and Cleopatra*; soldiers on the eve of battle hear music in the air and coming from under the ground (oboes play under the stage: *see* CELLARAGE) which they fear signifies bad luck. Music is played in the MASQUE performed to celebrate the betrothal of Miranda and Ferdinand in *The Tempest* and it plays an important part in the enchantment of Prospero's island. Prospero uses 'heavenly music' to work his magic and the invisible Ariel enchants Alonso and his companions with solemn music that sends them to sleep while the drunken Stephano celebrates his arrival on the island with an more prosaic sailor's song.

Musicians

Musicians appear on stage in several of Shakespeare's plays and sometimes their function is simply to add to the ceremonial atmosphere; for example, musicians play at the banquet aboard Pompey's galley in *Antony and Cleopatra*. Sometimes musicians are called for to aid romance. In *Cymbeline* they play for Imogen at the request of the loutish Cloten, who is trying to woo her, because he believes music will soften her heart towards him, and in *The Two Gentlemen of Verona* musicians serenade Silvia with the famous song 'Who is Silvia?'. In a scene of merry carousing in *King Henry IV, Part Two*, musicians are summoned to entertain Falstaff, who pays them for their pains. In *The Merchant of Venice*, Lorenzo calls for musicians to play to greet Portia on her return to Belmont and he speaks of the power that music has to soothe and calm. In the comedy *Much Ado About Nothing*, musicians play at Hero's tomb when Claudio sings 'Pardon, goddess of the night'.

In the tragedy *Romeo and Juliet*, three musicians are listed in the dramatis personae. They are the only musicians in Shakespeare's plays to be given names: Simon CATLING, Hugh REBECK and James SOUNDPOST, whose names all derive from musical instruments. They are hired to play at Juliet's wedding to Paris and are given some lines to speak although they do not actually play any music. When Juliet is discovered apparently dead, and they are no longer required, they say they will 'tarry for the mourners' instead.

Mustardseed

A minor character in *A Midsummer Night's Dream*, Mustardseed in one of the fairies in Titania's retinue. While Titania, bewitched and deluded, is in love with Bottom with his ass's head, Mustardseed waits on Bottom and scratches his hairy face for him. The name Mustardseed suggests a tiny creature and in Shakespeare's time, the part would probably have been played by a child actor from one of the royal choir schools. *See* BOY COMPANIES.

Mutius

A minor character in *Titus Andronicus*, Mutius is Titus' youngest son and the first of the family to die in the play's terrible cycle of revenge. When his sister Lavinia is promised to Saturnius as a wife, Mutius helps her fiance Bassianus to snatch her away. During the scuffle, Mutius stops his father from following Bassianus. Titus kills Mutius because he says his son has dishonoured the family by preventing the arranged marriage. Mutius' brothers want to bury him in the family tomb, but Titus says Mutius is not worthy of burial with his noble ancestors. Only when Titus' brother Marcus intervenes in the quarrel is Mutius laid to rest.

Myrmidons

Minor characters in *Troilus and Cressida*, the Myrmidons are Achilles' own band of particularly ruthless soldiers who kill Hector even though he is unarmed.

mystery plays

Medieval dramas, whose successors were still being performed during Shakespeare's lifetime. They evolved from the earlier MIRACLE PLAYS, but unlike them, were written in English. They were performed by members of guilds [associations of tradesmen] in a particular 'mestier' [occupation] (from which the word 'mystery' derives), who enacted bible stories in the open air and on movable stages. Mystery plays were the forerunners of much ELIZABETHAN DRAMA, sometimes written with rhyming dialogue and often involving SLAPSTICK humour. They were written in cycles of short plays, the most famous of which to have survived today is the York Cycle.

Nn

narrative
The account of events which in a play includes the ACTION that occurs on stage as well as OFF-STAGE action, such as a battle, which may be reported, for example by a messenger.

narrator
Someone who relates events but who does not appear as a central character in a play. The narrator may recount action that has occurred OFF-STAGE or, as the CHORUS, may describe events that have preceded the action of the play.

Nash, Thomas (1593-1647)
The first husband of Shakespeare's grand-daughter Elizabeth HALL.

Nashe, Thomas (1567-c. 1601)
A playwright, Nashe was also the author of a series of satirical pamphlets including one entitled *Pierce Pennilesse His Supplication to the Devil* (1592) which is said to have prompted Hamlet's comments on drunkenness. He collaborated with other unknown writers on a subversive play, *The Isle of Dogs* (1597), and was given a prison sentence, which he seems never to have served. *See* CENSORSHIP.

Nathaniel
A minor character in *The Taming of the Shrew*, Nathaniel is one of Petruchio's five servants. *See* SERVANTS AND SERVINGMEN.

Nathaniel, Sir
A comic character in *Love's Labour's Lost*, Nathaniel is a curate and a friend of Holofernes the schoolmaster whom he much admires. Like Holofernes, Nathaniel is pedantic and pompous, and he punctuates his conversation with Latin quotes and classical and biblical allusions. He takes part in the MASQUE of the *Nine Worthies* but has an attack of stage fright and runs off. Afterwards Costard describes him as a good neighbour, foolish perhaps, but a mild and honest man at heart.

National Theatre, The
A theatre in London founded by the actor Sir Laurence OLIVIER in 1963. The National Theatre began its life at the OLD VIC Theatre and moved to the new building on the South Bank in 1976. The theatre company is a large one and its wide repertoire of classic plays, including those by Shakespeare, is subsidized by the state.

Nell[1]
A minor character, Nell is a kitchen maid referred to in *The Comedy of Errors*. *See* LUCE.

Nell[2]
A minor, non-speaking character in *The Two Noble Kinsmen*, Nell is one of the Morris dancers; *see* COUNTRYWOMEN.

Nell, Hostess
A minor character in *King Henry V*, Nell is the former Mistress Quickly. *See* QUICKLY, HOSTESS.

nemesis
Punishment or retribution; the word derives from the name of the Greek goddess of vengeance who was called Nemesis.

Nerissa
A character in *The Merchant of Venice*, Nerissa is Portia's confidante and her lady-in-waiting. A lively companion, she discusses Portia's suitors with her and shares Portia's preference for Bassiano. When Portia disguises herself as a lawyer in order to defend Antonio, Nerissa accompanies her mistress to Venice dressed as a lawyer's clerk. There, she meets her lover Gratiano; in her male disguise she persuades Gratiano to give her a ring, an earlier present from her which he had vowed to keep for ever. Later, when she has returned to her true identity, she pretends to be angry with Gratiano because he has given away her keepsake.

Nestor
A legendary figure and a character in *Troilus and Cressida*, Nestor is one of the Greek commanders. He is an old man, respected by the Greeks despite his tendency to be long-winded, but he plays a small part in events. He joins the other leaders in trying to persuade Achilles to fight.

Nevil
The family name of the Earls of SALISBURY and WARWICK in *King Henry VI, Part Two*.

'new historicism'
A school of LITERARY CRITICISM.

New Place
A substantial property, the second largest house in Stratford at that time, which Shakespeare acquired in 1597 after he had made his fortune in London. Although presumably his family moved in straight away, Shakespeare himself was still living and working in London then and did not take up permanent residence at New Place until his retirement from the theatre in 1611. On his death, the house passed to his daughter Susanna HALL and it was subsequently inherited by her daughter Elizabeth. The original house was destroyed in 1759 when its owner, infuriated by the constant stream of visitors to the house, had it pulled down. The garden of New Place with its replica of an Elizabethan knot garden can still be visited.

Newington Butts Theatre
A theatre established around 1580 in the village of Newington in Surrey (now part of London) about a mile south of London Bridge. Little is known of the theatre's history but it was taken over by the theatrical entrepreneur Philip HENSLOWE during the 1590s

and the ADMIRAL'S MEN and the LORD CHAMBERLAIN'S MEN are recorded as playing there in 1594.

Nicanor
A minor character in *Coriolanus*, Nicanor is a Roman spy and a double agent. He meets Adrian, a Volscian spy, on the road and Nicanor informs him that there is unrest in Rome following Coriolanus' quarrel with the people and his banishment. Nicanor tells Adrian that it would be an ideal time for Aufidius to mount an invasion of Rome.

Nine Worthies, The
In a comic interlude in Love's Labour's Lost, a MASQUE, entitled *The Nine Worthies* is performed for the King and his court. The entertainment, organised by the schoolmaster Holofernes, is a celebration of the lives of nine notable figures from the past. Holofernes and his fellow masquers take the performance very seriously, but the proceedings are interrupted and only five 'worthies' make an appearance: Hector of Troy, Pompey the Great, Alexander, Hercules and Judas Maccabaeus.

Norfolk¹, Duke of
A historical figure (1415-1461) and a minor character in *King Henry VI, Part Three*, Norfolk is a supporter of King Edward and the Yorkist cause.

Norfolk², Duke of
A historical figure (c. 1430-1485) and a minor character in *King Richard III*, Norfolk is one of Richard's military commanders at BOSWORTH who is killed in battle. (see also SURREY)

Norfolk³, Duke of
A historical figure (1473-1554) and a character in *King Henry VIII*, the Duke of Norfolk is the Duke of Buckingham's son-in-law and a bitter opponent of Wolsey, whom he accuses of arrogance and ruthless ambition. When Buckingham is arrested, falsely accused of treason by Wolsey, Norfolk is eager to revenge himself on the Cardinal. He rejoices when Wolsey falls from grace, and informs his enemy that the King has ordered his house arrest. Norfolk, staunchly loyal to Henry, takes part in the christening procession for Princess Elizabeth.

The Duke of Norfolk is the same historical figure as the Earl of SURREY, who fought for Richard at Bosworth in *King Richard III*. His father died at Bosworth, and Surrey inherited the title of Duke of Norfolk from him.

Northumberland¹, Earl of, Henry Percy
A historical figure (1342-1408) and a character in *King Richard II* and *King Henry IV, Parts One and Two*.

In *King Richard II*, Northumberland, known also as Henry Percy, is the father of Harry Percy, surnamed Hotspur. At first a supporter of the King, Northumberland comes to believe that King Richard is unfit to rule and joins Bolingbroke's rebellion as one his main supporters, urging the other nobles to join the cause. Accused of treason, Northumberland declares that he is only helping Bolingbroke to recover his lost inheritance but he shows his true colours when he brutally forces Richard to read aloud the accusations that have been made against him by the rebels. Northumberland shows no mercy either when he separates Richard from his Queen and consigns Richard to Pontefract castle where he is murdered, and the Queen to banishment in France.

In *King Henry IV, Parts One and Two,* Northumberland, with his son Hotspur, are among the nobles rebelling against King Henry. In *Part One,* Northumberland is absent from the vital battle of Shrewsbury, where his son is killed, because he is ill. In *Part Two,* Northumberland hears of his son's death and in his grief he vows to put on his armour again for the rebel cause. However, the rebellion is not going well and his wife and his daughter-in-law persuade him instead to flee to Scotland where he is eventually defeated by the King's forces.

Northumberland[2], Earl of
A historical figure (1421-1461) and a minor character in *King Henry VI, Part Three,* Northumberland is a supporter of King Henry. Northumberland is furious when Henry agrees that the crown shall pass to Edward after his death, rather than to his own royal son and rightful heir. Northumberland is killed at the Battle of Towton.

Northumberland, Lady
A historical figure (died c. 1400) and a minor character in *King Henry IV, Part Two,* Lady Northumberland is the Earl of Northumberland's wife. After the death of their son Harry Hotspur (in *Part One*) she persuades her husband not to go to war and to flee to Scotland.

Nun
A minor character in *Measure for Measure,* the Nun, who is called Francisca in the stage directions, is a member of the convent that Isabella is about to enter. She listens to Isabella's comments about the rules of the religious order which Isabella thinks are too free and easy.

Nuncle
In *King Lear,* the affectionate nickname meaning 'old uncle' that the Fool gives to Lear.

Nurse[1]
A comic character in *Romeo and Juliet,* the Nurse is a member of the Capulet household who became Juliet's wet nurse when her own baby died. Good-natured but coarse, her conversation is full of sexual innuendoes and her crudity contrasts with Juliet's purity. She is devoted to Juliet and gladly acts as a go-between for the lovers and helps to arrange their secret marriage. The Nurse is the first to protect Juliet when Capulet, Juliet's domineering father, insists she should marry Paris. However, her limitations become apparent when she fails to appreciate the depth of Juliet's love for Romeo and finally advises her to consent to a bigamous marriage. When she goes to wake Juliet on the morning of her ill-fated second wedding, the Nurse as usual quibbles lewdly but her jokes quickly turn to lamentations when she discovers her young charge apparently dead. Her grief is predictably loud but nonetheless genuine.

Nurse[2]
A minor character in *Titus Andronicus,* the Nurse brings Tamora's new born child to its father Aaron with instructions that he must kill it. The child is black, proof of Tamora's infidelity with Aaron, and the Nurse says it must be got rid of in order to keep Tamora's

indiscretion secret from her husband Saturnius. Aaron saves the child but kills the nurse to ensure her silence.

Nym

A minor comic character in *The Merry Wives of Windsor* and *King Henry V*, Nym is one of Falstaff's companions.

 In *The Merry Wives of Windsor*, Falstaff asks Nym to deliver his love letters to the merry wives and when Nym refuses, Falstaff dismisses him. Nym is a dim-witted eccentric; he repeatedly uses the phrase 'that's my humour' and his style of speech confuses both himself and his listeners.

 In *Henry V*, the action of which takes place at a later date, Nym quarrels with his old friend Pistol who has married Mistress Quickly, the woman Nym had hoped to marry himself. He hears of Falstaff's death and joins the King Henry's army fighting in France. Falstaff's page describes Nym as a petty criminal and a coward and later reports that Nym has been hanged for stealing.

Nymphs

Nymphs appear as dancers in the MASQUE performed for Miranda and Ferdinand in *The Tempest*. (*See* SPIRITS) Nymphs also appear in the wedding procession of Theseus and Hippolyta in *The Two Noble Kinsmen*. One is described as carrying a garland of wheat, a symbol of fertility, and with her hair hanging loose as a symbol of virginity. Two other nymphs wear garlands of wheat.

Oo

O
See WOODEN O

Oatcake
A minor character in *Much Ado About Nothing*; *see* WATCHMEN.

Oberon
A character in *A Midsummer Night's Dream*, Oberon is King of the fairies and Titania's husband. Oberon and Titania are quarrelling over a mortal child, an Indian boy to whom Titania is devoted but who Oberon badly wants to be his page. Oberon is furious and bewitches the sleeping Titania so that she will fall in love with the first thing she sees when she awakes; he is hoping that the object of her love will be some vile creature and it turns out to be Bottom, with his ass's head. Once Titania has handed over the boy, Oberon, who can appear quite sinister but who has a kind heart, takes pity on her and releases her from the spell. Having restored harmony to the fairy world, Oberon sets about doing the same for the mortals who are wandering in his woods. He is particularly sorry for Helena, who is bearing the brunt of Demetrius' anger, and he uses his magic to create unity and happiness between the lovers.

octave
A group of eight lines in verse, connected by a particular pattern of rhyme. Shakespeare's SONNETS begin with an octave.

Octavia
A character in *Antony and Cleopatra*, Octavia is Octavius Caesar's sister. She is described by Enobarbus as pious and frigid, but she shows a genuine love for Antony and a desire to be a good wife to him. Octavia is a political pawn. Her marriage to Antony is arranged in order to cement the peace between the joint rulers of the Roman Empire, Antony, Caesar and Lepidus. However, despite her best efforts to heal the rift, the truce between Antony and Caesar breaks down and Antony deserts the patient Octavia for Cleopatra. When Cleopatra first hears of Antony's marriage to Octavia, she demands a description of her rival and her messenger tactfully tells her that Octavia is insignificant, ordinary looking and thirty years old, which in fact makes her younger than Cleopatra.

Octavius Caesar
A central character in *Antony and Cleopatra*; *see* CAESAR, OCTAVIUS.

off-stage
The part of a stage which is out of sight of the audience, for example the WINGS. Actions, such as battles which take place out of sight and are later recounted to the

audience, are referred to as taking place off-stage. An example is Macbeth's account of the murder of Duncan given to Lady Macbeth.

Office of the Revels
From 1581 onwards, the Office of the Revels also acted as a licensing authority for plays, censoring those which were thought to contain anything politically subversive, or morally suspect or blasphemous, and to whom companies of players had to apply for permission to perform. In 1606 the powers of the Office were extended to include the publication of plays.

The Office of the Revels eventually became a theatrical company. *See also* MASTER OF THE REVELS.

Officers
Minor characters who appear in several of Shakespeare's plays, few of whom have any notable personality. Their function, generally, is to make an announcement or make an arrest.

In *Coriolanus*, the Officers are minor officials who discuss Coriolanus, who is about to be made consul. They comment on his arrogant dislike of the common people of Rome, but they admire him because he serves his country without seeking to be popular. In *King Lear*, an Officer is ordered by the wicked Edmund to kill Cordelia and Lear. The Officer hangs Cordelia, but Lear survives and kills him in turn.

An Officer in *The Two Noble Kinsmen*, is a non-speaking part; *see* ARTESIUS.

Old Lady
A minor character in *King Henry VIII*, the Old Lady is Anne Bullen's CONFIDANT and friend. Earthy and cynical, the Old Lady informs King Henry of the birth of a child to his new wife, Anne, and craftily avoids a direct answer to the King's question as to whether the child is a boy or a girl. She flatters Henry by saying that the child resembles him; when the King gives her a small amount of money as her reward for such happy news, the Old Lady says that she had hoped her flattery would be better rewarded.

Old Man[1]
A minor character in *King Lear*, the good Old Man is the devoted servant who leads the blinded Gloucester onto the heath and gives him into Edgar's care.

Old Man[2]
A minor character in *Macbeth*, the Old Man is an elderly peasant who describes the evil omens that occurred when King Duncan was murdered.

Old Shepherd
A comic character in *The Winter's Tale*, the kindly Old Shepherd discovers the infant Perdita, abandoned on the shore of Bohemia with nothing but a box of treasures and letters, and brings her up as his own daughter. Sixteen years on, Perdita is being courted by Prince Florizel, and the Shepherd tries to explain to Florizel's murderously angry father, King Polixenes, that Perdita is not really a mere shepherd's daughter but a highborn young woman. The Old Shepherd is tricked out of the evidence that would prove his story true by the wily Autolycus, and is forced to flee to Sicilia with his son and the young lovers. There, Perdita's identity is finally proved, and the Old Shepherd

and his son are rewarded by her real father, King Leontes. The simple old man is delighted to have become a 'gentleman' and proudly shows off his new clothes.

Old Vic, The
A theatre founded in Waterloo, London in 1818. In 1898, LILIAN BAYLIS (1874-1937) took over management of the theatre and from 1914 she instituted a series of Shakespeare productions which became renowned. The NATIONAL THEATRE was based at the Old Vic from 1963 to 1976 before its move to the South Bank.

Oldcastle, Sir John
The original name of the character of Falstaff in *King Henry IV*. Shakespeare changed the name when the Oldcastle family objected to being associated with such a reprobate figure as Falstaff. The real Sir John (c. 1375-1417) was a soldier and politician and a companion of King Henry V, for whom he fought before he became king. Oldcastle joined the Lollards, an anti-Catholic movement, and in 1413 he was arrested and imprisoned for heresy. He escaped from the TOWER OF LONDON and led a Lollard rebellion against King Henry, a treasonable offence for which he was eventually hanged and burned.

Oliver
A character in *As You Like It*, Oliver is the elder son of Sir Rowland de Boys (now dead), and Orlando's brother. Oliver has inherited his father's wealth and lands, but keeps Orlando, a brother he says he never loved, in poverty. A self-confessed villain, he plots to have Orlando killed by the wrestler, Charles. Duke Frederick, the other villain of the piece, seizes Oliver's lands, and threatens to banish him unless he brings back Orlando, dead or alive, from Arden. Searching for his brother, Oliver falls asleep. Orlando discovers him by chance, and risks his own life to save Oliver from an angry lioness. Orlando's heroism transforms Oliver. He gives the family lands to his brother, and marries Celia, with whom he plans to spend a life of rural bliss in ARDEN.

Olivia
A character in *Twelfth Night*, Olivia is a Countess who extends hospitality to her uncle, Sir Toby Belch, and his boisterous drinking companions. Olivia is melancholy, mourning the loss of a brother (like Viola with whom she has a lot in common - even their names are similar) and she is icily indifferent to the advances of Duke Orsino, who loves her. However, when 'Cesario' (Viola in disguise) is sent by Orsino to pay court to Olivia on his behalf, her heart melts and she falls headlong in love with 'him'. She casts off all her former austerity and becomes quite reckless in her pursuit of Cesario. When she meets Viola's twin, Sebastian, whom she mistakes for Cesario, she sweeps him off to get married. Love has rekindled Olivia's zest for life, and at the end of the play, she is the only character to treat Malvolio with any degree of humanity.

Olivier, Laurence (Kerr) (1907–89)
A British film and theatre actor and director, Olivier joined the OLD VIC company in 1937, playing all the great Shakespearean roles to critical acclaim. He became Co-director of the Old Vic in 1944, Director of the Chichester Theatre Festival in 1962, and Director of the NATIONAL THEATRE from 1963 to 1973. Olivier's film credits include his highly praised *King Henry V* (1944), *Hamlet* (1948) and *King Richard III* (1955). He was knighted in 1947 and made a life peer in 1970. The Olivier theatre (one

of the three theatres forming the National Theatre complex on the South Bank in London) is named after him.

onomatopoeia
Language or words whose sound imitates the noise of the thing or action it describes. Examples are 'buzz', 'hiss', 'splash', 'clang'.

open stage
A raised stage which projects into an auditorium rather like an APRON STAGE and which does not have a PROSCENIUM ARCH or a curtain.

Ophelia
A central character in *Hamlet*, Ophelia is Polonius' daughter and Laertes' sister. Ophelia loves Hamlet, but her brother warns her against Hamlet's advances, and her father forbids her to see Hamlet altogether. Ophelia obediently complies with her father's wishes, while Polonius, indifferent to his daughter's feelings, interrogates her about Hamlet's behaviour and uses her as a barometer of Hamlet's mental state. As Hamlet's feigned madness increases, he develops at the same time a real disgust towards women and sex. He cruelly rejects Ophelia, abusing her, and ordering her to go into a nunnery. After her father is killed by Hamlet, Ophelia loses her mind. She sings songs of love and death, interspersed with snatches from bawdy ditties, and lovingly offers around flowers, which hold symbolic meanings for her. A victim of her father's meddling and Hamlet's obsession with revenge, Ophelia's death by drowning is later reported.

 The character of Ophelia may have been based on a real-life girl, Katherine Hamlet, who was drowned in the river in STRATFORD-ON-AVON when Shakespeare was sixteen years old. There was some doubt as to whether her death was an accident or suicide.

Orlando
The noble hero of *As You Like It*, Orlando is the orphan son of Sir Rowland de Boys. Orlando's jealous elder brother, Oliver, denies Orlando any share of the family wealth, and plots to have him killed. Orlando seeks refuge in the Forest of ARDEN, accompanied by a faithful old family servant, Adam, for whom he cares. Orlando is a romantic; he pines for Rosalind, whom he has only briefly met, and decorates the forest with poems praising her beauty. Nonetheless, he fails to recognize Rosalind in her disguise as the young 'Ganymede' when he meets her. He agrees to let 'Ganymede' cure him of his lovesickness; the two play out an elaborate and flirtatious game in which Orlando woos 'Ganymede' as if he were Rosalind. In an act of extraordinary heroism, Orlando saves Oliver's life. His brother is transformed by Orlando's goodness and gives him all his wealth. By now, Orlando's love for Rosalind has grown from shallow infatuation, to a deep and steadfast love, and they are married.

Orleans, the Duke of
A minor character in *King Henry V*, the Duke of Orleans is one of the overconfident French nobles who is contemptuous of the English. He jokes with the Dauphin before the Battle of Agincourt about the relative merits of horses and mistresses and longs to fight. He recognizes that the French are losing the battle but vows to fight on, and is eventually taken prisoner.

Orsino, Duke
A character in *Twelfth Night*, Orsino is the Duke of Illyria and a STOCK CHARACTER of conventional Elizabethan romance. A self-consciously melancholic lover, Orsino is pining for love of Olivia and instructs the disguised Viola to court Olivia on his behalf. It is not until the end of the play that Orsino realizes that his love for Olivia was mere infatuation and that it is Viola whom he truly loves; but not before a disturbing, if fleeting, moment of violence when he threatens to kill Cesario (the disguised Viola) to spite Olivia for her coldness towards him. When the mists of mistaken identity have lifted, Orsino and Viola can be married.

Osric
A minor character in *Hamlet*, Osric is a foppish courtier who is sent by Claudius to tell Hamlet of the proposed duel with Laertes. Osric is mocked by Hamlet for his ornate language in a brief interlude of COMIC RELIEF.

Oswald
A minor character in *King Lear*, Oswald is Goneril's villainous steward who is party to his mistress's plans to undermine her father, Lear, and then to cast him out. He is exultant when Kent is put in the stocks, and eagerly acts as a go-between for Goneril and her equally evil sister, Regan. Oswald believes that he will be rewarded by Regan if he kills the blinded Gloucester, but when the opportunity arises, Oswald is killed by Gloucester's son Edgar.

Othello
Title Character. The hero of *Othello* and a noble Moor, Othello is the commander of the Venetian army and much respected for his military prowess. Although he describes himself as inarticulate in matters of the heart, Othello has recently married Desdemona, whom he loves with an intense passion. He is a man of action who, perhaps naively, believes all men are as honest and honourable as he is himself. This belief and his jealous nature, are fatal flaws in Othello, both of which are exploited by Iago, the man who is bent on his ruin. Iago subtly undermines Othello's confidence in himself and his trust in his wife, until he is persuaded by Iago that Desdemona is being unfaithful. He is consumed by an uncontrollable jealousy and cruelly accuses her of infidelity. Deaf to her pleading and blind to her love for him, Othello smothers her. When he discovers Desdemona's innocence and realizes the enormity of his crime, he kills himself.

Othello is one of two central black characters in Shakespeare's plays; the other is AARON, Tamora's villainous lover in *Titus Andronicus*. Where Aaron is an archetypal villain, who resembles Iago in many ways, Othello is portrayed as fundamentally honourable, a man who is more sinned against than sinning. *See also* BLACK CHARACTERS.

Othello
One of Shakespeare's later tragedies (*see* TRAGEDY) written around 1602-04, it was first published in a QUARTO edition of 1622 and performed at Court in November of 1604.

The principal source of the play was a story by an Italian writer, Giraldi Cinthio (1504-73). The play explores themes of jealousy and suspicion, deception, revenge, racism, and uncontrolled passions. The action, in which TRAGIC IRONY plays a big part, is fast-moving.

SYNOPSIS : Desdemona has secretly married the Moor, Othello, in defiance of her father's wishes. Soon after, Othello, a military commander from Venice, is sent to defend Cyprus against the Turks accompanied by his lieutenant, Iago. Iago has been overlooked for promotion and is consumed with hatred and envy, both for his rival for the post, Cassio, and for Othello. Pathologically ruthless, Iago vows to ruin them both, and his scheming fuels the plot. Iago boasts of his evil intentions to the audience, but maintains the pretence of being an honest and true friend to those whom he is working to destroy. He tries to blacken Othello's name by telling Desdemona's father that Othello used witchcraft to win her. He discredits Cassio by exploiting a weakness for wine, and getting Cassio so drunk that he ends up in a brawl. Iago cleverly and subtly sows seed of doubt and suspicion in Othello's mind, hinting that Desdemona is having an affair. He arranges things so that it is Desdemona who pleads with Othello to show mercy to the disgraced Cassio, further undermining Othello's trust of her. Iago takes a handkerchief, which Othello had given to his wife as a keepsake, and plants it on Cassio, as supposed evidence of Cassio and Desdemona's guilt. Tragically, Othello is all too easily convinced of his wife's guilt. Overwhelmed by feelings of jealousy, he insults Desdemona in front of important visitors and later goes to her room and orders her to say her prayers. Despite her protestations of innocence, Othello smothers her. When Iago's plot is exposed by his wife Emilia, Othello realizes the horrific consequences of his lack of belief in Desdemona's goodness and he kills himself. When Iago's villainy is exposed he tries to make his escape, but he is arrested to be sent back to Venice for punishment. *See also* BLACK CHARACTERS.

Other Place, The
See ROYAL SHAKESPEARE COMPANY, THE.

Outlaws
Minor characters in *The Two Gentlemen of Verona*, a band of good-natured Outlaws, with their own code of honour, who capture the banished Valentine and make him their leader because he is handsome and educated.

Overdone, Mistress
A minor comic character in *Measure for Measure*, Mistress Overdone is a bawd [prostitute and brothel-keeper]. Under Angelo's strict new regime in Vienna, brothels are being stamped out and Mistress Overdone is arrested and sent to prison with her servant Pompey. Mistress Overdone belongs to the world of immorality and petty crime that Angelo would like to see eradicated from Vienna.

Ovid (43 BC-AD 17)
A Roman poet who began his career studying law. Many of his poems, such as *Amores* (c. 20 BC) and *Ars Amatoria* (6 BC), were written on the theme of love. *Metamorphoses* (AD 2) was a collection of Greek and Roman legends, which Shakespeare almost certainly read at school in Latin, and which he may have also known in an English translation (1565-67) by Arthur Golding. Shakespeare certainly drew on Ovid's work for *Venus and Adonis* and the tale of Pyramus and Thisbe in *A Midsummer Night's Dream*, as well as for the storyline of Lavinia's shocking rape in *Titus Andronicus*. In

Titus Andronicus, the mutilated Lavinia, who is unable to speak, uses a copy of *Metamorphoses* to indicate the identity of her attackers.

Oxford, Earl of
A minor character appearing in both *King Henry VI, Part Three* and *King Richard III*, Oxford is an ally of Queen Margaret in both plays. In *Henry VI*, Oxford joins forces with Warwick against King Edward; in *Richard III*, he fights with Richmond against the King at the Battle of BOSWORTH.

Oxford, 17th Earl of (1550–1604)
The title of Edward de Vere, a poet and courtier and a favourite of Queen Elizabeth, who became Lord Chamberlain in 1562. The Earl of Oxford took over the patronage of his father's company of players, OXFORD'S MEN, in 1580 and wrote plays for them to perform. Some scholars have tried to prove that the Earl of Oxford was the real author of Shakespeare's plays, but no firm evidence for this theory exists.

Oxford's Men
A company of players, established around 1580 with the Earl of OXFORD as their patron. It was not one of the most successful companies of the time, and seems to have survived by touring the provinces rather than appearing in any of the London theatres. In 1602, Oxford's Men merged with WORCESTER'S MEN.

oxymoron
An expression that combines words with opposite, or unalike meanings to create a striking effect. Romeo uses such expressions, demonstrating his highly charged emotional state: 'Why then, O brawling love! O loving hate! ... Feather of lead, bright smoke, cold fire, sick health! Still waking sleep, that is not what it is!' *Compare* ANTITHESIS; PARADOX.

Pp

Page[1]

A minor character in *King Henry IV, Part Two* and *King Henry V*; in *Henry IV*, Falstaff's Page is a quick-witted boy who was given to Falstaff by his friend Prince Hal. His small stature is referred to several times (he is ironically called 'giant') which may be because there was a particularly small boy in the acting company when the play was first performed. The character of Maria in *Twelfth Night* is also described as being small and her part may have been played by the same boy actor.

In *King Henry V*, Falstaff's page is referred to as BOY. Falstaff has died and the Boy goes off to the war in France as Pistol's page together with Falstaff's old associates Bardolph and Nym, whose criminal exploits he thoroughly disapproves of. The Boy speaks a little French and acts as a rather inadequate interpreter between Pistol and a French soldier who is captured. The Boy is left to guard the luggage and is treacherously killed by the French against all the rules of warfare.

Page[2]

A minor character in the INDUCTION that introduces *The Taming of the Shrew*. The Page, called Bartholomew, is a servant to the Lord who plans the elaborate practical joke on the drunken Sly. The Page dresses up as Sly's obedient 'wife' (foreshadowing the theme of the obedient wife in the play that follows), but excuses himself from Sly's bed by saying that the doctors have strongly recommended that Sly should sleep alone for a night or two.

Page, Anne

A character in *The Merry Wives of Windsor*, Anne is the lively and beautiful young daughter of Mr and Mrs Page. She is being courted by Dr Caius and Slender, but her heart belongs to Fenton, a romantic young gentleman who is also in love with her. Her mother would like her to marry the rich Slender while her father favours marriage with the elderly Doctor; her parents think Fenton is unsuitable as a husband because his social ranking is higher than hers. Anne resolutely refuses to be married off to either Slender or Dr Caius so each of her parents plots secretly for her elopement with their chosen suitor. Anne foils their plans when she and Fenton arrange their own secret marriage and in the happy resolution at the end of the play her parents give the young couple their blessing.

Page, George

A character in *The Merry Wives of Windsor*, Page is a solid citizen of Windsor and Mistress Margaret Page's husband. His wife, one of the 'merry wives', is being courted by Falstaff but Page is cheerfully unconcerned, in contrast to the jealous Ford whose wife is also the object of Falstaff's desires. Page favours Slender as his daughter Anne's future husband, believing that the young gentleman Fenton whom Anne loves belongs

to too high a social class to marry her. Although he makes a secret arrangement with
Slender to elope with Anne, Page good-naturedly accepts Fenton as his son-in-law when
he discovers that he and Anne have already married. Page assists in the wives' plan to
humiliate Falstaff, but once he has been properly punished, the hospitable Page invites
Falstaff to dine at his house.

Page, Mistress Margaret
A character in *The Merry Wives of Windsor*, Mistress Page is George Page's wife
(called Meg by her husband) and Anne's mother, and one of the 'merry wives'. Mistress
Page is a virtuous woman who is appalled at Falstaff's impudence when she receives a
love letter from him suggesting a secret meeting. She is further outraged when she
discovers that her friend Mistress Ford has had an identical letter from Falstaff.
Together the wives plan to pay him back. Mistress Page's role in the trick is to set up
meetings between Mistress Ford and Falstaff, and then to burst in on them with news
that the violently jealous Mr Ford is about to arrive. Mistress Page thoroughly enjoys
Falstaff's panic and discomfort on both occasions, and devises the grand finale of his
public humiliation in Windsor Park, but her inventive tricking of Falstaff is without
malice.

Page, William
A minor character in *The Merry Wives of Windsor*, William is the son of George and
Margaret Page, and Anne's young brother. William is a innocent schoolboy who is who
is tested on his Latin grammar by the Welshman Sir Hugh Evans.

Painter
A minor character in *Timon of Athens*; *see* POET AND PAINTER.

Palamon
One of the two heroes of *The Two Noble Kinsmen*, Palamon is Arcite's cousin and his
inseparable friend. They are very alike, and their lives run parallel. Taken prisoners of
war by Duke Theseus, Palamon and Arcite are confidant that they will survive
imprisonment, sustained by their deep friendship. However, the instant they both fall in
love with Emilia, they become bitter rivals. Freed from jail, Palamon furiously pursues
Arcite determined to fight for Emilia. In the fateful duel arranged by Theseus, Palamon
is beaten. He accepts his fate heroically, but before the executioner's axe falls, news
comes of Arcite's death. Palamon loses his friend, a loss he feels keenly, but lives to
marry the beautiful Emilia. Palamon is the more romantic of the kinsmen; According to
Arcite, he has a way with words and 'a tongue [that] will tame tempests'.

Pandar
A minor comic character in *Pericles*, the Pandar keeps a brothel in Mytilene with his
wife the Bawd. (The word 'pandar' means a pimp.) The Pandar buys the virginal Marina
from the Pirates, but he soon regrets his purchase when Marina's goodness leads his
clientele to become reformed characters, and drives all his custom away.

Pandarus
A legendary figure and a comic character in *Troilus and Cressida*, Pandarus is
Cressida's uncle (in Shakespeare's time, the word 'pander', sometimes spelt 'pandar',
meant a pimp). Pandarus takes pleasure, rather than money, from his match-making. He

arranges a meeting between Troilus and Cressida and even provides a chamber and a
bed for them to consummate their love. When Cressida is to be handed over to the
Greeks, Pandarus sentimentally laments the lovers' parting and intrudes on their
farewells, but when Cressida is unfaithful to Troilus, Pandarus seems merely irritated by
the whole affair. At the end of the play, Pandarus, who has been abused by Troilus for
being a shameful pander, reflects on his miseries, declares that soon he will be dead, and
that he will bequeath his sexual diseases to the audience.

Pandulph, Cardinal
A character in *King John*, Cardinal Pandulph is the Pope's representative, who demands
that King John accepts the Pope's candidate for Archbishop of Canterbury. When John
refuses, he is excommunicated. Pandulph threatens the King of France with
excommunication too if he does not reverse a newly-made peace treaty with John, and
go to war with England. Pandulph then persuades John to surrender the English crown
to him, in exchange for which he will talk the French out of invading England. Later,
Pandulph returns the crown to John, establishing the power the Pope has over England,
but he cannot stop the French invasion.

Pantaloon
Originally a STOCK CHARACTER from 16th-century Italian comedy (*see* COMMEDIA
DELL'ARTE), Pantaloon was a lustful and avaricious old man. In the comedy *As You
Like It*, Jaques refers to 'the lean and slippered pantaloon with spectacles on nose and
pouch on side' as a symbol of old age, and Gremio, a rich old man in *The Taming of the
Shrew*, is described in the stage directions as 'a Pantaloon'. The character of Polonius,
Ophelia's father in *Hamlet*, may derive from Pantaloon.

Panthino
A minor character in *The Two Gentlemen of Verona*, Panthino is servant to Proteus'
father Antonio, and suggests to his master that Proteus should go to Milan.

Papal Legate
A minor character in *King Henry VI, Part One*, the Papal Legate is sent by the Pope to
collect the money owed by the Bishop of Winchester; the payment is for the Bishop's
promotion to Cardinal. England was still a Roman Catholic country at the time the play
is set, but by Shakespeare's own time it was Protestant, and anti-Catholic feeling ran
high.

paradox
A statement which seems to contradict itself, but which in fact may be true. For
example, Juliet describes her love for Romeo, whom she has been educated by her
family to hate, as: 'My only love sprung from my only hate'. *Compare* ANTITHESIS;
OXYMORON.

parallelism
A situation in which two characters are placed in parallel or similar situations. For
example, in *King Lear* the fates of Gloucester and Lear who are both old, exiled and
betrayed, run parallel. *See* PIRITHOUS.

Paris[1]

A character in *Romeo and Juliet*, Paris is a nobleman who Juliet's parents wish her to marry, and whom Lady Capulet likens to a book with a handsome cover. He is a conventional, formal figure, a contrast to his rival the passionate and impulsive Romeo, but he is genuinely grief-stricken when he finds Juliet apparently dead in the tomb. He dies at Romeo's hands believing that he is defending Juliet's body from harm.

Paris[2]

A legendary figure and a minor character in *Troilus and Cressida*, Paris is one of the Trojan King Priam's sons whose abduction of the beautiful Helen from the Greeks sparked the war between Greece and Troy. Paris is a warrior but he is besotted with Helen and admits that her charms have sometimes prevented him from making an appearance on the battlefield.

Parolles

A character in *All's Well that Ends Well*, Parolles is Bertram's follower. Shallow and vain, he dresses in the height of fashion and pretends to be of noble blood. Parolles is cynical and unscrupulous, and Bertram's mother, the Countess, thinks he is a corrupt influence on her son. Certainly it is Parolles who encourages Bertram to reject Helena and go off to fight in Italy where he acts as a go-between for Bertam in his attempted seduction of Diana. Parolles, who boasts of his courage as a soldier, shows a distinct lack of heroism on the battlefield, and some of the nobles decide to play a trick on him to expose his cowardice. Pretending to be the enemy, they seize him and question him in a nonsense language. Parolles is thoroughly frightened, but he is a great talker (his name means 'words'), and skilfully lies and flatters his way to freedom. Parolles acknowledges that he has been fooled, but he is a realist and a survivor, and resolves to make his living in future as a FOOL at court.

Passionate Pilgrim, The

A collection of twenty poems, by various poets, which was first published in 1599 in a complete edition with William Shakespeare's name on the title page; only five of the poems, I, II, III, V and XVI, are known to be by Shakespeare. Of the rest, three are by other known writers and the remaining twelve are of unknown authorship. Shakespeare's poems, four of them sonnets, are on the themes of love and deception, youth and age. Poems I and II are versions of the Sonnets 138 and 144 and scholars are divided as to which of these four poems are the originals and which are revisions.

pastoral

A literary style which derives from ancient Greek literature, and which typically represents shepherds and shepherdesses in an idealized rustic setting, and in a state of uncorrupted simplicity. *As You Like It* is an example of a pastoral romance, although in the play Shakespeare parodies certain STOCK CHARACTERS of the genre in the comic rustics Audrey, Silvius and Phebe.

pathos

A quality in a situation that arouses feelings of deep pity and compassion in those who hear or read it. Examples are: Gertrude's description of Ophelia's death in *Hamlet,* and Tyrrel's poetic account of the death of the little princes in the TOWER OF LONDON in *King Richard III*.

Patience

A minor character in *King Henry VIII*, Patience is Queen Katherine's devoted lady-in-waiting. She cares tenderly for the dying Queen, and embodies the quality of her name.

Patricians

Minor characters in *Coriolanus*, Patricians were the aristocrats of Ancient Rome. Patricians are present in the Senate when Coriolanus is proposed as Consul, and in later crowd scenes. Their presence alongside the ordinary citizens of Rome highlights the class conflict in the play.

Patroclus

A legendary figure and a character in *Troilus and Cressida*, Patroclus is a young Greek warrior and close companion of Achilles whom he amuses with his wicked impersonations of the Greek commanders. He quarrels with Thersites who accuses Patroclus of being a male prostitute. When Patroclus is killed by Hector, Achilles is spurred into action; he returns to fighting and kills Hector in revenge.

Paulina

A character in *The Winter's Tale*, Paulina is Antigonus' wife and Hermione's out-spoken and generous friend. When King Leontes, in his insane jealousy, accuses Queen Hermione of infidelity, Paulina staunchly defends the wronged Queen. She rescues the newly-born Perdita from Hermione's prison and presents the baby to Leontes, once again holding her own against the King, despite his abuse and threats. Paulina is present at Hermione's trial and later announces the Queen's supposed death. When Leontes sees how blind he has been and is overtaken by remorse, Paulina feels pity for him and makes the King promise to let her chose another wife for him. During the sixteen years that pass while Perdita is growing up in Bohemia, Paulina faithfully cares for Hermione in secret and in the final scene of reconciliation, she engineers the dramatic dénouement in which Hermione appears as a statue that comes to life before the astonished Leontes.

Peaseblossom

A minor character in *A Midsummer Night's Dream*, Peaseblossom is one of the fairies in Titania's retinue. While Titania, bewitched and deluded, is in love with Bottom with his ass's head, Peaseblossom waits on Bottom and is given the task of scratching his hairy face.

Pedant of Mantua

A minor comic character in *The Taming of the Shrew*, the old Pedant [schoolmaster], who is passing through Padua, is drafted in by Tranio, Lucentio's clever servant, to play a part in the complex arrangements for Lucentio's secret marriage to Bianca. Tranio tells the Pedant that his life is in danger in Padua and suggests that he should disguise himself as Lucentio's father for safety's sake. In this guise, the Pedant tells Bianca's father that he gladly gives his blessing to his son's marriage. When Lucentio's real father appears on the scene, the Pedant does his best to bluster his way out of trouble but eventually flees for his life.

Pedro, Don
A character in *Much Ado About Nothing*; *see* DON PEDRO.

Pembroke¹, Earl of
A historical figure (c. 1146-1219) and a minor character in *King John*, the Earl of Pembroke accuses King John of murdering Arthur. He rebels against the King and joins the French invading England, but later returns to the King's side to save his own skin.

Pembroke², Earl of
A historical figure (d. 1469) and a minor character in *King Henry VI, Part Three*, Pembroke is a supporter of King Edward and the Yorkist cause.

Pembroke, 3rd Earl of (1580–1630)
The title of WILLIAM HERBERT, a courtier and literary patron, who was LORD CHAMBERLAIN from 1615 to 1625. He was briefly imprisoned after refusing to marry his mistress Mary Fitton (a Maid of Honour to Queen Elizabeth whom some believe to be the DARK LADY of the sonnets) when she bore him a child. It has been suggested that the Earl of Pembroke is the mysterious 'Mr W H' to whom Shakespeare's sonnets are dedicated.

Pembroke's Men
A company of actors founded c. 1590 under the patronage of the 2nd Earl of Pembroke (father of William Herbert above), who travelled around the provinces performing in great houses. In 1597 they leased the newly-built Swan theatre in London, but following the performance of the seditious play the *Isle of Dogs* later that year, the theatre was closed by the licensing authorities and some of the actors imprisoned. The company was never re-established at a London theatre and continued touring the provinces until it went bankrupt in 1593. Shakespeare probably wrote *Titus Andronicus* for them around 1592 and may briefly have been a member of the company before he joined the LORD CHAMBERLAIN'S MEN.

Penker, Friar
The real name of one of the churchmen who pretends to be a bishop in *King Richard III*. *See* BISHOPS.

pentameter
In verse, a metric line of five feet. *See* FOOT; IAMBIC PENTAMETER; METRE.

Percy, Henry
A character in *King Henry IV, Part One*; *see* HOTSPUR. Percy is the family name of the EARLS OF NORTHUMBERLAND.

Percy, Lady (Kate)
A historical figure (b. 1371), whose real name was Elizabeth Percy, and a minor character in *King Henry IV, Parts One and Two*. Lady Percy is Hotspur's high-spirited and affectionate wife. In *Part One* she playfully tries to persuade her husband not to leave for the war, and he teases her for refusing to sing to him. In *Part Two*, Lady Percy is a widow who speaks lovingly of her dead husband, and tries to persuade her father-in-law, the Earl of Northumberland, not to go to war against the King again.

Percy, Thomas, Earl of Worcester

A minor character in *King Henry IV, Part One*; *see* WORCESTER, EARL OF.

Perdita

A character in *The Winter's Tale*, Perdita is the long-lost daughter of King Leontes and Queen Hermione ('Perdita' means 'lost' in Latin). She was born to Hermione while her mother was in prison, accused by the insanely jealous Leontes of infidelity, but Leontes refused to believe that the infant Perdita was his child, and ordered the baby to be abandoned. Left on the inhospitable shore of Bohemia, she was discovered by an old shepherd who brought her up as his own daughter. Perdita makes her first appearance in the play, aged sixteen. She is loved by Florizel, a Prince of Bohemia, who is courting her in disguise because he believes her to be a simple shepherd girl. Florizel's father, Polixenes, furious that his son should be wasting his time with someone so unsuited to be a princess, forbids their marriage. The couple elope to Sicilia, where Perdita's true identity as a princess is revealed and the lovers are free to marry. Charming and beautiful, Perdita has little personality, but plays a significant part in the reconciliation and reunion at the end of the play.

performance

See PLAY PRODUCTION AND PERFORMANCE.

Pericles

Title Character. The title character of *Pericles*, Pericles, Prince of Tyre, is a good man who makes a series of journeys, suffering misfortunes which he bears with patience. He is a character to whom things happen, rather than someone who plays an active role in affairs. He visits Antiochus to woo the King's daughter, and he is horrified to learn that the King and his daughter have an incestuous relationship. He travels next to Tharsus, where he saves the country from famine with the contents of his ships, earning the gratitude of its rulers Cleon and Dionyza. Pericles is shipwrecked on his third journey, and washes up on the shores of Pentapolis where he falls in love with and marries King Simonides' daughter, Thaisa. Fate deals Pericles a cruel blow when he loses his beloved Thaisa at sea after she has given birth to their daughter, Marina. Fourteen years later, Pericles hears that Marina has died. He is plunged into deep despair, but is miraculously reunited with both his wife and his daughter at the end of the play.

Pericles

Shakespeare's first ROMANCE, *Pericles* was written around 1606-08, and first published in a QUARTO edition in 1609 although, surprisingly, it was not included in the First FOLIO edition of 1623. There is a debate among scholars as to whether Shakespeare wrote all of the play by himself or whether it was a collaborative effort. It was probably first performed in 1608, and was popular in Shakespeare's lifetime, playing repeatedly at the GLOBE THEATRE. The main source of the play was a 16th century version of *Confessio Amantis* (1393), the story of Apollonius of Tyre, by the medieval poet John Gower who appears as the CHORUS in the play.

The action of the play extends over sixteen years and is set in various countries. It is a fairy tale in which the narrative is more important than character development. Each act is introduced by a Chorus who also ends the play with an epilogue. The hero of *Pericles* makes a series of journeys in which he encounters different kinds of love and evil and experiences personal loss in a play that explores ideas of patience and redemption, and the nature of controlling destiny.

SYNOPSIS : Pericles, Prince of Tyre, seeking a wife, visits Antiochus where the King requires him to solve a riddle before he can marry his daughter. The answer to the riddle reveals that the King and his daughter have an incestuous relationship, and Pericles leaves in disgust. The King, anxious to ensure Pericles' silence, schemes to kill Pericles who is forced to flee. He arrives at Tharsus where, to the gratitude of Cleon and Dionyza, he is able to relieve a famine with the contents of his ships. Homeward bound, Pericles is shipwrecked at Pentapolis where he wins the hand of King Simonides' daughter Thaisa in a tournament. Returning to Tyre, Pericles and Thaisa are caught in a storm at sea, Thaisa gives birth to a daughter, Marina, but apparently dies in childbirth. Her body, encased in a watertight box and thrown overboard, washes up in Ephesus where a doctor revives Thaisa. Heartbroken at losing her husband and daughter, she becomes a nun at the goddess Diana's temple. Pericles takes the infant Marina to Tharsus and asks Cleon and Dionyza to bring her up as their own. When Marina grows into a beautiful young girl who outshines their own daughter, the wicked Dionyza plans her death, but just in time Pirates snatch Marina and carry her off her to Mytilene where they sell her to a brothel-keeper. Marina's innocence and purity have such a profound effect on the men who visit the brothel that they all become reformed characters. She is rescued by Lysimachus who decides that she is the perfect person to comfort Pericles, who has arrived at Mytilene and is mad with grief at the loss of his family. Marina tells him her story, and Pericles recognizes his long-lost daughter and is restored to happiness. The goddess Diana appears to Pericles in a dream and helps him to find Thaisa, and so the family are reunited. Marina marries Lysimachus, and Pericles and Thaisa return to Penatapolis to live in happiness for ever.

peripeteia
A sudden and unexpected reversal of fortune in a drama; an element which is found sometimes in comedy but more often in tragedy, and which may involve a hero's fall from grace. An example is Shylock's downfall in the court scene in *The Merchant of Venice* .

peroration
The conclusion of a speech; or sometimes an entire speech which is full of RHETORIC. An example is Mark Anthony's long speech from *Julius Caesar*: 'Friends, Romans, countrymen, lend me your ears'.

persona
Originally a word used to describe the mask worn by actors in the Greek Classical theatre, persona has come to mean the assumed character of the writer or of the narrator of a work as presented to the reader. Scholars argue, for example, as to whether the emotions expressed in the SONNETS are Shakespeare's own or whether he adopted a persona in writing them.

personification
A way in which an inanimate object or an abstract concept is described as having human qualities. For example:

> 'For never-resting Time leads summer on
>
> To hideous winter and confounds him there'.
>
> *Sonnet 5*

In *King Henry IV, Part Two*, the activity of spreading rumour is personified in the form of the character called Rumour who introduces the play.

Peter[1]
A minor character in *King Henry VI, Part Two*, Peter is apprentice to an armourer, Thomas Horner. He accuses his master of treason, and they are ordered to fight in single combat to discover the truth. Peter wins the fight and kills Horner who dies confessing his guilt.

Peter[2]
A minor character in *Romeo and Juliet*, Peter is a servant to the Nurse in the Capulet household. He is involved in scenes of bawdy and banter with the Nurse which provide light relief in the tragedy. Shakespeare almost certainly wrote the part for Will KEMP.

Peter[3]
A minor character in *The Taming of the Shrew*, Peter is one of Petruchio's servants. *See* SERVANTS AND SERVINGMEN.

Peter, Friar
See THOMAS, FRIAR.

Peter of Pomfret
A minor character in *King John*, Peter is a wandering prophet who predicts that King John will surrender his crown on Ascension Day. The King sends him to prison and orders him to be hanged. Peter's prophecy is partly fulfilled. On Ascension day, the King does in fact hand over his crown but it is returned to him by the Pope's representative, Pandulph.

Peto
A minor comic character in *King Henry IV, Parts One and Two*, Peto is one of Falstaff's drinking companions. In *Part One* he takes part in the highway robbery at Gad's Hill and in *Part Two* he acts as a messenger bringing bad news of the rebellion in the North.

Petrarch (Francesco Petrarca) (1304–74)
An Italian Renaissance poet and humanist thinker, who was drawn to the literature of ancient Greece and Rome, Petrarch was made Poet Laureate in Rome in 1341. He is perhaps best remembered for his sequence of lyrical sonnets expressing devotion to 'Laura' which were translated into English in the 16th century by Thomas WYATT, and inspired the development of the English or Shakespearean SONNET.

Petruchio
A character in *The Taming of the Shrew*, Petruchio is a rich nobleman in search of a rich wife. He is introduced to the notoriously shrewish [sharp-tempered] Katherina and,

although she is abusive and hostile when they meet, he is content to marry her because of her large dowry. Petruchio sets out to tame Katherina by behaving even more perversely and stubbornly than she does. He arrives at his wedding wearing clothes that are in tatters, pretends to be drunk and insults the priest. He sweeps his bride off to his country house where he denies her food, claiming that everything served up to them is inedible, and stops her from sleeping by tossing and turning in bed. All the time, Petruchio makes constant references to her sweetness until Katherina is not sure whether it is she or Petruchio who is mad. His technique is a winning one; they fall in love with each other and Katherina becomes a loving and obedient wife.

Phebe

A character in *As You Like It*, Phebe is a Shepherdess in the Forest of ARDEN. She is adored by a young shepherd, Silvius, but Phebe is unromantic and cold-hearted, and spurns him. Phebe is no beauty, and Rosalind, in her disguise as the young man 'Ganymede', advises Phebe to take Silvius while she can, but Phebe has fallen in love with 'Ganymede'. Phebe experiences for herself what it is like to suffer from an unrequited passion. When Rosalind reveals her identity as a woman, Phebe settles for Silvius.

Philario

A minor character in *Cymbeline*, Philario is Posthumus' devoted friend. He is Posthumus' host in Italy and tries to prevent him from making the rash and fatal bet with Iachimo over Imogen's fidelity. When apparent proof of Imogen's faithlessness is shown to Posthumus, Philario tries to persuade his friend not to believe the evidence and to remain calm.

Philarmonus

A minor character in *Cymbeline*, Philarmonus is a Roman soothsayer [fortune-teller] who interprets a dream (wrongly), foretelling that Cymbeline will be beaten in battle by the Romans. He also interprets Posthumus' dream in which the god Jupiter appears promising that Posthumus and Imogen, and Cymbeline and his sons, will all be reunited and that Britain will prosper.

Philemon

A minor character in *Pericles*, Philemon is a servant to the kind Lord Cerimon in Ephesus. He is dispatched to provide food and warmth for two wet and hungry visitors who have arrived at the house on a stormy night.

Philip

A minor character in *The Taming of the Shrew*, Philip is one of Petruchio's servants. *See* SERVANTS AND SERVINGMEN.

Philip, King of France

A historical figure (1165-1223) and a character in *King John*, Philip is an enemy of King John and would like to see the young Arthur (son of Richard I) on the throne of England instead. However, he agrees to make peace with England, and to seal the agreement, a marriage is made between his son the Dauphin, and John's niece, Blanche. The peace is short-lived. When King John is excommunicated by the Pope, the Pope's representative calls on Philip to defend the Roman Catholic church and make war again

with England. Philip has the support of two English rebel nobles, Pembroke and
Salisbury, until they discover a plot to murder them.

Philip the Bastard
See BASTARD.

Phillips, Augustine (d. 1605)
An actor and one of the twenty-six 'Principall Actors' listed in the First Folio edition
(1623) of Shakespeare's plays. Phillips was a member of Shakespeare's company of
players, the LORD CHAMBERLAIN'S MEN, formed in 1594, and was one of the original
HOUSEKEEPERS of the Globe Theatre. Phillips seems to have been a prosperous and a
generous man. In his will he left bequests to the HIRED MEN of the company, and the
sum of thirty shillings in gold to Shakespeare, Henry CONDELL and Christopher
BEESTON. He also left his velvet hose and taffeta doublet (*see* COSTUME), together with
his sword and dagger, and various musical instruments to other members of the
company.

Philo
A minor character in *Antony and Cleopatra*, Philo is one of Antony's followers. He
appears in the opening scene of the play discussing Antony's passion for Cleopatra, and
the consequent neglect of his duties in Rome, with Demetrius.

Philostrate
A minor character in *A Midsummer Night's Dream*, Philostrate is the pompous MASTER
OF THE REVELS at Duke Theseus' court in Athens who is in charge of organizing the
entertainments for Theseus' forthcoming marriage to Hippolyta. Philostrate tries to
persuade Theseus not to watch the production of *Pyramus and Thisbe* by Bottom and his
fellow actors as he thinks it is tedious and ludicrous.

Philoten
The name of Cleon and Dionyza's daughter in *Pericles*; she takes no part in the action.
Cleon and Dionyza have promised Pericles to bring up his daughter Marina as their own
but as she develops into a beautiful young girl who is so much more attractive than
Philoten, they plan to murder her.

Philotus
A minor character in *Timon of Athens*, Philotus is a servant to one of Timon's creditors
who tries unsuccessfully to get the payment due to his master from Timon.

Phoenix and the Turtle, The
An allegorical (*see* ALLEGORY) poem by Shakespeare, first published in 1601. The
poem is an elegy, or lament, on the death of the Phoenix, a mythological bird who rose
from the ashes and represents immortality, and his mate the Turtle (a turtledove in
Elizabethan English) who is a symbol of fidelity. They have been consumed by fire,
dying together so as to be joined in love for eternity. The poem celebrates their sacred
and idealized love; a select band of birds is called upon to sing an anthem to the sacred
passion of the lovers. The swan, 'in surplice white', takes the part of the priest in this
funerary celebration, while the black crow represents the mourners. The final section is
a *Threnos* [funeral song], consisting of six rhyming triplets, to the Phoenix and the
Turtle as symbols of beauty and truth.

Phrynia

A minor comic character in *Timon of Athens*, Phrynia with Timandra is one of
Alcibiades' mistresses. Together with Alcibiades, Phrynia and Timandra visit Timon in
his self-imposed exile in the woods. He hurls insults at the two women, who answer in
kind, before giving them money which he hopes will cause the damnation of them and
of everyone else.

Pinch, Doctor

A minor comic character in *The Comedy of Errors*, Dr Pinch is a thin-faced
schoolmaster and a quack doctor. He is described as a 'conjurer' [someone who could,
apparently, exorcise or remove evil spirits not, as in the modern sense, someone who
performs magic tricks] and Adriana calls on Pinch to exorcise the devil that she believes
has possessed her husband Antipholus. Pinch takes his pulse and solemnly advises that
Antipholus and his servant Dromio should be tied up and kept in a dark room. When
Antipholus and Dromio escape they get their revenge. They tie up Pinch, set fire to his
beard and then put out the fire by pouring water over him.

Pindarus

A minor character in *Julius Caesar*, Pindarus is Cassius's slave. At Philippi, Pindarus
mistakenly tells Cassius that one of the officers in his army has been captured. Rather
than face capture himself, Cassius resolves to commit suicide and asks for Pindarus's
help. In exchange, Cassius gives Pindarus his freedom and he runs away to somewhere
where he cannot be caught again by any Roman.

pirated editions

Plays published from a text that has been stolen or illegally acquired; pirated editions of
Shakespeare's plays are sometimes called 'bad' QUARTOS.

Pirates

Minor characters in *Pericles*, Pirates snatch Marina just as Cleon is about to kill her.
They take her on their ship to Mytilene and sell her to a brothel-keeper.

Pirithous

A character in *The Two Noble Kinsmen*, Pirithous is a old friend of Duke Theseus of
Athens, and accompanies the Duke everywhere; their friendship parallels the
relationship between the two noble kinsmen (*see* PARALLELISM). Pirithous officiates at
the tournament when Palamon and Arcite fight for the hand of Emilia, and describes the
magnificence of the knights. As Palamon lays his head on the block, after his defeat by
Arcite, Pirithous rushes in and stops the execution with the news that Arcite is dead.

Pisanio

A character in *Cymbeline*, Pisanio is Posthumus' clever and loyal servant who is more
level-headed than his master. When Posthumus is banished to Italy, Pisanio remains
with Posthumus' wife, Imogen, to whom he is equally faithful. Instructed by Posthumus
to kill Imogen, Pisanio is appalled. Instead, he organizes her escape with great
efficiency, providing her with Posthumus' clothing so that she can disguise herself as a
boy. He does his best to protect her from the murderous Cloten, and although he is
threatened with torture by Cymbeline, he keeps Imogen's whereabouts a secret. In the

final happy reconciliation, Pisanio explains to Posthumus and to the court that
everything he did was done in defence of Imogen.

Pistol

A comic character in *King Henry IV, Part Two*, *King Henry V* and *The Merry Wives of
Windsor*, Pistol is Falstaff's 'ancient' or second-in-command. He is a loud-mouthed
soldier, a bully who uses flowery and overblown language, even when he is being
insulting. He is named after a handgun which is explosive but not really dangerous and
in Shakespeare's time, the word 'pistol' also had sexual connotations which are
exploited in punning exchanges with Falstaff. In *Henry IV, Part Two*, Pistol quarrels
with Doll Tearsheet and takes pleasure in telling Falstaff that she has been thrown into
prison. His pleasure is shortlived because shortly after he too is hauled off with the rest
of Falstaff's followers to prison.

In *King Henry V*, Pistol has newly married Mistress Quickly. Following the death of
Falstaff, Pistol joins the King's army fighting in France together with his old
companions Nym and Bardolph, and predictably proves himself a coward. Pistol makes
contemptuous comments about the Welshman Fluellen who wears a leek in his hat as
his national emblem. Fluellen later makes Pistol pay for his abuse by forcing him to eat
the leek.

In *The Merry Wives of Windsor,* Pistol is accused by Slender of stealing his purse;
typically full of blood and thunder, Pistol refutes the charge with a hail of words.
Falstaff asks his friend to be the messenger in his love affairs, but Pistol thinks such a
task is beneath his dignity and refuses. When Falstaff angrily dismisses him, Pistol gets
his revenge by telling the violently jealous Master Ford that Falstaff is courting his wife.
Falstaff's response to Pistol's refusal to act as go-between is to turn down a request for a
loan; but Pistol has the last word. Disguised as a hobgoblin, he takes part in Falstaff's
public humiliation in Windsor forest.

pit

Part of an auditorium which, in a modern theatre, is the small space in front of and
below the level of the stage where the orchestra sits. In Elizabethan PLAYHOUSES, the
pit was the area in front of the stage where the GROUNDLINGS or penny-paying audience
stood for performances. The stage would have been at about shoulder height from the
floor, and there was no roofing to protect the groundlings from the weather; they would
have stood on mud or straw that was frequently wet. The word pit comes from 'cockpit',
the small arena where cock-fighting used to take place.

Pit, The
See BARBICAN THEATRE, THE.

place, unity of
See UNITIES.

plague, the
A usually fatal disease, the bubonic plague was carried by the fleas of the black rat and
was rife in Elizabethan England; in 1563, the year before Shakespeare's birth, 20,000
Londoners died of the plague and in the following year nearly a quarter of
Shakespeare's home town, Stratford-on-Avon, died. The disease spread with horrific

speed through the crowded and insanitary streets of London and the compulsory quarantine of sick families only accelerated its advance, despite the use of preventatives such as chewing orange peel or smoking tobacco. Outbreaks of the plague were a recurring cause of the closure of London theatres.

The plague has an important role in *Romeo and Juliet*. Friar Lawrence's messenger is unable to deliver the vital letter to Romeo which explains Juliet's pretended death, because he is disastrously delayed, quarantined during an outbreak of the plague.

Plantagenet
The name of the English royal family who reigned from 1154 to 1399, and who were called this because the family emblem was flowering broom, a shrub known as *planta genista* in Latin. King Henry II (1154-99), the first Plantagenet King, was succeeded in due course by other family members including King JOHN and RICHARD II. After Richard II's death in 1399, the dynasty was continued through the houses of LANCASTER and YORK, branches of the Plantagenet family. See the table of kings and queens in the Supplement.

Plantagenet, Richard
In *King Henry VI, Parts One, Two, and Three*, the name by which the DUKE OF YORK is known before he is given the title of Duke by the King. *See* PLANTAGENET *above*.

platt
In the Elizabethan theatre, a platt was a summary of the plot of a play, containing a list of stage directions and PROPS, that would have been displayed back stage in a playhouse for the stage manager and actors to consult.

play production and performance
In Shakespeare's time, trumpet fanfares announced the beginning of the performance of a play, and flags were flown from the tops of PLAYHOUSES to show that a performance was in progress. The action would have been almost continuous, and intervals, if there were any, would have brief. The pace was so fast, in fact, that plays which now take some three hours to perform took perhaps only two hours (the Chorus at the beginning of *Romeo and Juliet* speaks of 'the two hours traffic of our stage'). As there was no artificial lighting, except in private theatres such as the BLACKFRIARS THEATRE, performances took place during daylight hours, usually beginning around two o'clock in the afternoon; night scenes were indicated by characters carrying torches. At the end of the play a JIG, a kind of crude musical comedy, was often performed (*see separate entry*).

Little is known for certain about the details of play production, but scenery was almost certainly minimal; changes in time or location in the narrative usually being indicated in the dialogue. For example, we are told of the setting for *Twelfth Night* by a sea captain, who announces to the heroine Viola, 'This is Illyria, Lady'. A curtain may have been hung at the back of the stage, which would have been black when a tragedy was being performed, and there would have been easily portable, if sometimes elaborate, PROPS. The actors wore contemporary Elizabethan dress and costumes were costly and lavish.

The action may have been played out on different levels using the CELLARAGE beneath the stage and the balcony above the HEAVENS. It seems evident from the appearance of the god Jupiter in *Cymbeline*, who descends from the skies, that there was some kind of

machinery by which characters could be lowered from above the stage. Certainly the
large dimensions of the stage would have allowed battle scenes and fights to be enacted
with great vigour, and a gory realism was created with large quantities of sheep's blood
and entrails. Sound effects were used and thunder, which is an important element in a
play such as *Julius Caesar*, was suggested by drum rolls or by rolling a heavy canon
ball down a wooden trough, while dried peas were used to mimic the sound of rain or
hail. The devastating fire which burnt down the GLOBE theatre in 1613 was caused by
canon fired during a battle scene. *See also* ACTORS AND ACTING; CURTAIN; COSTUME;
LIGHTING; PLAYHOUSES.

play within a play
A drama enacted on stage by the characters in a play as part of the action. It may be
included simply for its entertainment value, for example the masque of Pyramus and
Thisbe in *A Midsummer Night's Dream*, or it may hold some deeper dramatic
significance, as in the play within a play in *Hamlet*. *The Taming of the Shrew* is a play
within a play performed by travelling actors to entertain the tinker Sly, but in modern
productions it is usually performed simply as a play in its own right and the INDUCTION
or introduction is left out.

Players[1]
Minor characters in *Hamlet*, a company of travelling players (*see* ACTORS AND ACTING)
arrive at Elsinore and are welcomed by Hamlet. He instructs them to perform *The
Murder of Gonzago*, a play about murder, which he hopes will prompt Claudius into
revealing his guilty conscience, and he advises them on acting techniques. The FIRST
PLAYER takes the part of the PLAYER KING while the SECOND PLAYER is the PLAYER
QUEEN.

Players[2]
Minor characters in *The Taming of the Shrew*, a company of players arrives at a Lord's
house when he is tricking the drunken Sly into believing that he is a gentleman who has
been asleep for fifteen years. The Lord, who recalls an earlier visit, welcomes them
warmly to his house and gives them his hospitality before they enact the 'pleasant
comedy' of *The Taming of the Shrew* for Sly.

playhouses
Theatres were more usually called playhouses in Shakespeare's time. Very little is
known for certain about the structure of Elizabethan playhouses; information has been
constructed from the few remains of known theatre buildings discovered beneath the
streets of London in recent years, and from contemporary documents that have survived,
such as the papers of the theatrical entrepreneur Philip HENSLOWE.

 Groups of travelling players had long been performing in municipal buildings, and in
the halls of great houses and universities, as well as in the open air. Only during the
Elizabethan age when COMPANIES OF ACTORS were required by law to form
partnerships under the patronage of a nobleman in order to avoid imprisonment for
'vagrancy', did these groups begin to stay in the same place for longer periods of time.
Some companies established themselves at local taverns which provided not only
accommodation but also a ready-made audience and where they performed in the
INN-YARDS. Many companies moved to London where new, purpose-built theatres were

beginning to appear, their designs owing much to the layout of inn-yards; the first, the THEATRE, was erected in 1576. As the censorious London authorities, the CITY FATHERS increasingly imposed restrictions on players and playwrights, theatres were built beyond the city limits.

There were two distinct types of theatre: **public** and **private**.

Public playhouses: Partially thatched wooden structures, they were usually circular or octagonal in design and built to accommodate audiences of anything up to 3,000 (although it was rare for a theatre to be filled to capacity for a performance). Three tiers of galleried seating around three sides of the theatre were roofed in, but the centre was open to the skies, allowing natural light to illuminate the otherwise unlit productions but leaving much of the AUDIENCE unprotected form the rain. There was an area in front of the stage known as the PIT where poorer spectators, the GROUNDLINGS, would stand, while the most exclusive seats were on the stage itself. Entrance money was collected by 'gatherers' as the audience went into the theatre.

The STAGE, an APRON STAGE, would have projected into the auditorium at about shoulder height from the ground. It would have been larger than most modern stages (the stage at the FORTUNE theatre was about 14m x 9m - the present stage at the Royal Shakespeare Theatre at Stratford measures about 11m across). The dimensions of the stage meant that, even in a large theatre like the GLOBE, an actor at the front of the stage would have been little more than 25m from the most distant member of the audience, so there would have been an easy intimacy between actors and spectators. In some theatres the staging was removable in order to provide an arena for bear-baiting and cock-fighting. There was a trapdoor in the stage which might, for example, represent a grave or the mouth of Hell, or through which characters such the ghost of Hamlet's father could rise or descend to the CELLARAGE (the space beneath the stage, which was also sometimes used for storage). There may have been a recessed, curtained area at the rear of the stage, an INNER STAGE, which could be used rather like the wings in a modern theatre for the actors' entrances or exits and also for scenes which took place in for example a cave or a tomb.

A roof or canopy above the stage, known as the HEAVENS, was supported by wooden pillars and was sometimes painted blue with a gold sun, moon and stars. Above and behind the heavens, there probably was a small hut known as the TIRING-HOUSE which housed props and costumes. In front of the tiring-house there was a balconied space for musicians and for the machinery used to lower or raise actors or props; this may also have functioned as battlements, for example, in *Hamlet* or the balcony in the balcony scene in *Romeo and Juliet*.

Private playhouses: Unlike public playhouses, these theatres were entirely roofed over and were more luxurious, and accordingly more expensive. They were considerably smaller, too, accommodating around 800 people, and were rectangular in design, sometimes having been converted from private dwellings or, as in the case of the BLACKFRIARS THEATRE from a convent. The cheapest seats were in the galleries around the sides of the auditorium; more expensive seating was provided in partitioned sections of the galleries, similar to a box in a modern theatre. Costlier yet, was seating on the stage itself where spectators sat on stools which could be hired for half-a-crown.

The stage design would have been similar to the public theatres but on a smaller scale, and performances would have been lit by candles suspended in candelabras from above.

The most notable private theatre in Shakespeare's time was the BLACKFRIARS THEATRE, but there were others at Whitefriars, and in a choir school near St Paul's cathedral. *See the table of playhouses in the Supplement.*

Plebeians

Minor characters in *Coriolanus* and *Julius Caesar*, Plebeians are the ordinary people of Rome, (as opposed to the PATRICIANS, the Roman aristocrats) who appear in crowd scenes.

In *Julius Caesar*, the Plebeians are the fickle citizens of Rome who comment on and respond to events. In the recent past, the people of Rome had loved Pompey who ruled them jointly with Caesar. Now they are welcoming Caesar back to Rome fresh from a triumph in battle in which he defeated Pompey. The Plebeians are easily swayed. After Caesar's death, Brutus address the crowd, speaking to them with the voice of reason, and they hail him as their new king. Mark Antony's speech immediately afterwards, appeals to their emotions, and the crowd respond to him by demanding Brutus' death as a traitor. The mob riot, and run into a poet called CINNA on his way to Caesar's funeral whom they kill because he has the same name as one of the conspirators although he protests his innocence. *See also* CITIZENS.

plot

The story or plan of a literary work, including the sequence and relationship of events as well as the revelation of character. Shakespeare borrowed most of his plots from other SOURCES such as chronicle plays. *Compare* ACTION; NARRATIVE; SUB-PLOT.

In the Elizabethan theatre, the BOOK-KEEPER would have written out the plot of a play with notes about PROPS and stage directions, etc., and hung it at the back of the stage to help actors who had to learn new plays all the time; this was called the PLATT.

Plutarch (c. AD 50-130)

An Ancient Greek philosopher and biographer, Plutarch's *Lives of the Noble Greeks and Romans*, a collection of 46 biographies of great Greek and Roman figures, was translated into English from a previous French translation by Thomas North in 1579. Shakespeare used Plutarch's biographies as the source for *Antony and Cleopatra*, *Coriolanus*, and *Julius Caesar*.

Poet and Painter

Minor characters in *Timon of Athens*, at the beginning of the play, a Poet and a Painter are each preparing works of art which will flatter Timon. They are hoping for financial reward. The Painter is more modest than the Poet whose verses, anticipating Timon's fate, describe the goddess Fortune first smiling on Timon and then, in a sudden change of mood, ignoring him. His poem is a allegorical (*see* ALLEGORY) account of Timon's story. When Timon goes into his self-imposed exile in the woods and discovers gold, the Poet and the Painter follow him and oozing with insincerity offer their services to him. Timon says he will give them gold if they will rid him of villains and goes on to say that each of them is a villain.

Poet

A minor character in *Julius Caesar*, the poet demands to see Brutus and Cassius after they have quarrelled and, in two lines of doggerel, advises them to be reconciled. A poet with the name of CINNA is killed by the PLEBEIANS on his way to Caesar's funeral because he bears the same name as the Cinna who is one of conspirators.

poetic justice
Appropriate retribution when the characters in a work are punished for wrong-doing, or rewarded for virtue.

poetic licence
A freedom to depart from the conventions of form, or historical or factual accuracy which a writer may exercise.

poetry
See VERSE; compare PROSE.

Poins, Edward (Ned)
A minor comic character in *King Henry IV, Parts One and Two*, Poins is one of Prince Hal's drinking companions at the Boar's Head Tavern. In *Part One*, the plan to rob Falstaff and the other thieves at Gad's Hill is Poins' idea. In *Part Two*, Poins suggests that he and Prince Hal should disguise themselves as servants in order to spy on Falstaff. Falstaff soon discovers them, but not before he has described Poins in unflattering terms to Doll Tearsheet.

Polixenes
A character in *The Winter's Tale*, Polixenes is King of Bohemia. Polixenes and King Leontes of Sicilia were childhood friends, and Polixenes is enjoying a visit to Leontes' court when Leontes, seized by an irrational and murderous jealously, accuses his wife Hermione and Polixenes of having an affair. Polixenes' life is threatened and he is forced to flee. When Leonte's wife gives birth to a daughter, Perdita, Leontes is convinced that the infant is Polixenes' bastard child. Sixteen years later, Polixenes learns that his son, Prince Florizel, is courting a shepherd girl (who is in fact the long-lost Perdita). He is furious that his son is wasting his love on someone so unsuited to be a princess and forbids the lovers to marry. They elope to Sicilia, where Perdita's true identity is discovered. In a final scene of reconciliation and reunion, Polixenes gives his blessing to Florizel's and Perdita's marriage, and makes his peace with Leontes.

Polonius
A character in *Hamlet*, Polonius is a councillor to the King of Denmark, and father of Laertes and Ophelia. Wordy and pompous, Polonius advises Laertes on behaviour and manners before his son leaves for France. He instructs Ophelia to repel Hamlet's advances, telling her that he does not trust the Prince. He takes an unhealthy interest in his daughter's relationship with Hamlet, and, as Hamlet appears increasingly unbalanced, Polonius uses Ophelia as a barometer of Hamlet's state of mind. He agrees to spy on Hamlet for King Claudius, and eavesdrops on Hamlet and Gertrude, hiding behind a curtain in Gertrude's bedroom. Hamlet hears a noise and runs his sword through the drapery killing Polonius. His death is a crucial event. Ophelia goes mad, grieving for her father, and Hamlet is exiled to England.

Although Polonius contributes so centrally to the tragedy in the play, he is a partly comic character, and may derive from the traditional STOCK CHARACTER of Pantaloon in the COMMEDIA DELL'ARTE.

Polydore
In *Cymbeline*, Polydore is the name Belarius gives to GUIDERIUS, Cymbeline's son whom he snatched as a young child.

polysyllabic
Words containing more than one syllable are described as polysyllabic. The word polysyllabic comes from the Greek words *poly* meaning 'many', and syllable. *Compare* MONOSYLLABLE.

Pomfret Castle
See PONTEFRACT CASTLE

Pompey (Pompeius Sextus)
A historical figure (75-35 BC), son of Pompey the Great, and a character in *Antony and Cleopatra*, Pompey is a naval commander. During Antony's absence in Egypt, he has been gaining power for himself; supported in his fight by pirates, he has taken control on the seas around Southern Italy and is approaching Rome. Caesar calls a truce with Pompey, who is given certain lands in exchange for ridding the seas of pirates, and the peace is celebrated in a drunken feast on board one of Pompey's ships. One of the pirates suggests that Pompey should cut the ship's cable during the feast and let all the Roman leaders drift out to sea, but he refuses. Peace is short-lived; Pompey is beaten in battle by Caesar shortly afterwards and executed.

Pompey
A comic character in *Measure for Measure*; Pompey, whose surname is Bum [slang for an idle fellow], belongs to the underworld of petty crime that the Duke would like to see eradicated from Vienna. He is Mistress Overdone's servant who serves ale, and acts as a pimp for her brothel. He is arrested by the constable Elbow on a rather vague charge, but vigorously protests his innocence and out-talks the already confused constable. He is set free but warned to mend his ways. Arrested a second time, Pompey ends up in prison where he finds he rather enjoys life as most of the inmates are his friends. He is pressed into service as an assistant to the executioner Abhorson, a role he cheerfully accepts. Pompey's bawdy wit and vitality provide light relief in the play's darker moments.

Pompey the Great (106–48 BC)
A famous general and statesman, Pompey the Great, ruled the Roman Empire jointly with Crassus and Julius Caesar, whose daughter he married. Pompey and Caesar each became ambitious for power and eventually civil war broke out and Pompey was defeated and later killed. Shakespeare's *Julius Caesar* opens with Caesar's triumphal return after a victory over two of Pompey's sons. The character of Pompey (Pompeius Sextus) in *Antony and Cleopatra* is the son of Pompey the Great.

In *Love's Labour's Lost*, the character of Pompey the Great features in the comical MASQUE of *The Nine Worthies* and is played by Costard who mistakenly refers to the character as 'Pompey the Big'.

Pontefract (Pomfret) Castle
A castle in northern England which features in two of Shakespeare's HISTORY PLAYS. In *King Richard II*, King Richard is imprisoned and murdered in Pontefract Castle and in *King Richard III*, Rivers, Grey and Vaughan are executed there.

Popilius Lena

A minor character in *Julius Caesar*, Popilius is a Roman senator [member of the state council]. Unaware of their plans to kill Caesar, Popilius meets the conspirators on their way to the assassination, and disconcerts Cassius by wishing him good luck in his affairs that day.

Porter

A minor character in *Macbeth*, the porter is the drunken keeper of the gate to Macbeth's castle who comments on the effects of drink in a short interlude of comic relief. He admits Macduff to the castle where the shocking murder of the King is about to be discovered, and imagines himself as the guardian to the gates of Hell. The character of the Porter, based on the gate-keeper to Hell in medieval MORALITY PLAYS would have been a recognizable figure to Shakespeare's audiences, and his appearance would carry the suggestion that Macbeth's world is a hellish one.

Porter and his Man

Minor characters in *King Henry VIII*, the Porter and his Man appear in a brief interlude of comic relief. They are guarding the entrance to the court from the unruly crowds who have gathered, hoping to see the christening of the infant Princess Elizabeth. The Porter says that a group of particularly riotous young men must be apprentice boy actors. The scene helps to create an atmosphere of occasion, and anticipates the enthusiasm of the ordinary people of England for their future Queen.

Portia[1]

A historical figure (b. before 46 BC) and a character in *Julius Caesar*, Portia is Brutus's devoted wife. She is concerned that her husband seems depressed and restless and begs him to confide in her. She says that as the daughter of one famous Roman, Cato, and the wife of another, she is a woman who can be trusted with any secret, and she shows him a self-inflicted wound on her thigh, in order to prove her strength of purpose. It seems likely that Portia, at some stage, learns of Brutus's involvement in the conspiracy against Caesar because later her concern for her husband rises to fever pitch. She sends a servant to the senate to see if anything unusual has occurred there. Portia's death is reported by Brutus before the battle of Philippi; he tells Cassius that she had become distracted and swallowed fire.

Portia[2]

The heroine of *The Merchant of Venice*, Portia is rich and beautiful. Her father's will stipulates that she must marry the man who chooses the right casket of three; one casket is gold, one silver, and one is made of lead. Portia, trapped by the terms of the will, is unimpressed by her suitors until Bassanio appears to court her. To her delight he chooses the right casket, but their happiness is interrupted when Bassanio's friend Antonio is arrested because of the non-repayment of Bassanio's debt (guaranteed by a pound of Antonio's flesh) to Shylock. Portia shows herself to be one of the most resourceful and intelligent of Shakespeare's heroines. Disguised as a young lawyer, she appears in court and pleads with Shylock to show mercy to Antonio in a speech of extraordinary poetic power. When that fails, she uses the letter of the law to defeat him. Portia shows little mercy to Shylock, demanding that he is stripped of all his wealth. Reunited with Bassanio, she reveals the part she played in saving the life of his friend.

Posthumus Leonatus (Leonates)
A central character in *Cymbeline*; Posthumus has married Imogen against King Cymbeline's wishes, and has been banished to Italy. Posthumus is an impulsive young man whose feelings fluctuate. He sighs for Imogen and boasts of her beauty and purity, rashly betting Iachimo that she will always remain a faithful wife. When he is given apparent proof of Imogen's infidelity, he is immediately overcome with murderous rage, and instructs his servant to kill her. Believing her dead, he is consumed with remorse and longs for his own death. He fights for Britain in a battle against the Romans, but he survives and is taken prisoner. Posthumus has a dream in his condemned cell in which the god Jupiter appears and promises that everything will turn out well in the end, which indeed it does. In the happy ending to the play, Posthumus is reunited with Imogen and reconciled with Cymbeline.

Potpan
A minor character in *Romeo and Juliet*; Potpan is one of the servants in the Capulet household who clears away the banquet. The character is named in the cast list but does not appear in the play except by mention.

prefigure
To foreshadow or suggest the forthcoming events in a literary work, by making a reference to them before they occur. For example: Juliet prefigures her own tragic fate early in *Romeo and Juliet* when she says 'My grave is like to be my wedding bed'.

Priam
A legendary figure and a minor character in *Troilus and Cressida*, Priam is King of Troy. He tries unsuccessfully to persuade Hector of the dangers of fighting Achilles.

Priest
A minor character in *Twelfth Night*, the priest performs the marriage between Sebastian and Olivia.

Prince Henry's Men
The name taken by the company of actors the ADMIRAL'S MEN when Prince Henry, King James I's son, became their patron in 1603.

Princess of France, The
A character in *Love's Labour's Lost*, the Princess of France is visiting the King of Navarre with her entourage. The purpose of her visit is to discuss with the King the return of land in Aquitaine to the King of France. She is an intelligent ambassador, and a level-headed young woman who rebukes one of her courtiers, Boyet, for flattering her. It is soon apparent that the King of Navarre has fallen in love with the Princess, despite his vow of celibacy. She joins the King's hunting party but is reluctant to be a 'murderer' and kill deer. When the Princess and her companions hear that they are to be courted by the King and his friends disguised as Russians, she mischievously suggests that they trick their suitors by wearing masks to confuse the young men. Grieved at news of her father's death, the Princess prepares to depart for France. Before she leaves, she orders the King of Navarre to live as a hermit for a whole year, in order to test the strength of his love for her.

Principall Actors
The 26 actors who were listed in the First FOLIO edition of Shakespeare's plays. They were: William Shakespeare, Richard BURBAGE, John HEMING, Augustine PHILLIPS, William KEMP, Thomas Pope (d. c. 1603), George Bryan (active 1586-1613), Henry CONDELL, William SLY, Richard Cowly (d. 1619), John Lowin (1576-1653). Samuel Crosse (active c.1604), Alexander Cooke (d. 1614), Samuel Gilburne (active 1605), Robert ARMIN, William Ostler (c. 1588-1614), Nathan FIELD, John Underwood (d. 1624), Nicholas Tooley (c. 1575-1623), William Ecclestone (active 1610-1623), Joseph Taylor (d. 1652), Robert BENFIELD, Robert Gough (d. 1624), Richard Robinson (d. 1648), John Shank (c. 1565-1636), John Rice (active 1607-1630).

private playhouse
An exclusive, expensive type of indoor Elizabethan theatre; *see* PLAYHOUSES.

problem play
The term 'problem play' was first used in 1896 by the Shakespearean scholar, Frederick S Boas in *Shakespeare and his Predecessors*. It is used to describe some of Shakespeare's plays which are difficult to categorize as belonging to the genres of either comedy or tragedy, notably *All's Well that Ends Well*, *Measure for Measure*, and *Troilus and Cressida*, because they have the happy ending required of a comedy but also include elements of tragedy. These plays, which have a bitter quality and exhibit a certain cynicism about sex, were written during the years 1602 to 1604 which scholars have speculated may have been a time of depression or personal crisis in Shakespeare's life. *See* TRAGI-COMEDY.

Proculeius
A minor character in *Antony and Cleopatra*, Proculeius is one of Caesar's followers who is trusted by Antony. He is sent by Caesar to capture Cleopatra and to prevent her from committing suicide. Proculeius advises Cleopatra to surrender to Caesar, promising that she will be treated kindly.

producer
In the modern theatre or in film, the producer is the person who has overall control of a film or stage production but who, in general, is not actively involved with the actors' performance, which is the job of the DIRECTOR.

prologue
Literally a foreword; a speech, usually a monologue, at the beginning of a play which is often given by a CHORUS who, in Shakespeare's time, would traditionally have worn black. The function of a prologue is to set the scene for the forthcoming action, as in the opening of *King Henry V* or *Romeo and Juliet*.

In *Troilus and Cressida*, the Prologue is named as a character in the cast list. He describes how the abduction of Helen from the Greeks by the Trojan prince Paris sparked the siege of TROY, which is the setting for the play. The Prologue, who is dressed in armour, is a humorous figure who suggests that war is a chancy thing.

In *King Henry VIII*, the Prologue introduces the play, warning the audience that if they are expecting to see a 'merry bawdy play' they will be disappointed, because what follows is serious spectacle. He also speaks the humorous EPILOGUE in which he hopes that those members of the audience who have remained awake, enjoyed the proceedings. Scholars who believe that Shakespeare wrote *Henry VIII* in collaboration with another dramatist, regard the Prologue's speeches as having been written by the collaborator.

The Prologue introducing *The Two Noble Kinsmen* tells the audience that the play is based on a story by Chaucer and, while he hopes that the next two hours will be entertaining ones, he is afraid that the play cannot hope to be as good as Chaucer's version. (Chaucer's account of the Palamon and Arcite story, *The Knight's Tale*, one of the *Canterbury Tales*, was written around 225 years before *The Two Noble Kinsmen* and was printed in 1478.)

prompter
Someone in who sits off-stage during performances and whose job is to whisper lines (if possible without the audience hearing) to an actor who has forgotten his words. The prompter (known as the BOOK-KEEPER or book-holder in the Elizabethan theatre) follows the text from a 'prompt' copy of the play.

props
A commonly used abbreviation for 'properties', which are all the movable objects that are used on stage as part of the action of the play, for example swords, letters, crowns, or food and drink.

Although in Shakespeare's time fixed scenery was minimal, numerous props were used and they were sometimes quite substantial items. The theatre manager Philip HENSLOWE kept lengthy lists of props which included such things as a tomb, a HELL MOUTH, a lion and two lions' heads, crowns, a black dog, a 'tree of golden apples', a wooden hatchet, and even the City of Rome.

proscenium arch
The word proscenium comes from the ancient Greek and means 'before the stage'. In Elizabethan times the proscenium was the principal acting area (*see* APRON STAGE); in modern theatres, the proscenium arch is an architectural feature, a high arch at the front of a stage which creates a frame for the SET and conceals the WINGS at the side and the FLIES above. There is a debate among scholars as to when exactly the proscenium arch first became part of theatre design, but it was probably not until the mid-17th century.

prose
Written or spoken language which, although sometimes rhythmic in sound, is unlike verse in that it does not have a regular metrical structure (*see* METRE) or a pattern of rhyming lines.

Shakespeare employs both prose and BLANK VERSE in his plays. Prose is often (though by no means always) the language of the more lowly characters and of the rustic comics, while verse is frequently the medium for heroes and heroines, kings and noblemen. In *King Henry IV*, for example, poetry is the language of the court and prose the language of the tavern. In *Othello*, Shakespeare uses poetry to express Othello's love for Desdemona, while the malevolent Iago frequently articulates his schemes in prose. In *Hamlet*, while all the hero's soliloquies are written in verse, Shakespeare uses prose as a subtle indicator of Hamlet's feigned 'madness', for example in his prose dialogues with Polonius.

prosody

The study of poetry and verse form, including METRE, RHYME, and structure. *See* SCANSION.

Prospero

A character in *The Tempest*, Prospero is a philosopher and a magician. Once Duke of Milan, he spent so much of his time in study that he neglected his duties as a ruler. He was deposed by his treacherous brother Antonio, and put to sea in a boat with his infant daughter, Miranda. They have lived in exile on an otherwise uninhabited island for twelve years, and in this kingdom, Prospero is a sternly controlling ruler. He is served by the spirit Ariel, and Caliban, a resentful and deformed savage, whom he has tried unsuccessfully to educate. Prospero uses his magic to whip up a storm that beings all his enemies to the island, where they are made to confront their crimes. He forgives them and allows them to return safely to their homes, and renouncing magic, returns to Milan to take up his duties as ruler. Prospero has discovered that there is good and bad in the world, and has become more humane. His name means 'to make successful or happy' in Latin, but in the end his success is only partial. Antonio remains unrepentant and Caliban is still an unreclaimed savage.

protagonist

The principal character, hero or heroine, in a play.

Proteus

A character in *The Two Gentleman of Verona*, Proteus loves Julia. He is ordered to Milan and the lovers pledge fidelity and exchange rings. In Milan, Proteus rejoins his friend Valentine who has fallen in love with Silvia, and as soon as he sees her, Proteus too is smitten by Silvia's beauty. Forgetting his promises to Julia and abandoning all loyalty to his friend, he sets out to win Silvia for himself. He betrays Valentine by telling Julia's father of a plan to elope, and when Valentine is banished, Proteus courts Silvia and gives her the very ring that Julia had given him as a keepsake. He pursues Silvia when she flees, and is so determined to possess her that he even threatens her with rape. Confronted by Valentine, who forgives him, Proteus is ashamed of his treachery to Valentine and to Julia, and suddenly realizes that it is Julia whom he really loves.

   The name Proteus comes from a Greek god who could change his shape at will, rather as Shakespeare's character can change his feelings towards others.

Provost

A character in *Measure for Measure*, the Provost is the head of the police in Vienna and the governor of the prison in which Claudio is held. He is a sympathetic character who asks Angelo to show mercy to Claudio and hopes that Isabella can persuade him to be lenient, but when the law demands that Claudio must be executed, the Provost prepares to do his duty. The disguised Duke suggests a plan to save Claudio's life and the Provost is reluctant to help until the Duke shows him proper letters of authority. The Duke afterwards rewards him with a promise of promotion for his help.

public playhouse

A type of open-air Elizabethan playhouse. *See* PLAYHOUSES.

Publius[1]

A minor character in *Julius Caesar*, Publius is a Roman senator [member of the state council]; he accompanies Caesar to the senate and witness his murder there. Afterwards, Brutus tells Publius that the conspirators do not intend to harm him or any other Roman citizen.

Publius[2]

A minor character in *Titus Andronicus*, Publius is Marcus Andronicus' son and Titus' nephew. When Titus is becoming increasingly distracted, Publius expresses concern for his uncle's welfare. Titus calls on Publius to help him to seize Tamora's sons Chiron and Demetrius.

Puck (Robin Goodfellow)

A character in *A Midsummer Night's Dream*, Puck is the Fairy King Oberon's attendant and his jester. He is a supernatural being who can circle the earth in forty minutes, change his appearance, and imitate voices. A goblin, a mischievous spirit of the woods, Puck is a practical-joker whose tricks are not always good-natured. According to one of the fairies, he delights in frightening the young maidens in the village, and he derives great pleasure from tricking the bewitched Titania. Puck is unrepentant when Oberon tells him he has made a muddle of his instructions to cast spells on the mortal lovers, and gleefully anticipates creating greater confusion as he leads the mortals a merry dance through woods.

pun

A usually humorous use of a word that sounds the same as another word but which has a different meaning. *See* QUIBBLE.

Puritan

A member of an extreme Protestant movement that emerged in the second half of the 16th century, and which was particularly opposed to what it saw as Roman Catholic abuses in the Church of England. Puritans' suspicion of religious ritual and ceremony was rivalled only by their fear and hatred of the theatre. When the GLOBE THEATRE burnt down in 1613, they saw this as a manifestation of God's displeasure. They regarded plays as the work of the devil, believing that tragedies would incite audiences to murder and violence, and that performances of comedies would lead to lax sexual morals. The idea of boys wearing women's' clothes was repugnant to the Puritans, as it contravened an instruction given in the Old Testament, and they abhorred the practice, prevalent in the early part of Queen Elizabeth I's reign, of performing plays on Sundays. Puritans were fundamentally opposed to HUMANISM and were natural enemies of dramatists like Shakespeare. The character MALVOLIO in *Twelfth Night* displays all the attitudes of a Puritan, and may have been based on a real individual known to Shakespeare.

Pyramus and Thisbe

The hero and heroine of the 'lamentable comedy' performed by Bottom and his fellow workmen at the wedding celebrations in *A Midsummer Night's Dream*. The story of Pyramus and Thisbe belongs to a famous love tragedy from Ovid's *Metamorphoses* (see OVID), and is similar to the plot of *Romeo and Juliet* but involves a lion rather than poison. During rehearsals, Bottom and his fellow actors discuss the part of the lion in the play and decide not to make the lion too ferocious for fear of frightening the ladies in the audience. This is a reference to a real life occasion, which Shakespeare must have known of, when a MASQUE was performed at Stirling Castle in Scotland before King James VI (the future King James I of England) involving a pride of lions which terrified the ladies.

Qq

Q., or q.
An abbreviation for QUARTO.

quarto
A piece of paper that is folded into four to make eight pages and then bound together to form part of a book. Many of Shakespeare's plays were printed individually in quarto form and such editions are sometimes referred to as first and second quartos, which means that they are the first and second editions of the play. 'GOOD' QUARTO editions are those printed from Shakespeare's own handwritten script (known as 'foul papers') or from the BOOK-KEEPER'S prompt copy which would have had additional notes about exits and entrances. 'BAD' QUARTOS were editions printed from texts which had been written down from memory by someone who knew the play and who then sold it to the printer. These pirated versions of the plays were usually printed without the dramatist's name appearing on them; they often had pieces of text missing and sometimes contained lines from other plays. (*See also* FOLIO).

Queen
A character in *Cymbeline*, the Queen is Cymbeline's second wife and Imogen's evil step-mother. The Queen had hoped her loutish son Cloten would marry Imogen, but Imogen has married Posthumus and remains infuriatingly loyal to her husband even though he is banished. The Queen pretends friendship towards Imogen but schemes to murder her. She acquires poison from the court doctor but he is suspicious of her and secretly substitutes a harmless sleeping drug. Unaware that her plans have been foiled, the Queen falls fatally ill and on her death bed she makes a full confession and admits that she had planned to poison Cymbeline whom she never loved. Despite her murderous intentions, the Queen's villainy is ultimately harmless and Cymbeline says of her that she was so charming and beautiful that it was impossible not to trust her.

Queen (Isabel)
A historical figure (1389-1409) and a character in *King Richard II*, the Queen of England (called Isabel in the cast list but not in the stage directions). The Queen is King Richard's loving wife and when Richard leaves for the war in Ireland, the Queen misses him, and feels anxious about something that she cannot identify. Her sorrows increase when news comes of Bolingbroke's rebellion. The Queen's ladies-in-waiting try to distract her and suggest a game of bowls in the garden, but the Queen prefers to hide behind a tree and eavesdrop on the royal gardeners. She overhears them talk of Richard's capture by Bolingbroke and turns angrily on the gardeners. The Queen goes to meet Richard on his way to the TOWER OF LONDON; her fate is to be banished to France and she bids her husband a tearful farewell as he is taken off to Pontefract Castle and his death.

Queens
Minor characters in *The Two Noble Kinsmen*, three Athenian Queens approach Theseus, Duke of Athens on his wedding day, pleading for help. Their husbands have been killed by the Theban army of King Creon, who is refusing to allow them to bury their dead. Theseus and his future wife Hippolyta, postpone the wedding in order to raise an army against Creon. In the ensuing battle, Palamon and Arcite are captured, but when Theseus is victorious, the Queens are able to give their husbands a decent burial.

Queen's Men, The or Queen Elizabeth's Men
This was a prominent company of actors for eleven years from 1585, when it was founded by Edmund Tilney, the MASTER OF THE REVELS at Queen Elizabeth's court. As well as performing for the Queen, the company toured the country and in 1587 they paid a visit to Stratford where it is quite likely that Shakespeare may have seen them as a young man. The company included the clown Richard TARLTON among its members.

quibble
Although today a quibble is an argument about something unimportant, in Shakespeare's time a quibble meant a pun or play on words; verbal humour arising from the fact that although two words may sound similar their meaning is entirely different. Puns were extremely popular with Elizabethan audiences and featured frequently in Shakespeare's comedies. Quibbles appear, too, in the comic moments of the tragedies; for example, a melancholic Romeo talks to Mercutio about dancing: 'You have dancing shoes with nimble *soles*, I have a *soul* of lead'. Shakespeare puns on his name 'Will' and 'will' as in 'willing' in sonnet 135.

Quickly, Hostess
A comic character in *King Henry IV, Parts One and Two* and *King Henry V*, Hostess Quickly is the landlady of the Boar's Head Tavern in Eastcheap, London where Falstaff and his drinking companions gather.

In *Henry IV, Part One*, the good-natured Hostess' role is a minor one. She is obviously fond of Falstaff, who owes her money for food and drink, and for a loan which she tries, unsuccessfully, to reclaim from him. In *Part Two*, Hostess Quickly is angry with Falstaff for the way he treats her and tries to get him arrested for debt. In her rage, she confuses her words (*see* MALAPROPISM) as she tells the Lord Chief Justice that Falstaff not only owes her money but that he has not honoured the proposal of marriage he made to her. Her fondness for Falstaff, her friend of twenty-nine years, is the kind-hearted Hostess Quickly's undoing; not only is she persuaded by him to drop legal action but he even succeeds in borrowing more money from her. When Prince Hal becomes King and imposes a new order on the kingdom, Hostess Quickly and her friend Doll Tearsheet are arrested after a brawl in the tavern and are hauled off to prison.

In *King Henry V*, Hostess Quickly appears as HOSTESS NELL and plays a minor role at the beginning of the play. She has married Falstaff's companion, Pistol, and speaks affectionately about Falstaff whom she has cared for on his deathbed. Pistol hears that she has died while he is fighting in France.

Quickly, Mistress
A comic character in *The Merry Wives of Windsor* who may or may not be the same character as Hostess Quickly in the *King Henry IV* plays. If she is the same character,

she has moved from London to Windsor where she is Dr Caius' talkative servant. A lot of the comedy arises out of Mistress Quickly's misuse of words but her role is largely that of go-between for the two merry wives in their tricking of Falstaff. She also helps to further the cause of all three of Anne Page's suitors. In the scene of Falstaff's final humiliation in Windsor Park, Mistress Quickly takes the Part of the Fairy Queen who instructs the children, disguised as fairies, in their ritual dance around the oak tree and tells them to burn Falstaff with their tapers.

Quince, Peter

A comic character in *A Midsummer Night's Dream*, Quince is a carpenter and one of the Athenian workmen who takes part in the performance of *Pyramus and Thisbe* at Duke Theseus' wedding celebrations. His name may derive from a 'quoin', a wooden wedge which a carpenter would have used to make a join. Quince is the director of the play who takes his job very seriously, patiently discussing the actors' objections with them; he is also its author who has to revise the script from time to time during rehearsals. When it comes to the performance of the play, Quince speaks the Prologue but his audience observes that he gallops through his speech barely pausing for breath.

Quiney, Thomas (1589–1655)

A Stratford wine merchant and tavern keeper who married Shakespeare's younger daughter JUDITH in 1616 (she was four years his senior). During their engagement a scandal erupted when Quiney was accused of adultery with a Stratford woman who had become pregnant. He was tried and fined for the offence but the marriage went ahead. They had three children, all of whom died young: SHAKESPER aged six months in 1617, RICHARD (1618-1639) and THOMAS (1620-1639). During the 1630s it appear that Quiney's business did not prosper; he was fined for allowing drunkenness in his tavern.

Quintus

A character in *Titus Andronicus*, Quintus is Titus' son. Quintus, with his brothers LUCIUS and MARTIUS, quarrels with his father over the burial of his youngest brother Mutius in the family tomb. Quintus and Martius are victims of the wicked Aaron's ingenious plotting. During a hunting expedition, Aaron leads the brothers to a pit where he claims to have seen a panther. Martius falls in and discovers the body of the murdered Bassianus and when Quintus tries to help his brother out he too falls into the pit. When they are discovered with Bassianus' body they are accused of his murder by Saturnius and executed.

Rr

Ragozine
In *Measure for Measure*, Ragozine is the name of a notorious pirate who has died in the prison where Claudio is held. He does not make an appearance in the play, but in the plan to save Claudio's life, his head is substituted for Claudio's and presented to Angelo.

rake
The degree of the slope from the back (upstage) to the front (downstage) of a stage, or of the seating in an auditorium.

Raleigh, (Ralegh) Sir Walter (1552–1618)
A politician, a daring explorer, and one of the age's greatest writers, Raleigh made pioneering expeditions to North America, from where he introduced potatoes and tobacco to England, and to Guyana in South America. He helped to shape the RENAISSANCE world in which Shakespeare wrote. For a time, Raleigh was a great favourite of Queen Elizabeth I, but later, suspected of intrigues, James I had him tried for treason and imprisoned with his wife and son in the TOWER OF LONDON in 1603. In 1616, he was released, and made an expedition to South America to seek the lost city of gold, El Dorado. When this failed, he was finally executed. Raleigh wrote vivid travel accounts, a *History of the World* (1614), political essays and poems, the best known of which is 'Cynthia', expressing his devoted loyalty to Queen Elizabeth I.

Rambures, Lord
A minor character in *King Henry V*, Lord Rambures is one of the French nobles who thinks the English are cowards, and is confident that the French can win the forthcoming Battle of Agincourt. He bets on the number of English prisoners the French will take but his confidence is misplaced; the French are beaten and Rambures is killed in the fighting.

Rannius
A character in *Antony and Cleopatra* who is mentioned in a stage direction as appearing with Enobarbus in a scene, but does not speak.

Rape of Lucrece, The
See LUCRECE.

Ratcliffe, Sir Richard
A historical figure (d. 1485) and a minor character in *King Richard III*, Ratcliffe is Richard's devious CONFIDANT who organizes the execution of Rivers, Grey and Vaughan and later, Hastings.

Reapers
Dancers who appear in the MASQUE in *The Tempest*; *see* SPIRITS.

Rebeck, Hugh
A minor character in *Romeo and Juliet*; a MUSICIAN who comes to play at Juliet's proposed wedding to Paris. His name derives from an early kind of violin called a rebec.

Red Bull, The
A Jacobean PLAYHOUSE, built around 1604 in Clerkenwell, now part of London, the Red Bull was notorious for its rowdy audiences. It was occupied until 1619 by Queen Anne's Men (formerly WORCESTER'S MEN), a theatrical company whose patron was King James I's wife, Anne.

refrain
A line or phrase repeated during a poem or song, usually at the end of a STANZA. In the song Feste the Clown sings at the end of *Twelfth Night*, the repeated lines 'With hey, ho, the wind and the rain' in the middle of each verse and 'For the rain it raineth every day' at the end of each verse, form a refrain.

Regan
A character in *King Lear*, Regan is one of Lear's villainous daughters. Unlike their younger sister Cordelia, the hypocritical Regan and Goneril have no objections to proclaiming love for their demanding father in order to win a share of his kingdom. Both sisters are ambitious for power, and ruthless, and while Regan may be less iron-willed than Goneril, she is ice-hearted, and plays her part in humiliating Lear and driving him out into the storm. She is aided by her evil husband, the Duke of Cornwall, whom she encourages when, with sickening cruelty, he gouges out Gloucester's eyes. After her husband's death, Regan has designs on the wicked Edmund as her lover and ally against Cordelia, but she finds herself a rival in love to her more powerful sister Goneril. Regan falls sick, poisoned by Goneril, and dies.

Reignier
A historical figure (1434-80) and a minor character in *King Henry VI, Part One*, Reignier is the Duke of Anjou and titular King of Naples, and father of Margaret of Anjou. He is portrayed as an over-confident and inept soldier in the play, reinforcing the idea that the English forces were superior to the French.

Renaissance
The word means 'rebirth' and describes the period of transition in European history from the 14th to the 16th centuries. This was marked by a radical shift in religious and philosophical thinking, and an extraordinary flowering of both arts and sciences. The Polish astronomer Copernicus (1473-1543) and the Italian scientist Galileo Galilei (1564-1642) investigated the nature of the physical world, while the English physician William Harvey (1578-1657) discovered the circulation of the blood.

The English Renaissance spanned the 16th century when, following the development of printing during the preceding century, ideas and knowledge could be spread and exchanged more rapidly than ever before. There was a revitalized interest in Classical learning and a new interest in England's recent history. The doctrine of HUMANISM emerged with its emphasis on secular education; and the arts burgeoned. Great names in music were the secular and church composers Orlando Gibbons (1583-1625) and William Byrd (1543-1614); Hans Holbein the Younger (c. 1498-1543) painted magnificent portraits at court while Nicholas Hilliard (1547-1619) was producing exquisite miniatures.

Most remarkable of all was the development of English literature. The English language itself was hugely expanded, enriched with words borrowed from French and from the Classical languages of Latin and Greek. Poets wove this new vocabulary into the language of everyday speech to create verses whose novel vitality and richness of imagery expressed their emotions more personally then ever before. This new linguistic bounty was evident too in the drama of the time, in particular the works of dramatists such as Marlowe and, supremely, Shakespeare. The Elizabethan SONNET form was born and provided a new discipline to inspire poets such as DRAYTON, RALEIGH, SIDNEY, SPENSER and Shakespeare, and BLANK VERSE was introduced as a new medium for dramatic verse. *See* ELIZABETHAN AGE; ELIZABETHAN DRAMA.

repertory company
A group of actors who work together on a long-term basis to perform a regularly changing repertoire of plays. In Shakespeare's time, all companies functioned in repertory, frequently changing their programmes (the average run of a play was a mere ten performances) to feed the voracious appetite of Elizabethan audiences for new plays. During February of 1596 the ADMIRAL'S MEN, for example, performed eleven different plays. This made enormous demands on the actors who had continually to learn new roles, while not for forgetting old ones. Examples of repertory companies in England today are the NATIONAL THEATRE and the ROYAL SHAKESPEARE COMPANY.

reported action
See ACTION.

resolution
The final phase of a work of fiction or drama, when a solution has been found for the conflicts, and mysteries have been solved. In tragedy, although the resolution may have tragic consequences, there is a sense of order restored, for example in *Hamlet* and in *Romeo and Juliet*. In comedy, less serious conflicts are resolved in a happy ending.

revels
See MASTER OF THE REVELS.

revenge play
A type of particularly bloodthirsty, melodramatic tragedy (see MELODRAMA), in which the hero sets out to right a wrong. Revenge tragedies were especially popular with Elizabethan audiences, and *The Revenger's Tragedy* (1607) by Cyril TOURNEUR and *The Spanish Tragedy* (c. 1594) by Thomas KYD were frequently performed. They were astonishingly violent and featured multiple killings, mutilation, ghostly appearances and madness. Enormous quantities of blood, and even sheep's intestines, specially acquired from abattoirs, were used and the stage was littered with corpses by the end of the play. Shakespeare's *Titus Andronicus* belongs to this genre, and *Hamlet*, though not strictly speaking a revenge tragedy, derives from its conventions.

Reynaldo
A minor character in *Hamlet*; Reynaldo is a servant instructed by Polonius to spy on his son Laertes while he is studying in Paris, to make sure he is not up to mischief.

rhetoric
Oratory; a way of using speech to influence or persuade the listener, often used by statesmen and politicians. There are examples of rhetoric in *Julius Caesar*; perhaps most famous, Mark Antony's speech: 'Friends, Romans, countrymen, lend me your ears'. Training in the art of rhetoric was an important part of the curriculum in Elizabethan schools (it may well have formed part of Shakespeare's education) and was an excellent preparation for a career as an actor.

rhetorical question
A question that is asked to which you do not expect an answer, but in order to emphasize a statement. For example: 'Shall I compare thee to a summer's day?' (Sonnet 18).

rhyme
The sound of an entire word, or final syllable of a word, when it is identical to another final syllable. For example, 'cow' rhymes with 'bough' although it is not spelt the same; but 'cow' does not rhyme with 'low' despite the identical spelling. Rhyme (although it is not an essential element of verse) is often combined with METRE to create a pleasing pattern, and can be employed by a poet to control emphases and reinforce meanings.

In verse, INTERNAL RHYME is found within a line of poetry and END RHYME at the end of the line. There are two types of rhyme, 'masculine' and 'feminine'; masculine rhyme consists of a single stressed syllable like 'car' and 'far', while a feminine rhyme is one in which a stressed syllable is followed by an unstressed one, for example 'knowing' and 'going'. The BLANK verse of Shakespeare's plays is usually unrhymed, although an early play such as *Romeo and Juliet* contains a great deal of rhymed verse. In *Twelfth Night* there is a RHYMING COUPLET at the end of each verse scene.

rhyme royal
A pattern of verse in IAMBIC PENTAMETER, in which each STANZA has seven lines, which was particularly popular with Elizabethan poets. It was first used by the English poet Geoffrey Chaucer (c. 1345-1400) and is sometimes known as the Chaucerian stanza. Shakespeare used rhyme royal for his two poems *A Lover's Complaint* and *Lucrece*.

rhyme scheme
The pattern of rhyming sounds at the end of lines of verse; in SCANSION this is denoted by letters of the alphabet. For example, if the third line rhymes with the first and the fourth line rhymes with the second, the line scheme will be shown as 'a b a b'.

rhyming couplets
Lines of verse which rhyme in pairs in an 'aa bb cc' RHYME SCHEME; Shakespearean SONNETS have a final rhyming couplet.

rhythm
An ordered pattern of stressed and unstressed syllables which creates a regular beat in verse. Rhythm can be an important element in dramatic verse: for example, a strong marching rhythm might signify a warlike subject, whereas a soft flowing rhythm might suggest a more reflective mood. In spoken verse, such as in dialogue, the speaker can to

some extent determine the strength of the rhythm of a passage by the way in which he emphasizes certain syllables, and by the length of pauses between words.

Richard, afterwards Duke of Gloucester
A historical figure (1452-1485) and a character in *King Henry VI, Parts Two and Three*; Richard is the same hunchback Richard who is crowned RICHARD III in the later play of that name. In *Henry VI, Part Two*, Richard is the Duke of York's younger son who is called upon by his father to lend support to the Yorkist claim to the throne. Lord Clifford refers to his crooked shape.

In *Part Three*, the hunchback Richard plays a larger part in affairs. He urges his father to seize the crown for himself and when his father is killed he vows to be revenged on his murderer Clifford. After his brother Edward is crowned King, Richard is given the title of Duke of Gloucester but although he continues to support Edward, a murderous scheme for taking the throne for himself is taking shape in his mind. He plans first to rid himself of his brother Clarence who is next in line to the throne. A bloodthirsty character, Richard kills the imprisoned King Henry and takes part in the killing of the Henry's young son the Prince of Wales.

Richard II, King of England (1367–1400)
Historical Figure. The historical King of England from 1377 to his death, and a PLANTAGENET, Richard succeeded to the throne when he was only ten; until his majority the country was governed by a council of rival nobles. In 1481, the young king successfully put down the Peasants' Revolt, showing remarkable courage in confronting the rioting mob. However, his reign saw continuing conflict with parliament and the powerful nobles, in particular his uncle John of Gaunt and the Duke of Gloucester. In 1397, in an attempt to establish unassailable authority, the king seized power from the nobles. He had Gloucester murdered, and banished other nobles, seizing their lands. These moves prompted his cousin Henry of Bolingbroke, Duke of Lancaster, who was one of those banished by Richard, to raise an army against the king. Henry Bolingbroke (the future HENRY IV) forced Richard to abdicate, imprisoned him in Pontefract Castle, where he was almost certainly murdered, and declared himself king. Richard II is the subject of one of Shakespeare's HISTORY PLAYS, *The Tragedy of King Richard II*. See the table of kings and queens in the Supplement.

Richard II
Title Character. A historical character (1367-1400) (see above), and the hero of Shakespeare's HISTORY PLAY *King Richard II*, Richard is weak and easily influenced by flatterers, and as the play opens, his popularity as King is in decline. He is suspected of arranging the murder of his uncle Gloucester sometime earlier, and his extravagance and mismanagement of the country are giving rise to discontent among his nobles. Richard, like other tragic heroes, lacks self-awareness and does not foresee the trouble that results from his seizure of Gaunt's land and property that are the rightful inheritance of Gaunt's son Bolingbroke. When Bolingbroke raises an army against him, Richard believes that as God's anointed (see DIVINE RIGHT OF KINGS) his position is unassailable; even when he begins to lose confidence, he still refuses to acknowledge his mistakes. Richard, by nature changeable, is not a fighter and Bolingbroke is easily able to overthrow him and seize the crown; Richard is arrested, and murdered at Pontefract Castle.

Richard II, King

One of Shakespeare's HISTORY PLAYS, *King Richard II* was written around 1595 and
first published in a QUARTO edition in 1597, but the scene of Richard's abdication was
left out, probably because a rather uncertain situation regarding claims to the throne at
the time made the subject of deposition a sensitive one. The play may have been first
performed before a private audience in 1595.

The primary source for the play was HOLINSHED'S *Chronicles* but the well-known
garden scene (*see* GARDENER) in the play was an invention of Shakespeare's. *Richard II*
is set in England and Wales between 1398 and 1400 and written entirely in verse, much
of it rhyming, and there is little comic relief. Unlike the other history plays, *Richard II*,
concentrates on Richard's personal drama rather than simply dramatizing the historical
events. It explores themes of Chivalry and the DIVINE RIGHT OF KINGS and the problem
of loyalty to a bad king. In 1601, when the Earl of ESSEX was plotting a rebellion
against Queen Elizabeth I, his followers paid Shakespeare's company to perform
Richard II, because Essex believed there were similarities between Richard's position
on the throne and Queen Elizabeth's.

SYNOPSIS : Before the action of the play, Richard had already become unpopular
with his people. There are rumours of his involvement in the murder of his uncle the
Duke of Gloucester, and discontent about his extravagance. He is a weak and
changeable King, surrounded by corrupt flatterers, who has plunged his country into
debt. The play opens with Bolingbroke, the King's cousin who mistrusts Richard,
accusing Mowbray of having a hand in the murder of Gloucester and challenging
him to single combat. Richard stops the fight before any blood is shed; he banishes
Mowbray for life and sends Bolingbroke into exile for six years. Bolingbroke's
father, John of Gaunt dies and Richard illegally seizes his assets in order to finance
his war in Ireland. When Bolingbroke hears of this he raises an army and returns to
England demanding the return of his inheritance. He also has his eye on the crown
and executes Richard's close advisors. Richard's confidence in his position as King
crumbles, and one by one his nobles desert him. He weakly capitulates and hands
over power to Bolingbroke. Bolingbroke has Richard arrested an imprisoned, and is
crowned King Henry IV. A handful of nobles still loyal to Richard conspire against
Bolingbroke but the plot is discovered. Richard is murdered by a noble who has
misunderstood a chance remark of Bolingbroke that he wants Richard killed, and
the play ends with Bolingbroke tormented with guilt planning to go on a pilgrimage
to the Holy Land to seek forgiveness.

Richard III, King of England (1452–1485)

Historical Figure. The historical King of England from 1483 until his death, and last of
the Yorkist kings, Richard fought with distinction in the WARS OF THE ROSES on the
side of the house of YORK. When he became Protector to his thirteen-year-old nephew
Edward V, he declared that the young prince was not a legitimate heir to the throne.
Richard imprisoned Edward with his brother, Richard Duke of York, in the TOWER OF
LONDON, where it has long been supposed he had them murdered. Despite his
competence as a monarch, the suspicions surrounding the deaths of the young princes
led to a decline in the king's popularity. In 1485 Henry TUDOR, Earl of Richmond, who
had a claim to the crown through the Lancastrian line (*see* LANCASTER, HOUSE OF),
raised an army against Richard who was defeated and killed at the battle of Bosworth.

In popular imagination, Richard III has remained the hunchbacked monster of Shakespeare's play. In fact, there is no evidence either that he was a hunchback (although the historian Holinshed (*see* HOLINSHED'S *Chronicles*) describes him as "crooke backed"), nor that he really was responsible for the murder of the princes in the Tower. Shakespeare, who was probably ignorant of the true facts, exaggerated the myth of Richard's blackhearted villainy in order to please Queen Elizabeth I. The Queen was a direct descendant of Henry Tudor who, with only a rather flimsy claim to the crown, had nonetheless seized it from Richard at Bosworth. It was important, therefore, for Elizabethan propaganda to portray Richard as an almost demonic figure, so that Henry could be seen in contrast as a heroic saviour whose moral right to the crown at least was unquestionable. Richard III (see below) is the subject of Shakespeare's play *King Richard III*. See the table of kings and queens in the Supplement.

Richard III (Duke of Gloucester)
Title Character. A historical figure (1452-85) (*see above*), and the charismatic hero of *King Richard III*, Shakespeare's Richard was born a hunchback and his deformities have made him bitter; with black humour, he confides in his audience that he is a villain. Richard lusts for power and plots to seize the crown of England for himself on the death of his brother King Edward. He sows seeds of suspicion between the King and his nobles, while playing the part of an innocent bystander, and plans the murder of any one who stands in his way. His brother Clarence is killed first, and his next victims are the two young heirs to the throne, Prince Edward and the Duke of York. Richard proclaims himself King, but his confidence begins to desert him, as one by one his remaining supporters join forces with the Earl of Richmond who is raising a rebel army. On the eve of the battle of Bosworth, Richard is visited by the ghosts of his victims who prophesy his death. For the first time, he has twinges of conscience, but events overtake him. He loses his horse in the battle and is killed by Richmond.

Richard III, King
One of Shakespeare's early HISTORY PLAYS, *King Richard III* is the fourth in the tetralogy [group of four interrelated works], *King Henry VI, Parts One, Two and Three* to *Richard III*. It was written around 1592-93 and first published anonymously in a QUARTO edition in 1597. Probably first performed in 1593, it seems to have been extremely popular during Shakespeare's lifetime. An adaptation by Colley CIBBER was widely performed in the 18th and 19th centuries. Main sources for the play were HOLINSHED'S *Chronicles* and *The History of King Richard the Thirde* (1513) by Sir Thomas More.

The play, set in England between 1483 and 1485, was written partly as a piece of political propaganda to please the Tudor Queen Elizabeth I. (*See* RICHARD III, KING OF ENGLAND *and* TUDOR.) It explores themes of superstition, evil and retribution, chaos and order. The play has its roots in the earlier morality plays with its personification of evil in Richard, who owes something to the character of 'Vice'.

SYNOPSIS : King Edward IV is dying and his brother Richard plots to seize the crown for himself. Richard makes a pretence of loyalty to the King, but stirs up enmities between the King and his courtiers. When another brother Clarence is sent to the TOWER OF LONDON by King Edward as a result of Richard's intrigue, Richard arranges for his murder. He uses his hypnotic charm to woo, and later marry, the reluctant Lady Anne whose husband the Prince of Wales was killed by Richard. On Edward's death, Richard dispatches everyone who stands in his way. His victims include the two young royal heirs to the throne, his nephews the Prince of Wales and the Duke of York, whom he sends to the TOWER OF LONDON stirring up rumours of their illegitimacy. Richard is proclaimed King at last. To make his position more secure, he first arranges for assassins to smother the two royal children in the Tower and then plans to be rid of his wife Anne, and to marry Elizabeth, the late King's daughter. King Richard grows uneasy. News comes that Henry TUDOR, the Duke of Richmond, is raising forces against him, and his allies begin to desert him, including the loyal Buckingham who is executed. Richmond's army marches to meet Richard's forces at BOSWORTH and on the eve of the battle, Richard is haunted by the ghosts of those he has killed. In the battle that follows Richard loses his horse and is killed by Richmond, who is declared King Henry VII, the agent of a new order in England.

Riche, Barnabe
Soldier and writer (c. 1549-1617), author of the *Farewell to Militarie Profession,* from which Shakespeare used the story of *Apolonius and Silla* in *Twelfth Night.*

Richmond, Earl of
A historical figure (1457-1509) and a character in *King Henry VI, Part Three* and *King Richard III*; in *Henry VI*, Richmond is a minor character who appears as a young boy. King Henry predicts that Henry Richmond will one day be King of England.

In *Richard III*, Richmond appears at the end of the play leading the rebellion against Richard and inspiring his troops to battle. Camped at the opposite end of the battlefield from Richard, he sleeps the sleep of the just while Richard is haunted by ghosts. Richmond kills Richard in hand to hand combat at the Battle of Bosworth and his victory redeems England from Richard's evil. He is proclaimed King and announces a new era of peace in an England ruled by the TUDOR family.

In history, Henry Tudor, the Earl of Richmond, became King Henry VII of England from 1485-1509.

Rivers, Lord
A historical figure (c. 1442-83) and a character in *King Henry VI, Part Three* and *King Richard III*; in *Henry VI* he is a minor character, brother to Lady Elizabeth Grey who marries King Edward.

In *Richard III*, Rivers' sister is now Queen Elizabeth. Rivers is executed by Richard simply because, as the Queen's brother, he may stand in the way of Richard's ambitions for the throne. His ghost appears to Richard in a dream on the eve of the Battle of Bosworth and prophecies the King's downfall.

Robert[1]
A minor character in *The Merry Wives of Windsor*, Robert is one of Mistress Ford's servants who is instructed to carry out Falstaff in the basket of dirty washing, and dump him in a muddy ditch, as part of the merry wives' trick on Falstaff.

Robert[2]
A minor character in *King John,* Robert Faulconbridge is Philip the Bastard's younger half-brother. He maintains that his brother is illegitimate and so is not entitled to inherit the family land and wealth. King John decides that Robert's claim is a just one, and allows him to keep the lands while his brother is given a knighthood instead.

Robeson, Paul (1898–1976)
A black American actor and singer, Paul Robeson was a political activist and socialist who spent a lifetime campaigning against racial prejudice. He graduated from Law school, but chose to go on the stage, making a name for himself in contemporary American plays. In 1930, Robeson came to London and played Othello opposite the English actress Peggy Ashcroft (1907-91) as Desdemona, to great acclaim. Othello was the only Shakespearean part Robeson ever played, but he repeated his London success in the role on Broadway in New York in 1943 and at Stratford-on-Avon in 1959.

Robin
A minor character in *The Merry Wives of Windsor,* Robin is Falstaff's page and probably the same character who appeared, without a name, as Falstaff's PAGE in the *King Henry IV* plays. Falstaff lends Robin to Mistress Page and the wives tell him about the trick they are going to play on his master. Robin is a lively boy who enters into the joke with great enthusiasm.

Robin Goodfellow
Another name for the character PUCK in *A Midsummer Night's Dream.*

Roderigo
A character in *Othello,* Roderigo was Desdemona's suitor before her marriage, and still loves her. He tells Desdemona's father of her elopement with Othello, and threatens to kill himself in despair at losing her. Iago sees a way to exploit the foolish Rodrigo in his plot to ruin Othello and Cassio, and urges Roderigo not to give up hope of winning Desdemona. Rodrigo is easily taken in by Iago, believing his story that Cassio and Desdemona are lovers, and that Iago will help him. He is persuaded to pick a quarrel with the drunken Cassio, and in the fight that follows, Rodrigo is hurt. Gradually, Rodrigo begins to suspect Iago, but Iago kills him to prevent exposure. Roderigo is an unpleasant character, but more a victim of villainy than a villain himself.

role
The part an actor plays on stage. The word possibly derives from the medieval name for the long roll of paper (sometimes as long as five metres) on which a play text was written.

role reversal
The act of exchanging one role for another, but without the intention to deceive and without actually putting on a disguise. In *King Henry IV, Part One,* Prince Hal and Falstaff take on different roles; Falstaff pretending to be the King exhorts Prince Hal to keep the company of the virtuous Falstaff. The Prince in his turn pretends to be the King, while Falstaff takes the part of Prince Hal. The 'king' warns his son against consorting with the reprobate Falstaff.

Roman plays

Shakespeare wrote four plays which are set in Ancient Rome: *Antony and Cleopatra*, *Coriolanus*, *Julius Caesar* and *Titus Andronicus*, all of which are tragedies. *Antony and Cleopatra* is a play about the hero's moral conflict, but *Coriolanus* and *Julius Caesar* are political plays. They have much in common with Shakespeare's HISTORY PLAYS in which there is unrest and corruption in the state which has at its head an unsatisfactory leader who is deposed. There is a new order at the end of each play and hope for a stable future. *Titus Andronicus* is above all a REVENGE PLAY, but the corrupt state of Rome, described as a 'wilderness of tigers' is one of its concerns. For all of the Roman plays, except *Titus Andronicus*, Shakespeare used as his source the *Lives of the Greeks and Romans* by the Greek biographer PLUTARCH, whose writings Shakespeare may have come across during his school days, and which he would certainly have known in a 16th century English translation.

romance

A work which is based on the PASTORAL tradition, but set in a world of chivalry and magic, with heroic characters, and the exotic locations of ancient legends. The heroes and heroines of a romance are the embodiment of virtue and beauty. Although it contains elements of a love story, a romance in this sense differs from the word romance as we use it today because it involves improbable incidents and characters that are remote from everyday life. Four plays of Shakespeare's later period, *Pericles*, *Cymbeline*, *The Winter's Tale* and *The Tempest*, are romances.

romantic comedy

A type of 16th-century COMEDY concerned with the love of an idealized young couple, for example Orlando and Rosalind in *As You Like It*.

Romeo

A central character in *Romeo and Juliet*, Romeo is the play's tragic hero. Romeo first appears as an Elizabethan STOCK CHARACTER, the melancholic lover, who is infatuated with Rosaline. When he meets Juliet, he is immediately overwhelmed by a far deeper and truer love. Because Romeo's family, the Montagues, are engaged in a bitter feud with Juliet's family, theirs is a forbidden love, but Romeo is passionate and impulsive, and the lovers marry in secret. When Romeo is reluctantly drawn into a fight with Juliet's cousin and kills him, he is banished to Mantua where he hopes eventually to be reunited with Juliet; instead he is wrongly informed of her death. Romeo hastens to Juliet's tomb, where despair makes him ruthless. He kills Paris and drinks the fatal poison. Romeo is not a reflective character, and although he is partly a victim of his own impetuosity, he is more a victim of circumstance. He refers to himself several times as being a pawn of fate and 'fortune's fool'.

Romeo and Juliet

One of Shakespeare's early tragedies (*see* TRAGEDY) which he probably began writing around 1591-92; it was first performed between 1594 and 1596, and first published in a QUARTO edition in 1597.

The primary source of the play was a popular narrative poem, itself based on earlier versions of the story, entitled *the Tragicall Historye of Romeus and Juliet* (1562) by Arthur Brooke. Shakespeare followed Brooke's poem closely but speeded up the action from several months to four or five days and added the character of MERCUTIO. The play, set in Italy, explores extremes of emotions, love and hate for example, and is full of contrasts such as light and dark, day and night. There is comedy in the play, with punning and bawdy jokes that highlight the difference between the pure romantic love of Romeo and Juliet and a coarser sexual one.

SYNOPSIS : Two families in Verona, the Capulets and the Montagues, are engaged in a long-running feud which is so bitter that even their servants fight in the streets. Juliet, a Capulet, and Romeo, a Montague, meet at a masked ball and unaware of each other's family names they fall in love. Because of the feud, they are forced into secrecy, and are married the next day by Friar Laurence. The Capulet and Montague feud still simmers and Romeo is drawn into a quarrel with Juliet's cousin Tybalt. Although he is reluctant to fight, Romeo kills Tybalt and is straightaway banished from Verona. Friar Laurence advises the distracted Romeo to stay with Juliet that night and then flee to Mantua and wait for a time when they can be reunited. Unaware of her marriage to Romeo, Juliet's parents are making arrangements for her to marry a young nobleman, Paris. Juliet in desperation consults Friar Laurence. Both he and Juliet's nurse advise her to make a second, bigamous marriage, but Juliet refuses. Friar Laurence provides her with a drug which will make her appear dead for forty-two hours. He promises to send word to Romeo to come in secret and fetch her from the family vault, where she will be laid out, and take her back to Mantua. On the morning of her proposed marriage to Paris, Juliet is discovered apparently dead, and is placed in the tomb. The Friar's message to Romeo fails to reach him in time, and learning that Juliet is dead and he hastens in despair to the Capulet tomb where he plans to be united with Juliet in death if not in life. Paris tries to stop Romeo from entering the vault, but Romeo kills him, and drinks a deadly poison. When Juliet awakes moments later, she is thrilled to find Romeo beside her. Her happiness is brief; she sees that he is dead and kills herself. As a result of the tragedy there is a reconciliation between the feuding families.

Rosalind

The romantic heroine of *As You Like It*, Rosalind is Duke Senior's daughter. When her father is banished to the Forest of ARDEN, Rosalind chooses to remain behind to be with her inseparable friend, Celia. Rosalind misses her father but she has an out-going nature, and is soon distracted from her sadness by meeting, and falling in love with Orlando. Exiled herself to the Forest of Arden, she adopts the disguise of a boy 'Ganymede', and meets Orlando again. She mischievously undertakes to cure him of his lovesickness, suggesting that he courts her as if she really were Rosalind. They engage in a flirtatious role play in which Rosalind, playing the part of Ganymede, pretends to be herself. Ganymede scorns romance, but Rosalind falls deeper in love. In the play's happy conclusion, Rosalind and Orlando are married.

 In Shakespeare's time, the comedy of the female Rosalind, disguised as a boy, pretending to be a girl, would have been heightened because the actor playing Rosalind would have been a boy.

Rosaline[1]

A character in *Love's Labour's Lost*, Rosaline is one of the French Princess's entourage visiting Navarre, where the King and his court have sworn to renounce the company of all women. One of the noblemen, Berowne, is struck by Rosaline's beauty and falls in love with her. She is every bit as sharp and witty as he is, and obviously enjoys the cut and thrust of their verbal sparring. Rosaline is not easily won over, and she jokes with her friends about the ways in which she might tease the love-sick Berowne. When Berowne and his companions court the French ladies, absurdly disguised as Russians, Rosaline, who is masked, pretends to be the Princess and is wooed by the King. Afterwards she mischievously suggests to the Princess that they keep up the pretence of not knowing the true identities of their Russian suitors for a bit longer. Rosaline imposes a harsh penance on Berowne, and says he must prove his love for her by tending the sick for a whole year.

Rosaline is described as having a dark complexion and it has been speculated that the character is associated with Shakespeare's DARK LADY OF THE SONNETS.

Rosaline[2]

A character in *Romeo and Juliet*, Rosaline is referred to in the play but makes no appearance. She is Capulet's niece and the object of Romeo's infatuation at the beginning of the play.

Rose Theatre, The

An Elizabethan PLAYHOUSE built at Bankside in London in 1587 by Philip HENSLOWE, on the corner of Rose Alley where there had once been a rose garden. It is possible that Shakespeare once acted at the Rose with the ADMIRAL'S MEN. The Rose was enlarged in 1592, but it was probably torn down around 1606; the site was excavated in 1989 and can be visited today.

Rosencrantz and Guildenstern

Two minor characters in *Hamlet*, Rosencrantz and Guildenstern always appear together and sometimes even speak in unison. Although they are former schoolfellows of Hamlet, they conspire against him with Claudius. They accompany Hamlet to England bearing a sealed letter from Claudius to the King of England ordering Hamlet's death. Hamlet uncovers the plot and sends Rosencrantz and Guildenstern to their deaths in his place.

Ross or Rosse

A minor character in *Macbeth*, Ross is a Scottish nobleman who brings the tragic news of the murder of Lady Macduff and her son to Macduff. Ross joins forces with Prince Malcolm against Macbeth.

Ross, Lord

A historical figure (d. 1414) and a minor character in *King Richard II*, Lord Ross is one of the nobles who support Bolingbroke. After the death of John of Gaunt, when King Richard seizes the dead man's assets to finance his war in Ireland, the nobles no longer trust him and Ross, with the Earl of Northumberland and Lord Willoughby, join Bolingbroke's rebellion.

Rossillion (Rousillon), Countess of
A character in *All's Well that Ends Well*, the Countess of Rossillion is Bertram's mother and guardian to the orphaned Helena. An affectionate mother, she is nonetheless appalled by her son's behaviour towards Helena whom she loves too. When Bertram abandons Helena, the Countess writes to her son in the hope that she can change his mind. She forgives Bertram and begs the King to show him the same forgiveness for his acts of youthful folly. The Countess is a warm-hearted character who has an easy relationship with members of her household, including the Clown who confides in her about his own plans to marry.

Rowe, Nicholas (1674–1718)
A lawyer, turned poet, actor, and playwright who became England's Poet Laureate in 1715. In 1709, Rowe produced an edition of Shakespeare's plays with the most comprehensive revisions and emendations that the plays had so far received. He worked from original texts, and divided the plays into scenes and acts; he added a DRAMATIS PERSONAE [cast list] for each play, as well as stage directions and headings to the scenes. He also provided a short and not altogether accurate biographical introduction to Shakespeare, based on tradition rather than hard fact. In it he states that Shakespeare went to school but left before his education was completed because of financial difficulties in the family. He also recounts the story that Shakespeare had to leave Stratford to avoid the wrath of a local landowner, Sir Thomas Lucy, whose deer the young William had poached.

Royal Shakespeare Company (also known as the RSC)
An English theatre company founded in 1875 to perform Shakespeare's plays exclusively. It is a REPERTORY COMPANY based in Stratford-upon-Avon and at the Barbican Theatre in London, and now performs works by playwrights other than Shakespeare as well. The company was originally based at the Shakespeare Memorial Theatre, Stratford, which was built in 1879 and almost completely destroyed by fire in 1926. The present riverside theatre was opened in 1932 and renamed as the Royal Shakespeare Theatre in 1961.

In 1986 the company built a new and smaller theatre, THE SWAN, inside the shell of what remained of the old Memorial Theatre. The OTHER PLACE opened in 1991 for performances by overseas theatre companies, plays by contemporary playwrights, workshops, and educational courses.

Artistic directors of the Royal Shakespeare Company have been: Sir Peter Hall (1960-68); Trevor Nunn (1968-78); Trevor Nunn and Terry Hands (1978-86); Terry Hands (1986-91), and Adrian Noble (1991-).

RSC
An abbreviation for the ROYAL SHAKESPEARE COMPANY.

round, theatre in the
See THEATRE IN THE ROUND.

Rugby, John
A minor character in *The Merry Wives of Windsor*, Rugby is Dr Caius' servant who is bullied by his master. Mistress Quickly says of Rugby that his worst fault is that he prays a great deal.

Rumour

A character in *King Henry IV, Part Two*, Rumour is an allegorical (see ALLEGORY)
figure, rumour personified, who introduces the play and is described as being 'painted
full of tongues'. He says rumour is a many-headed monster whose wagging tongues
deceive his listeners. Rumour functions as a CHORUS, giving the audience a true account
of the final events of *Part One* of *Henry VI*, in which the King's forces defeated the
rebels and Harry Hotspur was killed. He goes on to say that he has been spreading
rumours that the reverse is true, and so sets the scene for the opening action of *Part Two*
of the play, in which the rebels receive incorrect news that Prince Henry is dead and
Hotspur victorious.

run-on lines

See ENJAMBEMENT.

Russians

In *Love's Labour's Lost,* the King, Berowne, Longaville and Dumain disguise
themselves as Russians in the hope of successfully wooing the Princess of France and
her ladies. The Princess and her friends see through the ludicrous disguise and make fun
of them. It is possible that Shakespeare added the scene after an entertainment held at
the INNS OF COURT during Christmas 1594 in which there was a comic MASQUE that
featured characters of Russians. Elizabeth I had many diplomatic contacts with Tsar
Ivan the Terrible, and during Shakespeare's lifetime companies were set up to trade with
Russia.

Rutland, Edmund Earl of

A historical figure (1443-60) and a minor character in *King Henry VI, Part Three*,
Rutland is the Duke of York's youngest son. He is only a boy when he is savagely
murdered by Lord Clifford, who is avenging his father's death at the hands of the Duke
of York.

Rycas

A minor, non-speaking part in *The Two Noble Kinsmen*, Rycas is one of the villagers
who perform a Morris dance for Duke Theseus. *See* COUNTRYMEN.

Rynaldo (Rinaldo)

A minor character in *All's Well that Ends Well*, Rynaldo is the steward to the Countess
of Rousillon. *See* STEWARD.

Ss

sack
A kind of strong wine from Spain, like sherry, which was drunk in Shakespeare's time and which is Falstaff's favourite drink.

Sailors
Minor characters in several of Shakespeare's plays; Sailors often act as messengers. In *Pericles*, the Sailors on board the ship taking Pericles and Thaisa to Tyre are unafraid of the raging storm. However, they are superstitious men, and when Thaisa apparently dies giving birth to Marina, they are frightened that having a corpse on board will bring them bad luck. The Sailors insist that Thaisa, in her sealed box, is thrown overboard. Their intervention crucially affects events as it leads to Thaisa and Pericles' separation.

Salerio (Salarino)
A minor character in *The Merchant of Venice*, Salerio is a young Venetian gentleman and a friend of Bassanio and Antonio who tries to cheer up Antonio when he is feeling depressed. Later, Salerio brings the disastrous news to Bassanio that all Antonio's ships have been lost at sea.

Salisbury, Earl of[1]
A historical figure (c. 1350-1400) and a minor character in *King Richard II*, The Earl of Salisbury is one of a handful of nobles who remain loyal to King Richard, although he foresees the King's downfall. He is reported killed, fighting against Bolingbroke.

Salisbury, Earl of[2]
A historical figure (1388-1428) and a minor character in *King Henry V* and *King Henry VI, Part One*; in *Henry V*, Salisbury, a supporter of the King, fights at the Battle of Agincourt.

In *Henry VI, Part One*, Salisbury, a general in the English army, is killed by a cannon ball at Orleans. (Not to be confused with the Earl of Salisbury of *King Henry VI, Part Two* (*see below*).

Salisbury, Earl of[3]
A historical figure (1400-60) and a minor character in *King Henry VI, Part Two*, the Earl of Salisbury's family name is NEVIL, and he is not related to the Salisbury of *Part One*. Old Salisbury is an honest and loyal supporter of King Henry. He is sent by the Commons [representatives of the people] to demand that the Duke of Suffolk be banished for his treachery to the King. However, Salisbury is eventually persuaded by the arguments of the Yorkists (*see* YORK, HOUSE OF) that the Duke of York is the rightful heir to the throne of England, rather than Henry, and transfers his allegiance.

Salisbury, Earl of[4]
A historical figure (d. 1226) and a minor character in *King John*, the Earl of Salisbury is an English noble who turns against King John after the death of Arthur. Salisbury, with the Earl of Pembroke, joins the French army fighting against England but they return to John's side when they learn of a plot by the French King to have them killed.

Sampson
A minor character in *Romeo and Juliet*, Sampson is a servant in the Capulet household who is involved in a punning dialogue with Gregory in the opening scene. He fights with the servants of the Montague family and says he will show himself a 'tyrant', a reference perhaps to his heroic name.

Sands, Lord (Sir Walter Sands)
A historical figure (Sir William Sands d. 1540) and a minor character in *King Henry VIII*, Lord Sands appears first in the stage directions as Sir Walter Sands and only later as Lord Sands. This is because Shakespeare compressed the time span of the play and forgot that Sir Walter had been enobled during that time. Sands is a courtier, more interested in French fashions and court gossip than affairs of state. At the banquet held by Wolsey for the King, Sands gallantly entertains the ladies. In a more serious role, he is mentioned as accompanying Buckingham on the way to his execution.

satire
A literary composition that criticizes folly or vice, by making it ridiculous and funny. In *Twelfth Night*, Shakespeare satirizes a particular type of hypocritical PURITAN in the character of Malvolio.

Saturnius
A character in *Titus Andronicus*, Saturnius becomes Emperor of Rome when Titus refuses the title. Saturnius rewards Titus for his support by choosing to marry Titus' daughter, Lavinia but she is already betrothed to Saturnius' brother Bassianus who snatches her away aided by Titus' sons. Saturnius, in a fury, marries the vindictive Tamora instead. Tyrannical, but weak, Saturnius fears Titus' popularity with the people and allows himself to be manipulated by Tamora who is bent on personal revenge. She persuades Saturnius to make an outward show of reconciliation with Titus but schemes to have Bassianus murdered and Titus' sons blamed for his death. In the terrible cycle of revenge killings, Saturnius kills Titus and is himself killed by Titus' son Lucius.

Say, Lord
A historical figure (d. 1450) and a minor character in *King Henry VI, Part Three*, Lord Say is Treasurer of England. He shows courage when Jack Cade and his rebels march on London, remaining there after the King has left even though his own life is in danger. Say is captured by the rebels who list their grievances and blame him among other things for clothing his horse in finer fabric than Cade and his men could afford to wear. He pleads for his life but is beheaded by Cade's men.

Scales, Lord
A historical figure (c. 1399-1460) and a minor character in *King Henry VI, Part Two*, Lord Scales is the keeper of the TOWER OF LONDON who helps to drive the rebel Jack Cade and his men out of London.

scansion
The analysis of the structure of verse, and the patterns of its METRE and rhyme.

Scarus
A minor character in *Antony and Cleopatra*, Scarus is one of Antony's followers, an honourable man and a courageous soldier. He fights with Antony at the Battle of Actium and describes Cleopatra's disastrous flight. At Alexandria, despite his terrible wounds, Scarus fearlessly pursues Caesar's retreating forces. Cleopatra promises to give him a suit of golden armour as a reward.

scene
A section of a play during which the continuity of time and place is unchanged; a subdivision of an act.

Scene changes, as we know them, were largely an 18th-century invention - the first division of Shakespeare's plays into acts and scenes was in the edition edited by Nicholas ROWE in 1709; in Shakespeare's time, the action would have been more or less continuous. As there was a bare minimum of scenery, the numerous scene changes could have been rapidly accomplished with the actors, or sometimes a CHORUS, describing a passage of time or a change of location.

scenery
The materials used to create a representation on the stage of the physical setting for a play, apart from the PROPS. In Shakespeare's time the props were often elaborate and sizeable but fixed scenery would have been minimal, perhaps only a painted hanging at the back of the stage. The setting was more usually indicated within the text of the play; for example the Chorus in *King Henry V* asks the audience to imagine the battlefield of Agincourt, while Gower, the Chorus in *Pericles*, describes the stage as the deck of a ship in a storm. *See* PLAYHOUSES.

Schoolmaster
A Schoolmaster acts as Antony's ambassador to Caesar in *Antony and Cleopatra*; *see* AMBASSADOR.

Schoolmaster (Gerald)
A minor character in *The Two Noble Kinsmen*, the pedantic Schoolmaster organizes the Morris dance that is performed by the villagers (see COUNTRYMEN) for Duke Theseus. He calls on Athene, the goddess of wisdom, to help him before he delivers his pompous, rambling introductory speech to the Duke. The Jailer's Daughter says he is called 'Giraldo' and that he is Emilia's schoolmaster and full of absurd ideas.

Scottish Play, The
Another name for *Macbeth* which is often used by members of the theatrical profession. The play has traditionally been associated with bad luck, and there is a superstition in the theatre that mentioning its real name will bring misfortune.

Scrivener
A minor character in *King Richard III*, the Scrivener [official writer] spends eleven hours copying out the formal accusation made against Hastings. The Scrivener is

horrified at its contents; he knows that Hastings is blameless and that the accusations made against him are false.

Scroop, Richard, Archbishop of York
A historical figure (c. 1350-1405) and a character in *King Henry IV, Parts One and Two*; in *Part One* Scroop is a supporter of Hotspur and the other rebels who are fighting against King Henry. In *Part Two* Scroop, who appears in the cast list as Archbishop of York, plays a larger part. He continues to back the rebellion but he begins to express doubts about the rightness of the cause which seeks to depose a King who, bad though he may be, is nonetheless the Lord's anointed (see DIVINE RIGHT OF KINGS). He is persuaded that the rebels should make peace with the King by the treacherous Prince John. Like the other rebels he believes that the King will show mercy to them but he is arrested for treason and sentenced to death. Archbishop Scroop is the uncle of Henry, Lord Scroop of Masham in *King Henry V* (*see below*).

Scroop of Masham, Lord Henry
A historical figure (c. 1376-1415) and a minor character in *King Henry V*, Lord Scroop is one of the conspirators against the King. He urges Henry not to show mercy to a drunk man who has been committed to prison for the minor misdemeanor of insulting the King but Henry ignores his advice and orders the man to be freed. Shortly after, Scroop is himself accused of plotting against the King. Henry shows no mercy to a man whose crime is high treason and sentences Scroop to death.

Scroope (Scroop), Sir Stephen
A historical figure (d. 1408) and a minor character in *King Richard II*, Scroope is one of the few nobles who remain loyal to King Richard. He is the bearer of bad news to the King; he describes the popularity of Bolingbroke with the people of England, and tells Richard of the execution of his favourites, Bushy and Greene, and worst of all that Richard's uncle, the Duke of York, has joined forces with Bolingbroke.

Seacole
One of two minor characters in *Much Ado About Nothing; see* SEXTON, WATCHMEN.

Sebastian[1]
A character in *The Tempest*, Sebastian is King Alonso's brother. He is shipwrecked in the storm engineered by Prospero that brings all his old enemies to the magic island. There, he persuaded by the scheming Antonio to murder his sleeping brother and seize the crown of Naples for himself. Prospero casts a spell on the survivors of the shipwreck, imprisoning them in a kind of trance, before Sebastian can carry out his murderous intentions. Sebastian shows no real remorse at the end of the play nor any indication that he will reform.

Sebastian[2]
A character in *Twelfth Night*, Sebastian is Viola's identical twin brother. The twins have been shipwrecked on the shores of Illyria and Sebastian believes Viola has drowned. Befriended by Antonio who lends him his purse, Sebastian sets out to investigate his surroundings. In a series of comic confusions, he is mistaken for 'Cesario', the disguised Viola. His bewilderment grows when Olivia, making the same mistake about his identity, gives him a passionate greeting and sweeps him off to get married. In the scene

of final reconciliation, Sebastian is reunited with Viola. Sebastian's experiences largely mirror those of his sister, but where Viola as a woman has to resort to disguise and secrecy to survive, Sebastian is able to confront situations in a more straightforward way.

Second Player
A minor character in *Hamlet*, the Second Player is a member of the travelling company of actors who visit Elsinore. He probably takes the part of the 'Player Queen' in *The Murder of Gonzago* which is performed before the court.

Seleucus
A minor character in *Antony and Cleopatra*, Seleucus is Cleopatra's treasurer. Cleopatra asks Seleucus to confirm the contents of the inventory of possessions she has promised to hand over to Caesar. Much to his mistress's fury, Seleucus refuses to do so and tells Caesar that Cleopatra may have misled him by keeping some of her treasures back for herself.

Sempronius[1]
A minor character in *Timon of Athens*, Sempronius is one of the hypocrites who take advantage of Timon's generosity. When Timon is facing bankruptcy, he calls on Sempronius for a loan but Sempronius refuses, pretending to feel insulted because he is the last of Timon's friends to be approached. He is invited to attend Timon's last banquet when only warm water is served to the guests.

Sempronius[2]
A minor character in *Titus Andronicus*, Sempronius is one of the relatives who is present when Titus and his family shoot arrows carrying messages to the gods.

Senators
In Ancient Rome and Greece, Senators were members of the country's governing body. Senators appear in several of Shakespeare's plays as minor characters, law-makers and politicians. The Athenian Senators in *Timon of Athens* are cold-hearted and calculating; they refuse to help Timon when all his money has gone. They banish Alcibiades, whose only crime was to plead for mercy on behalf of a friend who killed someone in self-defence, saying that to show mercy is a sign of weakness. Alcibiades responds by threatening to conquer Athens and the Senators themselves have to beg him to spare the city and their lives.

Senecan tragedy
See TRAGEDY.

Senior, Duke
See DUKE SENIOR.

Sennois
A minor, non-speaking part in *The Two Noble Kinsmen*, Sennois is one of the villagers who performs a Morris dance for Duke Theseus. *See* COUNTRYMEN.

Sentry
See SOLDIER.

Sergeant
See SOLDIER.

Servants and Servingmen
Minor characters in Shakespeare's plays, Servants often act as messengers; they are frequently comic characters, such as the servants in *Romeo and Juliet*. Servants may embody goodness in a world where evil is rife. In *King Lear*, for example, Servants are horrified by the villainy of Regan and Cornwall and try to prevent the blinding of Gloucester; one of them is killed and the other fatally wounds Cornwall. In *Timon of Athens*, Timon's servants provide a contrast to the hypocritical aristocrats in his circle of so-called friends by remaining faithful to their master. When Timon is bankrupt, the Servants have to leave his household and the last of his money is shared among them. Timon's friends send their servants to try, in vain, to recover money owed by Timon to their masters. Servants often demonstrate a strong loyalty to their masters; in *King Richard II*, Sir Piers Exton's servant agrees with his master, who has understood Bolingbroke to say that he wants King Richard to be killed.

Three Servants appear in the INDUCTION of *The Taming of the Shrew*. They wait on the confused Sly, providing him with the kind of rich food and drink that he is quite unused to, and bringing him fine clothes to wear. They keep assuring him that he really is a nobleman who has been asleep for fifteen years.

Five servants of Petruchio have a role to play in his taming of the shrew, Katherina. In order to demonstrate how unpleasant her shrewish and abusive behaviour is, Petruchio himself kicks and abuses the Servants at his country house. The Servants are given names: Joseph, Nathaniel, Philip, Peter, Walter and Sugarsop.

In *Coriolanus*, Aufidius' Servingmen try to prevent Coriolanus entering the house, but he forces his way past them. Afterwards, the servants comment on his strength and pretend that they had realized all along that there was something superior about their visitor. Learning of Coriolanus' alliance with the Volscians, they express their admiration for him as a soldier and cheerfully anticipate the excitements of the forthcoming war with Rome.

Shakespeare created a range of characters based on the cunning servant, a stock character of the COMMEDIA DELL'ARTE. These characters are more developed that the Servants above, and are given names; for example Tranio the servant in *The Taming of the Shrew*.

Servilius
A minor character in *Timon of Athens*, Servilius is Timon's loyal servant. When Timon is bankrupt, he sends Servilius to ask Lucius for money, but a loan is refused. Servilius tells the servants of the other lords who come to demand the repayment of Timon's debts that his master is unwell.

sestet
A group of six lines in verse, connected by a particular pattern of rhyme. Shakespeare's SONNETS end with a sestet.

set
The arrangement of background SCENERY and PROPS on a stage, within and around which the play is enacted and which can be altered from scene to scene.

Sexton
A minor character in *Much Ado About Nothing*, the Sexton is called Francis SEACOLE. Presumably because he can read and write, he is chosen to make a written record of the accusations brought against Borachio and Conrade. He makes enough sense of Dogberry's confused account to realize that Borachio has been responsible for blackening Hero's name and that she is innocent. *See also* WATCHMEN.

Sextus Pompeius
A character in *Antony and Cleopatra*; *see* POMPEY.

Seyton
A minor character in *Macbeth*, Seyton is an officer who attends Macbeth as he begins to lose control before the fighting at Dunsinane. Seyton brings news that Lady Macbeth has died.

Shaa, Doctor
The real name of one of the churchmen who pretends to be a bishop in *King Richard III*; *see* BISHOPS.

Shadow, Simon
A minor comic character in *King Henry IV, Part Two*, Shadow is one of the unsuitable villagers whom Falstaff recruits for the army. He is chosen by Falstaff because, as his name implies, he is so thin that he will present a very small target for the enemy to hit.

Shagspere, Shakspere, Shakenschafte, Shaxspere
Alternative spellings of Shakespeare.

Shakespeare, Anne (1571–1579)
One of Shakespeare's younger sisters, Anne died in childhood. It is recorded that the family gave her an expensive funeral despite the fact that they were in some financial difficulty at the time.

Shakespeare, Edmund (1580–1607)
One of Shakespeare's younger brothers of whom little is known, Edmund was probably an actor in London. He may be buried in a Southwark church where the burial register has the description: "a player baseborn".

Shakespeare, Gilbert (1566–1612)
One of Shakespeare's younger brothers, Gilbert never married. He may have been a haberdasher in London for several years before returning to Stratford where he died.

Shakespeare, Hamnet (1585–1596)
Shakespeare's only son and twin sister of JUDITH, Hamnet was probably named after his godfather, Hamnet Sadler, who was a friend of Shakespeare's. Hamnet died at the age of eleven and it is possible that the moving speeches which Shakespeare wrote at about the same time for the character Constance in *King John* on the death of her young son Arthur, may reflect the poet's grief at the loss of his son.

Shakespeare, Joan (b. 1558)
Shakespeare's younger sister who died in early infancy. A second sister, also christened Joan, was born in the year following her death. *See* HART, JOAN.

Shakespeare, John (c. 1530–1601)

William Shakespeare's father, John, was the son of a tenant farmer in Snitterfield, a village near to Stratford. John left Snitterfield and became a business man in Stratford, probably a glover and tanner as well as a wool merchant, and married Mary ARDEN around 1557. He appears to have suffered some serious personal and financial reverses between 1576 and 1596 during which time, in 1578, he mortgaged part of his wife's inheritance. Perhaps partly due to his son's success, John ended his life in prosperity and as a property owner of some substance. He was granted a coat of arms in 1596.

Shakespeare, Judith (1585–1662)

William Shakespeare's elder daughter, Judith was the twin sister of Hamnet who died in childhood. In 1616 Judith married a Stratford tavern keeper, Thomas QUINEY who was four years her junior. They had three children, all of whom died young: SHAKESPER aged six months in 1617, and RICHARD aged eleven and THOMAS aged nineteen who both died in 1639. Judith's husband may have been a rather disreputable figure; he was fined for drunkenness and Shakespeare may have been concerned for his daughter's well-being since he altered his will in order to protect her inheritance from her husband.

Shakespeare, Richard (1574–1613)

One of William Shakespeare's younger brothers of whom nothing, other than the dates of his life, is recorded.

Shakespeare, Susanna

See HALL, SUSANNA.

Shakespeare, William (1564–1616)

A playwright, poet, and actor, Shakespeare was born in Stratford-upon-Avon in Warwickshire, probably on 23 April and, according to parish records, was baptized there three days later. He was the eldest son and third child of a businessman, John SHAKESPEARE and Mary ARDEN, the daughter of a well-to-do yeoman farmer. Eight children were born to the Shakespeares: Joan (b. 1558) who died in childhood, Margaret (1562-63), William, Gilbert (1566-1612), a second Joan (1569-1646), Anne (1571-79), Richard (1574-1613), Edmund (1580-1607) who became an undistinguished actor in London.

Little is known of Shakespeare's childhood. He almost certainly lived in the house in Henley Street, Stratford-upon-Avon, now known as The Birthplace, and he was probably educated at the local grammar school, a building which also still exists. There, according to later biographers, he would have learnt Latin and literature and perhaps some Greek and would have been introduced to classical drama. The school day would have been a long and rigorous one from six or seven in the morning until five or six at night for six days a week.

In 1567, Shakespeare's father held office as Bailiff of Stratford and as such was responsible for licensing the travelling companies of actors who visited the town. William would almost certainly have watched their plays in his leisure time and, since acting formed part of the Elizabethan school curriculum, it is not impossible that he may have acted in some school productions himself.

William probably left school before completing his education, perhaps aged about fifteen when his father was experiencing financial difficulties, and he may have spent some time helping his father run his business. Some biographers have suggested that following his schooling, Shakespeare became a school teacher, or possibly a tutor in a noble family where he might even have joined a company of actors attached to such a household. There is no evidence for this, except for Shakespeare's obvious familiarity with such families displayed for example in *Twelfth Night*. There is no evidence either that Shakespeare joined the army, which is sometimes suggested as a possibility, except that his history plays show a detailed knowledge of military procedure. It is not known either whether or not Shakespeare was brought up as a Protestant or a Roman Catholic.

What is certain is that in November 1582, Shakespeare married Anne HATHAWAY who was eight years his senior. The marriage by special licence seems to have been arranged in something of a hurry; Anne was three months pregnant at the time. The following year she presented William, a father at twenty, with a daughter Susanna (*see* HALL, SUSANNA); in 1595 twins, Hamnet (who died in 1596) and Judith (*see* QUINEY), were born. Little else is known of the first ten years of Shakespeare's married life.

He left Stratford in about 1585; legend, but not fact, has it that his departure was to avoid a charge of poaching deer from a local estate. It was probably around 1591 that he moved to London where Dr JOHNSON recounts he was hired to mind the horses of the gentry while they were in the playhouse. He was so good at the job, Johnson wrote, that he in turn hired other boys who became known as 'Shakespeare's Boys'.

In 1592, he met the Earl of Southampton who became his patron and it is known that in the same year he was writing plays for Philip HENSLOWE. He may also have been acting with PEMBROKE'S MEN as a HIRELING or with the tragedian Edward Alleyn's company of actors, the ADMIRAL'S MEN, but from the summer of that year, and for the next two years, London theatres were frequently shut down because of outbreaks of plague. During this period of theatrical inactivity, Shakespeare wrote the poems *Venus and Adonis* and *Lucrece*. By 1594, he was a leading member of the LORD CHAMBERLAIN'S MEN and was writing plays for them; he remained with the company for the rest of his life. A 17th-century critic suggested that Shakespeare was such a poor actor, a "better poet than player", that he was only allowed to play relatively small parts, such as the ghost of Hamlet's father.

In 1599, he became a part owner (with BURBAGE and KEMP among other members of the company) of the newly-built Globe Theatre, sharing in its profits. The Lord Chamberlain's Men became known as the King's Men following James I's accession to the throne in 1603. The company played frequently before the King and its members were given office with the Royal Household. Shakespeare became a GROOM OF THE CHAMBER (an unpaid post and honorary title conferred on royal players) and was given four yards of red cloth for his livery.

How often Shakespeare returned to Stratford to see his wife and family is not known, nor is the quality of his relationship with Anne. There is a story that on his journeyings between London and his home, Shakespeare would stop for refreshment at a particular Oxford inn in where he enjoyed an intermittent relationship with the landlady, Mistress Davenant by whom he had an illegitimate son called William (*see* DAVENANT, WILLIAM).

In 1596 John Shakespeare was granted a coat of arms, and his son was entitled thereafter to call himself 'gentleman'. Shakespeare seems to have been prospering on his own account. In 1597 he acquired New Place, the second largest house in Stratford

© *Guildhall Library, London*

William Shakespeare

and on the death of his father he inherited the Henley Street house. His success enabled him to buy 107 acres of good land some five years later, although he was still working and living in London.

 He was certainly in London in 1598 and appeared as a 'principal comedian' and as a 'principal tragedian' in 1603. He retired from acting in 1604 but he seems to have remained in London since he bought a house in Blackfriars in 1613. He certainly continued writing, producing some his great tragedies at about this time.

 Shakespeare died at the age of fifty-two of a fever supposedly caught at a convivial meeting with fellow playwrights DRAYTON and JONSON and was buried in the Parish Church of Holy Trinity at Stratford where his gravestone can still be seen. In his will he left his clothes to his sister Joan's sons, and a special silver and gilt bowl to his daughter Judith. The bulk of his estate went to his elder daughter Susanna. His wife Anne would automatically have received a life interest and a right to stay on in New Place, but particular mention was made that she should inherit the second-best bed. He also left money to various people, including the original members of the Lord Chamberlain's Men for memorial rings. Some hundred years later, an early biographer Nicholas Rowe wrote of the SWAN OF AVON that he was "a good-natur'd Man of great sweetness in his Manners".

Shakespeare's Plays

It is difficult to be precise about the dates of Shakespeare's 37 plays (38 if *The Two Noble Kinsmen* is included), although information can sometimes be gleaned from HENSLOWE's diaries which give dates of performances, or from the accounts of the MASTER OF THE REVELS. Shakespeare's plays can, however, be roughly grouped in to the EARLY, MIDDLE and LATE periods of his writing.

The early plays (1589-94)

These included four history plays (*King Henry VI, Parts One, Two and Three*, and *King Richard III*; four comedies (including *The Taming of the Shrew*), and two tragedies *Titus Andronicus* and *Romeo and Juliet*. As was common practice, Shakespeare's name as author of these first 10 plays did not appear on the text. From 1598, however, his name did appear on the printed plays.

The middle plays (1595-99)

During this period Shakespeare wrote his greatest comedies (five in all and including *A Midsummer' Night's Dream* and *Twelfth Night*); five history plays (including *King Henry IV, Parts One and Two*, and *King Henry V*), and the tragedy *Julius Caesar*.

The late plays (1600-13)

Shakespeare produced his greatest tragedies (seven in all, including *Hamlet, King Lear* and *Macbeth*) towards the end of his life; he wrote four comedies including *The Merry Wives of Windsor* and *Measure for Measure*, and four tragi-comedies including *The Winter's Tale* and *The Tempest*. See the table of Shaekespeare's plays in the Supplement.

Shakespeare's plays were hugely popular in his lifetime, but the first collected edition of his plays was not published until 1623, after his death. Known as the First FOLIO edition, it did not include *Pericles*. The plays continued to be published and performed in various forms, often adapted to placate the PURITAN regulators of the theatre. In 1709, a collection of them appeared which had been edited and amended by Nicholas ROWE, the first editor to divide the plays into acts and scenes. Other revised editions of the plays included a adaptation of *King Lear* by Nahum TATE (1652-1715) who gave it a happy ending, and a vandalized version of *King Richard III* by Colley CIBBER in 1700. 19th- and 20th-century editors have been more concerned to return to the original texts.

Shakespeare's Poems

Shakespeare's poetry includes two long narrative poems 'Venus and Adonis' (1593) and 'The Rape of Lucrece' (1594) which were dedicated to his patron Henry Wriothsley, the Earl of Southampton (for whom he also wrote one of his early comedies, *Love's Labour's Lost*). A love poem, 'The Phoenix and the Turtle' was written in 1601. The 152 sonnets were written during the 1590s and are concerned with love, the passing of time, and death. The first 126 were addressed to an unknown young man, possibly the 'Mr W H' who some believe was the Earl of Southampton. Sonnets 127 to 152, are written to a mysterious and fickle dark-haired lady; much scholarship has been devoted to discovering the identity of 'Mr W H' and the DARK LADY. *See* SONNET.

Shakespearean criticism

Dryden's 'Essay of Dramatick Poesie' (1668) was the first work of dramatic criticism to pay scholarly attention to the works of Shakespeare. In it, DRYDEN wrote of Shakespeare that 'he was a man who of all Modern and perhaps Ancient poets, had the largest and most comprehensive soul'. In 1709, Nicholas ROWE produced the first complete edited collection of Shakespeare's plays which included a brief critical and biographical introduction. Shakespeare's reputation continued to grow and in the course of the 18th-century many more editions of his plays followed with emendations and textual notes and several works of Shakespearean criticism appeared. The most famous of these, published in 1765, was *Preface to Shakespeare* by Dr JOHNSON, a lifelong devotee of Shakespeare. Johnson worked from the First FOLIO and applauded Shakespeare's gift for comedies (though he deplored his puns), and the way in which he mixed comedy with tragedy, and he defended Shakespeare's disregard of the three UNITIES. Johnson admired Shakespeare's genius as a creator of realistic characters, although he condemned him for loosely formed plots, for the blasphemy in some the plays and for putting dramatic effect before moral justice.

At the beginning of the 19th century, writers associated with the Romantic Movement focused on Shakespeare's characters and plots. The Romantic poet Samuel Coleridge (1772-1834) gave a series of lectures (published in 1807) which explored the characters as vivid individualized types. *Characters of Shakespeare's Plays*, published in 1817 by the writer and critic William Hazlitt (1778-1830), conveyed the dynamic effect of Shakespeare's creations in performance. Adaptations of Shakespeare's plays, such as Charles and Mary LAMB'S *Tales from Shakespeare* (1807) and Dr BOWDLER'S notoriously expurgated version of Shakespeare's plays *The Family Shakespeare* (1807-18), placed Shakespeare at the centre of Victorian literary culture. Elevation of Shakespeare as a heroic poet encouraged interest in him as a person, as seen in the Shakespearean scholar, Edward Dowden's, *William Shakespeare: a Critical Study of his Life and Art* (1875). The actor-manager, William Charles MACREADY focused interest in Shakespeare's works in performance. He worked to establish the authentic Shakespearean texts which were performed with historically researched, and elaborate, scenery.

At the beginning of the 20th century, the Romantics' focus on Shakespeare's characters culminated in A C BRADLEY'S *Shakespearean Tragedy*, which treated figures like Hamlet, Othello, Lear and Macbeth almost as real people. Subsequent Shakespearean criticism in the 20th century has made a movement against Bradley's 'biographical' approach, as typified in a witty essay entitled, 'How Many Children had Lady Macbeth?' (1933) by L C Knights. Criticism has tended to focus on the actual text; studies such as G Wilson Knight's *The Wheel of Fire* (1930) placed patterns of imagery at the heart of Shakespearean interpretation.

Shakespearean criticism since the 1960s has tended to analyze the text in isolation from its social or historic setting. Text is studied as a structured organization of linguistic signs, a kind of code to be deciphered by the reader. Structuralism, in particular, is a modern intellectual approach to texts which is less interested in the actual meaning of a work, than in how it achieves that meaning. 'New historicism' is a recent school of literary criticism which originated in the 1980s. It regards history, not as a fixed setting for a work of literature, but as a shifting background to it; history itself being a narrative that is open to interpretation in the same way that a critic might interpret the text of a play. *See* LITERARY CRITICISM.

Shakespearean sonnet
See SONNET.

Shallow, Robert
A comic character in *King Henry IV, Part Two* and *The Merry Wives of Windsor*, Justice Shallow is a country lawyer. In *Henry IV*, Shallow produces the unlikely collection of villagers from which Falstaff is to chose his army recruits and then invites Falstaff and his men to a cheerfully drunken evening at his house. Shallow is excessively talkative, shallow by name and shallow by nature, but he is a sociable and good-humoured old man who recounts and embroiders the exploits of his youth when he was at law school in London.

In *The Merry Wives of Windsor*, the character of Shallow is less clearly defined. He is angry with Falstaff whose men have beaten his servants and killed his deer. His dim-witted nephew Slender is staying with him and Shallow does his best to bring about a marriage between Anne Page and Slender. In his role as a lawyer Shallow tries to prevent the duel between Evans and Dr Caius taking place.

It has been suggested that the character of Justice Shallow is a portrait of Sir Thomas Lucy, a landowner living near Stratford from whom, legend has it, Shakespeare poached deer in his youth.

Shapes
Minor characters in *The Tempest*; *see* SPIRITS.

sharer
In Shakespeare's time, a member of a company of players who had a financial stake in the running of the company, in the expenses of play production, the hiring of actors and the commissioning of plays, as well as in the profits.

Shepherd
A minor character in *King Henry VI, Part One*, the old Shepherd is Joan La Pucelle's father. When Joan is condemned to death by the English she meets her father but refuses to acknowledge him, claiming that she is descended from kings. Hurt and angry, the simple Shepherd curses his daughter.

Shepherd
A character in *The Winter's Tale*; *see* OLD SHEPHERD.

Sheriff of Wiltshire
A minor character in *King Richard III*, the Sheriff escorts Buckingham to his execution.

Shoreditch
An area of London which in Shakespeare's time was outside the City limits, where the playhouses the CURTAIN and the THEATRE were built and which was said to be full of thieves and prostitutes. See the map of London at the back of the book.

Shylock
A character in *The Merchant of Venice*, Shylock is a Jew, an outsider in the Christian world of Venice. Although he asks to be treated with the respect due to any human being, he is regarded with contempt by the other characters. Shylock is a moneylender whose loan to Bassiano is guaranteed by the promise of a pound of Antonio's flesh.

When Shylock's daughter, Jessica, elopes with her Christian lover and escapes her possessive father's clutches, she takes his money and jewels with her. Shylock is as angry about the loss of his money as he is distraught at his daughter's disappearance. He vents his rage on Christians in general and Antonio in particular, demanding his pound of flesh when Antonio is unable to repay Bassiano's debt, and showing no mercy. Outwitted in court by Portia, he is stripped of his wealth and as a final humiliation, he is instructed to become a Christian. Shylock is the villain of the piece but he is also a victim for whom Shakespeare makes us feel some sympathy. He is an old man who loses everything; his daughter, his wealth and his religion.

The character of Shylock, one of Shakespeare's most memorable creations, owes much to a STOCK CHARACTER from earlier drama who would have been well-known to Elizabethan audiences. He is the miser, a comic villain who is a killjoy and a possessive father.

Sicilius Leonatus
A minor character in *Cymbeline*, Sicilius is not named in the cast list. He is Posthumus' father who appears as an Apparition to his son in a dream while he languishes in his condemned cell, and begs the god JUPITER to help. He is described in the stage directions as an 'old man, attired like a warrior'.

Sicinius, Velutus
A character in *Coriolanus*, Sicinius is one of the tribunes [representative of the people] with Brutus, who is given office following riots in the city over food shortages. Noisier than his colleague Brutus, he is described as an 'old goat' by Coriolanus. After Coriolanus has addressed the crowd and asked them to support him as consul, Sicinius and Brutus incite the mob to turn against the city's ruling class and the arrogant Coriolanus. They suggest hurling him off a rock to his death but they are overruled and Coriolanus is banished. In Coriolanus' absence, Sicinius reports that the city is peaceful and contented and that the tradesmen are happily singing in their shops. When Coriolanus returns intent on destroying Rome, the tribunes refuse to take any responsibility for the part they have played in putting their city in danger.

Siddons, Sarah (1755–1831)
An actress and perhaps the greatest tragedienne of all time, who was particularly renowned for her portrayal of Lady Macbeth. It was said that she could make audiences faint with the intensity of her acting. Aged twenty, she was the first actress to attempt the role of Hamlet, a part she continued to play for the next thirty years, despite her inappropriate age and increasing weight. *See illustration, opposite.*

Sidney, Sir Philip (1554–86)
A courtier, statesman and poet whose work influenced not only his contemporaries but subsequent generations of writers as well. His best known works are the series of sonnets 'Astrophel and Stella' (written c. 1580-84), 'Arcadia', and 'Apologie for Poetrie' which was the first work of English LITERARY CRITICISM; none of these were published in his own lifetime. Sidney was a nephew of Queen Elizabeth's favourite the Earl of LEICESTER.

Silence

A minor comic character in *King Henry IV, Part Two*, Justice Silence is a country
lawyer who, as his name implies, is naturally the opposite of his friend, the talkative
Justice Shallow. However, under the influence of drink at Shallow's party, Silence
breaks into song and at the end of the evening has to be carried to bed.

Silius

A minor character in *Antony and Cleopatra*, Silius serves as an officer in the army of
Ventidius, one of Antony's supporters. Silius tries to spur Ventidius on to greater
military glory by pursuing the fleeing enemy Parthians into Persian territory.

Silvia

A character in *The Two Gentlemen of Verona*, Silvia, a conventional young woman, is
loved by Valentine. Her father, the Duke, intends her to marry Thurio so she and
Valentine plan to elope. They are betrayed by Proteus and when Valentine is banished
Proteus tries to win Silvia for himself. Silvia spurns his advances and, showing resource
and courage, escapes from Milan to join Valentine. She is seized by a band of outlaws
and rescued by Proteus who claims her for himself as a reward and threatens her with
rape when again she refuses him. Silvia is reunited with Valentine and her father gives
his blessing to their marriage.

   Proteus serenades Silvia with the well-known song that Schubert later set to music,
'Who is Silvia?'.

Silvius

A character in *As You Like It*, Silvius is a romantic young shepherd in the Forest of
ARDEN. He is passionately devoted to Phebe, a shepherdess, but she does not return his
love; she has fallen in love with Rosalind in her disguise as the young man 'Ganymede'.
Silvius is duped into being Phebe's messenger when she writes a love letter to
'Ganymede', but in the end his patient adoration is rewarded. He is married to Phebe,
who grudgingly gives herself to him when she discovers Ganymede's identity.

Sarah Siddons, *artist: Sir William Beechey*

Simonides
A character in *Pericles*, Simonides is 'the good' King of Pentapolis and father of
Pericles' wife Thaisa. When Pericles is shipwrecked on the shores of Pentapolis he is
told by fishermen that Simonides is hosting a tournament for his daughter's suitors.
Pericles appears at the tournament in rusty armour and Simonides tells Thaisa that she
must not judge the inner man by his outward appearance. Thaisa falls in love with
Pericles and Simonides is delighted but before giving his formal approval to the
marriage he demands to know if Pericles' intentions towards Thaisa are honourable.
Simonides' death is reported by Thaisa as she and Pericles are reunited at the end of the
play, and Pericles declares that they will return to Simonides' kingdom and rule after
him. Simonides' love for Thaisa is in stark contrast to the incestuous relationship
between King Antiochus and his daughter.

Simpcox, Saunder
A minor character in *King Henry VI, Part Two*, Simpcox and his WIFE are fraudulent
beggars who the gullible King Henry meets at St Albans. Simpcox claims his sight has
been miraculously restored after years of blindness and he also pretends to be lame but
when his story is seen through by the Duke of Gloucester and he is threatened with
whipping he runs off. Both Simpcoxes are punished with a beating.

simile
A figure of speech that expresses the similarity of one thing to another, which is usually
introduced by the words 'as' or 'like'. The comparison is a way of illustrating a
particular quality about a person or thing. For example: 'She sat like Patience on a
monument, smiling at grief'.

Simple, Peter
A minor character in *The Merry Wives of Windsor*, Simple is Slender's servant who is as
dim-witted as his master.

Sinclo, John or Sincler (active 1590–1604)
An actor of whom nothing is known but whose name appears in several of the stage
directions in Shakespeare's plays. He seems to have played mainly minor roles, such as
one of the players in *The Taming of the Shrew* and apparently he was particularly thin. It
is possible that Shakespeare created for him parts such as Dr Pinch in *A Comedy of
Errors* and Shadow, one of the recruits in *King Henry IV, Part Two*, both of whom, as
their names imply, are described as being terribly bony.

Siward
A minor character in *Macbeth*, Siward is the Earl of Northumberland who leads the
army sent to Scotland by King Edward of England to help Malcolm defeat Macbeth. His
son YOUNG SIWARD is killed in single combat with Macbeth.

slapstick
A type of COMEDY which is based on physical rather than verbal humour (as when
Falstaff is put into the laundry basket and tipped into a stream in *The Merry Wives of
Windsor*). The word derives from a 'slap stick' which was a two-piece stick used by a
CLOWN to make a loud slapping noise on impact.

Slender, Abraham

A comic character in *The Merry Wives of Windsor*, Slender is Justice Shallow's dim-witted nephew. He is courting Anne Page and his suit is favoured by Anne's father as Slender is a young man of means. Slender sighs for love of Anne but is incapable of expressing his passion. He makes embarrassed conversation with her and his proposal is pathetically clumsy. Anne begs her mother not to marry her to such a fool but her father arranges in secret for Slender to elope with her. He is to meet Anne at night in Windsor Park where she will be with the others, disguised as fairies, who are playing the trick on Falstaff. Slender only discovers at the altar that he has made a terrible mistake and has run off with a boy dressed as a woman, who was substituted for Anne.

Sly, Christopher

A comic character who appears at the beginning of *The Taming of the Shrew* in the INDUCTION that introduces the play, Sly is a beer-swilling tinker with a variety of past careers from pedlar to bear-keeper. He is found by a hunting party, lying in a drunken stupor outside an inn and they decide to play an elaborate trick on him. They carry him off to a grand house nearby, dress him up in rich clothing and tell the inn boy to dress up as his wife. When he wakes, they convince Sly that he is a nobleman who has been mad for fifteen years and they lavish attention on him. A group of travelling actors arrives, and as part of the good-natured joke Sly is told that his doctors have recommended that he watches their play. He looks on with his 'wife' at his side as *The Taming of the Shrew* is enacted for them.

Sly, William (d. 1608)

An actor in Shakespeare's company of actors the LORD CHAMBERLAIN'S MEN, Sly is one of the 'PRINCIPALL ACTORS' listed in the First FOLIO edition of Shakespeare's plays. He was a HOUSEKEEPER [part owner] of the Globe and later of the BLACKFRIARS THEATRE. He took the part of his namesake 'Sly' in *The Taming of the Shrew* and he may have taken the role of Osric in *Hamlet*.

Smith the Weaver

A minor character in *King Henry VI, Part Two*, Smith is one of the followers of the rebel Jack Cade.

Snare

A minor comic character in *King Henry IV, Part Two*, Snare, together with Fang, is one of the constables who is sent to try to arrest Falstaff for debt.

Snout, Tom

A comic character in *A Midsummer Night's Dream*, Snout's name derives from his profession as a tinker in which he would have repaired snouts, or spouts, of kettles and jugs. Snout is one of the amateur actors in the MASQUE of *Pyramus and Thisbe* which is performed for Duke Theseus at his wedding. Not the most talented of actors, Snout is given the part of the 'Wall' to play.

Snug

A comic character in *A Midsummer Night's Dream*, Snug is a joiner [furniture maker and carpenter] and one of the Athenian workmen who takes part in the MASQUE of *Pyramus and Thisbe*. Snug is an enthusiastic member of Bottom's troupe of actors but, a slow learner, he is relieved to be given the part of the Lion in the play because he is only required to roar a lot. When *Pyramus and Thisbe* is performed for Duke Theseus as part of his wedding celebrations, Demetrius shouts out: 'Well roared, Lion!'.

Solanio and Solario
A minor character in *The Merchant of Venice*, Solanio is a young Venetian gentleman and a friend of Bassanio and Antonio. Together with his companion Solario, his main function is to comment on events.

Soldiers
Soldiers, Sentries and Sergeants appear as minor characters, who sometimes act as messengers, in several of Shakespeare's plays. In the HISTORY PLAYS and the ROMAN PLAYS, Soldiers may embody qualities of courage, or of cowardice, that may say something about the people for whom they are fighting. For example, French soldiers in the history plays are often portrayed as inept or cowardly, in order to make Shakespeare's case that the English fighting forces were superior and the English cause a just one. In the Roman Plays, Soldiers sometimes comment on the fighting abilities of the central figure, or his state of mind. In *Antony and Cleopatra*, for example, a Soldier in Caesar's army praises Antony, although he is his enemy.

soliloquy
A speech or a MONOLOGUE which is addressed by a character to the audience rather than to a fellow actor on the stage. It is spoken as if the character was in a confidential or reflective mood and expressing his inner thoughts aloud. Such confidences allow psychological insights into a character and may sometimes lead to a situation of DRAMATIC IRONY. This kind of intimacy between actor and spectator would have seemed quite natural in an Elizabethan playhouse, where the audience sat around three sides of the stage or even on it. The most famous example of a soliloquy is Hamlet's speech 'To be or not to be'.

Solinus
A minor character in *The Comedy of Errors*; *see* EPHESUS, DUKE OF.

Somerset, Duke of[1]
A historical figure (1403-44) and a character in *King Henry VI, Part One*, Somerset is a Lancastrian (*see* LANCASTER, HOUSE OF) and a supporter of King Henry against claims to the throne from the House of YORK. In a scene in the Temple Garden in London, Somerset chooses a red rose as his emblem while Richard Plantagenet, Duke of York, chooses a white one (*see* WARS OF THE ROSES). When the quarrel between the two men erupts again, King Henry tries to resolve it by dividing the military command between them. It proves to be a disastrous move as Somerset and York are so absorbed in their feud that they fail to provide proper support for the rest of the English army.

Somerset, Duke of[2]
A historical figure (1406-55) and a character in *King Henry VI, Part Two*. Somerset, loyal to King Henry, is appointed by him as Regent in France over his rival the Duke of York. When news comes that the territories in France are lost, York sneers at Somerset for his mismanagement of affairs. When York launches his own attack on the throne, he accuses Somerset of treachery and demands his removal. Somerset agrees to go to the

TOWER OF LONDON to appease York but actually he remains free and tries to arrest York for treason. His attempt to stop York is futile and Somerset is killed by him in the battle for the crown at St Albans.

Somerset, Duke of[3]

A historical figure (1436-64) and a minor character in *King Henry VI, Part Three*, Somerset is a supporter of King Edward and the Yorkist cause (*see* YORK, HOUSE OF), but he defects to King Henry's side after Edward's marriage to Lady Grey. He fights at the Battle of Tewkesbury and is captured and sentenced to death.

Somerville, Sir John

A minor character in *King Henry VI, Part Three*, Somerville is a supporter of the Earl of Warwick in his rebellion against King Edward.

Son

A minor character in *Macbeth*; *see* BOY.

Son that has killed his Father

A minor character in *King Henry VI, Part Three*, the Son has tragically mistaken his father's identity in the heat of battle and killed him. King Henry witnesses the Son's sorrow and grieves himself for the terrible loss of life the civil war has caused.

sonnet

A type of verse form which consists of fourteen lines either in a single stanza (unit of lines) or divided into a unit of eight lines (an octave) followed by six lines (a sestet). It is written in IAMBIC PENTAMETER with ten syllables to a line and has particular fixed patterns of rhyme. The SHAKESPEAREAN SONNET was developed in 16th-century England from the sonnets of PETRARCH. It is written in single stanza form and the RHYME scheme is *a b a b c d c d e f e f g g*, with the final couplet acting as a sort of EPIGRAM or comment.

Shakespeare's sonnets may or may not be autobiographical; they may express a personal view or the poet may have adopted a PERSONA, and it is possible that they were originally written for a private readership only. Most Elizabethan sonnets were simply stylized declarations of love, but Shakespeare invests his poetry with a unique vitality and originality. He also investigates other themes such as immortality and the passing of time. Versions of Sonnets 138 and 144 first appeared in *The Passionate Pilgrim* in 1599, but the collection as a whole was published in 1609 and privately circulated; they were written between 1593 and 1600. There is as much doubt about the exact date they were written as there is argument about the identity of the person or persons to whom they are addressed. There is also uncertainty about the order in which the sonnets were written which may well have been different from the order in which they now appear.

The sonnets are dedicated to a 'The onlie begetter of these ensuing sonnets Mr W H '. The first 126 describe quarrels and reconciliations in a friendship, which some scholars have suggested was a homosexual relationship, with the unknown W H, the 'fair friend', and the object of Shakespeare's affections. Sonnets 1 to 17 are concerned with persuading a young man to marry and produce an heir. Shakespeare gives as reasons for marriage the fact that the youth can achieve a kind of immortality by having children. These sonnets are linked by themes of time passing and by repetitions of rhymes, and some scholars believe that they may originally have been written as a single poem. Sonnets 18 to 31 are concerned with the young man's flawless beauty which is threatened by passing time; they are love poems, some containing suggestions of sexual desire. Sonnets 33 to 42 record an estrangement between the poet and the youth, apparently because he has been seduced by the poet's mistress - sexual passion has become more important than the ties of friendship between the two men. The poet expresses his feelings that he has been betrayed. In sonnets 37 to 42 the poet forgives his friend, deciding to hand over his mistress because the claims of the poet's friendship are stronger than those of the relationship with his mistress. Sonnets 43 to 58 express fears about the young man's inconstancy and numbers 59 to 75 examine the way in which poetry can ensure immortality as the poet looks forward to his own death. Sonnets 76 to 96 express changing moods - love and praise for his friend and anxieties about infidelity and a rival relationship with another poet whom Shakespeare fears is greater than he. Numbers 97 to 108 seems to have been written about a break from the young man, but the poet says that his love is stronger than ever. Numbers 109 to 126 are the last of the group which are addressed to the fair friend. In them the poet says that although he has been neglectful because his profession (as an actor) has been responsible for taking him out into the world, he has remained faithful to the young man.

The sonnets numbered 127 to 154 are concerned with an anonymous, faithless, dark-haired woman who aroused feelings of passion and guilt in the poet. Some of these poems are addressed directly to her and some are about the triangular relationship with the Dark Lady and Shakespeare's fair friend. There are poems about sexual desire, with innuendoes and puns and they express bitterness and abject misery and tell how the poet has fallen in love with this brunette, a musician. *See* DARK LADY OF THE SONNETS.

Soothsayers
Fortune-tellers, minor characters in several of Shakespeare's plays; in *Antony and Cleopatra*, the Soothsayer reads the palms of Charmian and Iras and predicts that Charmian will live longer than her mistress, Cleopatra. The Soothsayer accompanies Antony to Rome and warns him that Caesar will always prove the stronger. Both the Soothsayer's predictions are proved right. In *Julius Caesar*, the Soothsayer calls from the crowd to warn Caesar to beware of the Ides of March (15 March). Caesar dismisses him as a dreamer but Portia, Caesar's wife, speaks to the Soothsayer later and takes his warning more seriously. On his way to the Senate and to his death on 15 March, Caesar meets the Soothsayer one more time and is warned that though the Ides of March have come, they have not yet gone.

In *Cymbeline*, a soothsayer interprets dreams. *See* PHILARMONUS.

Soundpost, James
A minor character in *Romeo and Juliet*; Soundpost is one of the MUSICIANS hired to play for Juliet's wedding. A 'soundpost' is a small part of a stringed instrument, such as a violin; it is a wooden peg fitted between the back of the instrument and its belly, beneath the bridge.

sources
Nearly all Shakespeare's plays derive from other, earlier works. The Elizabethan appetite for new plays was so voracious that playwrights were driven to borrow material

from earlier texts and to invest these ready-made plots and STOCK CHARACTERS with new life rather than write entirely original material. Collaboration was quite usual among Elizabethan dramatists and borrowing other writers' work was not considered to be plagiarism as we understand it today.

Shakespeare, for example, adapted romances from Italian literature for comedies such as *All's Well that Ends Well*, *Much Ado About Nothing* and *Twelfth Night*. He drew on the historical accounts of Edward HALLE and HOLINSHED'S *CHRONICLES* for the histories but added memorable characters such as Falstaff. For the Roman plays, Shakespeare used North's translation of *Lives of the Greeks and Romans* by PLUTARCH, a series of biographical accounts of great figures of the past, such as Julius Caesar and Antony and Cleopatra. Less consciously, Shakespeare used tales from folklore for stories such as the taming of Katherina the 'shrew'.

Southampton, 3rd Earl of (1573–1624)
The title of Henry Wriothsley, (pronounced Risely), the Earl of Southampton was a friend and patron of Shakespeare to whom the two narrative poems 'Venus and Adonis' (1593) and 'The Rape of Lucrece' (1594) were dedicated. He was a highly educated man who wrote letters in Latin and who was known for his physical beauty. An explorer and politician, Southampton was a favourite of Queen Elizabeth's for a while until the discovery of his involvement in the Earl of Essex's abortive rebellion in 1601. He was sentenced to death but the sentence was commuted to life imprisonment on account of his youth. While in the TOWER OF LONDON he kept a black and white cat in order to control the rats. He was eventually freed by James I. There is speculation that the Earl of Southampton is the 'Mr W H' to whom Shakespeare's sonnets are dedicated. In a miniature portrait of Southampton aged 20/21, painted by Nicholas Hilliard in 1593/4, he is portrayed with rather feminine features and golden hair. *See also* ESSEX.

Southwark
A district of London, south of the river Thames which in Shakespeare's time included the BANKSIDE area. See the map of London at the back of the book.

Southwell, John
A minor character in *King Henry VI, Part Two*, Southwell is described as a priest in the cast list but he is involved in conjuring up the unholy spirits who advise the Duchess of Gloucester. Southwell is arrested and hanged.

Speed
A minor comic character in *The Two Gentlemen of Verona*, Speed is Valentine's page and a friend to Launce. He teases his master about his love for Silvia.

Spenser, Edmund (c. 1552–99)
A poet, Spenser is particularly remembered for his long allegorical poem 'The Faerie Queene', begun in 1579 (*see* ALLEGORY). The poem, in six books, is an account of the adventures undertaken by six knights, each of whom symbolize a particular virtue, such as truth or chastity. The poem makes allusions to the glories of Queen Elizabeth's reign and the Queen herself is referred to as 'Gloriana'. Spenser's other works include a series of twelve pastoral poems '*The Shepheardes Calendar*' (1579) and an elegy on Sir Philip SIDNEY, '*Astrophel*' (written c. 1591).

Spirits

Minor characters in *The Tempest*, the spirits come in different guises. They appear as SHAPES who, as part of Prospero's enchantment of his enemies, provide an illusory banquet for Alonso. They dance round the table to Ariel's soft music before carrying it off again. SPIRITS, in the shape of dogs, chase the drunken Stephano and his companions Trinculo and Caliban at Prospero's bidding. When Miranda and Ferdinand are betrothed, Spirits perform a celebratory MASQUE appearing as Roman deities. IRIS (messenger of the gods) calls on JUNO (Queen of Heaven and protector of marriages) to come down from the heavens. JUNO sings a song granting her blessing to the lovers and CERES (goddess of the fruits of the earth) promises plenty to the young couple. NYMPHS and REAPERS dance together and vanish suddenly after a signal from PROSPERO.

spondee

A metrical FOOT of two equally stressed syllables, such as 'Adam'.

Stafford, Sir Humphrey and William

Minor characters in *King Henry VI, Part Two*, Sir Humphrey and his brother William are sent to try to persuade Jack Cade and his men from continuing with their rebellion. Humphrey's haughty tones do little to pacify Cade and the brothers are killed by the rebels.

Stafford, Lord

A minor character in *King Henry VI, Part Three*, Stafford is a supporter of King Edward and the Yorkist cause. *See* YORK, HOUSE OF.

stage directions

Instructions to actors which are written into the text of a play and which tell them when to move to a particular part of the stage or to pick up PROPS or make an exit. In Shakespeare's time, some stage directions would have been added to the text by the BOOK-KEEPER and some perhaps by the author himself, but they would have been few; most existing stage directions in the texts of Shakespeare's plays have been inserted by later editors. The most startling stage direction in any Shakespeare play is 'Exit, pursued by a bear' in *The Winter's Tale*.

stage-keeper

A stage hand in the Elizabethan theatre who might sometimes be given a small part to perform and who was responsible for organizing the PROPS in a production of a play and supervising their arrangement.

stage manager

Someone in a modern theatre who is responsible for organizing the PROPS in a production of a play and supervising their arrangement.

Stanley, Earl of Derby

A historical figure (c. 1435-1504) and a minor character in *King Richard III*; at first Stanley is loyal to Richard, although he has an unsettling and prophetic dream about the King. After the execution of Hastings, he changes his allegiance to Richmond, but Richard suspects he might defect and takes Stanley's son as a hostage. Fortunately, the King's order to kill Stanley's son is never carried out. Stanley remains neutral at the

Battle of Bosworth and takes no part in the fighting. After the King is killed, Stanley presents the crown to Richmond.

Stanley, Sir John
A minor character in *King Henry VI, Part One*, Stanley escorts the Duchess of York to the Isle of Man where she is to be held in exile. He promises to treat her kindly.

Stanley, Sir William
A minor character in *King Henry VI, Part Three*, Stanley is a supporter of King Edward and the Yorkist cause. *See* YORK, HOUSE OF.

stanza
A unit of verse lines in a poem which are usually arranged in a regular pattern of length and number, often with a recurrent RHYME scheme.

Starveling, Robin
A comic character in *A Midsummer Night's Dream*, Starveling is a tailor and one of the Athenian workmen who takes part in the MASQUE of *Pyramus and Thisbe*. He takes the role of 'Moonshine' in the play which is performed for Duke Theseus as part of his wedding celebrations. Starveling, whose PROPS are a dog, a thornbush and a lantern, is a nervous performer on stage. He is so agitated by the comments of the audience that, forgetting his lines, he turns to them and simply tells them that he is the character 'Moonshine'.

 The name 'Starveling' may refer to a particularly thin actor, John SINCLO, a member of Shakespeare's company of actors at the time, who may have taken the part of the tailor.

Stationers' Company, The
In Shakespeare's time, an organization which was licensed by the government and whose members were publishers and printers. Once a text had been licensed, by the MASTER OF THE REVELS in the case of plays, members of the Stationers' Company could secure the right to publish it by registering its title with the STATIONERS' REGISTER and paying a fee. The Stationers' Company existed only to protect the rights of those in the book trade; authors had no copyright in their own work.

Stephano[1]
A minor character in *The Merchant of Venice*, Stephano is Portia's servant who tells Jessica and Lorenzo that Portia is about to arrive back at Belmont.

Stephano[2]
A comic character in *The Tempest*, the villainous Stephano is King Alonso's drunken butler who is shipwrecked on the shores of Prospero's magic island with his master. He floats ashore, appropriately enough, on a barrel of sack [sherry] and joins up with Trinculo, the King's jester, and the monstrous Caliban. Under the influence of enormous quantities of sack, the unlikely trio, led by Stephano, hatch a plot to kill Prospero and take over the island. Stephano, relishing the idea of being King of the island with Miranda as his Queen, puts on lordly airs and becomes increasingly authoritarian towards the submissive Trinculo and the doting Caliban. When Prospero confronts Stephano with his misdeeds, the butler admits he would have made a poor king and is pardoned.

Steward

A minor character in *All's Well that Ends Well*, the Steward whose name is given as Rynaldo in the cast list, manages the household of the Countess of Rousillon. He has observed that Helena is in love with Bertram and tells his mistress so. The Countess reproaches the Steward for allowing Helena to leave Rousillon and free Bertram from his marriage to her but the Steward says there is nothing he could have done to stop her.

Steward (Flavius)

A character in *Timon of Athens*; there is some uncertainty among scholars as to whether Shakespeare intended the character of Flavius and the Steward to be one and the same but it is generally assumed that they are. The Steward is Timon's servant who remains loyal to his master to the bitter end. He foresees the financial ruin that lies ahead of Timon and is aware that it is Timon's excessive generosity that is the cause of his bankruptcy, and tries to warn his master that his friends are unlikely to help him out of trouble. The Steward visits Timon is his self-imposed exile in the woods and although he is rebuffed by Timon at first, his master eventually recognizes that his Steward is the only honest friend he has. The Steward is the one character who is not changed by money and his belief in the ultimate goodness of Timon's nature is in contrast to Timon's own belief that human nature is rotten to the core.

stock character

A character type which embodies particular and well-defined characteristics such as a cunning servant, a jealous husband or a heroic prince. Romeo exemplifies many of the stock characteristics of a typical Elizabethan melancholic lover, while Hamlet has some of the attributes of the stock hero of a REVENGE TRAGEDY. The word 'stock' character derives from a permanent REPERTORY company in a theatre, known as a 'stock company'.

Strangers

Minor characters in *Timon of Athens*, the Strangers, one of whom is called HOSTILIUS, witness one of the crucial events of the play and comment on it, providing an independent view of Timon's generosity. They are present when Lucius, one of the hypocritical lords, refuses to help Timon with a loan and they condemn his ingratitude.

Strange's Men

An Elizabethan company of players. It is thought that Shakespeare himself may have acted with them and that he may have written *King Henry IV, Parts One and Two* for them to perform. This travelling company began to establish itself in London between 1580 and 1592, playing at court and at the Curtain and Rose theatres. The company was reorganized in 1594 and most of its members, probably including Richard BURBAGE and Will KEMP joined the newly formed LORD CHAMBERLAIN'S MEN.

Stratford-Upon-Avon

A town on the River Avon in Warwickshire, in central England, and the birthplace of William Shakespeare. It was founded in the early 14th century by the Bishop of Worcester and became a thriving market town. It has changed remarkably little since Shakespeare's time despite two serious fires in 1594 and 1595, and now has a population of some 25,000 people. Stratford was often visited by companies of touring players in Shakespeare's time: between 1573 and 1587 twenty-three travelling companies came to the town, and it is now the home of the ROYAL SHAKESPEARE COMPANY. It is a mecca for the thousands of visitors who come each year to see the Shakespearean sites, including Shakespeare's birthplace in Henley Street; New Place, the house where Shakespeare spent his retirement; his mother, Mary Arden's house in nearby Wilmcote, and the cottage in the village of Shottery where Shakespeare courted his future wife, Anne Hathaway. The grammar school where Shakespeare was almost certainly educated cannot be visited as it is still in use as a school.

Strato

A minor character in *Julius Caesar*, Strato is a solider in Brutus's army. Brutus asks him to help in his suicide after the battle of Philippi and when Octavius and his army arrive, Strato tells him that Brutus has taken his own life as an honourable alternative to capture. Octavius, who held Brutus in respect, asks Strato if he will now enter his service.

stress

An emphasis or accent which is put on a syllable in spoken language. In the word 'poetry', for example, the stress falls on the first syllable. In verse, it is the ordered pattern of weak [unstressed] syllables (shown as˘ in scansion) and stressed syllables (shown as ‾) that creates a particular rhythm such as that of IAMBIC PENTAMETERS in blank verse.

sub-plot

Part of the action of a play that exists as a separate entity from the main plot. Its function sometimes is to mirror the main action of the play. In *King Lear* for example, the central narrative concerns the story of Lear and his daughters while the sub-plot concerns the fate of Gloucester, whose story reflects Lear's own.

sub-text

An element in a work which may not be immediately obvious and which lies beneath the surface of a character's behaviour. An example of a sub-text in *King Richard III* is the King's bitterness about his deformity.

Suffolk, Duke of

A historical figure (d. 1545) and a character in *King Henry VIII*, the Duke of Suffolk is one of Henry's courtiers who opposes Wolsey. Honest and straightforward, Suffolk accuses Wolsey of such greed and ambition that the Cardinal has even arranged to have the image of his cardinal's hat to be stamped on the coins of the realm. Suffolk has an informal relationship with the King, playing cards with him until the early hours of the morning, but their friendship is threatened when Suffolk, with some misgivings, joins other nobles accusing the King's ally Cranmer of heresy and threatening him with imprisonment in the TOWER OF LONDON.

Suffolk, Earl of

A historical figure (1396-1450) and character in *King Henry VI, Parts One and Two*. In *Part One*, Suffolk is a supporter of the Lancastrian King Henry against the House of YORK but, a devious politician, he has ambitions of his own. Suffolk takes the French Margaret of Anjou prisoner. He strikes a bargain with Reignier, Margaret's father, in which Margaret will become Henry's wife and Queen of England while Reignier will be guaranteed certain French territories. Pretending to be loyal to the King, Suffolk woos Margaret on behalf of Henry and falls in love with her himself. When the royal marriage is agreed upon, Suffolk announces his intention of manipulating both the Queen and the Young King for his own purposes.

In *Part Two*, Suffolk presents Henry with his new bride, Margaret. Still scheming for his own ends, he plots to disgrace Gloucester by setting a trap for the Duke's wife, Eleanor, who reveals her own treacherous ambitions for power through her husband. In quick succession, Suffolk accuses the blameless Duke of Gloucester of treason, arrests him and has him murdered. Grief-stricken at the loss of his old friend Gloucester, the young King Henry banishes Suffolk. On the journey into exile, Suffolk's ship is seized by pirates and he is killed. *See* WHITMORE, WALTER.

Sugarsop
A minor character in *The Taming of the Shrew*, Sugarsop is one of Petruchio's servants. *See* SERVANTS AND SERVINGMEN.

Surrey
In *King Richard III*, the name of King Richard's horse, 'White Surrey', killed in battle at Bosworth.

Surrey, Duke of
A historical figure (1374-1400) and a minor character in *King Richard II*, the Duke of Surrey comes to the defence of the Duke of Aumerle who is accused by Lord Fitzwater of having a hand in the murder of the Duke of Gloucester. Surrey challenges Fitzwater to single combat.

Surrey, Earl of[1]
A historical figure (1381-1415) and a minor character in *King Henry IV, Part Two*, the Earl of Surrey is a supporter of the King.

Surrey, Earl of[2]
A historical figure (1443-1524) and a minor character in *King Richard III*, Surrey is one of Richard's general's at the Battle of Bosworth.

Surrey, Earl of[3]
A historical figure (d. 1544) and a minor character in *King Henry VIII*, the Earl of Surrey is the Duke of Buckingham's son-in-law, sent to Ireland by the Cardinal so that he cannot raise support for Buckingham against Wolsey's false accusations of treason. Surrey is an unrelenting enemy of Wolsey, and is delighted to hear news of his downfall.

Surveyor
A minor character in *King Henry VIII*, the Surveyor [manager of the Duke's estates] is not mentioned in the cast list but he appears in the scene of Buckingham's trial, and gives evidence against Buckingham. The reason for his treachery, as Queen Katherine reveals, is that the Surveyor was dismissed from his post because of complaints made against him by the Duke's tenants. The historical Surveyor, was in fact the Duke of Buckingham's cousin, Charles Knyvet.

suspension of disbelief
A phrase coined by the English poet and literary critic, Samuel Coleridge (1772-1834), who wrote of: 'That willing suspension of disbelief for the moment, which constitutes poetic faith'. He was describing our imaginative acceptance of a fiction or a drama, which we know is not actually true.

Sussex's Men
A company of actors in Shakespeare's time, founded by the Earl of Sussex in 1572 when he became LORD CHAMBERLAIN. The company performed regularly at Queen Elizabeth I's court for the next ten years. In 1593, Sussex's Men were superseded at court by the Queen's own company of players, the QUEEN'S MEN. In 1594, they played for the theatrical entrepreneur, Philip HENSLOWE in London, and performed *Titus Andronicus* as part of their repertory of plays. It is possible that Shakespeare acted with Sussex's Men at the beginning of his theatrical career, and that he wrote *Titus Andronicus* specially for them.

Swan, The
One of the largest public Elizabethan PLAYHOUSES at Bankside, London, the Swan was built in 1594. It was funded by Francis Langley, a London goldsmith, and the LORD CHAMBERLAIN'S MEN may have been the first company to play there. It was closed three years later by the city authorities following the presentation of a comedy, *The Isle of Dogs* by Ben Jonson and Thomas Nashe, which was deemed to be 'very seditious'. The players, who subsequently leased the theatre from Langley, were members of PEMBROKE'S MEN and some of their number including Ben Jonson were briefly imprisoned. The theatre was never officially reopened and it appears to have been used thereafter for various spectacles including the exhibitions of prize fighters. In 1596 Johannes DE WITT, a Dutch visitor to London drew an illustration of the interior of the Swan which gives an idea of the design of a typical Elizabeth Playhouse with its circular structure, APRON STAGE and tiered galleries. De Witt describes the Swan as seating 3,000 people.

Swan, The
A theatre in Stratford-upon-Avon, belonging to the ROYAL SHAKESPEARE COMPANY, which was built in 1986 inside the shell of what remained of the old Memorial Theatre that burned down in 1926. The Swan mainly stages plays from the 16th to the 18th century.

Swan of Avon, The
A name for Shakespeare coined by Ben JONSON in his Memorial Ode 'To the Memory of Shakespeare' whom he referred to as the 'sweet swan of Avon'.

syllable
A unit of sound in a word which contains a vowel sound; for example, 'ham' has one syllable and 'Hamlet' has two.

symbol
Something that is traditionally used to represent something else, which may either be an object, a person or an idea or quality; for example a crown can symbolize monarchy, white can denote purity. The symbol may be either something abstract or an object and

it is usually something which has particular, sometimes subtle, associations with the person or thing it represents. *Compare* METAPHOR; METONYMY; SYNECDOCHE.

synaesthesia
The way in which two or more senses can perceive a single object; for example, a colour that is something *seen* can be described as being 'loud' which is something *heard*. Synaesthesia is a form of IMAGERY.

synecdoche
A part of something that is used to represent that entire thing; for example, if someone says they have hungry *mouths* to feed, they actually mean hungry *people*. *Compare* METONYMY.

synonym
A word, or phrase which means almost the same as another word. For example, evil is synonymous with wickedness, virtue with goodness. *Compare* ANTONYM

syntax
The ordering of words in phrases and sentences governed by the rules of grammar in any language

Tt

tableau
A momentary stage picture created by a posed group of silent and motionless actors.

Taborer (Timothy)
A minor, non-speaking part in *The Two Noble Kinsmen*, the Taborer plays the drum (a tabor) for the Morris dancers who perform for Duke Theseus. *See* COUNTRYMEN.

Tailor and Haberdasher
Minor characters in *The Taming of the Shrew*, the Tailor and the Haberdasher are commissioned by Petruchio to make a beautiful dress and a cap for Katherina. As part of his plan to demonstrate how hateful Katherina's shrewish [bad-tempered] behaviour is, Petruchio rejects both gown and cap and sends the Haberdasher and the Tailor packing. He promises in a whispered aside that he will pay the Tailor nonetheless.

Talbot, John
A minor character in *King Henry VI, Part One*, John Talbot is the son of Lord Talbot (*see below*) who dies alongside his father in battle. Before his death, Lord Talbot grieves over John's dead body.

Talbot, Lord
A historical figure (c. 1388-1453) and a character in *King Henry VI, Part One*, Talbot is a professional soldier, a courageous patriot who serves his country and who alone among the nobles is not involved in stratagems to gain power. He inspires his troops and represents all that is best of England in the play, in opposition to Joan La Pucelle who is made to represent the weakness and immorality of the French. Talbot is captured and ransomed during the war but never daunted. He dies in battle when reinforcements fail to reach him in time as a result of the rivalry of Somerset and York. Betrayed by those on his own side, Talbot's death marks the beginning of a period of turmoil for England.

The Taming of the Shrew
One of Shakespeare's early comedies, written during the early 1590s, although there is some scholarly debate as to the exact dating. A play entitled *The Taming of A Shrew*, was known to have been performed in 1594 and published in a 'BAD' QUARTO edition in the same year, but it may either have been an earlier play from which Shakespeare's version derived, or an early version of his own work. *The Taming of the Shrew* proper, was first published in the First FOLIO of 1623 and printed from Shakespeare's FOUL PAPERS. The tale of the shrewish [sharp-tempered] wife is common to folklore, but the source of Bianca's story was an English version of an Italian comedy (*I Suppositi*, written by Ludovico Ariosto in 1509), entitled *Supposes* (1573), by George Gascoigne (c. 1530-77).

The play, set in Padua in Italy, revolves around a battle of the sexes in which men, apparently, come out the winner. However, it is important to read the play in the context of life in Shakespeare's time in which a wife was the property of her husband. It is also important to realize that the play is concerned with the growth of its central character because she is loved.

SYNOPSIS : In the Induction [introduction], Christopher Sly, a tinker, is discovered in a drunken stupor by a Lord and his hunting party who decide to play an elaborate trick on Sly. They take him home, surround him with luxuries and persuade him that he is a nobleman who has been mad for fifteen years. He is provided with a 'wife', really the Lord's page dressed in women's clothing, with whom he watches a company of travelling players perform *The Taming of the Shrew*.

In the play within a play, Baptista, a rich gentleman, has two daughters, Bianca who is sweet-natured and has a string of admirers, and Katherina whom no one will marry because of her reputation for being shrewish [sharp-tempered]. Baptista insists that Bianca must remain single until Katherina has found a husband. Lucentio, newly arrived in Padua, catches sight of Bianca and immediately falls in love with her. He disguises himself as a schoolmaster and under the pretence of teaching her Latin he wins her love. Baptista is greatly relieved when Petruchio, a rich, if apparently eccentric bachelor, announces that he will marry Katherina because she is rich. He seems unperturbed by her volatile temperament and carries her off to his country house, and sets about taming her. His technique is to behave as shrewishly as his wife; he sends back meals without eating them, hurls food at his servants, and prevents Katherina from sleeping at night. He intersperses his perverse behaviour with frequent references to Katherina's, sweet disposition until Katherina is thoroughly confused. Katherina and Petruchio return to Padua where they find that Lucentio, has outwitted his rivals, and secretly married Bianca. At a celebratory banquet, Petruchio and Lucentio make a bet as to which of their wives is the most obedient. Surprisingly, Katherina, now thoroughly 'tamed' and in love with her husband, obeys him instantly while the apparently submissive Bianca, who also loves her husband, refuses on the grounds that it is inappropriate to make a silly bet about her obedience.

Tamora

A character in *Titus Andronicus*, Tamora is the wicked Queen of the Goths. She has been captured by Titus, and brought to Rome together with her three sons and her lover, Aaron. Her eldest son Alarbus is killed, sacrificed to appease the spirits of Titus' dead sons, and Tamora swears vengeance. The Emperor, Saturnius, marries Tamora who continues to meet Aaron in secret. Tamora and Aaron frame Titus' sons for murder. She gloats when they are beheaded for the crime, and watches, pitiless, while her own sons rape and mutilate Titus' daughter, Lavinia. Tamora tells her weak and frightened husband that she will prevent an invasion that Titus' son, Lucius, is mounting against him. Disguised as 'Revenge', a spirit from Hell, she visits Titus, whom she believes insane, and suggests a way he can be revenged on his enemies. Titus sees through her disguise, and realizes that she is hatching a murderous plot against him. He kills her sons and cooks them in a pie which is served up to her at a feast. After she has eaten the pie, Titus tells her of its contents and kills her.

Tarlton, (Tarleton) Richard (d. 1588)

A famous comic actor in Shakespeare's time who played with the QUEEN'S MEN. He was noted for his ability to EXTEMPORIZE and may have been the subject of Hamlet's comment about clowns who 'speak more than is set down for them'. It is also possible that the Yorick referred to in Hamlet was based on Tarlton, who was one of the Queen's private jesters. It was said that he made her laugh so much on one occasion that she had to command him to leave the royal presence. Tarlton eventually fell into disgrace, however, for making jokes about the Queen's favourite courtier, LEICESTER.

Tarus (Taurus)

A minor character in *Antony and Cleopatra*, Tarus is a lieutenant-general in Caesar's army. At the Battle of Actium he is ordered by Caesar not to attack on land until the sea battle is won.

Tate, Nahum (1652–1715)

An English dramatist and poet who is only remembered now for his idiosyncratic adaptations of Shakespeare's plays, including a rewriting of *King Lear* with a happy ending. Tate's version was immensely popular and completely ousted Shakespeare's own text between 1681 and 1823 until the original was restored by Edmund KEAN. In Tate's version, Cordelia is widowed and marries Edgar; under their rule, harmony and order are restored in Britain and Lear lives with them into happy old age.

Tearsheet, Doll (Dorothy)

A comic character in *King Henry IV, Part Two* and *King Henry V*, Doll Tearsheet is Falstaff's hard-drinking, vulgar, lover. Her name suggests that she is a prostitute; Doll was a name often given to prostitutes in Shakespeare's time and 'Tearsheet' implies that she is active between the sheets. Although she is continually cursing and swearing at him, Doll is warm-hearted and genuinely fond of Falstaff. In *Henry IV, Part Two*, she is heartbroken when he has to leave to join the King's army. Doll's violent nature is her undoing. Charged together with Mistress Quickly for being involved in a murder, she is hauled off and thrown into prison.

The Tempest

Shakespeare's last romantic comedy, a TRAGI-COMEDY, *The Tempest* was written around 1610-1611 and was almost certainly one the first of Shakespeare's plays to be performed at the private BLACKFRIARS THEATRE soon after. It was played at court for King James I by the KING'S MEN in 1611 and formed part of the festivities for the marriage of his daughter Princess Elizabeth in 1613. It was first published in the First FOLIO of 1623. There is no known source for the plot, but it was written at a time of great interest in the exploration of the New World, and Shakespeare may have been influenced by accounts of those on board the *Sea Venture*, who were shipwrecked off the Bermudas on a voyage to America in 1609, and who landed safely on an island. Shakespeare was also influenced by the essays of Michel de Montaigne (1533-92), in particular one, translated into English in 1603, entitled 'Of Cannibals', in which he describes an ideal community in the newly discovered America.

The play is set on an imaginary island and includes magical tableaux, ghostly apparitions and music. It explores themes of social order, the supernatural, and the relationship between man and his so-called civilized world of art and learning, and the natural world, personified by the philosopher Prospero and the savage Caliban. Some 20th-century critical scholarship has commented on a relationship between *The Tempest* and colonialization and the institutionalized slavery of later generations. As in all of Shakespeare's comedies, there is a happy ending which results in reunion and reconciliation.

SYNOPSIS : Twelve years before the beginning of the play Prospero was Duke of Milan. His brother, Antonio, took advantage of Prospero's preference for philosophy over affairs of state and seized the dukedom for himself, aided by Alonso, King of Naples. Prospero and his three-year-old daughter Miranda were cast adrift in a boat and miraculously survived, washed up on the shores of a deserted island. The only inhabitants were the brutish Caliban, orphan son of the witch Sycorax, and Ariel, a spirit whom Prospero rescued from imprisonment by Sycorax in a tree. Ariel serves Prospero out of gratitude for his freedom while Caliban, who is at first treated with kindness by Prospero, is made to be his unwilling slave after an attempt to rape Miranda. Prospero uses his magic powers to call up a violent storm at sea in which all his old enemies are shipwrecked on the island's shores. Ferdinand, son of Alonso King of Naples, is washed up on Prospero's part of the island where he falls immediately in love with Miranda and she with him. On another shore, Alonso and his treacherous brother Sebastian, together with Prospero's wicked brother Antonio, search for Ferdinand. While Alonso mourns the loss of his son, Sebastian and Antonio are plotting to kill him and take his crown. Nearby, two other survivors of the shipwreck, Trinculo, a jester, and Stephano, a drunken butler, are plotting to kill Prospero and rule the island aided by Caliban who, under the influence of drink, comes to regard Stephano as a god. Prospero, who is aware of what is going on in his domain, uses his magic powers and with the help of Ariel brings everyone under his control. In a happy resolution of forgiveness and reunion, Prospero frees Ariel and blesses the marriage of Miranda and Ferdinand. He breaks his magic wand in two and throws his book of magic into the sea.

Terry, Dame Ellen (Alice) (1847–1928)
A Shakespearean actress who belonged to a large theatrical family and began her career on the stage at the age of eight, playing the part of the boy Prince Mamillius in *The Winter's Tale*. Among her greatest successes were the parts of Portia and Ophelia, characters she endowed with charm and sympathy; she played opposite Henry IRVING in many Shakespearean roles in London and America.

tetralogy
A series of four plays which are connected by a common theme. Shakespeare wrote two historical tetralogies: the first group consisting of *King Henry VI, Parts One, Two and Three* and *King Richard III* and the second comprising *King Richard II, King Henry IV, Parts One and Two*, and *King Henry V*. The common themes of these plays are the struggle for the English throne, the problems of kingship and the cycle of political order and disorder that characterized that particular period of English history.

Thaisa
A character in *Pericles*, Thaisa is Pericles' wife and Marina's mother. When Pericles arrives in Pentapolis, Thaisa is choosing a husband from one of the hopeful knights who

have come to court her. When she sees Pericles she falls in love with him on sight
although, dressed in rusty armour, he is outwardly less desirable than her other suitors.
Thaisa resolutely refuses to marry anyone other than Pericles and her father, King
Simonides, finally agrees. Thaisa gives birth to Marina in a storm at sea and is believed
to have died. She is cast overboard in a sealed box which is washed up at Ephesus,
where she is revived and cared for by Cerimon. Believing her husband and baby
daughter are lost to her, she vows to remain chaste for ever and joins the temple of the
goddess Diana (goddess of chastity). She is eventually reunited with Pericles and
Marina after Diana has appeared to Pericles in a dream.

Thaliard
A minor character in *Pericles*, Thaliard is a lord at the court of King of Antiochus.
When Pericles discovers that Antiochus has an incestuous relationship with his daughter
he leaves Antioch in disgust. The King orders Thaliard to follow Pericles to Tyre and
kill him. Thaliard feels duty bound to carry out the King's orders, but reluctant to
commit murder. He is relieved when he hears that Pericles has left Tyre and he can
pretend to Antiochus that his enemy has died at sea.

Theatre, The
The Theatre, built in 1576-77 by James BURBAGE, was the first purpose-built public
playhouse in London since Roman times. Circular in design, it was a wooden structure,
sited just outside the City of London, in Moorfields near Shoreditch. The location was
carefully chosen so that the LORD CHAMBERLAIN'S MEN, who leased it, could perform
plays there without having to seek permission from the City Fathers (*see* CENSORSHIP)
who would often prohibit performances. The Theatre was pulled down in 1598 and its
timbers were taken across the river Thames to form part of the new GLOBE THEATRE.
See PLAYHOUSES.

theatre in the round
The production of a play where the audience is seated in a circle around the stage, or
area in which the play is enacted. The performance usually takes place on the same level
as the audience is seated, for example on the floor rather than on a raised stage. Theatre
in the round, which creates a sense of intimacy that is similar to the Elizabethan
experience, has become increasingly popular in the 20th century.

theatres
See PLAYHOUSES.

Thersites
A legendary figure and a character in *Troilus and Cressida*, Thersites is a friend of
Achilles and a jester, who Achilles says is a privileged man. He mocks and insults the
Greek commanders who he says are fools, and pops in and out of the action, peppering
the characters with his bitter and vicious comments. Thersites is an unashamed rogue
who declares himself a bastard by birth and by nature. He is cynical about the world in
general and about the war in particular, but Thersites' role is also that of the FOOL who
sees clearly the follies of war.

Theseus[1]
A legendary figure and a character in *A Midsummer Night's Dream*, Theseus is a Greek
hero, the Duke of Athens and ruler of the city. Theseus and Hippolyta are about to

marry and plans for the wedding celebrations are being made. Theseus is a just but unbending head of state. Called upon to mediate between Egeus and his daughter Hermia over the matter of her marriage, Theseus advises Hermia to obey her father on pain of death. He softens towards the lovers in the end and decrees that their wedding shall take place alongside his own, and that the revels shall last for a fortnight.

Theseus[2]

A legendary figure and a character in *The Two Noble Kinsmen*, Theseus, Duke of Athens, is a warrior prince. About to marry Hippolyta, Theseus' wedding is interrupted by three widowed Queens imploring his help in burying their husbands, who have died fighting Creon, the tyrannical King of Thebes. Theseus nobly postpones his marriage to make war on Thebes. The Athenians are victorious and Palamon and Arcite, two Theban kinsmen, are captured by Theseus. A model of chivalry, he orders his prisoners to be given the best possible care, and later commutes Arcite's life sentence to one of banishment from Thebes. Theseus presides over the tournament in which the kinsmen fight for Emilia's hand. He sternly rules that the loser must die, but only because he realizes that it would be impossible for Palamon and Arcite ever to live in peace together. Theseus recognizes that human beings are the playthings of the gods, and must accept what fate decrees.

Thidias

See THYREUS.

Thomas, (Peter) Friar

A minor character in *Measure for Measure*, Friar Thomas helps the Duke disguise himself as a friar. Later the same character, but now called FRIAR PETER, assists the Duke to expose Angelo; he brings Isabella and Mariana before the Duke to give their evidence against Angelo.

Three Unities

See UNITIES.

thrust stage

See APRON STAGE.

Thurio

A minor character in *The Two Gentlemen of Verona*, Thurio is Valentine's foolish rival for Silvia's love, whom Silvia's father intends her to marry. Proteus pretends to help Thurio to woo Silvia, but Thurio's feelings are not seriously engaged and when Valentine challenges him to fight for Silvia's hand he beats a hasty retreat.

Thyreus

A minor character in *Antony and Cleopatra*, Thyreus is one of Caesar's followers and his messenger. After Antony's defeat at the Battle of Actium, Thyreus is sent by Caesar to make a peace treaty with Cleopatra. Cleopatra agrees to Caesar's terms but Antony arrives just as Thyreus is kissing her hand and, in a jealous rage, Antony commands Thyreus to be taken away and soundly whipped. In the First FOLIO and other early editions, Thyreus was called THIDIAS. This was the name Shakespeare originally gave to the character, but later editors of the plays substituted Thyreus as this was the name given by PLUTARCH (Shakespeare's source for the play) to a historical figure who was Caesar's representative.

Tilney, Sir Edmund (d. 1610)
The MASTER OF THE REVELS at Queen Elizabeth's court who held office from 1579 until his death. He was responsible for supervising entertainments for the Queen and for censoring and licensing plays for public performance.

Timandra
A minor comic character in *Timon of Athens*, Timandra is Alcibiades' mistress. Timandra and Phrynia (another mistress), together with Alcibiades, visit Timon in his self-imposed exile in the woods. Timon hurls insults at Timandra and Phrynia, calling them a pair of 'harlots', and they answer in kind before greedily taking the gold he offers them.

Time
The CHORUS in *The Winter's Tale* who introduces the pastoral section of the play at the beginning of Act IV. He tells the audience that sixteen years have passed since the preceding scene.

Time, Unity of
See UNITIES.

Timon
The title character of *Timon of Athens*, Timon is a rich Athenian, surrounded by flattering friends to whom he is extravagantly generous. His kindness, however, is double-edged; Timon expects his friends to be equally bountiful, and he is bad at repaying money he owes to them. Like Lear, Timon lacks insight; he cannot distinguish between his true friends and those who exploit him. When all his money has been spent, and his so-called friends have failed him, he becomes filled with hate. He holds a final banquet and serves up bowls of warm water, telling his guests to lap at their supper like the dogs they are. Timon becomes a hermit, and when digging for roots to eat he discovers gold. News of his new-found wealth travels and he is visited by some of his fortune-hunting friends, and the scum of society. He curses everyone and tries to corrupt them with the gold. Not even the loyalty of his faithful Steward or his one friend Alcibiades can comfort Timon. Filled with despair, he crawls into a cave and dies.

Timon of Athens
One of Shakespeare's late plays written around 1605, and a TRAGEDY; many scholars believe that Shakespeare never properly completed *Timon of Athens* and that he may have written it in collaboration with someone else. It was first published in the First FOLIO edition of 1623 in a version which is full of textual errors and almost certainly based on Shakespeare's original script (see FOUL PAPERS). There is no record of a performance in Shakespeare's lifetime; the first recorded performance was an adaptation of the play entitled *The History of Timon of Athens, the Man-hater* in 1678.

The main source for the play was PLUTARCH'S *Lives of Greeks and Romans*. The play, set in Athens in Ancient Greece explores the way in which wealth can affect friendship and examines the nature of love, and extremes of behaviour.

SYNOPSIS : Timon, a rich Athenian, is a man of extravagant generosity who showers his friends with gifts and entertains them lavishly. Only his faithful Steward, Flavius, and his servants are aware that the money is running out. Finding himself bankrupt, Timon confidently expects that his friends will lend him the money he needs. When they all refuse, he suddenly changes from a kindly benefactor to a bitter hater of mankind and goes to live as a hermit in a cave in the woods. Digging for roots to eat, he discovers gold and it is not long before news of his new-found wealth spreads. He is visited by thieves and prostitutes and by some of his former friends, all of whom he curses and insults. He presses gold on them in the hope that it will corrupt and destroy them. His loyal Steward, Flavius tries to help Timon who recognizes, too late, that Flavius is his honest friend. He too is sent away with gold but told he must never give a penny of it away, even to help the starving. The ruling Senators of Athens come to plead with Timon to return to the city, which is in danger of invasion; they promise him absolute power, but Timon refuses. The city of Athens is threatened by Alcibiades, Timon's only other true friend. Like Timon, Alcibiades has been in exile, banished by the Senators for daring to question their methods of justice. Alcibiades wants revenge, but he is persuaded by the Senators to make a peaceful entrance, and to punish only his personal enemies and those who have wronged Timon. News arrives that Timon has died of despair in his cave. Alcibiades laments Timon's death, and vows to make Athens a humane state where each individual acts for the general good of society at large.

tireman

In Shakespeare's time, a tireman was a member of a company of players who was responsible for the costumes and the PROPS, and also for the lighting in the private PLAYHOUSES such as the Blackfriars theatre. *See also* LIGHTING.

tiring-house

Part of an Elizabethan playhouse, the tiring-house was a curtained area at the back of the stage through which the players could make their entrances and exits. It was also used as a dressing room, an 'attyring house', and an INNER STAGE. *See* PLAYHOUSES.

Titania

A character in *A Midsummer Night's dream*, Titania is the Queen of the fairies and Oberon's wife. Titania and Oberon are involved in a quarrel about a young Indian boy, a CHANGELING, whom Titania has adopted and whom Oberon wants to have as his page. Their argument is so intense that it is affecting the weather but Titania, jealous and proud, refuses to give up the boy. In revenge, Oberon casts a spell on Titania which makes her fall in love with the first thing she sees on waking. Unfortunately for Titania she falls for the mortal Bottom whose head Puck has changed into an ass's head. She is absurdly devoted to her ass, and lavishes every luxury upon him until she is released from the spell. Thereupon, she happily makes peace with Oberon and joins with him in blessing the marriages of the mortals.

Titinius

A minor character in *Julius Caesar*, Titinius is a friend of Cassius and an officer in Cassius and Brutus's army. At the battle of Philippi, Titinius is sent to discover whether the approaching troops are friends or enemy forces. Cassius is wrongly informed that Titinius has been taken prisoner and believing that he too may be captured and disgraced, Cassius kills himself. When Titinius returns, he is shocked to find Cassius dead and kills himself with Cassius's sword.

Titus

A minor character in *Timon of Athens*, Titus is a servant of one of Timon's creditors. He presents a bill to Timon for the money owed to his master but is angrily turned away without being paid.

Titus Andronicus

The title character of *Titus Andronicus*, Titus is a military hero and an honourable man. He returns triumphant to Rome after defeating the Goths whose captive queen, Tamora, swears vengeance on him when he has her son killed. Her revenge is terrible. Titus' two sons, are framed for a murder and beheaded; his daughter, Lavinia, is raped and mutilated, and Titus is tricked into cutting off his own hand, supposedly as a ransom for his son's lives. Titus is nearly driven mad with grief and the shame that Lavinia's rape has brought on her and the family. Family honour is important to Titus, who killed his own son Mutius for trying rescue Lavinia from an arranged marriage, and in the bloody dénouement, he kills Lavinia to save her from living with her shame. Titus' real tragedy, however, is that he becomes as murderous and vengeful as his enemies. He kills Tamora's sons and in a cruel and macabre gesture cooks them in a pie which he serves up to Tamora before killing her. Titus, who has had his revenge, is killed by Saturnius.

Titus Andronicus

One of Shakespeare's ROMAN PLAYS and an early TRAGEDY, *Titus Andronicus* may have been written around 1593, or possibly as early as 1589. It was first published in a QUARTO edition in 1594 and possibly first performed in the same year (some scholars argue for a first performance as early as 1590) and was a great favourite with Elizabethan audiences. Over the centuries there has been a great deal of dispute among scholars as to whether Shakespeare wrote *Titus Andronicus* in collaboration with another dramatist. Some are reluctant to believe that Shakespeare could have written such an unremittingly cruel play with its multiple revenge killings, but it is important to remember that in Shakespeare's time the REVENGE PLAY, which was horrifically violent and bloodthirsty, was enormously popular with audiences.

A possible source for the play is a lost play entitled *Titus and Vespesian*, which was certainly performed in 1592, but the plot seems to have been largely Shakespeare's own invention, although it is evident that he was influenced by the gruesome works of the SENECA. The play, set in Ancient Rome, begins like Shakespeare's HISTORY PLAYS with a dispute about a new ruler and ends with a new order in Rome. It explores themes of extreme cruelty, including mutilation and cannibalism.

SYNOPSIS : The hero Titus returns to Rome in triumph after defeating the Goths. He is popular with the people, but he refuses the honour of being made Emperor, in favour of Saturnius, the late emperor's son. Titus has captured Tamora, Queen of the Goths, with her three sons, and he insists on the ritual sacrifice of her eldest son, Alarbus, to appease the spirits of his dead sons. Tamora vows to avenge Alarbus' death. She marries Saturnius, and aided and abetted by her lover the wicked Moor Aaron, sets out to destroy Titus. Aaron frames Titus' sons, Quintus and Martius, for murder and although Titus is tricked into cutting off his own hand in order to ransom them, they are beheaded. Titus' daughter Lavinia is seized by Tamora's sons, Chiron and Demetrius. Her husband is killed in front of her, and she is raped and horribly mutilated. They cut off her hands and cut out her tongue so that she cannot write or speak the names of her attackers. Titus, nearly mad with grief, becomes as vengeful as his enemies and orders his son Lucius and his brother Marcus to right the wrongs done to their family. Lucius raises an army of Goths to march on the Emperor Saturnius and depose him. Saturnius panics, but Tamora assures him that she will be able to persuade Titus to call off the attack. Disguised as 'Revenge', an evil spirit from Hell, she urges Titus to invite his enemies to a banquet where they will all be at his mercy. She, meanwhile, plans to kill Titus and Lucius. Titus sees through her disguise and her plan. He kills her sons, cooks them in a pie and serves it up to her at the banquet. When he has told her that she has eaten the flesh of her own sons, Titus kills Tamora and is immediately killed by Saturnius. Lucius kills Saturnius and is hailed as Rome's new emperor.

Titus Lartius
A character in *Coriolanus*, *see* LARTIUS, TITUS.

Topas
The name adopted by Feste in *Twelfth Night* when he disguises himself as a clergyman come to comfort Malvolio who has been locked up as a lunatic.

Touchstone
A comic character in *As You Like It*, Touchstone is a FOOL at the court of Duke Frederick, and a faithful servant and friend to Celia. When Celia and Rosalind go to live in the Forest of ARDEN, Touchstone accompanies them, willing to share their hardships. Touchstone's name derives from an Elizabethan word which described something that could be used to test the genuineness or value of anything else. Touchstone tests the world by poking fun at it, and his witty fooling loses nothing of its sharpness in the romantic world of Arden. He mocks Orlando's love poems with his own bawdy versions of them, and ridicules Corin and Rosalind's lovesickness. However, Touchstone himself falls in love with the plain Audrey, whose kindness and honesty he values, although claiming that his romance has more to do with lust than love.

Tourneur, Cyril (c. 1570/80–1626)
A soldier, diplomat and playwright, author of the blank verse REVENGE TRAGEDY *The Revenger's Tragedy* (1607) which was probably performed at the GLOBE THEATRE. The play owes much to *Hamlet*; in it, the hero is spurred to avenge the death of his mistress, using her skull which is poisonous as the agent of death. He poisons her murderer and then himself by kissing the skull's lips.

Tower of London
A castle in London built in the 11th century for use as a military base. By the 15th century, the Tower had become a huge complex and was used both as a royal residence, a military store, and a prison housing political prisoners. They often lived there in quite reasonable comfort but all too few emerged alive. The Tower is mentioned in several of Shakespeare's plays. In *King Henry VI*, the King is killed there and in *King Richard II* the King is condemned to the Tower (although he dies elsewhere). In *King Richard III*,

the Tower takes on a particularly sinister aspect. It is there that Richard's brother and his two nephews, the little Princes, are murdered.

tragedian
An actor or actress (tragedienne) who principally plays the central parts in tragedy.

tragedy
A serious and usually moral work, written in an elevated style, in which the outcome is a sad one, and which is principally concerned with the suffering and conflict experienced by its hero. Tragedy usually ends in the death of the central character, which results as much from some fatal flaw in his nature as from external events.

In the Middle Ages, 'tragedy' simply meant the downfall of a person of high degree, from happiness to grief. At the time Shakespeare was writing, tragedy was being influenced by Classical scholarship, in particular by works such as the *Poetics*, written in the 4th century BC by the Greek philosopher ARISTOTLE, who regarded tragedy as the highest form of poetry. The tragedies of Greek Classical drama originated in religious festivals, and portrayed noble heroes caught between the workings of the gods, and their own tragic flaws or weaknesses.

Elizabethan tragedy was also influenced by the plays of the 1st century Roman philosopher, Seneca, who established tragedy as a distinct form, with five acts that built up to a dramatic climax. SENECAN TRAGEDY with its themes of revenge was often horrifically bloodthirsty, though much of the violence was enacted offstage. *Gorboduc* (c. 1565), written in blank verse, was the first Senecean tragedy to be performed in England. The popular revenge tragedies of KYD, and the historical tragedies of MARLOWE, though modelled on the Classical tradition, burst with action and a new narrative energy.

Shakespeare's tragedies are psychological as well as moral dramas. His heroes, although men of importance, are complex characters who engage our sympathies as ordinary, flawed human beings and their downfall often affects the welfare of the society around them. At the core of the play is a conflict between the opposed forces of good and evil; in *Hamlet* the conflict is between the hero and Claudius, but the conflict also exists within Hamlet's soul.

Shakespeare was the first dramatist to include interludes of comedy in his tragedies. He wrote twelve tragedies which were first categorized as such in the First FOLIO edition of 1623; His best known are *Hamlet, King Lear, Macbeth,* and *Othello. See also* ARISTOTLE.

tragi-comedy
A work which is a combination of tragedy and comedy which contains serious elements but always has a happy ending. Shakespeare wrote several plays which can be categorized as tragi-comedies and which are sometimes referred to as his PROBLEM PLAYS: *All's Well That Ends Well, Measure for Measure, The Merchant of Venice,* and *Troilus and Cressida,* and the romances *Cymbeline, Pericles* and *The Tempest.*

tragic irony
A situation in which a character is unaware of the possible tragic consequences of an action, although these may be clear to the audience. An example is Othello's belief that his wife Desdemona is unfaithful, which the audience knows is unfounded.

Tranio

A central character in *The Taming of the Shrew*, Tranio is Lucentio's cunning servant whose character derives from the stock character of the HARLEQUIN of the COMMEDIA DELL'ARTE. It is Tranio's idea that Lucentio should disguise himself as the schoolteacher CAMBIO in order to woo the beautiful Bianca. Tranio is to take his master's place, and as he is well educated and speaks Latin, he is quite able to pass himself off as a gentleman. Pretending to be Lucentio, Tranio convinces Bianca's father that he is an eligible suitor, but he is told that he must have his father's permission before he can marry her. Tranio persuades a passing school teacher to impersonate his/Lucentio's father but nearly gets caught out when Lucentio's real father appears on the scene. Resourceful as ever, Tranio wriggles out of trouble.

travelling players

See ACTORS AND ACTING

Travers

A minor character in *King Henry IV, Part Two*, Travers is a follower of the Earl of Northumberland and one of the rebels fighting against King Henry.

Trebonius

A minor character in *Julius Caesar*, Trebonius is one of the conspirators against Caesar who is present when Caesar's assassination is planned. On his way to the Capitol and his death, Caesar asks Trebonius to be near him and Trebonius mutters under his breath that Caesar's friends will soon wish he had not been so near.

Tressel

A minor character in *King Richard III*, Tressel is a gentleman attending on Lady Anne.

trilogy

A series of three works which are connected by a common theme; for example Shakespeare's *King Henry VI, Parts One, Two and Three. Compare* TETRALOGY.

Trinculo

A comic character in *The Tempest*, Trinculo is Alonso's jester who is shipwrecked on Prospero's magic island in the storm, and separated from his companions. He takes shelter under the sleeping Caliban's cloak where he is discovered by the drunken butler Stephano. The unlikely trio band together and under the influence of large quantities of sack [sherry] they plot to kill Prospero and to take control of the island. Trinculo lacks Stephano's bravado and is quite content to take orders from him, calling him 'King' and flattering him in a comic imitation of life at court.

triumvirs

A triumvir is one of three rulers of the Roman Empire in *Antony and Cleopatra*. The 'triumvirate' consists of Antony, Caesar and Lepidus.

trochee

A stressed syllable followed by an unstressed one such as in 'Hamlet'.

Troilus

A legendary figure and the title character of *Troilus and Cressida*, Troilus is the son of
Priam, King of Troy and a young warrior. Weary of war, and pining for love of Cressida
whom he admires from afar, Troilus asks her uncle, Pandarus to arrange a meeting.
Troilus and Cressida fall in love but are soon parted when Cressida is handed over to the
Greeks. The lovers are heartbroken and promise to remain true to one another. Troilus
tells Diomedes, Cressida's Greek guardian, to treat her well, on pain of death, but he is
hurt and angry when he discovers that Cressida has allowed herself to be seduced by
Diomedes. Fuelled by his jealousy, and in defence of his own and Troy's honour, he
seeks out Diomedes and fights with him. Diomedes wins the fight and adds insult to
injury by sending Troilus' horse to Cressida as proof that he is the better man. At the
end of the play, Troilus, concerned with the fate of Troy now that Hector is dead, vows
to avenge his death.

Troilus and Cressida

One of Shakespeare's PROBLEM PLAYS, written around 1600-02, *Troilus and Cressida*
is difficult to categorize as either a tragedy, a comedy or a history play, or even a
SATIRE. It was first published in a QUARTO edition in 1609 and in the First FOLIO
edition of 1623 it was called a 'history'. It is thought possible that the play was written
for a particular private audience, perhaps the lawyers at the INNS OF COURT. *Troilus and
Cressida* was probably first performed publicly at the Globe Theatre by the LORD
CHAMBERLAIN'S MEN in 1603.

 Main sources for the play were Homer's *Iliad* translated into English by George
Chapman (c. 1566-1634) and *Troilus and Criseyde* by the English writer Geoffrey
Chaucer (c. 1345-1400). The play, set during the siege of Troy (*see* TROJAN WAR),
satirizes the glamour of war and explores themes of honour and dishonour, social and
moral order, and passing time; there are frequent references to disease.

SYNOPSIS : The Greek army is laying siege to the city of Troy to avenge the
capture of the famously beautiful Helen by the Trojan prince Paris. Within the walls
of Troy, Troilus admires Cressida from afar. Her sly uncle, Pandarus arranges a
meeting and the two fall instantly and passionately in love. The Trojan leaders
argue about whether they should return Helen to the Greeks and put an end to this
lengthy war. They decide to keep Helen, and the Trojan warrior Hector challenges
the Greek hero Achilles to single combat. Camped outside the walls of Troy,
Achilles is sulking and refusing to fight. The Greek commanders, angered by
Achilles' disregard for authority which has weakened the Greek fighting force,
manage to spur him into action by appealing to his vanity. They tell him that they
have chosen Ajax, another warrior, to fight Hector instead of him. Cressida's father
Calchas, a Trojan priest who has deserted to the Greeks, has made an arrangement
with them to return Cressida to him in exchange for a Trojan prisoner and the lovers
part, swearing to be faithful to one another. Diomedes, a Greek prince, is sent to
fetch Cressida and although she would like to be true to Troilus, Diomedes wins her
over and seduces her. Troilus, who has followed her, witnesses the moment when
she gives Diomedes a sleeve which he had given her as a keepsake when they
parted. Hurt and angry he promises to be avenged. Achilles is eventually stung into
action following the killing of his friend Patroclus by Hector. Achilles and Hector
fight, and although Hector proves the stronger he is finally killed by a treacherous

Achilles who chooses a moment when Hector is defenceless to surround him with his armed men. Pandarus rounds off events with a bitter EPILOGUE about the state of the world.

Trojan War
During the reign of Priam, King of Troy, in the 13th century BC, Priam's son Paris captured the famously beautiful Helen from her husband Menelaus of Sparta (an ancient Greek city state). To avenge the rape of Helen, the Greeks laid siege to Troy for nearly ten years before they finally overran the city. The ancient city of Troy was in Asia Minor, part of present-day Turkey. Its Latin name is ILIUM. Part of the story of the Trojan war is told in the *Iliad* by the Ancient Greek poet, Homer who lived in the 8th century BC.

Tubal
A minor character in *The Merchant of Venice*, Tubal is a Jewish friend of Shylock. He acts as a messenger telling Shylock about Jessica's extravagance in Genoa after her elopement with Lorenzo, and brings the more welcome news of the loss of Antonio's merchant ships at sea.

Tudor
The name of a Welsh dynasty, founded in the 15th century by Owen Tudor who married Catherine de Valois, the widow of King Henry V of England. Their son, Edmund, married a descendant of the Lancastrian John of Gaunt and the dynasty became a royal one when Edmund's son, Henry Tudor, Earl of Richmond, seized the crown from Richard III and declared himself King Henry VII in 1485. He in turn was succeeded by his son HENRY VIII (1509-1547), Edward VI (1547-53) and Mary I (1553-58). The childless Queen Elizabeth I (1558-1603) was the last Tudor monarch.

Shakespeare was at pains always to show the Tudor monarchy in a favourable light in his plays in order to flatter Queen Elizabeth, and justify the Tudors' position on the throne. It was important to demonstrate the moral and political legitimacy of Henry VII's somewhat flimsy claim to the crown, and his seizure of it from Richard III. See the table of kings and queens in the Supplement.

Tullus Aufidius
A character in *Coriolanus*; *see* AUFIDIUS, TULLUS.

Tutor to Rutland
A minor character in *King Henry VI, Part Three*, the Tutor is with Rutland when he flees from the Battle of Wakefield. He tries unsuccessfully to prevent Clifford from killing the boy.

Twelfth Night: or What You Will
One of Shakespeare's late comedies, written around 1599-1600 and first published in the First FOLIO edition of 1623, *Twelfth Night* was probably first performed in 1601.

Principal sources of the play were the story of *Apolonius and Silla* in *Farewell to Militarie Profession* by the soldier and writer Barnabe Riche (c. 1549-1617) and a version of an earlier short story by François de BELLEFOREST (1530-83). The play explores themes of delusion and disguise and different kinds of love.

SYNOPSIS : Identical twins, Viola and Sebastian, are shipwrecked on the shores of Illyria. They are separated and each thinks the other is dead. Viola, intrigued by a romantic story she hears surrounding Duke Orsino, disguises herself as a boy and calling herself 'Cesario', enters the Duke's employment as his page. Orsino is in love with Olivia and instructs Viola/Cesario to court her on his behalf. Unfortunately, Olivia falls violently in love with Viola/Cesario, while at the same time Viola is falling in love with her master, Orsino. A farcical situation develops and becomes increasingly complex when Sebastian appears on the scene and is mistaken by everyone for his twin sister. Olivia, believing he is Cesario, easily persuades Sebastian into getting married and angers Orsino as a result. In a happy resolution, Viola's identity is revealed and she and Sebastian are reunited. Orsino realizes that it is Viola whom he truly loves and they are married.

A comic subplot centres on members of Olivia's household, Sir Toby Belch, Sir Andrew Aguecheek, Maria and Feste. They have a long-running quarrel with the PURITAN Malvolio, Olivia's self-important and disapproving steward. They contrive his downfall in a plot involving a forged letter, apparently written by Olivia, inviting him to make love to her. His subsequent behaviour is so bizarre that he is treated as if he were a lunatic, and locked up. When Malvolio is eventually released, he swears vengeance on everyone.

The comedy in Shakespeare's time would have been heightened by the fact that the actor playing Viola would actually have been a boy, who was acting the part of a girl playing a boy.

Two Gentlemen of Verona, The

One of Shakespeare's early comedies, possibly his first, written sometime between 1590 and 1595 and first published in the First FOLIO edition of 1623. *The Two Gentlemen of Verona* was presumably performed during Shakespeare's lifetime, but there is no recorded performance until as late as 1762.

The source for the play was *La Diana Enamorada*, a Spanish romance by Jorge de Montmayor (c. 1521-61) to which Shakespeare added the comic characters of Speed and Launce. The play explores themes of love, friendship and betrayal.

SYNOPSIS : Two young gentlemen of Verona, Valentine and Proteus, are friends. Valentine wants to see the world and leaves for Milan, while Proteus, in love with Julia, remains behind until ordered by his father to go to Milan too. The lovers exchange rings as keepsakes, and when Proteus departs, Julia dresses as a boy 'Sebastian', and follows him in secret. When Valentine and Proteus meet again, Valentine has fallen in love with Silvia but her father, the Duke, intends her to marry Thurio. As soon as Proteus sees Silvia, he too is captivated by her and although he keeps his feelings hidden, Proteus is determined to win her for himself. Silvia and Valentine plan to elope but Proteus betrays them to the Duke who banishes Valentine. With the field clear, Proteus pays court to Silvia and when Julia/Sebastian arrives, unrecognizable in her guise as a boy, she overhears Proteus declaring his love for Silvia. Julia enters Proteus' service as his page and acts as a messenger between the lovers. Proteus asks 'Sebastian' to take a ring to Silvia as a token of his love; the ring is the very one that Julia had given to Proteus as a parting gift. Silvia scorns Proteus and leaves to rejoin Valentine. Accompanied by

Julia/Sebastian, Proteus pursues Silvia and rescues her from a band of outlaws, who earlier had captured Valentine and made him their leader. When Proteus demands Silvia's hand in marriage as his reward and threatens to rape her when she spurns him, Valentine steps in and curses his friend for his treachery. Proteus, full of remorse begs forgiveness, which Valentine willingly gives and even says he will give up Silvia for friendship's sake. Julia faints when she hears this and when she recovers and reveals her identity, Proteus suddenly realizes he truly loves her. In a happy resolution to the story, the Duke pardons the outlaws and blesses the marriage of Valentine and Silvia.

Two Noble Kinsmen, The

One of Shakespeare's late plays, a TRAGI-COMEDY, *The Two Noble Kinsmen* was almost certainly a collaborative effort between Shakespeare and the dramatist FLETCHER, although scholars argue as to how much of the play Shakespeare actually wrote. Written in 1613-14, it was first published in a QUARTO edition in 1634 with Shakespeare's and Fletcher's names on the title page. The play was probably first performed in 1613.

The source for the play (*see* PROLOGUE), a romance about chivalry and honour, is the *Knight's Tale* by Geoffrey Chaucer (1345-1400), itself a version of a Greek legend. Set in Athens and Thebes, the play explores themes of male friendship and rivalry, and chivalric honour.

SYNOPSIS : At his wedding, three Queens beg the Athenian Duke Theseus for help. Their husbands have died fighting the Theban army of the tyrannical King Creon, but Creon refuses to allow the widows to bury their dead. Theseus nobly postpones his wedding to go to war with Thebes; the Athenians are victorious and the Queen's husbands are buried with due ceremony. In the fighting, Palamon and Arcite, two young Thebans friends and cousins, are wounded and captured. They were proposing to leave Thebes when war broke out, but stayed to defend their country. In prison, Palamon and Arcite are well cared for by the Jailer and his Daughter. They long for freedom but console themselves up with the thought that locked away from the world, their lives will at least be virtuous ones. They are sure they will be sustained by their indestructible friendship. However, glancing out of their prison window they see the beautiful Emilia below, and both fall instantly in love with her. All earlier protestations of affection for one another are forgotten, and they become deadly rivals from that moment on. Arcite is freed from jail and banished from Thebes. In disguise he distinguishes himself, wrestling in the May Day games in Athens, admired by Emilia who takes him into her service. Palamon languishes in jail, but the Jailer's Daughter, who has fallen in love with him, helps him to escape. He pursues Arcite, intent on fighting him to the death but they are interrupted by Duke Theseus. It is decided that Palamon and Arcite must fight a duel, arranged and overseen by the Duke. The winner shall marry Emilia; the loser will die. Emilia waits in anguish to hear the outcome of the fight. Arcite wins, but just as Palamon lays his head on the executioner's block, news comes that Arcite is dying after a fall from his horse. With his dying breath, Arcite gives Emilia to Palamon, who loses his friend but gains a wife. See morris dancing.

Tybalt

A character in *Romeo and Juliet*, Tybalt is Juliet's cousin and a member of the Capulet family . The fiery Tybalt is always spoiling for a fight. At the masked ball he is only prevented from drawing his sword on Romeo by Capulet's intervention. The following day, Tybalt tries again to pick a fight with Romeo who, now that marriage to Juliet has made him Tybalt's cousin-in-law, refuses to be provoked into violence. Mercutio steps in to defend his friend Romeo's honour and when Tybalt kills him, Romeo at once retaliates, killing Tybalt. His death is the pivotal event in the middle of the play that leads to Romeo's banishment to Mantua and the subsequent tragedy.

Tyrrel, Sir James

A historical figure (1450-1502) and a minor character in *King Richard III*, Tyrrel is the ruthless nobleman who is instructed by Richard to arrange the murder of the little Princes in the TOWER OF LONDON. When he recounts their deaths to Richard afterwards, Tyrrel expresses remorse for the bloody deed.

Uu

Udall, Nicholas (1505–56)
A scholar and headmaster, Udall was the author of the first real comedy in English, *Ralph Roister Doister*, a verse play with music that was written for and performed by the boys of Eton College c. 1540.

Ulysses
A hero of Greek mythology and a character in *Troilus and Cressida*, Ulysses is a Greek prince who is convinced that war with the Trojans over the return of the beautiful Helen is pointless. The Greeks are losing the war and Ulysses, who is as much a philosopher as a warrior, believes that they have been weakened because society has abandoned the ordered rule ordained by the Heavens. He sees Achilles' defiance of authority as a symptom of this social disorder. Ulysses suggests to the Greek commanders that they should spur Achilles into action by arousing the base instinct of his jealousy rather than appealing to his honour. Ulysses is a voice of sanity in the war but can do little to change events.

Underwood, John (d. 1624)
An actor and a member of the KING'S MEN company of actors who probably joined the company in 1608, Underwood owned shares in the Globe theatre. His name appears as one of the twenty-six men listed as the 'Principall Actors' of Shakespeare's plays in the First FOLIO of 1623.

unities
The three unities of time, place and action were principles of dramatic structure, based on the theories propounded in the *Poetics*, a treatise by the Ancient Greek philosopher ARISTOTLE. The theory of the three unities states that the action of the play should be confined to a single plot (Unity of Action), a time span of a single day (Unity of Time), and a single location (Unity of Place). Shakespeare broke away from these conventions in his plays; in the 17th century, *The Winter's Tale* in particular was criticized for not adhering to the unities, but the 18th-century writer Dr JOHNSON praised Shakespeare for breaking with the tradition.

unstressed
An unstressed syllable is one which has a weak emphasis placed upon it. In the analysis of verse rhythm, it is denoted by the mark˘ written above the syllable. *See* FOOT, METRE, STRESS.

University Wits
The University Wits was a term that was coined in the 19th century. It describes a group of foremost, university educated, Elizabethan dramatists and pamphleteers, who by reason of their education influenced contemporary attitudes to the theatre and asserted

the worth of a profession that had hitherto been regarded as lowbrow and improper. Among their number were Robert GREENE, Thomas NASHE and Christopher MARLOWE.

upstage
A word to describe the rear part of the stage, which may be higher than the front of the stage if there is a RAKE. An actor who stands upstage holds a commanding position; he or she is said to 'upstage' a fellow actor if he draws the audience's attention away at an inappropriate moment.

Ur-Hamlet
A pre-Shakespearean version of *Hamlet* believed to have existed but which has long been lost. *Ur-Hamlet* may have been a REVENGE PLAY by Thomas KYD, entitled *Hamlet,* that was performed by the company of players, the LORD CHAMBERLAIN'S MEN in 1594.

Ursula (Ursley)
A minor character in *Much Ado About Nothing*, Ursula is a gentlewoman who attends Hero. She is a light-hearted young woman who cheerfully plays her part in tricking Beatrice into the belief that Benedick loves her.

Urswick, Sir Christopher
A historical figure (1448-1522) and a minor character in *King Richard III*, Sir Christopher is a supporter of Richmond who acts as a messenger between him and Stanley before the Battle of Bosworth.

Vv

Valentine[1]
A minor character in *Titus Andronicus*, Valentine is mentioned in the cast list as Titus' kinsman [relative]. He plays no part in the action but is present when Tamora's sons Chiron and Demetrius are captured by Titus.

Valentine[2]
A minor character in *Twelfth Night,* Valentine is a gentleman who attends Duke Orsino and acts as a go-between for him in his unrequited suit of Olivia (his name is a suitable one for a messenger of love).

Valentine[3]
The hero of *The Two Gentlemen of Verona* and friend of Proteus, the suitably-named Valentine is a romantic young man who wants to see the world. He travels to Milan where he falls in love with Silvia. The lovers plan to elope but are betrayed by Proteus who has also fallen in love with Silvia. Valentine is banished and seized by a band of outlaws who make him their leader because he is educated and handsome. Silvia, seeking Valentine, is captured by the same outlaws and then by Proteus who demands her hand in marriage as his prize. Valentine confronts Proteus with his treachery but forgives him; he is so unselfish that he even offers to give up Silvia to Proteus. In the final happy resolution the Duke blesses Valentine's marriage to Silvia.

Valeria
A minor character in *Coriolanus*, Valeria is a friend of Coriolanus' wife, Virgilia, and a Roman aristocrat. A talkative young woman, she visits Virgilia and does her best to comfort her in her anxiety over Coriolanus's safety. Valeria cheerfully praises Coriolanus' young son Martius who has been mutilating butterflies. She accompanies Virgilia and Volumnia when they visit Coriolanus to beg him not to invade Rome.

Valerius
A minor character in *The Two Noble Kinsmen*, Valerius is a gentleman of Thebes, and Arcite and Palamon's friend. He tells the Kinsmen, who are planning to leave Thebes, that war with Athens is imminent and that they must stay to fight.

Varrius[1]
A minor character in *Antony and Cleopatra*, Varrius is one of Pompey's followers. He brings Pompey the bad news that Antony is shortly expected to arrive in Rome.

Varrius[2]
A silent minor character in *Measure for Measure*, Varrius is mentioned in the cast list as a gentleman in the Duke's entourage and appears with him.

Varro
One of Timon's creditors in *Timon of Athens*; Varro does not appear in the play but his two SERVANTS make a vain attempt to recover the money owed to their master.

Varrus (Varro)
A minor character in *Julius Caesar*, Varrus is a soldier in Cassius and Brutus's army at Philippi. Brutus orders Varrus and Claudio, to spend the night in his tent before the battle of Philippi in case they are needed to take messages to Cassius. When Caesar's ghost visits Brutus, they cry out in their sleep but neither man actually sees the ghost.

Vaughan, Sir Thomas
A historical figure (d. 1483) and a minor character in *King Richard III*, Vaughan is one of Queen Elizabeth's allies who is executed at Pontefract.

Vaux
A historical figure (d. 1523) and a minor character in *King Henry VI, Part Two*, Vaux brings news of the Cardinal's dying agonies to Queen Margaret.

Vaux, Sir Nicholas
A historical figure (d. 1523) and a minor character in *King Henry VIII*, Vaux escorts the condemned Duke of Buckingham to his execution and arranges for his prisoner to be treated with the dignity due to someone of his rank.

Velutus, Sicinius
A character in *Coriolanus*; *see* SICINIUS, VELUTUS.

Venice, the Duke of[1]
A minor character in *The Merchant of Venice*, the Duke of Venice presides over the court of law in Venice; he hears the case that Shylock brings against Antonio and welcomes Portia to the court in her guise of lawyer. He dispenses justice as the law allows, showing some degree of mercy to Shylock, sparing his life but decreeing that his estate shall be confiscated.

Venice, the Duke of[2]
A minor character in *Othello*, the Duke is the ruler of Venice who appoints Othello as commander in Cyprus. He listens to Brabantio's accusations that Othello has used witchcraft to persuade his daughter Desdemona into marriage and advises him to draw a veil over the past.

Ventidius[1]
A historical figure (c. 90-38 BC) and a minor character in *Antony and Cleopatra*, Ventidius is one of the most loyal of Antony's followers. He successfully puts down a rebellion in Parthia but refuses to pursue the enemy further; he does not want to jeopardize his career by being seen to do more in battle than Antony.

Ventidius[2]
A minor character in *Timon of Athens*, Ventidius is one of the many false friends of Timon who exploit his generosity. When Ventidius is arrested for debt, Timon pays what he owes so that he can be freed. Ventidius subsequently inherits a fortune and offers to repay Timon, who tells him that he paid the debt out of love and as a gift.

When later Timon is in need of money and appeals to Ventidius to help him, Ventidius refuses.

Venus and Adonis
A narrative poem by Shakespeare and dedicated to Henry Wriothsley, Earl of SOUTHAMPTON, *Venus and Adonis* was so popular during Shakespeare's lifetime that it was reprinted eight times. It was probably written during 1592, a year when playwrights were not in demand as London theatres had been closed following an outbreak of the PLAGUE. Shakespeare used as his source *Metamorphoses*, a poem by the Latin poet OVID. The poem is constructed in 199 verses of IAMBIC PENTAMETERS and is a typical exercise in Elizabethan literary conventions.

 The poem recounts the story of Venus's obsessive love for Adonis which, despite the tragic outcome, Shakespeare treats as a romantic comedy.

SYNOPSIS : Adonis, a youth of incomparable beauty, is the object of Venus' keen desire. She tries to seduce him with honeyed words but Adonis, whose enthusiasm for hunting is far greater than his interest in love, is unresponsive. Even Adonis' stallion is more lustful than his master and spying a desirable young mare prances off in pursuit. Adonis, disgusted at losing his mount, continues to resist Venus's entreaties. Venus swoons and Adonis, fearing she has died, tries to rouse her with kisses, but when she revives he protests that he is too young to become her lover and declares his intention to hunt boar the next morning. Venus begs him not to indulge in so dangerous a sport and prophesies his death but Adonis, contemptuous of her love, strides off into the night. The next morning, Venus hears sounds of the hunt and is grief-stricken to discover Adonis dead, killed by the boar. She vows that henceforth love shall be a force for mischief, for suspicion, jealousy and war. Adonis's body melts into the ground and a flower springs up in its place. Venus plucks it and placing it in her bosom is transported up into the skies by silver doves.

Verges
A comic character in *Much Ado About Nothing*, Verges is a headborough [officer of the parish] and Dogberry's enthusiastic second-in-command. An honest, if somewhat dim-witted, old man Verges takes part in the arrest of Borachio and Conrade but is always out-talked by Dogberry.

Vernon
A minor character in *King Henry VI, Part One*, Vernon is a follower of Richard Plantagenet and the house of YORK. He suggests that white and red roses should be the emblems of the supporters of the rival houses of LANCASTER (red roses) and York (white roses).

Vernon, Sir Richard
A historical figure (d. 1403) and a minor character in *King Henry IV, Part One*; loyal to Hotspur, Vernon is one of the rebels fighting against King Henry who gives a vivid description of the approach of the royal forces led by Prince Hal. He is captured in the final battle and sentenced to death.

verse

Verse or poetry is any composition that is written with a recurring pattern of stresses (*see* METRE) and sometimes with a recurring pattern of rhyme. Verse is the oldest form of literature and had been the medium for story-telling and drama long before Shakespeare began to write; even accounts of contemporary events were often told in ballad form and in song. Verse is also a synonym for a STANZA. *See* BLANK VERSE; PROSODY.

Vice

A stock figure from medieval MORALITY PLAYS, Vice was the deceitful and cunning character who attempted to corrupt the hero and to persuade him to become evil. The role of Vice was often a comic one; he openly admitted his villainy to the audience and entertained them with bawdy jokes. In the later morality plays of the 16th century, Vice gradually came to resemble the FOOL. The character of Vice formed the basis for a number of Shakespeare's villains, most notably Richard III who even describes himself as being 'like the formal Vice'.

villain

A central character in a play, the villain is usually in conflict with the hero or heroine, and both embodies and instigates evil of some sort or other; an example is Iago in *Othello*. Richard III, although technically the hero of the play of that name, is also its self-confessed villain whose intentions throughout are entirely malign.

 The word villain derives from 'villein', meaning a low-born peasant, an unprincipled person who is disposed to criminal acts.

Vincentio

A minor character in *The Taming of the Shrew*, Vincentio is a rich citizen of Pisa, a merchant, and Lucentio's father. Lucentio's servant Tranio has persuaded a passing schoolteacher to impersonate Vincentio in his scheme to smooth the way to his master's marriage with Bianca. When the real Vincentio arrives in Padua and goes to Lucentio's house he is startled to find himself accused of being an imposter. Before he is hauled off to prison, Lucentio arrives and explains matters and begs his father's forgiveness.

Vincentio, the Duke

A central character in *Measure for Measure*; *see* DUKE.

Viola

The resourceful heroine of *Twelfth Night* and Sebastian's identical twin sister, Viola is shipwrecked on the shores of Illyria and fears her brother is dead. She hears the romantic story of Duke Orsino's unrequited love for Olivia and, resolving to make the best of her misfortune, disguises herself as a boy called 'Cesario' and enters Orsino's employment as a page. Orsino instructs Viola to court Olivia on his behalf with the unforeseen consequence that Olivia falls in love with 'Cesario'. Viola is the only character to understand the absurdity of her situation when, trapped in her disguise and terrified, she is forced to fight an absurd duel with Sir Andrew Aguecheek, another rival for Olivia's affections. Viola, meanwhile, has fallen in love with Orsino but her love, like her identity, must remain a secret that she can only give voice to in private. When Sebastian unexpectedly appears Viola's true identity is at last revealed and she and Orsino are married.

Violenta
A silent minor character in *All's Well that Ends Well*, Violenta is a friend of the Widow Capilet who is named in the cast list.

Virgin Queen, The
The 'Virgin Queen' was a name given to Queen Elizabeth I who never married.

Virgilia
A character in *Coriolanus*, Virgilia is Coriolanus's wife, whom Coriolanus clearly loves. Virgilia is quiet (Coriolanus refers to her as his 'gracious silence') and a rather nervous person, easily overawed by her dominating mother-in-law, Volumnia. Coriolanus goes off to war and Virgilia is so desperately concerned for his safety that she resolves not to leave her house until he returns. On his return home, she welcomes him with tears in her eyes. Gentle where Volumnia is aggressive, Virgilia successfully begs her husband and father of their son Martius, not to conquer Rome.

Volscians (Volces)
A warrior tribe in *Coriolanus* who, led by Aufidius, make war on Rome. When the Roman soldier Caius Martius conquers the Volscian town of CORIOLI, he is given the name of 'Coriolanus' as a reward for his courage. A Volscian spy named ADRIAN, meets a Roman spy named Nicanor on the road and learns that Coriolanus has been banished from Rome.

Voltemand (Voltimand)
A minor character in *Hamlet*; Voltemand is a courtier who, with Cornelius, is sent by Claudius to the King of Norway to try to prevent the King's nephew Fortinbras from launching an invasion of Denmark. They return with a message of friendship from Fortinbras.

Volumnia
A character in *Coriolanus*, Volumnia is Coriolanus' aristocratic and arrogant mother. Dominating and controlling, she is the power behind Coriolanus whom she has brought up to be a fearless warrior. Volumnia has nurtured Coriolanus' contempt for the common people of Rome which she shares but, ambitious for him to become consul and better able than Coriolanus to compromise, she cynically urges him to play the hypocrite and ask for the people's support with pretended humility. When Coriolanus is preparing to conquer Rome, Volumnia pleads with him to reconsider. She begs him to think of his family's fate and appeals to his pride by pointing out that if he subdues Rome his name will be hated by future generations. It is Coriolanus' tragedy that he yields to his powerful mother; persuaded by her he betrays Aufidius and his fate is sealed.

Volumnius
A minor character in *Julius Caesar*, Volumnius is a soldier in Cassius and Brutus's army and an old school friend of Brutus. After the battle at Philippi, Brutus asks Volumnius to help him to commit suicide but Volumnius says his friendship for Brutus makes it impossible.

Ww

Waiting Woman
A minor character in *The Two Noble Kinsmen*, the Waiting Woman and Emilia are talking together, discussing which flower is the most fitting emblem for virginity, when Arcite and Palamon catch their first sight of Emilia from the prison window.

Walter
A minor character in *The Taming of the Shrew*, Walter is one of Petruchio's servants. *See* SERVANTS AND SERVINGMEN.

Wanamaker, Sam (1919–1993)
An American actor, Sam Wanamaker, visited London in 1949 and was disappointed to find only a bronze plaque on the site of the old GLOBE Theatre. From that moment on he devoted his energies to the creation of a faithful reproduction of the Globe. The project took over forty years to complete but his vision was finally realized when the new Shakespeare's Globe theatre was declared open in 1996.

Wars of the Roses
Thirty years of civil war (1455-85) between two powerful factions and rival claimants to the English throne, the Houses of LANCASTER (whose emblem was a red rose) and of YORK (whose emblem was a white rose). The Wars of the Roses began during the weak rule of the Lancastrian Henry VI (1422-61/71) when Richard, Duke of York made a bid for the crown. He was unsuccessful but was appointed protector during the period of Henry's mental breakdown (1453-54) and again from 1455 to 1456. For the rest of Henry's reign and from 1461-70 and again from 1471-83, when Edward IV (son of the Duke of York) was on the throne, the wars continued with periodic but bitter fighting and brutal executions. The thirteen-year-old King Edward V acceded to the throne in 1483 and when later that year he died in suspicious circumstances with his brother in the Tower of London, his uncle Richard III took the throne. The Wars of the Roses ended on the field of Bosworth where Richard III, the last Yorkist king, was killed, making way for Henry VII to establish the new TUDOR dynasty. The Wars of the Roses form the background to Shakespeare's plays *King Henry VI Parts One, Two and Three* and *King Richard III* and are foreshadowed in a fictitious scene in *King Henry VI, Part One* when Richard Plantagenet, soon to be Duke of York, picks a white rose while Somerset for the House of Lancaster chooses a red one.

Wart, Thomas
A minor comic character in *King Henry IV, Part Two*, the aged Wart is one of the simple villagers whom Falstaff recruits for the army. Wart is pitifully thin and dressed in tatters and Falstaff at first rejects him as being too decrepit. However, when he is running out of suitable candidates for his army, Falstaff finally enlists Wart and gives him a sixpence.

Warwick, Earl of[1]

A historical figure (1382-1439) and a minor character in *King Henry IV, Part Two* and *King Henry V*, Warwick is loyal to the crown. In *Henry IV, Part Two*, Warwick is the King's adviser who defends Prince Hal to his father assuring him that he will reform.

In *Henry V*, Warwick fights in France for the King and is present at the Battle of Agincourt.

Warwick, Earl of[2]

A historical figure (1428-1471) and a character in *King Henry VI, Parts One, Two and Three*; in fact Shakespeare combines two separate historical Earls of Warwick to create the character in his own version of history.

In *Part One* the Earl of Warwick declares his loyalty to Richard Plantagenet. He takes a white rose as a sign of his support and presents a petition to King Henry urging the King to restore the title of Duke of York to Richard. A professional soldier, Warwick nonetheless shows some degree of sympathy towards Joan La Pucelle when she is condemned to be burned to death.

In *Part Two*, Warwick, the Earl of Salisbury's son, expresses his grief at the loss of territories in France and vows to win the lands back for England. Father and son, whose family name is NEVIL, confirm their allegiance to the Duke of York and his cause and York promises to make Warwick the greatest man in England when he is King. Warwick fights for York with distinction at the Battle of St Albans and celebrates their famous victory.

In *Part Three*, Warwick becomes the mainstay of support for Edward and Richard after their father the Duke of York has been killed. When Edward is crowned King, Warwick is sent to France to arrange a marriage between Edward and the French King's sister-in-law, Bona, which will cement a political union and further secure Edward's position on the throne. In Warwick's absence, Edward hastily contracts a marriage at home with Lady Grey and when Warwick learns of this he is so angry at Edward's casual treatment of the French and his own diplomacy, that he immediately abandons his support for Edward and joins King Henry's cause instead. It is a lost cause, and Warwick is eventually killed in battle.

Watchmen

Three comic characters in *Much Ado About Nothing*, named Hugh Oatcake, George Seacole and Francis Seacole - the latter being the only one who can read and write. They are recruited by Dogberry who instructs them on how to carry out their duty as night watchmen. They are a dim-witted trio but nonetheless they manage to arrest Borachio and Conrade for their part in framing the innocent Hero and the Watchmen's testimony against the villains is crucial in clearing Hero's name.

Webster, John (c. 1580–c. 1634)

An actor and playwright who collaborated with fellow dramatist Thomas DEKKER in writing comedies, Webster is better known for his tragedies, for example the REVENGE PLAYS *The White Devil* (c. 1608) and the *Duchess of Malfi* (c. 1614).

Welsh Captain, A

A minor character in *King Richard II*; *see* CAPTAIN.

Westminster, the Abbot of
A minor character in *King Richard II*; *see* ABBOT OF WESTMINSTER.

Westmoreland, Earl of[1]
A historical figure (1364-1425) and a character in *King Henry IV, Parts One and Two* and *Henry V*; in *King Henry IV, Part One,* Westmoreland is a military leader and a loyal supporter of King Henry and his role is a minor one. In *Part Two*, Westmoreland remains strongly loyal to the King. He supports Prince John when he pretends to make peace with the rebels and later arrests the rebel leaders for treason.

In *Henry V*, Westmoreland is a supporter of the King and a courageous leader of the English army at the Battle of Agincourt. He knows that the English are outnumbered by the French but believes it an honour to fight for his country no matter what the cost.

Westmoreland, Earl of[2]
A historical figure (c. 1404-1484) and a character in *King Henry VI, Part Three*, Westmoreland is a member of the House of LANCASTER. He is a supporter of King Henry who is angered by the King's decision to bequeath the throne to the Duke of York rather than to his own son and heir.

'W H, Mr'
The initials of an unknown man to whom the 1609 QUARTO edition of Shakespeare's sonnets are dedicated. The dedication reads: 'To the onlie begetter of these ensuing sonnets Mr. W. H. all happiness and that eternity promised by our ever-living poet the well-wishing adventurer in setting forth'. The identity of 'Mr W H' has never been established. He may be William Herbert, Earl of Pembroke, to whom the First FOLIO edition of Shakespeare's plays was dedicated, or Shakespeare's patron HENRY WRIOTHSLEY, EARL OF SOUTHAMPTON (but why reverse the initials H W?). One argument (though not necessarily a convincing one) against either of these men being the dedicatee is that it would seem strange to address an earl as 'Mr'. Another candidate is SIR WILLIAM HERVEY who it is sometimes suggested asked Shakespeare to write the sonnets in the hope of persuading the Earl of Southampton to marry. The playwright Oscar Wilde (1854-1900) held the theory that 'Mr W H' was a fellow actor of Shakespeare, WILLIAM HUGHES, but it is also possible that the 'onlie begetter' of the poems may simply have been the go-between, a London printer who obtained the sonnets for the publisher, whose name was WILLIAM HALL. It has even been proposed that the initials may have stood for WILLIAM HATHAWAY, Shakespeare's brother-in-law or, even less likely, for 'William Himself'. There is speculation that the relationship between Shakespeare and Mr W H may have been a homosexual one.

Whately, Anne
The name of a mysterious, so far unidentified woman who appears in the Stratford marriage records of 1582 as the bride of one William Shakespeare on the same day as the registration of Anne Hathaway and Shakespeare's licence to marry. Registered as living at Temple Grafton, near Stratford, Anne Whately may indeed have existed or it is possible that, given the vagaries of Elizabethan spelling, the clerk entered the name of Anne Hathaway in the records in a transposed form as 'Whately'.

Whitefriars
A district of the City of London off Fleet Street, which in Shakespeare's was a notoriously rough area. It took its name from the Whitefriars monastery.

Whitefriars Theatre
A private playhouse in Shakespeare's time, built in 1608 on the site of the Whitefriars monastery in the City of London. The Whitefriar's Theatre was established by Michael DRAYTON as a venue for the CHILDREN OF THE KING'S REVELS, but was never as successful as its rival the BLACKFRIARS THEATRE and fell into disuse after 1621.

Whitmore, Walter
A minor character in *King Henry VI, Part Two*, Whitmore is an avenging pirate whose first name, 'Walter', would have been pronounced 'water' in Shakespeare's time. He captures and kills Suffolk, so fulfilling a prediction that Suffolk will die by water.

Widow
A minor character in *The Taming of the Shrew* who marries Hortensio. Hortensio had hoped to marry Bianca but, disappointed in love, he turned to the rich Widow instead. Hortensio is confident that he can manage his new wife as well as Petruchio manages his, but she turns out to be as disobedient a character as the unreformed Katherina.

Widow Capilet (Capulet)
A minor character in *All's Well that Ends Well*, the Widow Capilet keeps the inn in Florence where Helena stays. She tells Helena that she comes from a good family but that she has fallen on hard times. The Widow is worried about her daughter, Diana, who is being courted by Bertram. She has no illusions about Bertram's motives and willingly helps Helena in her plan to substitute herself for Diana in bed. The Widow's willingness may have something to do with the fact that Helena offers her a considerable sum of money for her assistance.

Wife
A minor character in *King Henry VI, Part Two*, the Wife is married to the imposter Simpcox. *See* SIMPCOX.

William
A minor comic character in *As You Like It*, William is a CLOWN, a rustic figure and a man of few words who dotes on Audrey the goatherd in the Forest of ARDEN. He is sent packing by Touchstone who threatens to kill him, before he can speak more than a few words.

Williams, Michael
A minor character in *King Henry V*, Williams is a soldier in the King's army fighting in France. On the eve of the Battle of Agincourt he argues with the disguised King Henry, whom he does not recognize, as to the rightness of England's war with France. The King and Williams agree to fight it out later and exchange gloves, each promising to wear them in their hats as identification. After the battle, the King notices Williams but gives the identifying glove to Fluellen and sends him to fight in his place. Just as Fluellen and Williams are about to fight, King Henry appears and explains matters. He pardons Williams for disagreeing and fills his glove with money.

Willoughby, Lord

A minor character in *King Richard II*, Lord Willoughby is one of the nobles who support Bolingbroke. When John of Gaunt dies and King Richard seizes the dead man's assets to finance his war in Ireland, the nobles no longer trust the King and Willoughby, together with Lord Ross and the Duke of Northumberland, joins Bolingbroke's rebellion.

Winchester, Bishop of; later Cardinal Beaufort

A historical figure (1374-1447) and a character in *King Henry VI, Parts One and Two*: in *Part One* Winchester is politically ambitious. Throughout the play he quarrels with the Duke of Gloucester, Protector of the Kingdom during King Henry's childhood, who accuses him of neglecting his religious duties. Their quarrel begins at the funeral of Henry V and becomes so bitter that their retainers fight in the street. When King Henry tries to broker a peace between them, Winchester publicly agrees to a truce while privately declaring his intention to ignore it. The Bishop of Winchester crowns Henry King at Paris.

In *Part Two*, Winchester is known as CARDINAL BEAUFORT. He schemes with Suffolk to bring about the downfall of his old enemy the Duke of Gloucester and when Gloucester's wife is arrested for witchcraft they accuse the old Duke of conspiring with her in a bid for power. Gloucester is disgraced but the Cardinal and Suffolk want him permanently out of the way and the Cardinal offers to hire a murderer. Suffolk actually commits the murder but the Cardinal is stricken by a sudden illness and his deathbed ravings reveal a guilty conscience.

wings

Areas to the side of a modern stage which are hidden by the PROSCENIUM ARCH and through which actors make their entrances and exits.

Winter's Tale, The

One of Shakespeare's later plays, a TRAGI-COMEDY, which was written around 1609-10; it was first published in the First FOLIO edition of 1623, the last play in the Comedy section. *The Winter's Tale* was probably first performed at the GLOBE THEATRE in 1611 and the KING'S MEN are known to have put on the play as part of the celebrations for the wedding of the Princess Elizabeth in 1613.

The principal source of the play was *Pandosto, or the Triumph of Time* (1588), a romantic novel by Robert GREENE. Shakespeare added some new characters, including the comic Autolycus, and gave the play a happy ending. The play explores the themes of jealousy, redemption and the effect of passing time.

> SYNOPSIS : Polixenes, King of Bohemia is visiting his childhood friend King Leontes in Sicily. Polixenes is due to return home but Leontes begs him to stay longer. When Hermione, Leontes' wife, echoes his request Leontes suddenly erupts into a passion of insane jealousy and accuses her of having an affair with Polixenes. Leontes makes plans to poison his old friend and orders Camillo to carry out the murder but Camillo warns Polixenes and the two of them flee to Bohemia. Leontes has Hermione thrown into prison where she gives birth to a daughter, Perdita, whom Leontes rejects and orders to be abandoned in some deserted place. Antigonus takes the infant princess to Bohemia and leaves her on the shore where

she is discovered by a shepherd who takes her home and brings her up as his own. Leontes is told by the Oracle that Hermione is innocent but when he hears that his son Mamillius and Hermione are dead he suddenly realizes how he has wronged Hermione and falls into an anguish of remorse.

The middle section of the play, a PASTORAL comedy, takes place in Bohemia sixteen years later. Perdita has grown into a beautiful young woman and is being courted by King Polixenes' son Florizel who, believing Perdita is a simple shepherdess, is wooing her in disguise. Polixenes forbids Florizel to marry Perdita, so they sail to Sicilia where they are welcomed by Leontes who eventually discovers that Perdita is his daughter and blesses their marriage. Leontes is shown a 'statue' of Hermione by her companion Paulina. He is unaware that Paulina has been caring for Hermione in secret during the intervening years and is astonished when the 'statue' (who is the real live Hermione) apparently comes to life. In the happy resolution to the play, Leontes is reunited with Hermione and reconciled with his old friend Polixenes.

wit

The modern meaning is 'sharp humour'; in Shakespeare's day *wit* meant intelligence.

For example, Sir Andrew Aguecheek's comment in *Twelfth Night*:

> 'I have no more wit than a Christian or an ordinary man has: but I am a great eater of beef, and I believe that does harm to my wit'.

Witches

The three supernatural and sinister sisters in *Macbeth* who establish an atmosphere of evil at the opening of the play and who fatally inspire Macbeth's murderous ambitions. They hail Macbeth as Thane [chieftain] of Cawdor (a title that he is soon to possess) and foretell among other things that he will become King of Scotland. When Macbeth is crowned King, he seeks out the witches to ask them how he can safeguard his position. They summon up ghostly apparitions who promise that Macbeth can only be harmed by someone not born of a woman and that he will be safe until Birnam Wood moves to Dunsinane castle. Although these predictions seem impossibilities they actually describe Macbeth's eventual destruction.

In HOLINSHED'S *Chronicles*, the source for the plot of *Macbeth*, the supernatural apparitions that appear to Macbeth are described as fairylike. Shakespeare may have turned them into the malign and ugly witches of his play in order to please James I of England who felt strongly about the evils of witchcraft and wrote a treatise on it.

Wolsey, Cardinal

A historical figure (c. 1475-1530) and a character in *King Henry VIII*, Shakespeare's Wolsey is presented from the outset as a man of greed, pride, and ruthless political ambition; a 'holy fox' who has a 'witchcraft over the King'. His power is such that he raises taxes in the King's name, but without informing the King, and has Buckingham arrested and condemned on a trumped-up charge of treason. Wolsey opposes Henry over the royal marriage, adamant that the King shall not marry Anne Bullen. His enemies conspire against him, and when the King discovers the extent of Wolsey's deceit and his personal wealth, he is made to return the great seal of his office, and retire from the court. Denied power, Wolsey is humbled, and his life becomes one of genuine penitence and meditation; he dies regretting that he did not serve God better.

Wolsey is a character who, in the view of the people of Shakespeare's Protestant England, embodies everything that was bad about Roman Catholicism, and his malign influence over Henry serves to free the King himself from blame.

women actors
In Shakespeare's time women were forbidden by law to perform in public, they only acted in MASQUES and other such private entertainments. It was not until 1660, when King Charles II was restored to the throne and the theatres in England were reopened, that women appeared on stage. It is probable that the first professional actress to appear on the London stage was Mrs Margaret Hughes (d. 1719), who took the part of Desdemona in *Othello* in December 1660. *See also* ACTORS AND ACTING.

Wooden O, The
The name given by the Chorus at the beginning of *King Henry V* to the circular, wooden theatre building, probably the GLOBE THEATRE, in which the play was originally performed.

Woodville
A minor character in *King Henry VI, Part One*, Woodville is Lieutenant of the TOWER OF LONDON who is instructed by the Bishop of Winchester to refuse entry to the Duke of Gloucester.

Wooer
A character in *The Two Noble Kinsmen*, a friend of the Jailer, the Wooer loves his Daughter and hopes to marry her. When the Jailer's Daughter, who loves Palamon, is driven mad with grief at losing him, the faithful Wooer does his best to help her recover her wits. On the suggestion of the Doctor, the Wooer pretends to be Palamon, patiently courting the Daughter, and granting her every wish. The Wooer's devotion is rewarded; the Daughter is reported recovered, and about to marry.

Worcester, Earl of, Thomas Percy
A historical figure (1343-1403) and a minor character in *King Henry IV, Part One*, Worcester is Hotspur's uncle and one of the original plotters of the rebellion against King Henry. When the King tries to make peace, Worcester deliberately fails to tell his fellow rebels of the King's terms. He is captured at the battle of Shrewsbury and sentenced to death.

Worcester's Men
A company of actors in Shakespeare's time, originally formed under the patronage of the Earl of Worcester, Worcester's Men toured the provinces between 1555 and 1585 and visited Stratford several times during Shakespeare's youth. They took over another company, OXFORD'S MEN, in 1602 and became established as one of the foremost theatre companies in London playing at the ROSE theatre for Philip HENSLOWE. In 1605, King James I's wife, Anne, became their patron and, as the Queen Anne's Men, they played at the RED BULL theatre until 1619.

Wriothsley, Henry
See SOUTHAMPTON, EARL OF.

Wyatt, Thomas (c. 1503–1542)
A courtier and poet who translated some of the sonnets of PETRARCH from Italian into English and, subsequently adopting the form for his own poetry, was responsible for introducing the SONNET form to England.

Xx Yy Zz

Yorick
In *Hamlet*, the name of the King of Denmark's jester. Hamlet discovers Yorick's skull in the graveyard and recalls how Yorick played with him as a child. It is possible that Yorick was based on Richard TARLTON, who was one of the Queen's private jesters.

York, Archbishop of
A character in *King Henry IV, Parts One and Two*; *see* SCROOP, RICHARD.

York, Archbishop of
A historical figure (1423-1500) and a minor character in *King Richard III*, the Archbishop of York is a friend of Queen Elizabeth who offers to help her to sanctuary.

York, Duchess of[1]
A historical figure (1355-1393) and a minor character in *King Richard II*, the Duchess of York is married to the Duke of York to whom Richard hands over the reins of power while he is away fighting the war in Ireland. The Duchess discovers that her son, the Duke of Aumerle, is conspiring against the life of Bolingbroke, newly crowned King Henry IV. She pleads with Henry to pardon her son and spare his life.

York, Duchess of[2]
A historical figure (1415-1495) and a minor character in *King Richard III*, the Duchess of York is the mother of Richard and his brothers Edward IV and Clarence. She recognizes that her son Richard is a villain.

York, Duke of[1], Edmund Langley
A historical figure (1341-1402) and a character in *King Richard II*, the Duke of York is a respected elder statesman and the King's uncle. He is critical of the way Richard is ruling England, but he faces the dilemma of many characters in Shakespeare's history plays: the problem of the DIVINE RIGHT OF KINGS. York believes that any crime against the King is a crime against God so he remains loyal to Richard despite doubts as to his ability to govern the country. Richard goes to the war in Ireland and asks York to manage the country during his absence. When Bolingbroke returns from exile and seizes Richard's crown, York reacts angrily but he is unable to stop the tide of events and, as a true patriot, he feels obliged to transfer his allegiance to the new King of England. Loyal now to the new King Henry, York discovers that his son, the Duke of Aumerle, is conspiring with others against the king and is the first to denounce him.

York, Duke of[2]
A historical figure (1373-1415) and a minor character in *King Henry V*, the Duke of York is a supporter of the King; a courageous soldier who asks to be allowed to lead the army, he is killed at the Battle of Agincourt. The same character appears in *King*

Richard II, an earlier play, but before he has been given the title of Duke of York; in *Richard II*, he is known as the Duke of AUMERLE.

York, Duke of[3]
A historical figure (1473-1483) and a character in *King Richard III*, the Duke of York is one of the little Princes in the TOWER OF LONDON. Aged about ten, he is the younger brother of Prince Edward and second in line to the throne. In the play he jokes and plays with his uncle, Richard, and rides on his back. He is afraid of the sinister Tower where he is horribly murdered and later appears as a ghost to haunt Richard on the eve of the Battle of Bosworth. There is no historical evidence that Richard was actually responsible for his death.

York, Richard Plantagenet, Duke of
A historical figure (1411-1460) and a character in *King Henry VI, Parts One, Two and Three*: in *Part One*, the character appears as RICHARD PLANTAGENET in the dialogue until the title of Duke of York is restored to him by King Henry, after which he is known as YORK.

In *Part One*, the Lancastrian King Henry is on the throne but the Duke of York has designs on the crown for himself. In the Temple Gardens in London, York's supporters chose a white rose as their emblem while the opposing faction of Lancastrians, represented by Somerset, who are loyal to the King, chose a red rose. This marks the beginning of a long-running quarrel between York and Somerset which affects the War in France and prepares the way for the events of the WARS OF THE ROSES in *King Henry VI, Part Three*. York learns from the dying Mortimer that as a Plantagenet he has a rightful claim to the Throne and King Henry unwittingly furthers York's cause by giving him back his title of Duke of York. The King gives York command of part of the army in France but York is absorbed in his quarrel with Somerset, who commands another section of forces, and between them they betray Talbot by failing to send him vital reinforcements.

In *Part Two*, York declares his hand. He makes his intention of taking the crown for himself clear to the Earls of Warwick and Salisbury and wins their support for his cause. When a rebellion breaks out in Ireland, York is given command of an army and sent to quell it. He seizes the opportunity to use the army for his own ends and when Jack Cade's rebellion erupts in England, York returns with his own forces. He confronts King Henry and announcing his claim to the throne he meets the King's army at St Albans where he is victorious.

In *Part Three*, York makes an agreement with King Henry that Henry will remain King but that on his death the crown will pass to York and his heirs. The agreement is short-lived; York is soon persuaded by his ambitious son Richard to make another bid for the crown. In a battle between the armies of Richard and Queen Margaret Richard is captured. He is taunted and humiliated by Margaret who puts a paper crown on his head and jeers at him over the death of his young son Rutland before she kills him.

York, The House of
An English royal dynasty, a branch of the PLANTAGENET family, which was founded by Edmund, the first Duke of York (1385-1402) and fourth son of Edward III. While the mentally unstable Lancastrian Henry VI (1422-61/71) was on the throne, Richard, the

second Duke of York, made a bid for the crown in 1454 so instigating the WARS OF THE ROSES. Although his bid was unsuccessful, he was made protector for the period of Henry's illness and inability to rule. After the Duke of York's death in 1460, his son was crowned the following year as Edward IV, the first Yorkist king. He was succeeded in turn by his thirteen-year-old son Edward V in 1483, whose uncle King Richard III seized the crown later that year. Richard III was the last Yorkist king, who died at the Battle of Bosworth in 1485. *See* LANCASTER, THE HOUSE OF.

Yorkshire Tragedy, A

A tragedy published in 1608 with William Shakespeare's name as author on the title page. The play was included in the third FOLIO edition of his plays in 1664, but it is now considered unlikely to have been written by him and does not belong to the Shakespeare canon.

Young Lucius

Titus' grandson in *Titus Andronicus*; *see* LUCIUS, YOUNG.

Young Martius

See MARTIUS, YOUNG.

Young Siward

A minor character in *Macbeth*; *see* SIWARD.

SUPPLEMENT

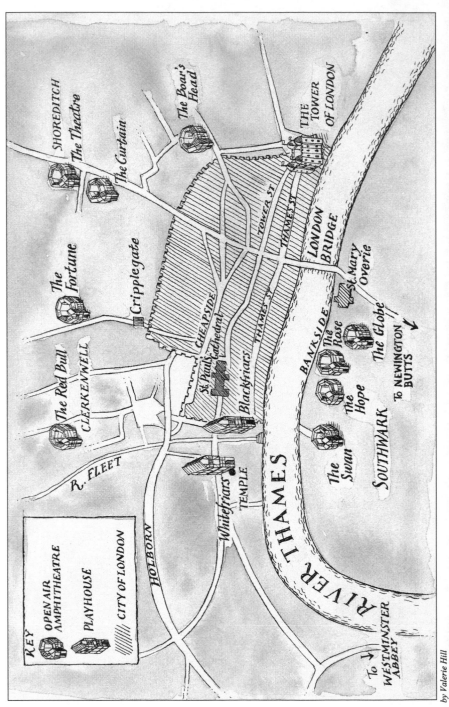

Theatres in Elizabethan London

by Valerie Hill

A CHRONOLOGY OF SHAKESPEARE'S LIFE AND TIMES

1558	Elizabeth I crowned Queen of England
1564	William Shakespeare born
1576	The opening of the first purpose-built theatre, **The Theatre**, in London since Roman times
1582	William Shakespeare marries Anne Hathaway
1583	Birth of Shakespeare's daughter, Susanna
1585	The Queen's Men perform in Stratford
1590	Shakespeare working in London, writing and acting with Burbage's company of players at The Theatre
1592	First performances of Shakespeare's *King Henry VI, Parts One and Two* in London
1592-94	An outbreak of plague closes the London theatres
1593	Christopher Marlowe dies
1593-94	Shakespeare's poems *Venus and Adonis* and *The Rape of Lucrece* published
1596	Hamnet Shakespeare dies.
	The Shakespeare family are granted a coat of arms
1597	Shakespeare buys New Place, the second largest house in Stratford
1598	The building of the Globe Theatre begins
1599	The Globe Theatre opens
1601	Shakespeare's father, John Shakespeare, dies
1603	Queen Elizabeth I dies. James I crowned King of England
1605	The Gunpowder Plot, a failed attempt to blow up the Houses of Parliament
1607	Shakespeare's daughter, Susanna, marries John Hall
1608	Shakespeare's mother, Mary Arden, dies
1609	Shakespeare's *Sonnets* published
1610-11	Shakespeare writes his last play, *The Tempest*
1613	The Globe Theatre burns to the ground
1614	The rebuilt Globe Theatre reopens
1616	Shakespeare's daughter, Judith, marries Thomas Quiney.
	Shakespeare writes his will.
	William Shakespeare dies
1619	Richard Burbage dies
1623	Shakespeare's wife Anne dies
	The *First Folio* edition of Shakespeare's plays published

CHRONOLOGICAL LIST OF SHAKESPEARE'S PLAYS

While there are some records that give us the dates of first performances of Shakespeare's plays, it is difficult to be precise about when the plays were actually written and there is considerable debate among scholars of the subject. The table below lists the plays in the order in which they were probably written with the probable dates of their composition.

The Two Gentlemen of Verona	1590-91
The Taming of the Shrew	1590-93
King Henry VI, Part One	1590-91
King Henry VI, Part Two	1590-92
King Henry VI, Part Three	1590-92
Titus Andronicus	1590-93
(Edward III	1592-93)
King Richard III	1592-93
The Comedy of Errors	1593-94
Love's Labour's Lost	1594-95
King Richard II	1595
Romeo and Juliet	1591-96
King John	1591-96
A Midsummer Night's Dream	1594-96
The Merchant of Venice	1596-98
King Henry IV, Part One	1596-98
The Merry Wives of Windsor	1596-98
King Henry IV, Part Two	1597-98
Much Ado About Nothing	1598
King Henry V	1598-99
Julius Caesar	1599
As You Like It	1598-1600
Hamlet	1599-1601
Twelfth Night	1599-1601
Troilus and Cressida	1600-02
Measure For Measure	1603-04
Othello	1603-04
All's Well That Ends Well	1603-05
Timon of Athens	1605
King Lear	1605-06
Macbeth	1606
Antony and Cleopatra	1606-08
Pericles	1606-08
Coriolanus	1607-08
The Winter's Tale	1609-10
Cymbeline	1606-10
The Tempest	1610-11
King Henry VIII	1612-13
The Two Noble Kinsmen	1613-14

ENGLISH KINGS AND QUEENS 1327-1603

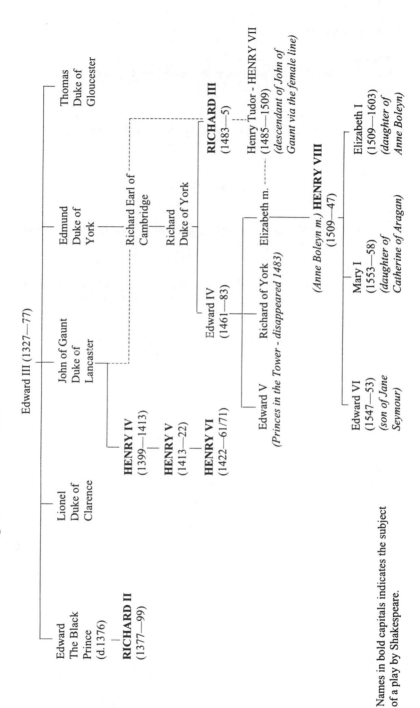

Names in bold capitals indicates the subject of a play by Shakespeare.

PUBLIC PLAYHOUSES

The Theatre
The first to be built in 1576, it was later pulled down and its timbers used to build the Globe.

The Curtain
Built in 1577 beyond the limits of the City of London; it survived well into the 17th century.

Newington Butts
Built by 1580 about a mile south of London Bridge.

The Rose
Built on Bankside in 1587 by the theatrical entrepreneur Philip Henslowe. The site of this theatre was excavated in 1989.

The Swan
Built around 1595, it was one of the largest theatres of its day in London but only survived for three years before it was closed in 1597 by the **City Fathers**.

The Globe
Built on Bankside in 1599, from the timbers of the demolished Theatre, for the Lord Chamberlain's Men to whom Shakespeare was attached; it burned down in 1613.

The Fortune
Built in 1599/1600, it burned down in 1621 and was rebuilt in brick in 1625.

The Red Bull
Built circa 1604 in Clerkenwell, it was in use until the 1660s.

The Hope
Built in 1614 on the site of the old Bear Garden, it doubled as a theatre and bear-baiting arena.

BIBLIOGRAPHY

The Macmillan Casebook Series of Shakespeare's plays. General editor A E Dyson

The Arden editions of plays and poems

Abrams, M.H., *A Glossary of Literary Terms*, Fourth Edition. New York: Holt, Rinehart and Winston, 1981

Baldwin, Thomas Whitfield, *The Organization and Personnel of the Shakespearean Company*. New York: Russell & Russell. 1961

Bate, Jonathan, *The Genius of Shakespeare*. London: Picador, 1988

Bate, Jonathan and Jackson, Russell, eds., *Shakespeare, an Illustrated Stage History*. Oxford: Oxford University Press, 1996

Blake, N. F., *Shakespeare's Language: An Introduction*, London: Macmillan Press Ltd, 1983

Blakemore Evans, G. (ed.), *Elizabethan-Jacobean Drama*, A New Mermaid Background Book. London: A & C Black, 1989

Boyce, Charles, *Shakespeare A-Z*, New York; Roundtable Press, Inc, 1990

Bradley, A. C., *Shakespearean Tragedy*, London: Macmillan & Co, 1957

Cook, Judith, *Women in Shakespeare*. London: Virgin Books, 1985

Chambers, E. K., *The Elizabethan Stage Volumes I-IV*, Oxford: Oxford University Press, 1974

Davis, W. Robertson, *Shakespeare's Boy Actors*. London: J M Dent & Sons Ltd

Dover Wilson, John, *Life in Shakespeare's England*. London, Pelican Books, 1951

Eagleton, Terry, *Literary Theory, An Introduction*. Oxford: Basil Blackwell, 1983

Ford, Boris (ed.), *The Age of Shakespeare, Volume 2*, The New Pelican Guide to English Literature. London: Penguin, 1982

Freud, Sigmund, *Art and Literature, Volume 14*, The Pelican Freud Library. London: Penguin Books, 1985

Granville-Barker, Harley and Harrison, G B (eds.), *A Companion to Shakespeare Studies*. Cambridge: Cambridge University Press, 1934

Gray, Martin, *A Dictionary of Literary Terms*. London: Longmans 1992

Halliday, F. E., *A Shakespeare Companion 1564—1964*. London: Gerald Duckworth & Co Ltd, 1964

Harrison, G.B., _Introducing Shakespeare_, Harmondsworth: Penguin, 1966

Hartnoll, Phyllis, _The Theatre; A Concise History_. London: Thames and Hudson, 1985

Holinshed, R., _Holinshed's Chronicle As Used in Shakespeare's Plays_, Allardyce & Josephine Nicoll eds. London: Everyman's Library, J M Dent & Sons Ltd, 1975

Honan, Park, _Shakespeare A Life_, Oxford: Oxford University Press, 1998

Joseph, B. L., _Elizabethan Acting_, Oxford: Oxford University Press, 1951

Kiernan, Victor, _Shakespeare: Poet and Citizen_, London: Verso, 1993

Kott, Jan, _Shakespeare Our Contemporary_, Methuen & Co Ltd, London, 1975

Leach, Susan, _Shakespeare in the Classroom_, Buckingham: Open University Press, 1992

Lee, Sidney, _A Life of William Shakespeare_, London: Oracle, 1996

Levi, Peter, _The Life and Times of William Shakespeare_. London: Papermac, 1989

Mann, David, _The Elizabethn Player_, London: Routledge, 1991

Muir, Kenneth, _Shakespeare's Sonnets_, Unwin Critical Library, London: George Allen & Unwin Ltd 1982

Nagler, A.M., _Shakespeare's Stage_. New Haven: Yale University Press, 1964

Neale, J.E., _Queen Elizabeth I_, London: Penguin Books, 1960

O'Connor, Garry, _William Shakespeare; A Life_, London: Hodder & Stoughton, 1991

Phillips, Graham & Keatman, Martin, _The Shakespeare Conspiracy_, London: Century, 1994

Powell, Anthony (ed.), _Brief Lives_ by John Aubrey, London: The Cresset Press, 1949

Raine Ellis, Annie (ed.), _The Early Diary of Frances Burney 1768-1778_. London: G. Bell & Sons, 1930

Rowse, A L , _Discovering Shakespeare_, London: Weidenfeld and Nicholson, 1989

Sales, Roger (ed.), _Shakespeare in Perspective_, London: Ariel Books 1982

Sams, Eric, ed., _Shakespeare's Edward III_, London: Yake University Press, 1996

Schoenbaum. S., _William Shakespeare; A Compact Documentary Life_. Oxford: Oxford University Press, 1987

Sher, Antony, _The Year of the King_. London: Chatto & Windus, The Hogarth Press, 1985

Spencer, T. J. B., _Shakespeare: A Celebration_. London: Penguin Books, 1964

Spencer, T.J. B., *Shakespeare's Plutarch*, London: Penguin 1964

Stokes, Francis Griffin, *Who's Who in Shakespeare*. London: Bracken Books, 1989

Strachey, Lytton, *Elizabeth and Essex; a Tragic History*. London: Chatto & Windus, 1932

Thomson, Peter, *Shakespeare's Theatre*, London: Routledge, 1992

Tillyard, E. M. W., *Shakespeare's History Plays*. London: Penguin Books, 1969.

Tillyard, E. M. W., *Shakespeare;s Problem Plays*. London: Pelican, 1985

Trevelyan, G M, *English Social History*. London: Longman, Green & Co, 1944

Ward, A.C., *Specimens of English Dramatic Criticism XVII-XX Centuries*. Oxford: Oxford University Press, 1945

Waldman, Milton, *Elizabeth and Leicester*. London: Wm Collins Sons & Co Ltd 1946

Wells, Stanley, ed., *The Cambridge Companion to Shakespeare Studies*. Cambridge, Cambridge University Press, 1992

Wells, Stanley, *Shakespeare a Dramatic Life*, London; Sinclair-Stevenson, 1994

Wells, Stanley, ed., *Shakespeare in the Theatre*. Oxford: Clarendon Press, 1977

Wickham, Glynne, *Early English Stages 1300 to 1600*. Vol Two, Part I. London: Routledge & Kegan Paul, 1963

Woudhuysen, H. R. ed., *Samuel Johnson on Shakespeare*. London, Penguin Books, 1989